Asia-Gulf Economic
Relations in the 21st Century:
The Local to Global Transformation

Asia-Gulf Economic Relations in the 21st Century: The Local to Global Transformation

Edited by
Tim Niblock
with Monica Malik

First published 2013
by Gerlach Press
Berlin, Germany
www.gerlach-press.de

Cover Design: www.brandnewdesign.de
Set in ACaslonPro by Dataworks, Chennai, India
www.dataworks.co.in
Printed and bound in Germany by
Freiburger Graphische Betriebe
www.fgb.de

Bibliographic data available from German National Bibliography
http://d-nb.info/1028505930

ISBN13: 978-3-940924-10-0 (hardcover volume)
ISBN13: 978-3-940924-11-7 (eBook)

Contents

Introduction

Tim Niblock

The concerns of this book are with the shift in the balance of the global economic order which has been taking place – a shift which has become increasingly apparent over the past five years. A steady move of industrial capacity from West to East has occurred; the rates of economic growth of key Asian countries have outstripped (many by a high margin) those of advanced Western economies; the financial crisis that the Western world has experienced since 2008 has severely weakened Western economies while barely denting the rates of growth of some Asian countries; and a range of Asian countries have come to play a central role in global investment, whether through their sovereign wealth funds or private/public corporations and companies. Lucrative construction contracts, oil concessions, and development projects—which Western companies dominated in the past—are now being won by Asian companies.

The role of the Gulf region has been of particular significance in the current re-structuring of the global economy. In some respects the Gulf, itself part of Asia, constitutes one dimension of the shift in economic power. Despite the problems faced by Dubai in 2008-10, the Gulf economies have continued a rapid rate of expansion through the financial crisis; their sovereign wealth funds and major corporations have gained a central role in global investment flows; and they have acquired a key stake in a significant sector of global industrial production: petrochemicals.

In another respect, the re-direction of the economies of the Gulf states is reflective of, rather than part of, the critical shift of economic power from West to East. The economies of the Gulf have traditionally been closely linked to those of the Western world. Yet most oil now flows East, not West, and the development of the petrochemical industry (the cornerstone of the Gulf economies' hope for a future as industrial powers) is also now more dependent on Asian than Western markets. How the Gulf countries balance and manage their relationships with East/South/Southeast Asia and the West is, therefore, an important issue for the future for all of the parties involved (the Gulf countries, the West, and non-Middle Eastern Asia).

Nonetheless, it is inaccurate to represent the re-structuring of the Gulf's global economic relationships as a simple matter of Western decline and Asian growth. While an overall shift has indeed taken place, the shift is not simply from West to East. Asian countries themselves relate to the global change in different ways. An analysis of Gulf-Asia[1] trade, for example, reveals that not all Asian countries have benefited in the same way. The key factor in the direction of Gulf trade is that the share accounted for by industrialized and newly-industrialized countries (whether Western or Asian) has declined relative to that of particular industrializing countries. As will be shown in Chapter One, the share accounted for by Japan has declined as much (and perhaps more so) than have the shares of the major Western trading nations. The key industrializing countries that have gained substantially in market share are China and India. In 2011, China for the first time dislodged Japan from its long-established ranking as the second largest trading partner of the Gulf countries, and was only just behind the European Union. Contrary to widespread perceptions, moreover, it is India and not China whose trade has been growing most dramatically in the years since 2005, although India's trade started from a lower base.

Yet the pattern just described, where industrialised countries (whether Western or Asian) are losing market share to industrialising countries, does not do justice to the significance of Asia's growing role in the global economy. East Asia, and to some extent parts of South-East Asia and South Asia, are becoming highly integrated economically. In the words of Girijesh Pant, in Chapter Six of this book, these areas "have increasingly evolved as key elements in global production processes.." At the same time as being closely integrated into global markets, they are also "hugely mutually dependent" on eachother. Japanese companies, for example, have invested heavily in China, India and South-East Asia. The products of their overseas operations register as the products of the host country, not as Japanese products. When these products are exported, therefore, they will not figure as Japanese exports but as the exports of China, India or elsewhere. The large number of cars with Japanese brand names on the roads of Gulf states, therefore, is not necessarily evidence of large-scale Japanese exports to the country concerned. Where the Japanese brand-name car has been produced in another Asian country this is, rather, an indication of the economic weight of Asia as a whole in the new balance of economic power – including the industrialised Asian countries whose trade trends seem to mimic those of Western countries. The cases where Western companies manufacture in Asia and export to the Gulf are more limited.

Although there has been considerable work done on the relationships between individual Gulf and Asian countries, there has previously been no attempt to cover the overall relationship – bringing in all of the 8 Gulf countries and all the Asian countries which have substantial economic relations with the Gulf region. Information and analysis of how relations are developing between one Asian country and one Gulf country (most commonly China and Saudi Arabia), however, are of limited value in explaining how the global economic balance is changing. The strengthening of one Gulf-Asia relationship may be accompanied by the weakening of another such relationship. An overall perspective is what is needed in order to comprehend how Gulf-Asia developments are transforming the balance of global economic relations. This is what this book is seeking to achieve. On the side of the Gulf, the 6 Gulf Cooperation Council countries are covered (although not each GCC state has a chapter to itself), as well as Iran and Iraq. On the side of Asia, all of the Gulf's major Asian trading partners are included, in addition to some states which have a significant stake in the region but (as yet) limited trade. Turkey and Russia, both straddling the Europe-Asia divide, are brought in by virtue of their particular form of engagement with the Gulf states – affecting the Gulf-Asia relationship although perhaps marginal to it.

Chapter One provides statistics and analysis which create three different comparative perspectives: placing Gulf-Asian economic relations in the context of the overall global economic relations of Gulf states; documenting the share/significance of each Gulf state in the Gulf-Asian economic relationship; and similarly covering the share/significance of each of the major Asian countries in the Gulf-Asian relationship. While the focus is on Gulf-Asia, comparisons are also made with US and EU trade with the Gulf region, so as to show the changing weight of the Gulf's trading relationships over time. Chapters Two and Three cover the two Gulf countries whose engagement with Asia has been most significant internationally: Saudi Arabia and Iran. Chapters Four and Five cover Turkey and Russia.

India is covered in Chapters Six and Seven. The close interaction of economic and political factors are stressed, and emphasis is given to how India's Gulf involvement links in with wider Indian foreign policy initiatives. Chapters Eight, Nine, Ten and Eleven cover a wide variety of different dimensions of Chinese involvement in the Gulf region: the significance of China's economic relationship with the Gulf Cooperation Council states; the particular relationship with Iran; the manner in which China's Muslim communities have (or have not) enhanced the effectiveness of China's relations with the Gulf region; and the historical and cultural resonances which impinge on the relationship today.

Chapters Twelve and Thirteen cover the relations between the Gulf and two significant countries in South-East Asia: Singapore and Malaysia. In both cases, there are factors outside of the narrowly economic which have impinged on relations. In the case of Singapore, this has centred around the idea of Singapore as a developmental model from which others can benefit; in the case of Malaysia it is based more on cultural/religious linkages. Chapter Fourteen is devoted to South Korea's involvement in the Gulf. The Korean role now goes beyond the economic, and it is of note that South Korean trade with the Gulf has increased more strongly than that of any other industrialised country. Chapters Fifteen and Sixteen are devoted to Japan's relations with the Gulf. The extent of Japan's economic engagement is documented in great detail, but the political dimensions which mould the relationship are also made very explicit.

The pattern which emerges from the different cases is that a many-layered relationship is developing between the Gulf region and Asia. The interaction between the two has come to be of considerable importance to both. There is a strong basis for the Gulf to become integrated into the wider framework of a rapidly-expanding Asian economic hub. The synergies created by this process would be of critical importance not only to the countries concerned but also to the global economy. Nonetheless there are political issues within the Gulf and within Asia which could inhibit such a development. Much may depend on the ability of the states concerned to negotiate realistic solutions to issues in dispute. All the states concerned may gain from a pro-active Asian role in resolving conflict through collectively-agreed security arrangements.

The chapters in this book originated as papers to a 3-day workshop, entitled "Asia and the Gulf", held at the Gulf Research Meeting in Cambridge in July 2012. The meeting was organised by the Gulf Research Centre. The editor wishes to thank not only the Gulf Research Centre for having enabled this workshop to be held, but also to thank all of the participants who took part in the occasion. Their comments enriched the consideration of the papers which went forward for publication as chapters.

Endnote

1   For ease of expression, the term "Gulf-Asia" will be used in this text to signify the relationship between the states of the Gulf and those of non-Gulf Asia. The problematic nature of the term, however, should be borne in mind. It is an important theme of this book that the Gulf needs to be viewed as an integral part of Asia, where closer links are a natural development (with historical roots) rather than an intrusion into customary economic interaction.

Chapter One

Gulf-Asia Economic Relations,
Pan-Gulf and Pan-Asia Perspectives

Tim Niblock

1. Introduction

This chapter is intended to give an overall perspective of the economic relations between Gulf and Asian countries. The intention is to provide statistics and analysis which enable three different dimensions of comparison. These are: the relative importance of Gulf-Asian economic relations as part of the overall global economic relations of Gulf states; the share/significance of each Gulf state in the Gulf-Asian economic relationship; and the share/significance of each of the major Asian countries in the Gulf-Asian relationship. These various elements can, in turn, be grasped through three different sets of measures: oil and gas dependence (the extent to which any Asian country is dependent on the Gulf for its supply of hydrocarbons, and the extent to which any Gulf state is dependent on Asian demand for hydrocarbons); the flow of trade in both directions; and the nature and extent of investments and contracting undertaken by Asian companies in the Gulf, and by Gulf countries in Asia.[1] The perspective needs to take account of trends and not just current figures, as these will enable an assessment of how significant the relationships may be in the long-run.

2. The Hydrocarbon Dimension: Gulf States' Production and Global Share

The dependence of most Asian countries (as, indeed, most Western countries) on imported oil and gas to satisfy their energy needs has, of course, been critical to the economic relationships which have developed. It is, therefore, important to begin by situating Gulf oil production within the wider setting of overall global energy production.

Global oil production in 2010 stood at 87.4 million barrels a day (henceforth b/d). This constituted an increase of 3.1% over the previous year, and came after two years of depression or recession in the Western and some other economies. The annual production total was the highest recorded. The global oil trade had expanded by 2.2% in 2009. The most substantial export growth was from the Former Soviet Union (7.2%), followed by the Middle East (2.6%). The growth in oil production and consumption was part of a wider trend towards higher energy production and consumption. In fact, oil production was growing less fast than the overall average in primary energy consumption. The latter grew by 5.6% between 2009 and 2010 – the strongest such growth since 1973. The fastest rise in the consumption of primary energy came from biofuels (13.8%), coal (7.6%) and natural gas (7.4%). Oil, however, makes up 33.6% of all energy consumption in the world, with coal coming second at 29.6%, and natural gas at 23.8%.[2]

The Gulf's proven oil reserves constituted 54.0% of the global total at the end of 2010.[3] The proportion of the global total accounted for by the Gulf states has declined over the past 20 years, as a result of new discoveries elsewhere. In 1990, the percentage was generally put at about 60%. Nonetheless, the Gulf share remains very substantial, and may increase in the future when new estimates of the extent of Iraqi oil reserves are made and confirmed. What is critical, moreover, is not just the size of proven reserves but also the potential to retain or increase levels of production and oil export in the future. Gulf oil production in 2010 accounted for 26.1% of global oil production and 28.3% of oil exports – substantially less than the share of proven oil reserves.[4] Setting the 26.1% production share against the 54% share of global reserves, it follows that the rate of depletion of Gulf oil reserves is less than exists elsewhere, leaving more available for future production and export. Moreover, what is also important is the proportion of a country's or region's oil production which is available for export, rather than being absorbed by home consumption. In the case of the Gulf that proportion currently stands at about 70% (although home consumption is growing substantially), which is a lot more than that found in most other oil producing countries. For states eager to promote their medium- and long-term access to substantially increased oil supply, therefore, the Gulf is bound to be a – and probably *the* – key area of interest.

The shares which different Gulf states have in proven oil reserves, the current rate of production, and the likely period over which existing reserves could last (given current rates of production) can be seen from Table 1.1. Saudi Arabia, with 19.1% of global reserves, and currently producing 40.8% of all the oil produced in the Gulf, clearly occupies a central role in the oil market.

Table 1.1: Gulf Proven Oil Reserves, Rates of Production, and Years Remaining (2010 figures)

	Proven Reserves thousand million barrels	Share of Global Reserves %	Rate of Production mill. b/d	Reserves/Production Ratio Years remaining
Iran	137.0	9.9	4.2	88.4
Iraq	115.0	8.3	2.5	100+
Kuwait	101.5	7.3	2.5	100+
Oman	5.5	0.4	0.9	17.4
Qatar	25.9	1.9	1.6	45.2
Saudi Arabia	264.5	19.1	10.0	72.4
UAE	97.8	7.1	2.8	94.1
Total Gulf	747.2	54.0	24.5	n/a

Source: *BP Statistical Review of World Energy, June 2011*, pp 6 and 8.

Note 1: Bahrain is not included in this list as production and reserves are very limited.

Note 2: The estimates on oil reserves and oil production given here follow the definitions given in footnote 3. If the Canadian oil sands were included in the percentages for proven reserves, the proportion accounted for by Gulf states would be significantly less. With the inclusion of tar sands Canada has the third largest oil reserves in the world, after Saudi Arabia and Venezuela. Saudi Arabia's share of proven resources would then stand at 17.3% rather than 19.1%, and the figures for the other Gulf oil producing countries would be reduced proportionately. The overall figure for all Gulf oil proven reserves would come to slightly less than 50% of the world total.

With reserves expected to last for 72.4 years at current rates of production, it is bound to retain this central role through most of this century. At present, moreover, it has a spare oil-producing capacity of some 2.5 million b/d, such that it could satisfy short-term increases of demand for its oil. It is expected to retain a buffer of spare capacity through to 2020, at least.[5] Nonetheless, the proven reserves of Iran, Iraq, Kuwait and the UAE are also very substantial and, given the lower rate of current extraction, are expected to last longer than Saudi Arabia's. It is widely expected that estimates of Iraq's proven reserves will increase as a result of the new explorations which are currently being undertaken or are envisaged. At present, however, all of these states have relatively limited spare capacity. In the case of the smaller states, Kuwait and the UAE, this is because they have little incentive to increase production – their financial needs are covered by the existing level of revenues, and it is in their interest to conserve their reserves for the long-term.

With regard to natural gas, the Gulf states also possess substantial reserves but not quite so critical a position in global supply. As can be seen from Table 1.2 they collectively account for about 40% of global natural gas reserves, but only 13.9% of daily production. Only 4 of the Gulf states are currently exporting natural gas: Iran, Qatar, the UAE and Oman. Saudi Arabia is currently consuming all of the natural gas it produces, and Iran consumes the major part of its natural gas production. The only two states which have the potential to be major producers of natural gas in the long run are Qatar and Iran, which between them account for about three-quarters of the Gulf's natural gas reserves and 29.3% of global reserves. Qatar is currently the world's third largest gas producing country, after Russia and Norway. The volume of Russia's production in 2010, however, was about twice as great as Qatar's. It seems likely that the other Gulf states, besides Qatar and Iran, will use most of their natural gas for domestic purposes and will not figure strongly in export markets.

Table 1.2: Gulf Natural Gas Proven Reserves, Share of Global Production and Years Remaining (2010 figures)

	Share of Global Proven Reserves	Daily Production as a Share of Global Production	Reserves/Production Ratio Years remaining	Exports mill. cubic metres
Bahrain	0.1%	0.4%	16.7	0.0
Iran	15.8%	4.3%	*	7,870
Iraq	1.7	*	*	0.0
Kuwait	1.0%	0.4%	*	0.0
Oman	0.4%	0.8%	25.5	11,540
Qatar	13.5%	3.6%	*	94,810
Saudi Arabia	4.3%	2.6%	95.5	0.0
UAE	3.2%	1.6%	78.3	7,010
TOTALS	40.0%	13.9%		

Sources: For columns 1-3, BP *Statistical Review of World Energy, June 2011*, pp 20 and 22; and for column 4, See CIA, "Country Comparison: Natural Gas: Exports" in *World Factbook*, continuously updated, accessed March 2012 at www.cia.gov/library/publications/the-world-factbook/rankorder/2183rank.html

Note: There are no official estimates for the starred boxes.

The manner in which Gulf hydrocarbons affect the relationships between Gulf and Asian states, however, is not affected by present perspectives alone. Every Asian state which is likely to import substantial quantities of oil or gas in the future has to take into account the longer perspective: what the size of its own demand will be in future decades, how that will be affected by changing demand from other countries, and how much supply will be available from oil-producing countries in different parts of the world. Energy security needs to be seen in the long term, and states have to plan for that long-term and view their external relationships accordingly. The "long-term" which will be considered here is the period through to 2030, mainly because this is a time-span used by international energy analysts in making predictive projections on energy production and consumption.

Overall primary energy consumption, on the base of a median projection[6], is expected to grow by about 39% over the 2010-2030 period. This reflects underlying trends in population and income growth: world population over this period is expected to grow by 1.4 billion, with real income rising by about 100%.[7] The rate of growth in primary energy consumption is nonetheless rather lower than that for the previous 20 years, which was approximately 45%. The deceleration of consumption growth reflects the fact that energy efficiency (energy per unit of GDP) rises with the level of industrial development. As would be expected, therefore, most of the increase in energy consumption will be in those states which are industrialising rather than those with an established industrial infrastructure. In fact, energy consumption by non-OECD countries is expected to rise by about 68% by 2030, averaging 2.6% per annum, and to account for about 93% of all growth in energy consumption. The corresponding growth for the OECD countries is no more than 6% over that 20-year period, and in fact actually declines in the years after 2020.[8] There can be little doubt, therefore, that energy needs in industrialising Asia will be a significant concern of governments in the region.

Between different forms of primary energy, the prediction is that there will be a slow move away from oil and towards gas and non-fossil fuels (with renewables growing fastest). The share of oil in current primary energy supply is expected to fall by 2030 from its present 33.6% to a point where it converges with gas and coal at about 26-27% each.[9] Nonetheless, the demand for oil will increase overall, and will remain a critical source of energy supply. Demand for global liquids (mainly crude oil, but also including a small element of biofuels and other liquids) is expected to rise by 16.5 million b/d by 2030. Increasing demand in non-OECD Asia would come to 13 million b/d, while demand in the OECD, having peaked in 2005, would decline by about 4 million b/d.[10] The consumption of oil in non-OECD countries (both Asian and non-Asian) would overtake OECD consumption around 2015. China would constitute the largest element in the growth in oil consumption, with consumption rising from about 8 million b/d in 2010 to some 17.5 million b/d in 2030. It would by then have overtaken the US and become the largest oil consumer in the world – despite the fact that oil currently constitutes only some 20% to China's overall energy needs.[11]

An additional supply of 16.5 million b/d of global liquids, therefore, will be needed overall by 2030. This is attainable and, although there will be significant changes in the nature and sources of the supply, the Gulf states remain central to the provision of the supply. Declining oil production in the established fields of Europe, Asia Pacific and North America will be partially offset by newly-developed or developing fields in Brazil and the former Soviet Union. This, however, leaves the gap caused by rising demand. Some additional supply will come from biofuels, oil shale and oil sands, but some 75% of the increased supply will need to come from OPEC – whether as crude oil or natural gas liquids. This would leave OPEC with a larger share of world liquids production than it has at the moment; the percentage would rise from 40% to 46%. A substantial part of the increased OPEC supply would need to come from the Gulf states. Saudi Arabia, which has spare capacity for producing an extra 2.5 million b/d at the moment, might be expected to supply about 3 million by 2030, and Iraq, which currently has very ambitious (and probably unrealistic) plans to increase production capacity to some 12.5 million b/d, could also supply some 3 million b/d (additional to the 2.5 million which it produces at present).[12]

3. Asian Countries as Markets for Gulf Hydrocarbons[13]

China's need for increased supplies of oil has been given considerable attention by outside observers. This need is substantial and is likely to become more so. China is itself a major producer of oil—in 2008 it ranked as the fifth largest in the world. Nonetheless, its demand for oil first exceeded supply in 1993, and its dependence on imported oil has increased steadily since then. In 2009, oil imports for the first time exceeded local production, accounting for 52% of the oil consumed in the country, and the percentage accounted for by imports is expected to rise to 54% in 2010.[14] Chinese oil production is expected to begin to decline after 2020, at which time oil imports are expected to account for about 64% of consumption. Between 2010 and 2030 China will need, according to IEA estimates, to import an extra seven million barrels-a-day (b/d) on top of the 3.8 million it was importing in 2009.[15]

There are many reasons why obtaining the extra seven million may be problematic. Other rapidly industrializing countries will also be looking to increase their oil imports, and some analysts believe that global oil production has little potential to increase significantly above the c. 86 million b/d produced at the time of writing. Levels of investment in the oil industry may also be insufficient to support increased production (in part because with higher prices, oil producers have less incentive or need to accelerate the depletion of their oil reserves).

Of course, the Gulf is not the only area from which China will be able to draw supplies. At present (2011), Angola is the second largest supplier of oil to China, and that supply is likely to increase in the future. There is also potential in other parts of Africa, in Central Asia and the Caucasus, and in new areas where oil exploration has recently appeared promising, such as off the coast of Brazil. In some regions China may be able to access oil supplies that Western countries are unable to access for political, geographical, or environmental reasons. Nonetheless, the reality is that most of China's additional oil supply will have to come from the Gulf. This is not only because almost two-thirds of the world's proven oil reserves are located there (with depletion dates outstripping those of all other producers), but also because the gap between local consumption needs and production capacity are greater in the Gulf than elsewhere—despite the fact that consumption is rising quickly in Gulf countries. The Gulf producers, then, will have more oil to sell on international markets than other producers.

The dependence on Gulf oil also applies to India. According to the U.S. Energy Information Administration (EIA) statistics, India was consuming some three million barrels-a-day of oil in 2009, compared to the eight million consumed by China. Whereas China was itself producing 3.9 million b/d, however, India was only producing 880,000 b/d, such that imports accounted for 70% of India's oil supply as opposed to 52% of China's. The 2009 EIA International Energy Outlook estimates that India will be consuming an extra two million b/d of oil by 2030, while China will be consuming an extra seven million. Both countries are therefore in need of substantially increased quantities of oil, and it seems likely that a significant amount will need to come from the Gulf. The extent to which world oil production will be able to expand to meet such substantial increases in demand is a contentious issue. Specialists, oil companies, and international energy organizations have conflicting views about the stage at which the world will encounter "peak oil."

While it may seem that China and India are destined to be in severe competition over Gulf oil, in fact the situation is little different from that which affects many other countries (in Asia as elsewhere). Japan has very limited domestic reserves of oil and a high (although falling) demand for it; South Korea has no domestic reserves at all. The economies of many other countries are, and will for long remain, dependent on Gulf oil, and the global community has a collective interest in ensuring that Gulf oil is accessible to all who need it.

As far as Southeast Asia is concerned, each of the countries has a different balance between demand for, and domestic supply of, oil. Figures for 2009 will be given here. Only Singapore relies entirely on imports to cover its oil consumption (927,000 b/d); only Malaysia produces more oil than it consumes (578,000 b/d, as against 554,000); Indonesia has relatively small oil import needs at present (with production at 946,000 b/d and consumption at 1,268,000); and Thailand relies mainly on imports (with production at 238,000 b/d and consumption at 940,000). EIA projections for the growth of oil consumption in the region are that by 2035 oil consumption will have doubled while oil production will have declined. The quantities of oil concerned, however, are relatively limited, giving these countries more flexibility over sourcing their oil supplies than India and China have.

In natural gas, projected to be the fastest growing fossil fuel in the period through to 2030, production levels are expected to rise in most parts of the world except for Europe. The share of the Middle East (mainly the Gulf) in global natural gas production will grow from 12% in 2010 to 19% in 2030.[16] Despite the increase, the Atlantic and Pacific basins will remain more substantial producers of natural gas than the Middle East. The amount of Middle East natural gas available for export, moreover, will be limited by the sharp rise in local consumption. The Middle East is the second-fastest growing market for natural gas in the world (after Asia), with consumption rising at 3.9% per annum. Much of the Gulf's natural gas production, then, will be for local consumption, especially in power generation, and as a feedstock and power source for the burgeoning petrochemical industry.

The expansion of natural gas consumption in Asia is expected to be 4.6% per annum, substantially more than the increase in production. China has substantial natural gas reserves of its own, and production from these is expected to rise by 6% per annum. China will still need increased imports, however, as its oil consumption is expected to rise by 7.6% per annum.[17] In 2030 it is expected that China will be consuming almost as much natural gas as the European Union does today, with natural gas imports having increased 14-fold over the 2010-2030 period. This is in itself not surprising as China is expected by then to be the largest economy in the world. The 12th Five-Year Plan signalled that China would now focus on non-coal energy sources, and natural gas is one part of that.[18] China will account for some 56% of all the growth in Asian gas consumption. Natural gas consumption in India is expected to grow by 4.7% per annum, with imports needed to cover about 30% of total natural gas consumption.[19]

4. Analyzing Asia-Gulf Trade

The tables and charts in the appendices to this chapter have been developed on the basis of the IMF's direction of trade statistics. The countries whose trading relations with the Gulf are covered have been chosen with a view to laying bare the key shifts in trading "weight": China, India, Japan, and South Korea are the countries that account for the largest portion of Asian Gulf trade; the EU and the United States are the two major non-Asian global trading nations/blocs with substantial trading interests in the Gulf; and the four South-East Asian countries covered together with Pakistan provide evidence of how other Asian economies are responding to the growing opportunities of Gulf trade. Indonesia, Malaysia, Singapore and Thailand are the South-East Asian countries with the largest (albeit fairly limited) stakes in Gulf trade.

On the Gulf side, all of the eight Gulf states are covered. It is, as mentioned above, important to take cognisance of the whole picture. The weight which an Asian country attaches to relations with any individual Gulf country may depend on how its interests there balance with its interests in other Gulf states. It has been suggested by some, for example, that if relations between Saudi Arabia and Iran deteriorate further (within the context of a wider international confrontation with Iran) Asian countries may be driven to decide where their interests and priorities lie. It may no longer be possible to maintain the line which most Asian countries have previously pursued, namely that "economic relations should be based on mutual economic interest alone". A combination of regional antagonism and Western pressure could force an Asian country to decide whether its economic interests in one Gulf country are sufficiently important to risk a politically-driven retaliation damaging its interests in another.

The years presented here are intended to show how trading weight has changed over time: 1990 represents the period before China's (and to some extent India's) trading relationship with the Gulf states developed in any substantive way; 2000 marks the beginning of the period of substantial growth in Asia-Gulf trade; 2005 sees a new stage of growth, fostered in part by the rising price of oil and in part by the impact of World Trade Organization (WTO) accession which now covered most of the states involved in Gulf trade, at both ends; 2008 marks the high point of the rise in oil prices (at least in the first half of the year), with all its implications for Gulf trade. The figures

13

for 2009 show the impact of the global financial crisis, with the consequent drop in the value of world (and Gulf) trade, and those for 2010 and 2011 show the developing trends once the global economy began to show signs of recovery. As each of the four last years has, for different reasons, been idiosyncratic, it was deemed important to cover the data for all four. An assessment of the overall trends needs to show how boom conditions, retrenchment, and recovery all affect the balance.

The terms "industrialized," "newly-industrialized," and "industrializing" are used here to characterize the level of development of different economies. How states should be classified in this regard can be problematic, especially as the character of economies during rapid growth changes very quickly. For the purpose of this paper, the EU, United States, and Japan are classified as industrialized; South Korea and Singapore are classified as newly-industrialized; and China, India, Indonesia, Malaysia, and Thailand are classified as industrializing. It should be borne in mind that the research covers the 1990-2011 period, over which time there has been substantial development.

The key trends in Gulf trade that emerge from the statistics will be presented under three headings: Changing Balance of Gulf Trade Globally; The Share of Gulf Trade Conducted with Each of the Gulf's Major Trading Partners (China, India, Japan, South Korea, the EU, and the United States); and The Gulf Trade of Southeast Asian Countries and Pakistan Gulf Trade (relative to each other and relative to the Gulf's major trading partners). The first of these sections, although not related directly to Asian trade, is necessary so as to give perspective on which Gulf states have the potential to provide major markets for it.

5. The Development and Changing Balance of Gulf Trade Globally

The data reveals some important trends in Gulf trade globally. Over the whole period since 1990 Saudi Arabia and the UAE have accounted for more than half of all Gulf trade with the outside world. The proportion has remained relatively stable at around 60% - sometimes a little more, sometimes a little less. Most of the Gulf's trade with the outside world, then, is conducted by just two of the eight countries (Tables 1.3-1.9).

Within the Saudi-UAE composite share, moreover, the contribution from each country has steadily shifted over the past 20 years. Whereas in 1990 the value of Saudi Arabia's global trade came to more than twice that of the UAE's, and remained substantially higher into the first decade of this century, the annual trade values of the two countries have been very similar in the years since 2005.

Indeed, in 2009 for the first time the value of UAE total trade exceeded that of Saudi Arabia. In 2010 and 2011, Saudi Arabia regained the top position, largely due to the rise in oil prices. Saudi Arabia's oil exports are, of course, substantially higher than those of the UAE (Tables 1.3-1.9).

When population size is taken into account, there is clearly a significant imbalance in trade per head of population. Jointly the populations of Saudi Arabia and the UAE (inclusive of migrants) constitute 23.9% of the total Gulf population: 36.8 million out of 155.2 million.[20] That of the UAE individually comes to no more than 8.1 million (5%) of the total. In 2011, then, the UAE with 5% of the population of the region accounted for just less than 30% of Gulf external trade (Table 1.9).

The rising importance of the UAE in Gulf trade, moreover, is yet greater than is suggested by the figures mentioned above. As has been noted, the strength of Saudi Arabia's trading position reflects the scale of Saudi Arabia's hydrocarbon exports. Imports in recent years have constituted less than 30% of total Saudi trade. For the UAE, taking an average of the last four years (2008-11), imports have made up roughly 50% of its total trade. In 2011, the value of UAE imports came to $212.6 billion, while the value of Saudi imports stood at only $127.5 billion (Table 1.13). The expansion of UAE trade, then, reflects much more than the rising price of oil. It provides evidence of the UAE's emergence as the major trading hub of the region. In every year since 2008, the UAE has accounted for about 38% of all Gulf imports (Tables 1.11-1.13). The percentage increase in the value of UAE imports in 2011 alone was 28%. Some of the goods imported into the UAE are classified as "re-exports", where goods are offloaded in the UAE and immediately sent on to other regional markets. These, however, are not the only goods which eventually end up elsewhere in the region. Others are sold to the markets of neighbouring countries as part of the commercial operations of UAE businesses.

Iran comes third in the trade value ranking. Its population of 75.6 million accounts for about almost half of the total population of the Gulf region – substantially more than twice that of any other Gulf state. This population preponderance over other Gulf states, however, is not reflected in the country's weight in international trade. Its share of total Gulf trade has, in fact, declined over the past two decades. In the early 1990s, Iran came second only to Saudi Arabia in the size of its external trade, accounting for about 20% of all Gulf trade. Now it comes third. It has been substantially outpaced by the UAE as well as Saudi Arabia, each of whose external trade stands at more than twice that of Iran. Since 2005 Iran's share of Gulf trade has fluctuated between 14% and 15% of the total (Tables 1.5-1.9). Clearly Western and UN sanctions on Iran have constituted a major reason why Iran's global trade has failed to grow as quickly as the global trade of other Gulf states. When Iran eventually frees itself of sanctions its share of Gulf global trade may be expected to rise rapidly.

Qatar and Kuwait occupy the fourth and fifth positions. Relative to their small population sizes (Kuwait 2.9 million, and Qatar 1.9 million), their external trade is substantial. Qatar's external trade in 2011 was worth $127.1 billion, and Kuwait's $109.3 billion (Table 1.9). Up to 2010, Kuwaiti trade had always been in excess of Qatar's, but the sharp rise in Qatari exports of liquefied natural gas (LNG) in 2011 has now put Qatar ahead. In view of the huge investments in the natural gas sector which the Qatari government has made, it is likely that Qatar's external trade will retain this lead in future years. Qatar's production of natural gas has increased more than 6-fold since 2005. Current developments in Qatar are also substantially boosting imports, although at present Kuwait's imports remain marginally higher.

Iraq's share of Gulf trade with the outside world remains substantially below the level it had reached prior to the 1990 occupation of Kuwait. Despite the size of Iraq's population and its infrastructural needs, the country's external trade in 2011, valued at $104.4 billion, only constituted 7% of Gulf trade (Table 1.9). For a major oil-producing country, with a population of 33.7 million (23% of the Gulf's population), a higher level of trading activity would have been expected. This provides evidence of the slow rate of economic rehabilitation and recovery in Iraq since the 2003 war. The major weakness affecting exports has, of course, been the oil industry, where oil production has only recently exceeded the 2.5 million barrels-a-day level maintained prior to the 2003 war (approximately the same rate of production as in 1980). Exports have consequently failed to burgeon. Iraqi exports remained lower than those of all other Gulf states with the exception of Bahrain and Oman. If Iraq succeeds in reconstituting its oil production on the basis of investments which are currently underway or in prospect, then the scale of Iraq's external trade could, of course, be transformed. The final months of 2011 and the first months of 2012 have in fact seen a substantial rise in Iraqi oil production, suggesting that Iraq could soon have a larger share of Gulf trade.

Bahrain and Oman have the smallest shares of the Gulf's external trade. With the exception of Qatar they also have small populations: Oman 2.9 million and Bahrain 1.4 million (the smallest Gulf state by population and also by land area). The value of Oman's external trade in 2011 was $70.2 billion, and that of Bahrain was $41.2 billion (Table 1.9). Although these figures are low relative to other Gulf states, external trade per head of population is nonetheless quite high. Oman's external trade per head of population is considerably higher than, and Bahrain's at a similar level to, that of Saudi Arabia.

6. The Share of Gulf Trade Conducted with Each of the Gulf's Main Trading Partners (China, India, Japan, South Korea, the European Union, and the United States)

As already indicated, the overall trend has been for some Asian countries to obtain a substantially increased share of Gulf trade. To characterize this as Asian gain against Western loss, however, is misleading. Some Asian countries have not significantly increased their shares. This will be apparent from the material presented in section 5 as well as in this section.

Over the three decades prior to 2010, the European Union (and earlier the European Community) consistently held the largest share of Gulf trade (Tables 1.3-1.8). For most of this period the EU share was substantially more than that of any other Gulf trading partner. Its nearest competitor over this period was Japan, but the gap between EU and Japanese trade was very substantial, mostly between 25% and 50%. In 2009 the EU share was about 50% higher, and in 2010 29%. The shares of all other countries were substantially less (Tables 1.7 and 1.8). Despite the widespread impression that US economic interests in the Gulf are predominant, therefore, this is not reflected in the pattern of trade. The leading US position in some other aspects of the Gulf's external relations is not present in the trading relationship. Strategic presence, educational engagement and two-way investment clearly have limited implications for trade, at least in this instance.

The significance of the EU's trade with the Gulf is increased by its composition. In 2009 65% of the trade consisted of EU exports to the Gulf (Table 1.14). The comparative imports-to-exports figures for the United States, Japan, and South Korea in the same year were 49%, 25%, and 25%, respectively. Whereas the largest part of Japanese and South Korean trade with the Gulf consists of their import of oil, the EU and to some extent the United States have been more successful in creating balanced economic relationships. In these relationships, the Gulf states constitute important markets for EU/US goods. The proportion of EU trade made up by exports fell to 55% in 2011, but the drop reflects simply the rising price of oil and the impact which this had on the value of EU imports. All the Gulf's other trading partners were affected in a similar way (Table 1.14).

Nonetheless, despite the continued size and significance of EU, Japanese and US trade with the Gulf, the rate of growth of this trade has been relatively slow. Indeed, for all three countries, the increase has been lower than that of Gulf trade globally. This comes across clearly in all of the post-2000 time-periods covered in Table 1.15. Between 2005 and 2009, for example, the figures are: EU 9%, Japan 0%, and the United States 8%, as against an overall increase of 38% in global Gulf trade. Notable here is the zero increase registered by Japan. It can be noted that over the 2000-2008 and 2005-11 periods, the increase in Japanese trade with the Gulf was rather more positive (Table 1.15, second and third columns). This, however, is misleading. In 2008 Japan imported a larger-than-usual quantity of oil from the Gulf at a time when the prices were very high, and the same applies in 2010 and 2011 (Tables 1.8 and 1.9). The imbalance between the exports and imports side of trade, therefore, became greater. South Korea's trade falls into a slightly different category than the other 3 trade partners covered in this section. Mostly the rate of increase has been below the average for Gulf trade globally, but the margin has been narrower and in some time-periods has slightly exceeded the global average (Table 1.15, column 2).

Chinese and Indian trade with the Gulf has followed a very different course to that of the advanced industrial powers. It has been growing exponentially. The remarkable percentage increase over the 2000-2008 period (Table 1.15, column 3) is partly attributable to the relatively low levels of trade the two countries had with the Gulf before 2000, but the high increase after 2005 is more reflective of future trends. For both countries, the increases have been many-fold greater than the growth in EU, U.S., Japanese, or South Korean trade with the Gulf (Table 1.15). Between 2005 and 2011, China's trade grew by 334% and India's by 673%, while the figures for the four advanced industrial powers covered were South Korea 151%, US 88%, Japan 62%, and EU 38%.

The relative weight of outside countries in Gulf trade is being transformed as a result of the sharp differential in the rates of growth. In 2009, China and India became the third and fourth largest trading partners of the Gulf respectively, having displaced the US and South Korea from these positions (Table 1.9). They retained third and fourth positions in 2010, while in 2011 China moved up to become the second largest, with Japan going down to third. For the first time, moreover, EU-Gulf trade in 2011 only had a narrow margin over China-Gulf trade: $196.7 billion as against $194.9 billion. Japan-Gulf trade, furthermore, was only marginally before India-Gulf trade: $168.6 billion as against $165.5 billion. In 2009, the United States stood sixth in the ranking. In 2010 it moved up to fifth, overtaking South Korea, but the long-term trend has been for South Korean trade with the Gulf to increase more rapidly than U.S. trade. In line with this, South Korea regained the fifth position in 2011, with a margin of $134.1 billion as against $118.3 billion.

China and India are now substantial exporters to the Gulf as well as importers from it (Table 1.14). As with the EU and the United States, they (especially China) have established substantial markets for their own goods in the Gulf states. In the last few years China and India have been substantially ahead of Japan and South Korea in terms of the proportion of their Gulf trade made up by exports. The economic relationships, therefore, are not shaped solely around their need for oil but involve a more symbiotic set of exchanges. This, indeed, is part of the economic strategy the Chinese government has been pursuing in the Gulf region since the 1990s.[21] Multi-faceted relationships are likely to have dynamics that sustain them in the long term, which may be lacking in relationships based on the export/import of a single commodity.

Among the various trends in the trade of the Gulf's major trading partners, one has attracted very little attention among international observers. While much attention has been paid to China's growing economic presence in the region, little has been given to India's. Yet over the period since 2000 the rate of growth of India's Gulf trade has consistently outstripped that of China. Table 1.15 shows that whatever time-spans are taken (2000-2008, 2005-2009, or 2005-2011), the growth of India's trade has been substantially higher than China's. In the critical period after 2005 the rate has consistently been about twice has high, with the single exception of 2010-2011 (Tables 1.8 and 1.9). In the latter year the figures are skewed by the sudden rise in China's imports of oil from the Gulf – with imports from Iran, in particular, more than doubling. In 2010 India's Gulf trade had, for the first time since the 1990s, overtaken that of China by a very narrow margin (Table 1.8), but in 2011 China's trade regained the lead. If Iran is left out of account, the Gulf trade of India in 2011 was approximately equal to that of China, and both exceeded the Gulf trade of the European Union.

The leading Gulf trade partner of each of the outside states covered here has mostly been Saudi Arabia or the UAE. Nonetheless there have been some significant differences in the distribution of trade (Tables 1.3-1.9). The leading trade partner of China, Japan, South Korea, and the US has been Saudi Arabia. The predominance of EU trade has shifted between Saudi Arabia and the UAE. For India the UAE has held the leading position. The latter relationship has been particularly notable. Over the past three years India's trade with the UAE has been at least twice its trade with Saudi Arabia, accounting for about 46% of all India's trade with the Gulf. Since 2010 India has displaced the EU (and all other countries) as the UAE's leading trading partner. The margin of India's dominance in the market, moreover, is substantial (Tables 1.8 and 1.9).

Some other characteristics and trends in the trading patterns are also of interest. In 2011, Iran moved up to second place (after Saudi Arabia) in China's Gulf trade; Iraq was the only country where the US was the leading trading partner; China was Oman's leading trading partner (just as it had been for most of the previous decade); Japan and South Korea retained leading positions in Qatari and Kuwaiti trade; EU trade was well spread across the region, but only in Bahrain did it hold the leading position (Table 1.9).

7. The Gulf Trade of Southeast Asian Countries and Pakistan

The four Southeast Asian countries constitute a useful comparative grouping, in terms both of the similarities/differences among them, and those between them and the Gulf's other trading partners. They have historically had only a limited engagement in the Gulf, whether in trade, investment, strategy or population movement. Relative to the Gulf's major trading partners, the engagement remains limited. They are, however, fast-growing economies with rapidly expanding roles in international trade. Existing trends in their Gulf trade throw some light on how the trade may develop in the future.

Other Southeast Asian states have even smaller trading relationships with the Gulf states and are therefore not covered here. In one case, that of the Philippines, the limited trading relationship is surprising. In terms of overall contact, the Philippines is substantially more engaged in the Gulf than any other Southeast Asian country. Figures from the Philippines Overseas Employment Administration for 2009 put the total number of Filipinos in the Gulf at 2,290,161. This would put Filipinos as the third largest expatriate community in the region, after Indians and Pakistanis. Filipino overseas employment is better documented than that of Pakistanis (where there are significant numbers of non-registered migrants), which leaves open the possibility that the Filipino and Pakistani communities in the Gulf may be of a similar size. Despite this substantial Filipino presence in the Gulf, and the educational and cultural organization maintained by the community, trade between the Philippines and the Gulf is very limited.

Pakistan fits into a rather different category. Its engagement with the Gulf region has been very substantial. Historically there have been close links between the Gulf and the territories which now form part of Pakistan. Population movements, in both directions, have been present throughout recorded history, and in the mid-1980s it was estimated that Pakistanis (then totaling about 2 million in the GCC states alone) constituted the largest expatriate grouping in the region. Since then, the number has not increased as rapidly as has that of Indians (now about 6 million), but remains substantial. Some estimates put the total at around 2 million, and some at 3.5 million. A realistic figure may be about 3 million. Among this number are some who hold significant positions in commercial, governmental and military fields. As a result of military agreements between Pakistan and some Gulf states, there has at times been a significant military involvement in some of the armed forces of the GCC states. Nonetheless, Pakistan's trading relationship has not been commensurate with the wider engagement. Trade has been rather more substantial than in the case of the Southeast Asian states, but Pakistan has not by any means reached the level of being one of the Gulf's major trading partners.

Turning now to the specific trends and characteristics, the four Southeast Asian countries that account for the major part of Southeast Asia's trade with the Gulf collectively make up a relatively limited share of Gulf trade. This share has stood at about 7% for most of the period since 2005. The share was slightly higher in 2000, but had been lower in 1990. In 2011 it fell to 6.2%, mainly because of the greater relative impact which higher oil prices were having on the trade of the Gulf's major trading partners (Tables 1.3-1.9). While the overall growth of Southeast Asia's trade with the Gulf has not differed greatly from increases in Gulf trade globally, however, they do not all follow the same pattern.

Throughout the period from 1990 to 2010, Singapore had the biggest share of the Gulf trade. Up to 2000, in fact, Singapore accounted for more Gulf trade than all of the three other countries put together (Tables 1.3-1.9). Singapore's lead over the other Southeast Asian states, however, has steadily weakened in the period since 2000. The percentage increases in Singaporean trade with the Gulf have all been well below the global average increases in Gulf trade, over all three of the time periods covered in Table 1.15. The rates of growth have generally been more comparable to those of the EU, the US, South Korea and Japan, than to those of the other Southeast Asian countries. There is clearly no similarity with the expansionary pattern of Indian and Chinese trade with the Gulf. Singapore therefore fits into the pattern of the other industrial and newly-industrialized countries covered in the previous section: still occupying a leading position relative to others in its (in this case Southeast Asian) grouping, but gradually losing share to the industrializing countries in the same grouping.

The growth of Thailand's and Malaysia's trade with the Gulf has consistently exceeded average increase in global trade with the Gulf, while Indonesia's has been slightly below. As shown in Table 1.15, column 2, the rates of growth of trade with the Gulf for the four countries between 2005 and 2011 were: Singapore 41%, Indonesia 128%, Malaysia 154%, and Thailand 157%. The increase in the Gulf's global trade over that period was 136%.

Reflecting the differential in the rates of growth, the gap between the overall value of Singaporean trade with the Gulf and that of other Southeast Asian states has steadily declined over recent years, and in 2011 for the first time Thailand became the Gulf's leading trading partner in Southeast Asia. Figures for that year (see Table 1.9) are: Thailand $35.0 billion, Singapore $32.5 billion, Malaysia $16.0 billion, and Indonesia $14.6 billion. Given the pattern of growth over recent years, it seems probable that Thailand will retain the leading position for the near future. This, of course, should not be surprising. Although Singapore has had (and continues to have) a higher rate of GDP growth than Thailand, Thailand has a much larger population: 67 million, as against 5.4 million.

The composition of Southeast Asian trade with the Gulf varies considerably. Most of Singapore's trade with the Gulf consists of oil imports. In 2011, only 16% of its trade consisted of Singaporean exports to the Gulf, while the comparative percentages for Indonesia, Malaysia, and Thailand were 33%, 50%, and 26% respectively (Table 1.14, column 2). This, clearly, reflects the absence of any indigenous crude oil production in Singapore, despite consuming more oil than any other Southeast Asian state with the exception of Indonesia. Malaysia and Indonesia, on the other hand, are significant (but not self-sufficient) oil producers, and Thailand is a smaller-scale producer. The comparative figures for daily crude oil production/consumption for the four countries for 2011 were: Singapore 0/1183 bbl; Thailand 224/985 bbl, Malaysia 512/543 bbl, and Indonesia 918/1322 bbl.[22] Given Singapore's need for imported oil, it is unlikely that Malaysia or Indonesia will overtake Singapore in the ranking of Gulf trading partners at this stage.

Nonetheless, the changing trade patterns are not explained entirely by the need for oil. Since 2009, the exports of both Thailand and Malaysia to the Gulf have exceeded those of Singapore. Thailand is steadily consolidating its lead as the main Southeast Asian exporter to the Gulf, but with Malaysian exports to the Gulf also rising significantly. Indonesia's exports to the Gulf are substantially smaller, lagging behind those of all the other Southeast Asian states covered here. There is, however, some reason to believe that this could soon change. The 2010 and 2011 statistics show a substantial rise in Indonesian trade with Saudi Arabia and a lesser but significant rise in trade with the UAE. This reflects the potential of, and changes in, the Indonesian economy: a growth rate close to 6% per annum over the past five years; a large population to underpin a broadly-based industrialization; and a growing need for imported oil (with Indonesia's oil demand now significantly exceeding its domestic oil supply). The latter characteristics are reminiscent (but not identical) to those that applied to China and India when their Gulf trades first began to expand rapidly.

The primary Gulf trading partners of all of the Southeastern states are Saudi Arabia and the UAE (Tables 1.11-1.13). Singapore and Indonesia have had rather stronger trading relations with Saudi Arabia than with the UAE, while for Thailand and Malaysia it has been the other way round. Trading relations with other Gulf states have been very limited, with the exception of Singapore's oil imports from Qatar and Kuwait. Singapore has no quantifiable trade with either Iran or Iraq.

As noted earlier, Pakistan's Gulf trade is lower than would expected, given the country's long-standing links with the region (Table 1.16). Two-thirds of the trade is with Saudi Arabia and the UAE and consists mainly of oil imports. Relative to Southeast Asian countries, Pakistan's Gulf trade in 2011 was higher than that of Malaysia and Indonesia, but less than that of Thailand and Singapore. Yet, given that Pakistani international trade overall is relatively limited, the share of it going to (or coming from) the Gulf is higher than that of most of the other countries covered in this chapter. About 27% of all Pakistani trade was accounted for by the Gulf states in 2011, as against about 22% of all Indian trade. The rate of increase in the last two years (between 2009 and 2011) came to 42%, which suggests that it may have entered on a new projectory.

8. Investments and Contracting

The category of non-trade economic relations comprises a whole range of activities and undertakings, such as investment, construction contracts, co-production arrangements, and franchising agreements. They are difficult to quantify comparatively, and cross-national year-by-year comparisons are complicated by the irregular flows or resources required for particular projects, and sometimes by the unreality of attributing "national origin" to investments due to the transnational nature of many companies. In this paper, there will only be a cursory overview of this field of activity. Individual papers presented to the GRM workshop, focusing on individual Asian countries, provide a more appropriate framework for presenting the relevant material. It is, nonetheless, worth a mention here – to gauge whether shifts in trade (oil and non-oil) are counterbalanced by differing patterns of non-trade activity. The focus here is on the Gulf's major Asian economic partners: China, India, Japan and South Korea.

a. China

There has been a significant flow of investments between China and the Gulf, together with a large number of contracts won by Chinese companies operating in the Gulf. The most significant Chinese investments have been in Saudi Arabia, with a quite a high level of investment in Iran, and some significant projects in all of the other Gulf states (Iraq, Kuwait and the UAE in particular). There are currently about 80 projects in Saudi Arabia where Chinese companies are active, with a value of $12.5 billion, and some 90 Chinese businesses are present in the country. About 20,000 Chinese workers are employed on construction projects undertaken by Chinese companies. The construction of the Haramain Railway in Mecca has been regarded as a prestigious symbol of Chinese engagement in the region, even though the undertaking was loss-making to the Chinese holding company concerned. China also has a significant involvement in oil exploration and/or extraction in Iran, Iraq and Saudi Arabia. Conversely, there has been significant Gulf investment in China. The most substantial such investment is the Saudi ARAMCO/ExxonMobil/Sinopec joint investment in refining and petrochemicals in Fujian. Other Saudi companies (in particular SABIC) have also been involved, and there has in addition been refining or petrochemical-linked investment from Kuwait and the UAE, as well as other Saudi companies.

b. Japan

Japanese companies are well-established investors in most of the Gulf states, and its total investment in the Gulf is almost certainly larger than that of any other Asian country. Indeed, total investments were rising sharply through the middle of the last decade, but with some subsequent reduction as a result of the global financial crisis and in the wake of the earthquake and tsunami which hit Japan in March 2011. Much of the investment has been in major projects, such as the petrochemical project at Rabigh in Saudi Arabia and oil exploration. The range of fields of investment, moreover, has been wide with some significant investments in water and other infrastructural fields. Significant links exist between the financial sectors of Japan and the states of the GCC. Japanese companies have played a prominent role in construction in most of the Gulf states, with involvement in some major undertakings – including the Dubai metro. There has been a certain amount of Gulf investment going to Japan, such as the purchase by Dubai

International Capital of a stake in Sony Corporation. This, however, remains relatively limited.

c. India

India's investment in the Gulf has been relatively limited, although it is steadily increasing. Indian companies, however, have been increasingly active in construction contracts, especially in the field of infrastructure. The converse flow of investment has also been limited. There is, nonetheless, substantial indication that the latter is set to undergo rapid growth. Some of the latter has been caused by Gulf investors becoming wary about investing in Europe due to political/economic uncertainties over the Euro, and seeing India as providing opportunities for more profitable investment. A $1 billion vehicle for joint investment between India and Saudi Arabia was set up in 2009. In 2012 the Indian government agreed to allow qualified foreign investors to invest in Indian capital markets, and Gulf investors were expected to take benefit from this.

d. South Korea

South Korean investment in the Gulf states has been relatively limited, but is now acquiring substantial significance due to the crucial areas in which Korean investors have been active. South Korea's winning of the contract to construct the UAE's first nuclear power plants, with investment as part of the package, is particularly important and could be followed by similar success elsewhere in the Gulf (although not in Iran or perhaps Saudi Arabia). There is also strong South Korean involvement in the electric power sector and in semiconductors in the UAE, as also in petrochemicals and refining. South Korean construction companies have won many of the key construction contracts in the Gulf. Investment flows in the opposite direction have been limited.

9. Conclusion

The Gulf states are now becoming more integrated into an Asian framework than they have been in the past. To see this as a move toward the eclipse of Western interests in the region, however, would be misleading. The most fundamental change is represented by the reduced share of trade taken by industrialized countries and the increased share taken by two industrializing countries: India and China. Rather than focusing on the West to East shift, it is more useful to focus on the manner in which the different Asian countries relate to the Gulf and how these may impinge on the position of established interests there.

Appendix

Table 1.3: 1990 Gulf Trade (General) $ billion

	Bahrain	Saudi Arabia	UAE	Qatar	Oman	Kuwait	Iraq	Iran	TOTAL
China	0.0	0.5	0.6	0.0	0.0	0.1	0.0	0.2	1.3
India	0.1	1.3	1.3	0.1	0.1	0.5	0.4	0.6	4.4
Japan	0.3	12.1	9.9	2.2	0.6	2.4	1.1	5.9	33.5
South Korea	0.1	2.4	1.5	0.2	0.2	0.6	0.0	1.1	6.1
EU	0.7	17.3	5.8	0.8	1.3	3.5	5.9	24.6	59.9
US	0.3	11.2	1.9	0.2	0.4	1.0	3.7	0.4	19.1
Indonesia	0.0	0.4	0.1	0.0	0.0	0.1	0.2	0.1	0.9
Malaysia	0.0	0.2	0.2	0.0	0.0	0.0	0.1	0.1	0.6
Singapore	0.0	2.5	1.6	0.1	0.2	0.5	0.0	0.3	5.1
Thailand	0.0	0.6	0.6	0.1	0.0	0.2	0.1	0.2	1.8
World	4.5	68.5	33.4	4.9	6.8	12.6	16.8	38.0	185.5

Compiled by the author from IMF Direction of Trade Statistics

Table 1.4: 2000 Gulf Trade (General) $ billion

	Bahrain	Saudi Arabia	UAE	Qatar	Oman	Kuwait	Iraq	Iran	TOTAL
China	0.1	2.0	2.4	0.4	3.2	0.6	0.9	2.2	11.8
India	0.3	1.9	2.5	0.2	0.2	0.7	0.1	0.7	6.6
Japan	0.4	16.0	15.9	5.6	2.8	5.2	0.6	5.5	52.0
South Korea	0.3	9.8	5.5	2.1	1.6	2.7	0.7	2.9	25.6
EU	1.3	23.3	11.6	1.3	1.1	5.0	5.0	13.1	66.7
US	0.8	18.8	3.6	0.7	0.4	3.5	5.8	0.3	33.9
Indonesia	0.0	1.9	0.7	0.0	0.0	0.8	0.1	0.2	3.7
Malaysia	0.0	0.9	0.6	0.1	0.4	0.1	0.0	0.2	2.3
Singapore	0.0	4.1	1.9	0.9	0.3	1.4	0.0	1.4	10.0
Thailand	0.0	1.3	2.1	0.3	1.0	0.4	0.3	0.5	5.9
World	11.3	105.4	66.3	14.8	15.7	26.1	18.3	41.3	299.2

Compiled by the author from IMF Direction of Trade Statistics

Table 1.5: 2005 Gulf Trade (General) $ billion

	Bahrain	Saudi Arabia	UAE	Qatar	Oman	Kuwait	Iraq	Iran	TOTAL
China	0.3	15.6	11.5	0.9	4.5	1.6	1.8	8.5	44.9
India	0.4	3.2	13.1	1.2	0.8	0.9	0.2	1.6	21.4
Japan	0.7	40.3	28.2	11.5	3.8	8.2	0.5	10.5	103.8
South Korea	0.4	16.8	12.1	8.1	4.1	5.9	0.7	5.3	53.4
EU	2.2	44.2	44.2	3.9	2.5	8.9	7.5	29.1	142.5
US	0.8	35.1	10.7	1.5	0.9	6.1	10.3	0.3	66.0
Indonesia	0.1	3.0	1.3	0.1	0.2	1.3	0.1	0.3	6.4
Malaysia	0.1	1.9	2.7	0.1	0.4	0.4	0.1	0.6	6.3
Singapore	0.4	8.4	6.3	2.2	0.5	3.5	0.0	1.7	23.0
Thailand	0.2	4.7	6.4	0.7	0.5	0.4	0.4	0.3	13.6
World	22.1	214.3	197.7	35.4	27.3	51.1	30.5	94.1	672.5

Compiled by the author from IMF Direction of Trade Statistics

Table 1.6: 2008 Gulf Trade (General) $ billion

	Bahrain	Saudi Arabia	UAE	Qatar	Oman	Kuwait	Iraq	Iran	TOTAL
China	0.8	40.1	30.1	2.6	12.2	6.5	2.6	26.5	121.4
India	1.9	27.1	49.1	3.8	2.0	10.9	9.2	15.3	119.3
Japan	1.4	54.9	54.5	21.5	7.4	16.1	1.6	18.7	176.1
South Korea	0.8	36.5	23.8	13.5	6.9	11.8	4.2	12.2	109.7
EU	3.6	64.1	58.7	12.4	4.4	14.5	15.1	39.2	212.0
US	1.4	65.5	18.5	2.6	2.0	9.7	23.3	0.8	124.8
Indonesia	0.3	5.7	2.3	0.2	0.1	1.8	0.3	1.0	10.7
Malaysia	0.2	3.2	6.4	0.5	1.0	0.9	0.2	1.5	13.9
Singapore	0.3	14.3	10.3	6.9	1.0	6.2	0.0	1.9	40.9
Thailand	0.3	8.7	12.8	2.4	2.9	0.6	0.5	0.9	29.1
World	41.1	419.4	395.1	83.6	58.1	104.3	78.0	189.5	1370.0

Compiled by the author from IMF Direction of Trade Statistics

Table 1.7: 2009 Gulf Trade (General) $ billion

	Bahrain	Saudi Arabia	UAE	Qatar	Oman	Kuwait	Iraq	Iran	TOTAL
China	0.7	31.3	22.9	2.2	5.7	4.9	5.0	20.7	93.4
India	0.8	17.4	36.7	4.4	3.4	7.6	5.8	11.8	87.9
Japan	1.0	31.5	27.9	16.2	5.7	9.5	1.6	10.3	103.7
South Korea	0.6	22.2	13.9	9.0	4.3	8.0	4.3	9.6	71.9
EU	3.1	44.7	43.1	12.2	3.7	9.3	12.1	27.8	156.0
US	1.2	33.0	14.7	3.4	2.0	5.7	10.8	0.4	71.2
Indonesia	0.1	3.9	1.6	0.3	0.1	1.4	0.0	0.9	8.3
Malaysia	0.2	1.9	4.7	0.9	0.6	0.4	0.2	1.0	9.9
Singapore	0.4	8.2	7.9	4.4	0.7	2.6	0.0	1.9	26.1
Thailand	0.2	5.7	8.8	1.9	2.3	0.7	0.3	1.2	21.1
World	32.3	265.5	269.8	69.0	42.0	66.0	59.1	134.7	938.4

Compiled by the author from IMF Direction of Trade Statistics

Table 1.8: 2010 Gulf Trade (General) $ billion

	Bahrain	Saudi Arabia	UAE	Qatar	Oman	Kuwait	Iraq	Iran	TOTAL
China	1.1	41.3	27.3	3.2	9.9	8.1	9.7	18.8	119.4
India	0.9	23.7	50.3	5.8	5.1	10.2	8.4	15.2	119.6
Japan	1.2	39.7	34.7	21.0	7.5	10.9	3.5	12.4	130.9
South Korea	0.6	24.3	15.0	10.0	4.8	9.0	4.3	10.3	78.3
EU	2.7	48.7	42.1	16.0	4.3	9.3	11.8	32.6	167.5
US	1.8	42.4	13.9	3.9	1.9	8.1	13.3	0.3	85.6
Indonesia	0.2	5.2	2.1	0.6	0.3	1.3	0.1	1.2	11.0
Malaysia	0.3	2.4	5.7	1.1	0.7	0.5	0.2	1.3	12.2
Singapore	0.3	11.1	10.0	5.2	0.9	2.6	0.0	2.4	32.5
Thailand	0.3	7.5	11.1	2.2	2.8	0.8	0.5	0.8	26.0
World	40.7	330.7	321.3	87.6	55.9	81.7	74.7	172.6	1165.2

Compiled by the author from IMF Direction of Trade Statistics

Table 1.9: 2011 Gulf Trade (General) $ billion

	Bahrain	Saudi Arabia	UAE	Qatar	Oman	Kuwait	Iraq	Iran	TOTAL
China	1.4	51.3	37.0	5.6	14.6	10.6	13.7	43.8	194.9
India	1.6	30.3	76.0	8.8	5.9	13.8	13.9	15.2	165.5
Japan	1.2	53.1	47.2	28.5	7.8	13.4	3.8	13.6	168.6
South Korea	0.9	41.3	21.4	19.4	5.9	17.0	10.0	18.2	134.1
EU	3.2	49.2	54.8	23.3	5.0	9.7	15.7	35.8	196.7
US	1.8	59.5	19.8	4.3	3.7	10.3	18.5	0.3	118.3
Indonesia	0.1	6.5	2.6	0.7	0.6	1.4	0.8	1.9	14.6
Malaysia	0.2	4.7	7.6	0.6	0.4	0.9	0.2	1.4	16.0
Singapore	0.3	17.0	15.7	7.1	1.4	3.5	0.0	0.0	32.5
Thailand	0.8	9.2	16.2	2.6	3.0	1.1	0.8	1.2	35.0
World	41.2	457.2	454.8	127.1	70.2	109.3	104.4	225.3	1589.5

Compiled by the author from IMF Direction of Trade Statistics

Table 1.10: 1990-2009 Gulf Trade Totals $ billion

	1990	2000	2005	2008	2009
China	1.3	11.8	44.9	121.4	93.4
India	4.4	6.6	21.4	119.3	87.9
Japan	33.5	52.0	103.8	176.1	103.7
South Korea	6.1	25.6	53.4	109.7	71.9
EU	59.9	66.7	142.5	212.0	156.0
US	19.1	33.9	66.0	124.8	71.2
Indonesia	0.9	3.7	6.4	10.7	8.3
Malaysia	0.6	2.3	6.3	13.9	9.9
Singapore	5.1	10.0	23.0	40.9	26.1
Thailand	1.8	5.9	13.6	29.1	21.1

Compiled by the author from IMF Direction of Trade Statistics

Table 1.11: 2009 Gulf Imports $ billion

	Bahrain	Saudi Arabia	UAE	Qatar	Oman	Kuwait	Iraq	Iran	TOTAL
China	0.5	9.2	20.5	1.0	0.9	1.7	2.0	8.7	44.5
India	0.3	4.1	22.7	0.6	1.1	0.8	0.5	2.1	32.2
Japan	0.5	5.9	7.1	1.8	2.7	1.4	0.3	1.8	21.5
South Korea	0.3	4.2	5.5	1.4	0.6	0.8	0.9	4.4	18.1
EU	2.6	30.1	38.4	8.1	3.1	5.7	4.1	16.0	108.1
US	0.7	11.9	13.3	3.0	1.2	2.1	2.0	0.3	34.5
Indonesia	0.0	1.1	1.4	0.1	0.1	0.1	0.0	0.6	3.4
Malaysia	0.1	0.9	3.1	0.6	0.5	0.2	0.2	0.8	6.4
Singapore	0.1	0.8	4.1	0.3	0.2	0.2	0.0	0.7	6.3
Thailand	0.2	2.0	2.7	0.4	0.4	0.4	0.3	0.9	7.3
World	9.2	92.8	152.0	22.8	17.9	19.1	23.7	60.0	397.5

Compiled by the author from IMF Direction of Trade Statistics

Table 1.12: 2010 Gulf Imports $ billion

	Bahrain	Saudi Arabia	UAE	Qatar	Oman	Kuwait	Iraq	Iran	TOTAL
China	0.9	11.4	23.4	0.9	1.0	2.0	4.0	12.2	55.8
India	0.3	4.8	29.1	0.6	1.2	1.0	0.6	2.3	39.9
Japan	0.6	7.1	8.1	1.3	3.4	1.6	0.3	2.9	25.3
South Korea	0.3	4.3	5.5	1.5	0.6	0.8	0.9	4.4	21.3
EU	2.0	30.0	36.7	7.0	3.8	5.7	3.7	15.7	102.6
US	1.4	12.8	12.8	3.5	1.2	3.1	1.8	0.2	36.8
Indonesia	0.0	1.3	1.6	0.1	0.1	0.1	0.1	0.1	3.4
Malaysia	0.1	1.0	3.6	0.7	0.5	0.2	0.2	0.9	6.3
Singapore	0.1	0.9	4.2	0.2	0.1	0.2	0.0	0.4	6.1
Thailand	0.1	2.3	3.1	0.3	0.6	0.3	0.5	0.6	7.8
World	11.2	103.0	165.6	22.5	22.9	21.6	27.5	70.3	444.6

Compiled by the author from IMF Direction of Trade Statistics

Table 1.13: 2011 Gulf Imports $ billion

	Bahrain	Saudi Arabia	UAE	Qatar	Oman	Kuwait	Iraq	Iran	TOTAL
China	1.0	16.3	29.5	1.3	1.1	2.3	4.2	16.3	72.0
India	1.0	6.7	42.2	0.5	1.4	2.5	0.9	3.0	58.2
Japan	0.5	7.2	8.2	1.1	3.1	1.5	0.4	1.9	23.9
South Korea	0.3	7.7	8.0	0.5	1.0	1.6	1.7	7.9	28.7
EU	2.2	30.2	44.7	6.6	4.1	4.8	4.7	15.0	112.3
US	1.3	15.2	17.5	3.1	1.6	3.0	2.7	0.3	44.7
Indonesia	0.0	1.6	1.9	0.1	0.2	0.1	0.2	0.9	5.0
Malaysia	0.1	1.4	4.8	0.2	0.2	0.3	0.1	0.9	8.0
Singapore	0.1	1.0	5.1	0.3	0.2	0.2	0.0	0.0	6.9
Thailand	0.2	2.5	3.0	0.3	0.6	0.4	0.7	1.1	9.4
World	11.5	127.5	212.6	24.1	25.8	25.2	36.6	94.6	557.9

Compiled by the author from IMF Direction of Trade Statistics

Table 1.14: 2009 and 2011 Proportion of Exports in the Gulf Trade of Trading Partners

	2009	2011
China	48%	39%
India	38%	35%
Japan	25%	14%
South Korea	25%	22%
EU	65%	55%
US	49%	38%
Indonesia	38%	33%
Malaysia	67%	50%
Singapore	23%	16%
Thailand	33%	26%
World	43%	35%

Compiled by the author from IMF Direction of Trade Statistics

Table 1.15: Percentage Increases in Gulf Trade, by Trading Partners

	2005-9	2005-11	2000-8
China	107%	334%	908%
India	314%	673%	1600%
Japan	0%	62%	238%
South Korea	36%	151%	323%
EU	9%	38%	217%
US	8%	88%	213%
Indonesia	33%	128%	173%
Malaysia	67%	154%	600%
Singapore	13%	41%	310%
Thailand	50%	157%	383%
World	38%	136%	359%

Compiled by the author from IMF Direction of Trade Statistics

Table 1.16: Pakistan Gulf Trade, 1990-2011 $ billion

	1990	2000	2005	2009	2011	Combined Exports and Imports
Bahrain *Exports*	0.0	0.1	0.0	0.1	0.2	0.3
Imports	0.0	0.0	0.0	0.1	0.1	
Saudi Arabia *Exports*	0.5	1.0	2.6	3.2	5.3	5.9
Imports	0.1	0.1	0.2	0.5	0.6	
UAE *Exports*	0.1	1.0	2.4	3.1	5.2	7.4
Imports	0.1	0.3	1.4	1.6	2.2	
Qatar *Exports*	0.0	0.0	0.2	0.2	0.3	0.6
Imports	0.0	0.0	0.0	0.2	0.3	
Oman *Exports*	0.0	0.0	0.0	0.2	0.4	0.6
Imports	0.0	0.0	0.1	0.2	0.2	
Kuwait *Exports*	0.4	1.2	1.2	1.6	2.7	2.8
Imports	0.0	0.0	0.0	0.1	0.1	
Iraq *Exports*	0.0	0.0	0.0	0.0	0.0	0.1
Imports	0.0	0.0	0.0	0.1	0.1	
Iran *Exports*	0.2	0.3	0.3	0.9	1.5	2.0
Imports	0.0	0.0	0.1	0.4	0.5	
World *Exports*	7.7	10.4	25.2	32.4	46.6	74.2
Imports	5.5	8.9	15.2	19.6	27.6	

Compiled by the author from IMF Direction of Trade Statistics

Endnotes

1   One aspect of the economic relationships is not covered here, namely remittances transferred to non-Gulf Asian countries from Gulf countries. Coverage of these is left to the country-based chapters in this book. It should be noted, however, that these are very substantial for some Asian countries and insubstantial for others. Remittances form a significant part of the economic relations which Gulf countries have with India, Pakistan and South-East Asian countries, for example, but only an insignificant part of the economic relations with most of the other Asian countries covered in this book.

2   All of the statistics in this paragraph are taken from *BP Statistical Review of World Energy, June 2011* (London: BP Distribution Services, 2011), pp. 2-8, and 41.

3   "Oil reserves" as used here includes not only crude oil but also gas condensate, natural gas liquids and oil sands "under active development". "Oil production" includes oil coming from crude oil, oil shale, oil sands, and natural gas liquids (NGLs) where this is recovered separately.

4   See CIA, "Country Comparison: Oil Production" and "Country Comparison: Oil Exports", in *World Factbook,*, continuously updated, accessed March 2012 at https://www.cia.gov/library/publications/the-world-factbook/rankorder/2173rank.html

5   *BP Energy Outlook 2030* (London: BP Distribution Services, 2011), p. 37.

6   The median, as used here, is referred to by BP in its projections as "'to the best of our knowledge', reflecting our judgements of the likely path of global energy markets to 2030". *Ibid*, p. 6.

7   *Ibid.*, p. 9.

8   All figures on future energy consumption given here are taken from *Ibid*, pp. 13-17.

9   *Ibid.*, pp. 17-23.

10 *Ibid.*, p. 27-29.

11 *Ibid.*, p. 33.

12 The figures in this paragraph are taken from *Ibid*, pp. 35-37.

13 As it would not be possible to cover all Asian countries in this section and the next, primary attention will be given to China and India (for reasons already stated), with significant attention also to Japan, South Korea and Southeast Asia.

14 *China Briefing*, 13 February 2010. Available at http://www.china-briefing.com.

15 Similar figures are produced by the U.S. Energy Information Agency (EIA). See EIA, "Short-term Energy Outlook," Washington, D.C.: U.S.-EIA, March 2009, Section 3a.

16 Except where otherwise indicated, the projections on oil production given in this paragraph are taken from *BP Energy Outlook 2030* (London: BP Distribution Services, 2011), pp. 47-57.

17 EIA, *World Energy Outlook 2011: Are we Entering a Golden Age of Gas?* (Special Report), (Washington: EIA, 2011), pp. 48-56.

18 *Ibid.*

19 *Ibid.*

20 Population figures for the Gulf states vary considerably from source to source. All population figures in this chapter are taken from the data available from the United Nations Department of Economic and Social Affairs (Population Division). Accessed 21 June, 2012, http://esa.un.org/unpd/wpp/panel-population.hti.

21 This is documented in Chapter 3.

22 US Energy Information Administration, "Independent Statistics and Analysis". Accessed 30 June 2012, http://205.254.135.7/countries/country-data.cfm?fips=ID&trk=p1

Bibliography

Alterman, Jon, and Garver, John. *The Vital Triangle: China, the United States and the Middle East*. Washington: CSIS, 2008.

BP. *BP Energy Outlook 2030*. London: BP Distribution Services, 2011.

BP. *BP Statistical Review of World Energy, June 2011*. London: BP Distribution Services, 2011.

Central Intelligence Agency. "Country Comparison: Oil Production" and "Country Comparison: Oil Exports", in *World Factbook,* continuously updated, accessed March 2012 at https://www.cia.gov/library/publications/the-world-factbook/rankorder/2173rank.html

China Briefing. 13 February 2010. Accessed at http://www.china-briefing.com

Davidson, Christopher. *The Persian Gulf and Pacific Asia: from Indifference to Interdependence*. London: Hurst, 2010.

International Energy Agency. "Collaboration with India and China on Oil Security". Paper presented at the IEA/ASEAN/ASCOPE Workshop, Session 3, 6 April 2004.

International Monetary Fund. *Direction of Trade Statistics 2011*. Washington: International Monetary Fund, 2012.

Kemp, Geoff. *The East Moves West: India, China, and Asia's Growing Presence in the Middle East* Washington, D.C.: Brookings Institution Press, 2010.

Liangxiang, Jin. "Energy first: China and the Middle East". *Middle East Quarterly* 12 (2005).

Madani, Abdallah. "Indo-Saudi Relations, 1947-97: Domestic Concerns and Foreign Relations". PhD Diss., University of Exeter, 2003.

Madsen, Julian. "Iran in China's Strategic Calculus". *Gulf-Asia Research Bulletin*, 2 (2007).

Niblock, Tim. "China's Growing Involvement in the Gulf: The Geopolitical Significance," in *Multidimensional Diplomacy of Contemporary China*, edited by S.Shen and M.Blanchard, 207-231. New York: Lexington Books, 2010.

Pasha, A.K. *India, Iran and the GCC States: Political Strategy and Foreign Policy*. New Delhi: Manas Publications, 2000.

US Energy Information Administration, "Independent Statistics and Analysis". Accessed 30 June 2012. http://205.254.135.7/countries/country-data.cfm?fips=ID&trk=p1

U.S. Energy Information Agency (EIA), "Short-term Energy Outlook". Washington, D.C.: U.S.-EIA, March 2009.

U.S. Energy Information Agency, *World Energy Outlook 2011: Are we Entering a Golden Age of Gas?* (Special Report). Washington: EIA, 2011.

Chapter Two

The Growing Roles of Asian Powers in the Gulf: A Saudi Perspective

Naser al-Tamimi

1. Introduction

Since the 9/11 terrorist attacks Saudi Arabia has been seeking to rebalance its relations with the world major powers. As a result, the Saudis have been pursuing a "hedging strategy" toward the United States, by developing a more robust relationship with Asian powers, particularly China. Furthermore, the uprisings that swept the Arab countries in 2011 and resulted in the overthrowing of some Arab leaders could have very serious implications for Saudi Arabia's foreign affairs in the long term.

These political developments were coupled with change in the geopolitical landscape of the world's energy demand/supply. First, Saudi Arabia is facing a significant shift in demand from West to East. Second, Saudi Arabia's dominant role in the world oil supply could be altered by: (a) the development of the large new unconventional oil reserves in North America; (b) unrestrained domestic fuel consumption within Saudi Arabia itself; (c) a substantial increase in Iraqi production, with significant spare capacity.

Within this context, Riyadh's three main foreign policy objectives have been to[1] (a) maintain a strategic partnership with the United States, which is fundamental to its security; (b) maximise its global and regional political influence through its financial and Islamic "soft power"; and (c) maximise the economic and geopolitical benefits from being the most important oil producer in the world and *de facto* leader of OPEC. When these three objectives cannot be accommodated simultaneously, national security takes precedence. In other words, Saudi Arabia prefers an outcome that protects its special relationship with the United States over alternative outcomes that would imply higher economic benefits or global and regional influence.[2] However, in the last decade the economic and political calculation of Saudi Arabia has been complicated by many domestic and international factors which may require new policies. The combination of global structural shifts and local political transitions raises a critical question: what will be the strategic and economic implications of an eastward shift in focus by Saudi Arabia? This chapter argues that although Saudi Arabia does continue to rely on the United States in its defence policy, in the longer term, changes in the local, regional and international environment coupled with growing integration of Saudi Arabia's economy with Asian economies could push the Kingdom to diversify its political agenda and security arrangements.

2. Saudi Arabia's Security: Changing Dynamics

During the Cold War and Iraq's challenge in the 1990s, the US–Saudi relationship has been characterised as "oil for security," and the Saudis managed to balance their three foreign policy strategic objectives to protect their national security.[3] However, the terrorist attacks of 9/11 put a strain on this relationship and complicated the Saudi calculations. It caused both Riyadh and Washington to re-evaluate their "special relationship."[4] It was no longer realistic to imagine that Saudi religious influence could be used to promote US security and political interests within the region.[5] It is in this context that Riyadh has begun courting an Asian alternative.[6] As a result, the Saudis have been pursuing a "hedging strategy" toward the United States, by developing a more robust relationship with China.[7] A Saudi analyst summarised the Kingdom's position when he told the *Financial Times* that the new political issues arose as a factor for the Kingdom after the 9/11 attacks on the US strained relations with traditional allies in the West. He added: "The relationship with the US will always be strong…It's a long relationship and we cannot ignore it whatever happens. But after the September 11 attacks, when we started looking around, nobody was there because we had never built relationships with Russia or China [and India later on]. And we thought: Let's build bridges with other countries."[8]

Saudi Arabia has recognised that increased diversity of its oil exports and movement away from its heavy reliance on the American market has both economic and political benefits. Saudi Arabia cannot ignore the increased energy needs among Asian countries, notably China and India. Furthermore, by distancing itself from a disproportionate reliance on the US energy market, Saudi Arabia will be in a better position to extricate itself from the political costs of a close relationship with the United States.[9] Indeed, over the last decade, Saudi Arabia has diversified its foreign policies by shifting the focus from the West to the East as a response to changing international and regional situations. This is partly a means to neutralise American pressure, and partly because Asian economies, particularly China and India, have developed rapidly.[10]

US-Saudi relations have improved dramatically since the post-9/11 period. Nevertheless, Riyadh and Washington differ, often widely, on preferred strategies. In this regard a secret document sent by David Rundell, Deputy Chief of the US Mission in Saudi Arabia, and leaked by "*WikiLeaks*" in November 2010 summarises the Saudi American differences in very interesting words:

> The Saudis have three principal issues areas of concern about US policies: (a) As the author of the 2002 Arab Peace Initiative, King Abdallah risked his personal prestige to advocate a comprehensive Middle East peace as the "strategic option" for the Arabs, only to be frustrated by what he saw as US reluctance to engage over the next seven years. (b) Similarly, in the Saudi view, we ignored advice from the King and Foreign Minister against invading Iraq. In the words of Saudi Foreign Minister Prince Saud Al-Faisal, "Military intervention in Iraq and Afghanistan has tilted the (regional) balance of power towards Iran." (c) Finally, the US debate over whether and how to engage Iran has fuelled Saudi fears that a new US Administration might strike a "grand bargain" without first consulting Arab countries bordering the Persian Gulf.[11]

Adding to the complications, the strain on the relationship with the US was further exacerbated during the protests across the Arab world in the spring of 2011. These differences surfaced strongly in 2011 due to the Saudi king's anger at Washington's response to uprisings across the Arab World, especially its abandonment of Hosni Mubarak, the deposed Egyptian president, who was a long-time Saudi and US ally. In May 2011, Saudi grievances were laid out in a *Washington Post* op-ed by

Nawaf Obaid, a senior fellow at the King Faisal Center for Research and Islamic Studies headed by former Saudi intelligence chief Prince Turki al-Faisal. Describing a "tectonic shift" in the Saudi-US relationship, he argues that: "Riyadh intends to pursue a much more assertive foreign policy, at times conflicting with American interests."[12] He went on to say: "For more than 60 years, Saudi Arabia has been bound by an unwritten bargain: oil for security...American missteps in the region since September 11, an ill-conceived response to the Arab protest movements and an unconscionable refusal to hold Israel accountable for its illegal settlement building have brought this arrangement to an end."[13]

The current Saudi calculations are driven by a deep fear and suspicion of expanding Iranian influence. Saudi leadership has begun to look at all regional security issues through the prism of their fears about growing Iranian influence. They see Iran's activities as dangerously provocative, not only in Iraq, but also in Syria, Lebanon, Palestine, Bahrain, Yemen, parts of Africa, and Southeast Asia.[14] Indeed, the perceived Iranian "threat" moved again to Riyadh's top list of priorities. Concerned about a possible rise in Iran's regional influence and a decline in the status of the moderate Arab camp, the Saudis are pursuing an active diplomacy (Syria is a good example) aimed at leveraging the changes in the Arab world in their favour.[15] From the Saudi point of view, the inability to coerce Iran looks like American weakness. Add to this the withdrawal of US forces from Iraq, which is seen in Riyadh as a terrible error, and the result is that the United States appears in fact to be abandoning the arena to Iran.[16]

These developments could have very serious implications in the long term. The first issue, deterioration of the US-Saudi relationship, could cause Saudi Arabia to consider nuclear proliferation to deter foreign aggression independently of US security assurances. This scenario would only be likely if the Saudi leaders completely lost confidence in the US promise of protection during crises. Secondly, in the event of a nuclear breakout by Iran, Saudi Arabia would feel compelled to build or acquire its own nuclear arsenal.[17] Riyadh's view that the Iranian threat is serious and immediate was recently expressed by diplomatic cables obtained by *WikiLeaks* and published by the *Guardian* newspaper that revealed Saudi King Abdullah had privately warned Washington in 2008 that if Iran developed nuclear weapons "everyone in the region would do the same, including Saudi Arabia."[18] Whether Saudi Arabia relied on its emerging nuclear power programme to manufacture nuclear weapons (which would take approximately a decade), or tries to get help from Pakistan, in both cases China will play a vital role.[19] Finally, as Saudi leaders take popular sentiments into account, it will become more difficult for the governments to disregard the reactions of domestic audiences on important economic and security issues in order to satisfy the policy demands of the United States. Consequently, a close relationship with the United States may no longer be sustainable, or it might come at a cost of losing significant domestic support. Either way, the payoff from cooperating with the United States may decrease, making alternative policy choices more attractive.[20] This has been an important factor in pursuing the relations with China (and India) in order to assure the Saudi public in regard to the balanced foreign policy of their country. Within the backdrop of these strategic dynamics, do the Saudis have a viable alternative to relying exclusively on an American defence umbrella?

Currently, there is no substitute for the American defensive umbrella in the Gulf region and there is no evidence which suggests that the US-Saudi relationship will sour in the near future. Despite tensions, there is no crisis in the relationship. Plans are proceeding for the United States to sell Saudi Arabia US$60 billion in arms over the coming years. US advisers are helping the Saudi Interior Ministry build a 35,000-man "special facilities security force."[21] Washington and Riyadh have coordinated the efforts to manage a transition of power in Yemen.[22] Both countries currently share similar concerns about Iran and Syria, and seek to calm oil markets to prevent further pressure on the global economy.[23] Yet, Riyadh's concerns about the Arab Spring are similar to its concerns after the 9/11 terror attacks: that the events would have a negative impact on the Kingdom's image in the United States, and that in the long run, the willingness of the United States to defend Saudi Arabia would be damaged.[24] How, then, does the "Asian alternative" fit within the context of Saudi calculations?

i. **The Perceived Iranian Threat.** With recent developments in the Arab World, Saudi Arabia remains fearful of the ability of Iran to destabilise the Saudi regime. The security and stability of the Saudi regime remain of the utmost importance. Given Iran's constraints and limited timetable, Saudi Arabia is more likely to stay committed to the US security framework in the region -- for lack of better options.[25] Here China, India and the other Asian powers still lag far behind America, which remains the Saudis' military mainstay. In this context, John Garver, a professor at the Georgia Institute of Technology (Atlanta), argues that: "Middle Eastern authoritarian regimes that survive the upheaval -- especially Saudi Arabia -- may well look upon China as a more reliable supporter than the U.S....But the problem is that China is simply not prepared, materially or psychologically, to meet the security needs of those countries."[26] The presence of American troops in the Gulf, though no longer on Saudi soil, reassures the Saudis, since it can bank on America's presence.[27]

ii. **Military Power.** Asian countries' relations with Saudi Arabia remain fundamentally commercial and have not moved to a strategic level whereby one Asian power (in particular China or India) could play a role in safeguarding Saudi security.[28] From Riyadh's perspective, China, India and other Asian powers do not have the same capability to project power globally as the United States does and therefore cannot provide the same security assurances against the international threats Saudi Arabia faces, particularly from Iran and domestic terrorism. Even if the Chinese and Indians had the capability to project power globally, the Saudis may question the reliability of both countries' security assurances due to the long relations they have had with Iran. In this regard, only India has direct military ties with the Gulf States, and those ties are presently low-key in scope and purpose.[29] Japan, which has the least military presence, does not seek a direct relationship in the Gulf defence establishments. Japan's strategic relationship with the US remains a central pillar of its foreign policy.[30] South Korea's engagement with the Middle East has focused primarily on energy imports and construction. Seoul's foreign policy has been driven principally by deterrence and defence requirements vis-à-vis North Korea.[31] Therefore, it is difficult to see, based on current trends, any Asian military role that would supplement, let alone supplant, the current dominant position of the United States.[32]

iii. **Terrorism.** Al-Qa'ida remains a major Saudi security concern. The authorities crushed a violent militant campaign in 2003-06, but many al-Qa'ida operatives have since joined their counterparts in Yemen. Riyadh fears the turbulence in Yemen may allow al-Qa'ida to entrench itself in territory now beyond government control.[33] In this regard, the Saudis view Asian powers (China in particular) as a weak alternative for US support against the threats the Saudi Kingdom faces on the domestic front from terrorism, or from instability in Yemen. For example, in 2009, during the Saudi military's two months' campaign against Yemeni Houthi rebels, the Kingdom turned to the US for emergency provision of munitions, imagery and intelligence to help them operate with greater precision. According to a secret US diplomatic cable sent in December 2009 and released by *WikiLeaks*, the US Ambassador to Saudi Arabia, James B. Smith, acknowledged that the US supplied Riyadh with "stocks of ammunition for small weapons and artillery."[34] He later approved using US satellites to target the Yemeni rebels near Saudi Arabia's southern border.[35] Prince Turki al-Faisal also acknowledged that the U.S. was training a 35,000 strong facilities security force. He said that: "these troops come from across the Kingdom and receive extensive training through a US technical training program. This specialized force, which did not exist before 2005, has the exclusive responsibility of guarding all energy installations against both internal and external threats."[36]

Although Saudi Arabia believes that the emerging Asian countries, especially China and India, are not an alternative to the United States militarily in the short and medium terms, the Saudis are seeking to leave most of their options open. There are several other strategic and political factors that are pushing Saudi Arabia to develop closer relations with Asia - in particular China. First, the main catalyst for any Saudi decision to develop nuclear weapons is likely to be the concern raised over Iran's nuclear ambitions. Former senior US diplomat Dennis Ross confirmed publicly for the first time on May 30, 2012, that Saudi Arabia's King Abdullah had explicitly warned the US that if Iran obtains nuclear weapons, Saudi Arabia would seek to do so as well. King Abdullah told Ross during a meeting between the two in April 2009 that: "If they get nuclear weapons, we will get nuclear weapons."[37] Ross' direct quote of the Saudi king appears to be the first public confirmation of the Saudi position, with the threat of a Middle East nuclear arms race if Tehran acquires a nuclear bomb.[38]

Second, the Kingdom, already the largest supplier of oil to China, Japan, South Korea and India, is building new refineries and increasing exports with the aim of strengthening political and economic ties with Asia's growing economic giants. These petro-political partnerships are a key to Saudi Arabia's efforts to contain Iran's political influence and military growth, especially its nuclear program.[39] Thirdly, through the lens of the Saudi leaders, China (and maybe India) could be regarded as a valuable source of support as Riyadh develops a response to the challenge of the Arab Spring and continues on a path of cautious and selective economic liberalisation while seeking to deflect US pressure in the area of political reform.[40] Here, the Saudi king is basing his effort on two main pillars: education and economic diversification.[41] Serious political reform, therefore, will not figure high on Saudi Arabia's list of priorities in coming years. Saudi Arabia's reaction to the Arab uprisings has largely been to move in the other direction, with increased spending on security rather than promoting greater democratic participation.[42] Indeed, Saudi Arabia's response to the Arab Spring over the past two years suggests that it has significant concerns, and has therefore been acting in a counterrevolutionary manner, mobilising all kinds of forces. It has devoted resources to helping to crush Bahrain's uprising, supporting the Syrian rebels against the Assad regime, and encouraging religious establishments to discredit democracy, democratic transitions, and popular protests. It has managed to turn crisis into opportunity, although the gains may be short-term and uncertain.[43] As current popular pressure mounts in Saudi Arabia for political and social reform, China's (and the other Asian powers') silence on Saudi domestic affairs and its intervention in Bahrain makes it seem a more agreeable partner to the Saudi ruling elite than a United States that is increasingly insistent on democratic reforms in the region.[44]

3. The Look-East Policy: Rising Interdependence

These political developments were coupled with change in the geopolitical landscape of the world's energy demand/supply and the Saudi domestic agenda. Saudi Arabia derives much of its power from its important role as the "central bank" of the international oil market.[45] Saudi Arabia's ability to single-handedly alter the price of oil gives the Kingdom significant geopolitical power. The Kingdom has used its ability to lower the price of oil to its geopolitical advantage on many occasions over the decades. With this oil superpower stature comes the bargaining power that Saudi Arabia enjoys on the international stage, including its new and prized position in the G-20.[46]

However, Saudi Arabia is facing internal and external challenges which could have a significant impact on its position as a leader in the global oil market. First, it is facing a significant shift in demand from West to East. Demand from the customers which Riyadh has supplied for the past five decades is stagnating. However, energy-hungry Asian nations, such as India and particularly China, are taking their place, refocusing Saudi Arabia's attention eastward. Second, Saudi Arabia's dominant role in the world oil supply could, as mentioned above, be altered by; (a) the development of the large new unconventional oil reserves in North America; (b) unrestrained domestic fuel consumption within Saudi Arabia itself; (c) a substantial increase in Iraqi production, with significant spare capacity. All of these factors may lead to increased cooperation between Saudi Arabia and Asian powers.

3.1 Saudi Arabia's Oil Exports: Shifting Demand

Oil demand is shifting from the developed world to the developing world, and Asia is expected to account for much of the growing demand during the next two decades. According to a BP forecast, by 2030 China and India will be the world's largest and 3rd largest economies and energy consumers, jointly accounting for about 35% of the global population, GDP and energy demand.[47] The focus of growth in both energy demand and supply switches away from the OECD. Nearly 90% of global energy demand growth will be in non-OECD countries.[48] According to the IEA's *World Energy Outlook (2011)*, global liquids demand (oil, bio-fuels, and other liquids) is likely to rise by 16 mb/d, exceeding 103 mb/d by 2030. Growth will come exclusively from rapidly-growing non-OECD economies; China (+8 mb/d), India (+3.5 mb/d) and the Middle East (+4 mb/d) together account for most of the net global increase. OECD demand has likely peaked in 2005, and consumption is expected to decline by 6 mb/d.[49]

Table 2.1: Primary Oil Demand 2010-2035 (Selected Countries)

	IEA: Projections, (New Policies Scenario[50])					mb/d
	2010	2015	2020	2025	2030	2035
US	18.0	17.8	16.8	15.8	15.1	14.5
Europe	12.7	12.5	12.0	11.5	11.0	10.6
Asia	17.7	20.5	22.5	24.9	27.5	29.9
Japan	4.2	4.0	3.7	3.5	3.3	3.1
China	8.9	11.1	12.2	13.4	14.5	14.9
India	3.3	3.6	4.2	4.9	6.0	7.4
World oil Demand	86.7	90.8	92.4	94.4	96.9	99.4

Source: adapted from IEA, World Energy Outlook (November 2011)

The International Energy Agency predicts China's oil imports will increase by more than two-and-a-half times over the period 2010-2035 to reach 12.6 mb/d in 2035, nearly twice the level of Russia's oil exports, or around one-third of OPEC exports, in the same year.[51] Its import dependence increases from 56% in 2011 to 84% in 2035.[52] Within this context, Saudi Arabia has increasingly recognised that Asia will provide the region's largest and fastest-growing oil export markets in the future. Already, two-thirds of Saudi Arabia's oil exports go East to Asia, reflecting this profound shift in the balance of global oil. Indeed, the bulk of the Kingdom's exports of crude oil and refined products during 2011 went to Asia and the Far East region. The region received over 62 per cent of the Kingdom's total crude oil exports (see Table 2.2) and 58.0 per cent of total exports of refined products.[53] As Table 2.2 shows, Saudi Arabia's crude oil exports to Asia doubled between 1989 and 2011, while the exports to the US and Western Europe declined dramatically.

Table 2.2: Saudi Crude Oil Exports by Region, 1989-2011 (%)

	North America	South America	Western Europe	The Middle East	Africa	Asia and the Far East	Oceania	Total
2011	18.1%	1.0%	12.3%	3.9%	2.3%	62.1%	0.3%	100%
2010	18.2%	1.0%	9.9%	4.4%	2.2%	64.1%	0.7%	100%
2005	20.1%	0.9%	16.7%	4.2%	3.2%	54.5%	0.01%	100%
2000	25.2%	0.9%	21.1%	2.6%	3.4%	45.7%	0.6%	100%
1995	21.9%	2.3%	26.0%	3.5%	1.5%	43.8%	0.8%	100%
1990	29.2%	3.6%	23.1%	4.7%	1.9%	36.1%	0.7%	100%
1989	31.2%	2.9%	26.3%	5.7%	0.3%	31.9%	1.4%	100%

Source: Adapted from Saudi Arabian Monetary Agency Annual Report 46 & 47 (December 2011 & July 2010). All percentages were calculated by the author. The figures for 2011 are taken from OPEC, Annual Statistical Bulletin, (2012: 47)

The growing importance of Asia represents a fundamental shift in the geopolitics of oil. Saudi officials are increasingly recognising that China will soon become the biggest purchaser of Saudi oil (and India will also figure prominently in the near future).[54] ARAMCO's president and CEO, Khalid al-Falih, agrees with that assessment: "We believe this is a long-term transition…Demographic and economic trends are making it clear — the writing is on the wall. China is the growth market for petroleum."[55] With one of the world's most developed energy sectors in terms of infrastructure and operating efficiency, Saudi Arabia is not desperate to attract foreign investment to help expand its capacity to produce and export oil. Instead, Saudi Arabia is keen on identifying a stream of steady, long-term demand, an urgent priority as the United States and other Western countries look to decrease their consumption of oil and incrementally adopt conservation methods and alternative fuels.[56]

3.2. Saudi Arabia's Dominant Global Oil Power: The New Challenges

Saudi Arabia is facing internal and external challenges which could have a significant impact on its position as a leader in the global oil market. The first challenge stems from the rapid increase in global hydrocarbon production. As has been indicated in section 1, new sources of supply are emerging. A recent study by Harvard University shows that oil production capacity is surging in the United States and several other countries at such a fast pace that global oil output is likely to increase nearly 20 per cent by 2020, possibly leading to a collapse in oil prices. While the Western Hemisphere could become oil self-sufficient by 2020, Iraq's oil output could also substantially increase as its security stabilizes.[57] In North America, five incremental sources of liquids growth could make the region the largest source of new supply in the next decade: oil sands production in Canada, deepwater in the US and Mexico, oil from shale and tight sands, natural gas liquids (NGLs) associated with the production of natural gas, and bio-fuels. Putting these together, North America as a whole could add over 11 mb/d of liquids from over 15 mb/d in 2010 to almost 27-m b/d by 2020-22.[58]

These important developments come as the demand in the US for major petroleum products has fallen substantially between 2005 and 2011. Over the last six years, net oil imports have fallen by 33% to average 8.4 million barrels per day (mb/d) in 2011.[59] In 2011, the United States consumed 18.8 mb/d of petroleum products, down 2 mb/d or 9% since 2005.[60] US imports of oil from Saudi Arabia and other Gulf countries have already fallen from a peak of 2.76 mb/d in 2001 to 1.86 mb/d in 2011.[61] Domestic production of oil and related liquid fuels was 9.2 mb/d in 2011, up 1.8 mb/d or 24% since 2005.[62] As a result of lower consumption and higher production, the need for imported oil fell. Net imports fell from 60% of domestic consumption in 2005 to 45% in 2011.[63] Going forward, demand could fall by as much as an additional 2 mb/d due to demographic changes, policies on fuel efficiency and the mass commercialization of new technologies.[64] IHS Cambridge Energy Research Associates estimate that the fall could reach three million barrels per day.[65] On the other hand, the Harvard study predicts that the United States could increase oil production by 3.5 mb/d and conceivably produce a total of 11.6 mb/d of crude oil and natural gas liquids per year by 2020, making it the second largest oil producer in the world, after Saudi Arabia.[66]

The reduced vulnerability of the United States — and the world market — to oil price spikes also has deep consequences geopolitically, including the reduced strategic importance to the US of the oil- and natural gas-producing countries worldwide.[67] Even if US import needs are higher than projected, these will easily be met by its neighbours plus its own domestic production. The US will still have a geopolitical interest in the Gulf, but the region's strategic importance as an oil supplier will plummet. The shift in oil sources means the global supply system will become more resilient, American energy supplies will become more secure, and the US will have more flexibility in dealing with crises.[68]

The resurgence in US hydrocarbon production has serious potential repercussions for Saudi Arabia.[69] For the United States, the changing dynamics of its own domestic supply and demand, coupled with fiscal and strategic realignments, will give rise to questions over the value of long-standing security arrangements in the Gulf.[70] In a period of strained military budgets, fatigue among the US public with engagement in the Middle East, and a focus on Asia as the centre of strategic priority, there is likely to be pressure on the United States to either curtail its presence in the region or to share the burden of providing security.[71] Furthermore, with the US economy less dependent on Middle East oil, and broader US foreign policy priorities undergoing a "pivot" to Asia, the American and European energy companies may see the prospects of a diminishing presence on the part of their regional guarantor.[72]

Saudi Arabia's energy officials acknowledge that the country's dominant role in world oil supply has been altered by large new reserves in North America, sapping the urgency to develop the Kingdom's own reserves.[73] In one of the documents leaked by *Wikileaks*, Saudi Prince Abdul Aziz Bin Salman, the Assistant Petroleum Minister and senior Royal Family member, recently summarised Saudi concerns about the long-term outlook for international energy markets during a conversation with the US Ambassador in Saudi Arabia, James B. Smith:

> Prince Abdulaziz said it is important for Saudi Arabia to think through whether the United States is becoming a mature market, like Europe ("Which has been dead for years" as an energy market). Prince Abdulaziz said that Saudi Arabia needs to know what role the US will be willing to have Saudi Arabia play, [in the two decades]. He asked, in effect, if we will "green" Saudi Arabia out of the US market. Abdulaziz asked if there is any chance to refit Saudi production to make Saudi oil more welcome, or will the US decide it must replace all imported oil? Saudi Arabia will have to think what kind of shift will be required in terms of finding other markets, namely in Asia. Prince Abdulaziz made clear that, as the oil markets shift, so do the politics. Bilateral trade with China has more than tripled, and China will soon be Saudi Arabia's largest importer. Saudi Arabia has also committed significant investments in China, including the US$ 8 billion Fujian refinery.[74]

Furthermore, Saudi ARAMCO's Khalid al-Falih was the first Saudi official to acknowledge that unconventional oil was set to shift the energy balance of power and cut US dependence on Middle East crude.[75] In a speech at the KAPSARC Inaugural Energy Dialogue in Riyadh on 21 November 2011, he stated that "The abundance of resources and the more 'balanced' geographical distribution of unconventional energy sources have reduced the much-hyped concerns over 'energy security' which once served as the undercurrent driving energy policies and dominated the global energy debate."[76]

The second challenge is that Saudi Arabia's place in the world oil market could be threatened by unrestrained domestic fuel consumption.[77] Saudi Arabia's ability to stabilize the international oil market by turning export volumes up or down would be damaged, with spare capacity used up to maintain export volumes.[78] Saudi Arabia is now the world's sixth-largest consumer, using more than a quarter of its 10 mb/d output.[79] According to analysts at Riyadh-based Jadwa Investment, oil demand in the Kingdom rose by 22 per cent between 2007 and 2010, outpacing China's oil demand growth rate despite the Chinese economy expanding almost three times faster.[80] The CEO of Saudi ARAMCO admitted that unless internal demand is controlled the amount of oil left for export could fall by 3 mb/d to less than 7 mb/d by 2028.[81]

Table 2.3: Saudi Arabia's Oil Consumption

	Domestic Consumption		mb/d
IEA	Jadwa Investment (Forecast)		
2011	2015	2020	2025
2.87	3.1	3.9	5.1

Source: Adapted from IEA (Oil Market Report, September 2012) & Jadwa Investment (July 2011)

The third challenge is that although Saudi Arabia will continue to be the largest oil producer in the region, Iraq is expected to experience the largest growth in production over the next two decades.[82] Iraq's oil production potential is immense, but exploiting it depends on consolidating the progress made in peace and stability in the country and success in attracting infrastructure investment.[83] The IEA predicts that Iraq's production will jump to 4.2 mb/d by 2015 and could reach around 6 mb/d in 2020,[84] while a Harvard study suggests that Iraq's production capacity could total 7.6 mb/d by 2020.[85] In this regard, rising Iraqi output could alter the balance of political power within OPEC and challenge Saudi Arabia's current leadership. An Iraq with significant spare capacity would challenge Saudi Arabia's dominance in the oil market. Increased Iraqi production could potentially undermine Saudi Arabia's leverage over other OPEC producers. Even if Iraq was not able to match total Saudi production, it would rank as the second or third largest producer globally, a position of considerable power.[86] In this context Jareer Elass and Amy Jaffe from the James A. Baker III Institute for Public Policy, Rice University, argue that:

...It is in the Kingdom's long-term geopolitical and security interests to maintain its leadership role in the global oil arena. Riyadh's ability to threaten other oil producers that it could flood the oil market is a critical aspect buttressing its leadership role inside OPEC and gives the country regional clout as well. Saudi Arabia's ability to single-handedly alter the price of oil gives the Kingdom significant geopolitical power, and it has used its ability to lower the price of oil to its geopolitical advantage on many occasions over the decades. With this oil superpower stature comes much of the global influence that Saudi Arabia enjoys on the international stage".[87]

3.3. The Developing Saudi Response

There are three lines of response which Saudi Arabia is currently developing an answer to the challenges. First, it is seriously considering the introduction of nuclear and renewable energy as an option to counter the challenge as well as to diversify the industrial structure for the nation's sustainable development.[88] The announcement was made in December, 2011 by the Minister of Commerce and Industry Abdullah Zainal, who said 375 billion riyals (US$100 billion) would be spent on building 16 nuclear power plants to generate electricity in different parts of the Kingdom.[89] Accordingly, Saudi Arabia has signed memoranda of understanding (MoUs) with several countries with experience in building nuclear plants - including France, Russia, South Korea, China and Argentina - over the last few years.[90] Saudi Arabia expects to finalize its atomic energy plans in 2012 but the US nuclear industry may miss out on multi-billion dollar contracts turning into a reality unless Washington and Riyadh sign a non-proliferation deal soon. From the Saudi perspective, Asian countries would be very attractive partners to build a nuclear energy industry. Additionally, they would be useful to address a broad range of needs Saudi Arabia has, such as technologies, training of human resource, investment, high standard for safety and security, sensitive long term vision and R&D, and so on. Most important of all, with Iran's nuclear program remaining unresolved, Saudi Arabia may keep its nuclear options open, and China may be an important player in this area.

Second, Saudi Arabia is participating in oil processing and storage projects in Asia. These are to improve access to markets and protect Saudi Arabia's future oil shares in the region. ARAMCO plans to build refineries in Asia as part of a spending programme to double refining capacity in 2015,[91] and in a bid to become the supplier of choice for the booming economies of Asia.[92] More than a half of the Kingdom's refining capacity (including refineries under construction), 4.019 mb/d, currently lies outside the Kingdom in the US, South Korea, China and Japan. The company will spend US$90 billion over the next five years to increase refining capacity to 6 million barrels a day. Most of the capacity to be added above the five-year target will be at refineries in Asia, with the bulk of that in China. ARAMCO seeks to tap increasing consumption in China, Asia's biggest energy user, by forming joint ventures with local partners.[93]

In this regard, the opening of the Fujian Refining & Ethylene Project in Quanzhou in November 2009 is enabling ARAMCO to ship 200,000 barrels of refined products per day. The Saudi company is also looking to invest in a second Chinese refinery, producing 200,000 barrels a day (bpd) of refined products in the Yunnan Province. Furthermore, in January 2012, ARAMCO and the Sinopec Group of China signed a $8.5 billion joint venture to set up an ultramodern, highly sophisticated, full-conversion oil refinery in Yanbu (Saudi Arabia).[94] Called simply *YASREF*, the Yanbu Aramco Sinopec Refining Co. Ltd. intends to begin production in the second half of 2014, processing 400,000 barrels of heavy crude a day. Saudi Aramco will hold a 62.5 per cent stake in the plant while Sinopec Group will own the remaining 37.5 per cent.[95] Furthermore, in 2011, Petro Rabigh, Saudi ARAMCO's equity venture with Sumitomo Chemical, completed its second full year of commercial operations. The second phase of the venture, Petro Rabigh Phase II, has reached the advanced stages of a joint feasibility study and all major "invitation to bid" packages have been released to the market. The integrated complex will introduce a diverse slate of products from petrochemical commodities to specialty products, many of which are new to the Kingdom.[96]

Additionally, in February 2012, the South Korean company S-Oil (in which Saudi ARAMCO owns the largest single stake, with 35 per cent of the shares), signed a 20-year contract to buy crude from Saudi Arabia as South Korea is seeking to secure its supplies.[97] S-Oil's refining capacity is 669,000 bpd and Saudi Aramco currently supplies almost all of the crude it processes into fuels.[98] India's Reliance has also invested in a refinery and a petrochemicals project in Saudi Arabia, and India's state-owned energy firm, Oil and Energy Gas Corporation, is engaging Saudi Arabia as its equity partner for a refinery project in the Indian state of Andhra Pradesh.[99] Saudi ARAMCO has also agreed to lease storage tanks from Japan Oil, Gas and Metals National Corp (JOGMEC) for the storage of Arabian crude oil at Japan's Okinawa storage facilities.[100] The added storage capacity gives ARAMCO a bigger cushion against disruption of supply through the Strait of Hormuz.[101] Under the deal, Saudi ARAMCO will be allowed to store up to 3.8 million barrels.

The deal will run for three years, starting in February 2011 and ending in December 2013, in order to allow Japan to restock its crude oil reserves.[102]

Third, Saudi Arabia is seeking to diversify its economy. The Kingdom's government sees its strategic and energy future as revolving around becoming a global economic and energy power, based on being a dominant global supplier not only of oil but also of other energy-based commodities,[103] at least in the chemicals and fertilisers sectors. Saudi Arabia currently accounts for 7 per cent of global supply of basic and intermediary products[104] and is committed to producing 10 per cent of the world's petrochemicals output by 2015.[105] Another goal is for Saudi Arabia to become the newest plastics hub by increasing its share of the global plastics petrochemical industry from 1-2 per cent today to 15 per cent in 2020.[106] In this regard, there are now 62 projects ongoing in the Saudi petrochemical sector valued at roughly US$63 billion. Saudi Arabia needs to find growing markets for petrochemicals over the next decades.[107] The Kingdom also needs to build its market knowledge in Asia. Currently, over 50% of the country's petrochemical production is exported to Asian economies with China being the largest destination.[108] China offers important economic advantages to Saudi Arabia's downstream expansion into the wider region.[109] Saudi Arabia gains benefit from open access to China's domestic market and to investment opportunities.[110] According to data from the Saudi Arabian Statistics Department, non-oil exports (mostly petrochemicals and plastics) increased by 31 per cent to $47.07 billion in 2011 compared to $35.88 billion in 2010. China was at the top of the Kingdom's importers list with $5.97 billion worth of imported products.[111] Japan (with the US), on the other hand, was a forerunner of Saudi Arabia in the petrochemical industry and, therefore, benefits Saudi producers with technological transfer in the form of FDIs and assistance, rather than exporting and investment opportunities.[112]

Last but not least, Saudi Arabia has identified energy efficiency as a key national priority and sees renewable energy sources as supplementing existing sources. There is a growing push within the Kingdom to develop and apply clean energy technologies and to reduce dependence on oil consumption. The government appears to be following four main tracks at the time of writing – reforming electricity pricing; regulating and helping industry to increase efficiency; planning to introduce renewable energy sources and infrastructure; and planning to add nuclear power.[113] Japan (as also South Korea) has one of the most energy-efficient economies in the world, which has resulted in lower energy intensity and brought the benefits of greater security of supply and improved balance of payments.[114] Japan (and South Korea) could assist in improving energy efficiency and conserving energy consumption in Saudi Arabia. Additionally, the Kingdom aims to get more than a third of its peak-load power supply, or about 41 gigawatts (GW), from the sun (solar energy) within two decades at an estimated cost well over US$100 bn.[115] China today is the world leader in renewable energy as it was responsible for almost a fifth of the global total investment volume, spending US$52 billion on renewable energy in 2011.[116] One example that has impressed Western specialists is China's takeover of the growing global solar panel market, not on the basis of cheap labour, but by coordinated planning and, increasingly, innovation.[117] Thus, China's experience in this field will be very useful for Saudi Arabia's solar programme.

4. Conclusion

The relationship between Saudi Arabia and Asia suggests (at least for now) that this is an energy-economic partnership, not a military-political alliance. Riyadh's economic interests are the driving force behind the expansion of the Asia-Saudi relationship. The chapter has shown that Saudi Arabia's objectives in the Asia-Saudi relationship are framed around economic interdependence, but with some other dimensions emerging. Its energy strategy is not a strategy to exclude the United States, but rather a strategy to go where the market growth is. Saudi Arabia sees a need to diversify its political relations as a result of the complexity of US-Saudi relations, and is also hoping that closer Asia-Saudi relations will constrain the Sino- (or Indian-) Iranian relationship. As stated earlier, the Saudis would like to see decreased Sino-Iranian military relations and gain Chinese support for tougher action in the event of Iran continuing to pursue its nuclear program.

For Saudi Arabia, maintaining good relations with the United States remains its key foreign policy objective, given the long-standing economic and military ties between the two countries. Saudi Arabia and China recognise that, for at least the next decade, the United States will remain the only country in the world capable of projecting substantial amounts of conventional military and soft powers into the Middle East. Meanwhile, Saudi relations with China are still in their infancy and it is uncertain which precise direction they will take. It is unlikely, for example, that now or in the immediate future Saudi Arabia would seek to use China's weapons as a military alternative to those of the United States.[118] But should the United States put some distance between itself and the region, or a rift develop between Saudi Arabia and the US,[119] Riyadh is likely in the longer term to seriously consider parallel political-security arrangements.[120] Given its enormous wealth and military weakness, it is a safe bet that Saudi Arabia will invest in multiple strategic arrangements that help guarantee the continuity of the regime.[121]

Endnotes

1   See: Songying Fang, Amy Myers Jaffe and Ted Temzelides. "New Alignments? The Geopolitics of Gas and Oil Cartels and the Changing Middle East," *James A. Baker III Institute for Public Policy, January* 23, 2012. Accessed January 28, 2012. www.bakerinstitute.org/.../EF-pub-GasOilCartels-012312.pdf. - Nawaf Obaid. "Saudi Arabia: The Kingdom in a Post "Arab-Spring" Environment," *King Faisal Center for Research & Islamic Studies,* February, 2012. Accessed February 15, 2012. http://www.slideshare.net/SUSRIS/saudi-arabia-post-arabspring-environment.

2   Ibid.

3   Patrick Conge and Gwenn Okruhlik. "The Power of Narrative: Saudi Arabia, the United States and the Search for Security." *British Journal of Middle Eastern Studies,* 36:3, (2009): 359-374.

4   Tim Niblock. *Saudi Arabia: Power, Legitimacy and Survival* (London: Routledge, 2006), 167

5   *Middle East Online.* "Blix briefs EU on Iraq." January 16, 2003. Accessed December 22, 2011. http://www.middle-east-online.com/english/?id=4009.

6   Harsh V. Pant. "Saudi Arabia Woos China and India," *Middle East Quarterly* 4 (2006): 45-52.

7   Flynt Leverett and Jeffrey Bader. "Managing China-US Energy Competition in the Middle East," *The Washington Quarterly,* 29:1 (2005): 187-201.

8   Andrew England. "Chinese trade flows along new Silk Road." *Financial Times,* December, 14, 2009. Accessed February 14, 2012. http://www.ft.com/cms/s/0/c9a93230-e8d4-11de-a756-00144feab49a.html#axzz1sfvJr7Ct.

9   John Keefer Douglas, et al. "Rising in the Gulf: How China's Energy Demands Are Transforming the Middle East," *The Fletcher School Journal,* spring 2007. Accessed December 25, 2011 http://fletcher.tufts.edu/Al-Nakhlah/Archives/spring2007.

10   Guofu Li, "China in the Middle East," (Paper prepared for the Fourth Dialogue on U.S.-China Relations in a Global Context, Washington DC, May 12, 2009), Accessed January 5, 2012. http://www.gwu.edu/~sigur/research/uschina.cfm.

11   *Wikileaks.* "Scenestter Senator Bond's April 6-8 visit to Saudi Arabia," March 31, 2009. Accessed December 28, 2011. http://www.wikileaks.org/cable/2009/03/09RIYADH496.html.

12   Nawaf Obaid. "Amid the Arab Spring, a U.S.-Saudi split," *The Washington Post,* May 16, 2011. Accessed December 27, 2011. http://www.washingtonpost.com/opinions/amid-the-arab-spring-a-us-saudi-split/2011/05/13/AFMy8Q4G_story.html?wprss=rss_homepage.

13   Ibid.

14   *Wikileaks.* "Scenestter Senator Bond's April 6-8 visit to Saudi Arabia."

15   Yael Yehoshua. "Saudi Arabia Cautiously Navigating Conflict with Iran amid Arab Spring Storm," *The Middle East Media Research Institute,* December 23, 2011. Accessed January 15, 2012. http://www.memri.org/report/en/0/0/0/0/0/0/0/5946.htm.

16   Yoel Guzansky. "Saudi Activism in a Changing Middle East," *Strategic Assessment,* 14:3 (2011), 65.

17   Thomas Lippman. "Nuclear Weapons and Saudi Strategy," *The Middle East Institute,* January 2008. Accessed January 13, 2012. http://www.mei.edu/content/nuclear-weapons-and-saudi-strategy.

18   Jason Burke. "Riyadh will build nuclear weapons if Iran gets them, Saudi prince warns," *The Guardian*, June 29, 2011. Accessed December 29, 2011. http://www.guardian.co.uk/world/2011/jun/29/saudi-build-nuclear-weapons-iran?INTCMP=SRCH.

19   Richard Weitz. "Evaluating the Proposed Saudi Arabian Arms Deal," *Second Line Defence*, October 16, 2010. Accessed January 3, 2012. http://www.sldinfo.com/evaluating-the-proposed-saudi-arabian-arms-deal/

20   Songying Fang, Amy Myers Jaffe and Ted Temzelides. "New Alignments? The Geopolitics of Gas and Oil Cartels and the Changing Middle East".

21   F. Gregory Gause III. "Saudi Arabia in the New Middle East," *The Council on Foreign Relations (CFR)*, Special Report No. 63 December 2011. Accessed January 20, 2012. http://www.cfr.org/saudi-arabia/saudi-arabia-new-middle-east/p26663?co=C009603.

22   Ibid.

23   Jeffrey Fleishman. "Mideast upheaval knocks Saudi Arabia off balance," *Los Angeles Times*, March 29, 2012. Accessed March 30, 2012. http://articles.latimes.com/2012/mar/29/world/la-fg-saudi-worries-20120330.

24   Guzansky, "Saudi Activism in a Changing Middle East," 66.

25   *Stratfor*. "Annual Forecast 2012," January 11, 2012. Accessed January 15, 2012. http://www.stratfor.com/forecast/annual-forecast-2012.

26   Chris Buckley. "China to stay a low-key gambler in Middle East," *Reuters*, March 1, 2011. Accessed February 7, 2012. http://af.reuters.com/article/commoditiesNews/idAFTOE71N06E20110301?sp=true.

27   *The Economist*. "Saudi Arabia and China," December 9, 2010.

28   *Moscow Times*. "China-Gulf relations: nothing but business: Interview with Abdulaziz Sager, the Chairman of the Gulf Research Center based in Dubai," February 14, 2011. Accessed January 6, 2012. http://english.ruvr.ru/2011/02/24/45983843.html.

29   Geoffrey Kemp, "*The East moves West,*" 232.

30   The Economist Intelligence Unit. *Country Report: Japan.* (London: EIU, January, 2012), 5.

31   Chung Min Lee, "Coping with Giants: South Korea's Responses to China's and India's Rise," in *Asia responds to its rising powers: China and India, ed.* Ashley J. Tellis, et. al. (Washington DC: The National Bureau of Asian Research, 2011), 160.

32   Kemp, "*The East moves West,*" 232.

33   Angus McDowall. "Key political risks to watch in Saudi Arabia," *Reuters*, March 27, 2012. Accessed March 31, 2012. http://af.reuters.com/article/energyOilNews/idAFL6E8EMA0V20120327?sp=true.

34   *Wikileaks*. "SITREP on Saudi Military Operations against Houthis," December 7, 2010. Accessed January 18, 2012. http://wikileaks.ch/cable/2009/12/09RIYADH1687.html.

35   Ibid.

36   Prince Turki Al-Faisal, "A Tour d' Horizon of the Saudi Political Seas," (Speech at the Institute for Defence Studies and Analyses, December 15, 2011.) Accessed January 17, 2012. http://idsa.in/keyspeeches/ATourdHorizonoftheSaudiPoliticalSeas.

37   Chemi Shalev. "Dennis Ross: Saudi king vowed to obtain nuclear bomb after Iran," *Haaretz*, 30 May 2012. accessed 31 May 2012. http://www.haaretz.com/news/diplomacy-defense/dennis-ross-saudi-king-vowed-to-obtain-nuclear-bomb-after-iran-1.433294.

38   Ibid.

39   Aaron Mattis. "Oil Sheik-Down: Saudi Arabia's Struggle to Contain Iran," *Harvard International Review*, Spring 2010, 10-11.

40   John Keefer Douglas, et al. "Rising in the Gulf".

41   Christopher Clary and Mara E. Karlin. "Saudi Arabia's Reform Gamble," *Survival* 53:5, October-November 2011, 16.

42   James Gavin. "Creating a lasting reformist legacy in Saudi Arabia," *MEED*, 56:6, February 10, 2012, 30-13.

43   Michael Coleman. "Talk Studies Arab Spring, Saudi Fears," *Journal Washington Bureau on,* March 17, 2012. Accessed March 19, 2012. http://www.abqjournal.com/main/2012/03/17/politics/talk-studies-arab-spring-saudi-fears.html.

44   *Ergo.* "The Waning Era of Saudi Oil Dominance".

45   Fang, Jaffe and Temzelides, "New Alignments? The Geopolitics of Gas and Oil Cartels and the Changing Middle East".

46   Ibid.

47   BP. "Energy Outlook 2030".

48   "World Energy Outlook 2011", 69.

49   Ibid.

50   The *New Policies Scenario (IEA)* takes account of the broad policy commitments that have already been announced and assumes cautious implementation of national pledges to reduce greenhouse gas emissions by 2020 and to reform fossil-fuel subsidies.

51   Ibid., 92.

52   Ibid.

53   Saudi Arabian Monetary Agency. *47ᵗʰ Annual Report.* (Riyadh: SAMA, December, 2011), 144.

54   David Blair. "Oil supplies: Politics in the way of ambitions in Asia," *Financial Times*, September 29, 2011. Accessed January 26, 2012. http://www.ft.com/cms/s/0/0c0fc8b0-e08a-11e0-bd01-00144feabdc0.html.

55   Jad Mouawad. "China's Rapid Growth Shifts the Geopolitics of Oil," *New York Times*, March 19, 2010. Accessed January 2, 2012. http://www.nytimes.com/2010/03/20/business/energy-environment/20saudi.html.

56   Jon Alterman and John Garver. *The vital triangle: China, the United States, and the Middle East.* (Washington DC: Centre for Strategic and International Studies, 2008), 58.

57   Leonardo Maugeri. "Oil: The Next Revolution," Harvard University, July 3 2012. Accessed July 4, 2012. http://belfercenter.ksg.harvard.edu/publication/22144/oil.html.

58   Edward Morse et al. *Energy 2020: North America, the New Middle East?* (New York: Citi Investment Research Analysis, March 20, 2012), 3.

59   Neelesh Nerurkar. "U.S. Oil Imports and Exports," *US Congressional Research Service*, April 4, 2012. Accessed April 7, 2012. www.fas.org/sgp/crs/misc/R42465.pdf.

60   Ibid.

61   *See: EIA.* "U.S. Imports by Country of Origin". http://www.eia.gov/dnav/pet/PET_MOVE_IMPCUS_A2_NUS_EPC0_IM0_MBBLPD_A.htm.

62   Neelesh Nerurkar. "U.S. Oil Imports and Exports".

63   Ibid.

64   Morse. "Energy 2020," 32.

65   Daniel Yergin. "America's New Energy Security," *Wall Street Journal*, December 12, 2011. Accessed January 8, 2012. http://online.wsj.com/article/SB10001424052970204449804577068932026951376.html?mod=googlenews_wsj.

66   Oil: The Next Revolution," 36.

67   Morse. "Energy 2020," 32.

68   Yergin, "America's New Energy Security".

69   Brookings Doha Energy Forum (2012 February). *Energy Security Initiative Report 2012.* (Washington: The Brookings Institution), 16.

70   Ibid., 18.

71   Ibid., 10.

72   Ibid.

73   Khalid Al-Falih, President and CEO of Saudi ARAMCO, "Resetting the energy conversation: the need for realism," (Speech at KAPSARC Inaugural Energy Dialogue, Riyadh, Saudi Arabia, November 21, 2011), accessed February 3, 2012. http://www.saudiaramco.com.

74   *U.S. Secret Cables.* "What concerns Saudi Arabia about the future of Energy and Climate Change," *Wikileaks.* October 10, 2010. Accessed January 18, 2012. http://wikileaks.org/cable/2010/02/10RIYADH213.html #.

75   Ibid.

76   Ibid.

77   Glada Lahn and Paul Stevens. "Burning Oil to Keep Cool: The Hidden Energy Crisis in Saudi Arabia," *Chatham House,* December 2011. Accessed January 6, 2012. http://www.chathamhouse.org/publications/papers/view/180825.

78   Ibid.

79   *The Economist.* "Oil prices: Keeping it to themselves," March 31, 2012. Accessed April 1, 2012. http://www.economist.com/node/21551484.

80   Brad Bourland and Paul Gamble, "Saudi Arabia's coming oil and fiscal challenge," *Jadwa Investment,* Riyadh, July 2011.

81   *Reuters* (London) October. 12, 2011.

82   Ibid., 98.

83   Ibid., 131.

84   Ibid., 134.

85   "Oil: The Next Revolution," 36.

86   *Ergo.* "The Waning Era of Saudi Oil Dominance".

87   Jareer Elass and Amy Myers Jaffe, "Iraqi Oil Potential and Implications for Global Oil Markets and OPEC Politics," *James A. Baker III Institute for Public Policy, Rice University* July 2011. Accessed January 8, 2012. http://www.rice.edu/energy/publications/EF-pub-IraqFutureElassJaffe-072611.pdf.

88   *Ministry of Strategy and Finance, the Republic of Korea.* "Policy Recommendations for Economic Development in Priority Areas of the Kingdom of Saudi Arabia," Seoul: Korea Development Institute, 2011, 29.

89   Housam Matar. "Saudi Nuclear Program: A Mirage of Progress," February 9, 2012. Accessed February 10, 2012. http://english.al-akhbar.com/content/saudi-nuclear-program-mirage-progress.

90   Amena Bakr. "U.S. firms may miss out as Saudi nuke plan advances," *Reuters,* April 25, 2012. Accessed April 26, 2012. http://in.reuters.com/article/2012/04/25/saudi-nuclear-idINDEE83O0CY20120425.

91   Wael Mahdi. "Saudi Aramco to Invest $200 Billion in Refining, Exploration," *Bloomberg,* January 16, 2012. Accessed January 17, 2012. http://www.bloomberg.com/news/2012-01-16/saudi-aramco-to-invest-200-billion-in-refining-exploration.html.

92   Adal Mirza. "Riyadh looks to the long term," *MEED,* 54:3, January 15, 2010, 24-25.

93   Ibid.

94 Siraj Wahab. "Aramco, Sinopec sign SR32bn Yanbu refinery deal," *Arab News*, January 15, 2012. Accessed January 16, 2012. http://arabnews.com/economy/article563458.ece.

95 Ibid.

96 ARAMCO. *Saudi Aramco Annual Review 2010*. Riyadh: ARAMCO 2011, 29.

97 *S-OIL*. "S-OIL signs 20-year long-term crude supply contract with Saudi Aramco," February 9, 2012. Accessed February 10, 2012. http://www.s-oil.com/siteEng/index.asp.

98 Ibid.

99 Pant. "India's Relations with Iran," 66.

100 DiPaola Anthony. "Aramco Confirms Lease of Japan Crude Storage Capacity," *Bloomberg*, February 9, 2011. Accessed January 11, 2012. http://www.bloomberg.com/news/2011-02-09/aramco-confirms-lease-of-japan-crude-storage-capacity-update1-.html.

101 Ibid.

102 Business Monitor International, *Japan Oil & Gas Report Q4 2011*. (London: BMI, 2012), 13.

103 Philip Andrews-Speed et al. *The New Energy Silk Road: the Growing Asia–Middle East Energy Nexus*. (Washington DC: The National Bureau of Asian Research, 2009), 8.

104 *Saudi National Commercial Bank*. "Saudi Petrochemical Sector Review," September 2011. Accessed January 22, 2012. *www.menafn.com/updates/research_center/saudi.../ncb180911.pdf*.

105 James Drummond. "Gulf States urged to make petrochemical goods," *Financial Times*, December 19, 2011. Accessed December 20, 2011. http://www.ft.com/cms/s/0/f62ec8aa-2a37-11e1-b7f2-00144feabdc0.html#axzz1h686TEiI.

106 *Wikileak*s. "Saudi Investment Authority Outline Ambitious Plans," January 21, 2010. Accessed January 18, 2012. http://wikileaks.org/cable/2010/01/10RIYADH97.html.

107 John Sfakianakis. *Saudi-China Trade Relations*. Riyadh: SAAB Bank Research Notes.

108 *Aljazira Capital*. "Saudi Petrochemical Sector," July 2011. Accessed January 23, 2012. *www.aljaziracapital.com.sa/jaziracapital/report_file/ess/SEC-8.pdf*.

109 Ibid.

110 Yamada, Makio. "Gulf-Asia Relations as "Post-Rentier" Diversification? The Case of the Petrochemical Industry in Saudi Arabia," *Journal of Arabian Studies* 1:1 (June 2011), 101.

111 *Arab News*. "Saudi Arabia's 2011 exports hit USD 47b," May 19, 2012. Accessed May 20, 2012. http://www.menafn.com/menafn/1093514667/Saudi-Arabias-2011-exports-hit-USD-47b.

112 Yamada, Makio. "Gulf-Asia Relations as "Post-Rentier" Diversification? The Case of the Petrochemical Industry in Saudi Arabia", 113.

113 Glada and Stevens. "Burning Oil to Keep Cool The Hidden Energy Crisis in Saudi Arabia," 14.

114 Ibid, 34.

115 *Gulf Times*. "Saudi battles heat, dust to build solar power, save oil," May 27, 2012. Accessed May 28, 2012. http://www.gulftimes.com/site/topics/article.asp?cu_no=2&item_no=508171&version=1&template_id=48&parent_id=28.

116 United Nations. *Global Trends in Renewable Energy Investment 2012*. (Frankfurt: UNEP Collaborating Centre for Climate & Sustainable Energy Finance, 2012, 21.

117 Noam Chomsky. "Losing' the world: American decline in perspective, part 1," *The Guardian*. February 14, 2012. Accessed February 17, 2012. http://www.guardian.co.uk/commentisfree/cifamerica/2012/feb/14/losing-the-world-american-decline-noam-chomsky.

118 Ian Bremmer. "Washington's stark choice: Democracy or Riyadh," *Financial Times*, March 18, 2011.

119 Guzansky, "Saudi Arabia Nuclear Hedging".

120 Guzansky, "Saudi Activism in a Changing Middle East," 67.

121 Guzansky, "Saudi Arabia Nuclear Hedging".

Bibliography

Aaron Mattis. "Oil Sheik-Down: Saudi Arabia's Struggle to Contain Iran," *Harvard International Review*, spring 2010, 10-11.

Adal Mirza. "Riyadh looks to the long term," *MEED*, 54:3, January 15, 2010.

Aljazira Capital. "Saudi Petrochemical Sector," July 2011. Accessed January 23, 2012. www.aljaziracapital.com.sa/jaziracapital/report_file/ess/SEC-8.pdf.

Amena Bakr. "U.S. firms may miss out as Saudi nuke plan advances," *Reuters*, April 25, 2012. Accessed April 26, 2012. http://in.reuters.com/article/2012/04/25/saudi-nuclear-idINDEE83O0CY20120425.

Amy Myers Jaffe. "The Americas, Not the Middle East, Will Be the World Capital of Energy," *Foreign Policy* 188, September 2011.

Andrew England. "Chinese trade flows along new Silk Road." *Financial Times*, December, 14, 2009. Accessed February 14, 2012. http://www.ft.com/cms/s/0/c9a93230-e8d4-11de-a756-00144feab49a.html#axzz1sfvJr7Ct.

Angus McDowall. "Key political risks to watch in Saudi Arabia," *Reuters*, March 27, 2012. Accessed March 31, 2012. http://af.reuters.com/article/energyOilNews/idAFL6E8EMA0V20120327?sp=true.

Arab News. "Saudi Arabia's 2011 exports hit USD 47b," May 19, 2012. Accessed May 20, 2012. http://www.menafn.com/menafn/1093514667/Saudi-Arabias-2011-exports-hit-USD-47b.

_____. "Saudi-India relations," January 6, 2012. Accessed January 21, 2012. http://arabnews.com/opinion/editorial/article559276.ece.

ARAMCO. *Saudi Aramco Annual Review 2010*. (Riyadh: ARAMCO 2011)

_____. *Saudi Aramco Annual Review 2010*. Riyadh: ARAMCO 2011

Gawdat Bahgat. "A Nuclear Arms Race in the Middle East: Myth or Reality?" *Mediterranean Quarterly* 22:11 (2011), 27-40.

David Blair. "Oil supplies: Politics in the way of ambitions in Asia," *Financial Times*, September 29, 2011.

BP. "Energy Outlook 2030," January 2012. Accessed January 19, 2012. http://www.bp.com/sectiongenericarticle800.do?categoryId=9037134&contentId=7068677.

Brad Bourland and Paul Gamble, "Saudi Arabia's coming oil and fiscal challenge," (*Jadwa* Investment, Riyadh, July 2011).

Brookings Doha Energy Forum (2012 February). *Energy Security Initiative Report 2012*. (Washington: The Brookings Institution).

Business Monitor International, *Japan Oil & Gas Report Q4 2011*. (London: BMI, 2012).

_____. *South Korea Defence & Security Report*. (London: BMI, 2010).

Chemi Shalev. "Dennis Ross: Saudi king vowed to obtain nuclear bomb after Iran," *Haaretz*, 30 May 2012. accessed 31 May 2012. http://www.haaretz.com/news/diplomacy-defense/dennis-ross-saudi-king-vowed-to-obtain-nuclear-bomb-after-iran-1.433294.

Chris Buckley. "China to stay a low-key gambler in Middle East," *Reuters*, March 1, 2011. Accessed February 7, 2012. http://af.reuters.com/article/commoditiesNews/idAFTOE71N06E20110301?sp=true.

Christopher Clary and Mara E. Karlin. "Saudi Arabia's Reform Gamble," *Survival* 53:5, October-November 2011.

Chung Min Lee, "Coping with Giants: South Korea's Responses to China's and India's Rise," in Asia *responds to its rising powers: China and India, ed.* Ashley J. Tellis, et. al. (Washington DC: The National Bureau of Asian Research, 2011).

Daniel Yergin. "America's New Energy Security," *Wall Street Journal*, December 12, 2011. Accessed January 8, 2012. http://online.wsj.com/article/SB10001424052970204449804577068932026951376.html?mod=googlenews_wsj.

David Blair. "Oil Supplies: Politics in the Way of Ambitions in Asia," *Financial Times*, September 29, 2011. Accessed January 26, 2012. http://www.ft.com/cms/s/0/0c0fc8b0-e08a-11e0-bd01-00144feabdc0.html.

DiPaola Anthony. "Aramco Confirms Lease of Japan Crude Storage Capacity," *Bloomberg*, February 9, 2011. Accessed January 11, 2012. http://www.bloomberg.com/news/2011-02-09/aramco-confirms-lease-of-japan-crude-storage-capacity-update1-.html.

Edward Morse et al. *Energy 2020: North America, the New Middle East?* (New York: Citi Investment Research Analysis, March 20, 2012).

EIA. "South Korea Country Energy Profile," October 2011. Accessed January 15, 2012. http://205.254.135.7/countries/cab.cfm?fips=KS.

F. Gregory Gause III. "Saudi Arabia in the New Middle East," *The Council on Foreign Relations (CFR)*, Special Report No. 63 December 2011. Accessed January 20, 2012. http://www.cfr.org/saudi-arabia/saudi-arabia-new-middle-east/p26663?co=C009603.

Flynt Leverett and Jeffrey Bader. "Managing China-US Energy Competition in the Middle East," *The Washington Quarterly*, 29:1 (2005): 187-201.

George Friedman. "Saudi Arabia: A Balancing Act," *Stratfor*, January 30, 2004. Accessed January 2, 2012. http://www.stratfor.com/weekly/saudi_arabia_balancing_act.

Glada Lahn and Paul Stevens. "Burning Oil to Keep Cool: The Hidden Energy Crisis in Saudi Arabia," *Chatham House*, December 2011. Accessed January 6, 2012. http://www.chathamhouse.org/publications/papers/view/180825.

Gulf Times. "Saudi Battles Heat, Dust to Build Solar Power, Save Oil," May 27, 2012. Accessed May 28, 2012. http://www.gulftimes.com/site/topics/article.asp?cu_no=2&item_no=508171&version=1&template_id=48&parent_id=28.

Guofu Li, "China in the Middle East," (Paper prepared for the Fourth Dialogue on U.S.-China Relations in a Global Context, Washington DC, May 12, 2009), Accessed January 5, 2012. http://www.gwu.edu/~sigur/research/uschina.cfm.

Harsh V. Pant. "India's Relations with Iran: Much Ado about Nothing," *The Washington Quarterly* 34:1 (2011).

_____. "Saudi Arabia Woos China and India," *Middle East Quarterly* 4 (2006): 45-52.

Housam Matar. "Saudi Nuclear Program: A Mirage of Progress," February 9, 2012. Accessed February 10, 2012. http://english.al-akhbar.com/content/saudi-nuclear-program-mirage-progress.

Ian Bremmer. "Washington's Stark Choice: Democracy or Riyadh," *Financial Times*, March 18, 2011.

International Energy Agency. Oil Market Report. Paris: IEA, September 2012.

_____. *World Energy Outlook 2011*. Paris: IEA, November 2011

Jad Mouawad. "China's Rapid Growth Shifts the Geopolitics of Oil," *New York Times*, March 19, 2010. Accessed January 2, 2012. http://www.nytimes.com/2010/03/20/business/energy-environment/20saudi.html.

James Drummond. "Gulf States urged to make petrochemical goods," *Financial Times*, December 19, 2011. Accessed December 20, 2011. http://www.ft.com/cms/s/0/f62ec8aa-2a37-11e1-b7f2-00144feabdc0.html#axzz1h686TEiI.

James Gavin. "Creating a Lasting Reformist Legacy in Saudi Arabia," *MEED*, 56:6, February 10, 2012.

Jason Burke. "Riyadh Will Build Nuclear Weapons if Iran Gets Them, Saudi Prince Warns," *The Guardian*, June 29, 2011. Accessed December 29, 2011. http://www.guardian.co.uk/world/2011/jun/29/saudi-build-nuclear-weapons-iran?INTCMP=SRCH.

Jeffrey Fleishman. "Mideast Upheaval Knocks Saudi Arabia Off Balance," *Los Angeles Times*, March 29, 2012. Accessed March 30, 2012. http://articles.latimes.com/2012/mar/29/world/la-fg-saudi-worries-20120330.

John Keefer Douglas, Matthew B. Nelson, Kevin L. Schwartz "Rising in the Gulf: How China's Energy Demands Are Transforming the Middle East," *The Fletcher School Journal*, spring 2007. Accessed December 25, 2011 http://fletcher.tufts.edu/Al-Nakhlah/Archives/spring2007.

John Sfakianakis. *Saudi-China Trade Relations* ‖ . (Riyadh: SAAB Bank Research Notes, 2009).

Jon Alterman and John Garver. *The vital triangle: China, the United States, and the Middle East.* (Washington DC: Centre for Strategic and International Studies, 2008)

Khalid Al-Falih, President and CEO of Saudi ARAMCO, "Resetting the Energy Conversation: the Need for Realism," (Speech at KAPSARC Inaugural Energy Dialogue, Riyadh, Saudi Arabia, November 21, 2011), accessed February 3, 2012. http://www.saudiaramco.com.

Leonardo Maugeri. "Oil: The Next Revolution," Harvard University, July 3 2012. Accessed July 4, 2012. http://belfercenter.ksg.harvard.edu/publication/22144/oil.html.

Michael Coleman. "Talk Studies Arab Spring, Saudi Fears," *Journal Washington Bureau on*, March 17, 2012. Accessed March 19, 2012.http://www.abqjournal.com/main/2012/03/17/politics/talk-studies-arab-spring-saudi-fears.html.

Middle East Online. "Blix Briefs EU on Iraq." January 16, 2003. Accessed December 22, 2011. http://www.middle-east-online.com/english/?id=4009.

Ministry of Strategy and Finance, the Republic of Korea. "Policy Recommendations for Economic Development in Priority Areas of the Kingdom of Saudi Arabia," (Soul: Korea Development Institute, 2011)

Moscow Times. "China-Gulf Relations: Nothing but Business: Interview with Abdulaziz Sager, the Chairman of the Gulf Research Center Based in Dubai," February 14, 2011. Accessed January 6, 2012. http://english.ruvr.ru/2011/02/24/45983843.html.

Nawaf Obaid. "Amid the Arab Spring, a U.S.-Saudi split," *The Washington Post*, May 16, 2011. Accessed December 27, 2011. http://www.washingtonpost.com/opinions/amid-the-arab-spring-a-us-saudi-split/2011/05/13/AFMy8Q4G_story.html?wprss=rss_homepage.

_____. "Saudi Arabia: The Kingdom in a Post "Arab-Spring" Environment," *King Faisal Center for Research & Islamic Studies*, February, 2012. Accessed February 15, 2012. http://www.slideshare.net/SUSRIS/saudi-arabia-post-arabspring-environment.

Neelesh Nerurkar. "U.S. Oil Imports and Exports," *US Congressional Research Service*, April 4, 2012. Accessed April 7, 2012. www.fas.org/sgp/crs/misc/R42465.pdf.

Noam Chomsky. "Losing the World: American Decline in Perspective, Part 1," *The Guardian*. February 14, 2012. Accessed February 17, 2012. http://www.guardian.co.uk/commentisfree/cifamerica/2012/feb/14/losing-the-world-american-decline-noam-chomsky.

P. K. Abdul Ghafour, "Kingdom is World's 8th High Growth Economy," *Arab News*, June 15, 2012. Accessed June 16, 2012. http://www.arabnews.com/economy/kingdom-world%E2%80%99s-8th-high-growth-economy.

Patrick Conge and Gwenn Okruhlik. "The Power of Narrative: Saudi Arabia, the United States and the Search for Security." *British Journal of Middle Eastern Studies*, 36:3, (2009): 359-374.

Philip Andrews-Speed et al. *The New Energy Silk Road: the Growing Asia–Middle East Energy Nexus*. (Washington DC: The National Bureau of Asian Research, 2009).

Prince Turki Al-Faisal, "A Tour d' Horizon of the Saudi Political Seas," (Speech at the Institute for Defence Studies and Analyses, December 15, 2011.) Accessed January 17, 20212. http://idsa. in/keyspeeches/ATourdHorizonoftheSaudiPoliticalSeas.

Rakesh Sharma and Santanu Choudhry. "Iraq Replaces Iran as India's Second-Largest Crude Oil Supplier," *The Wall Street Journal*, May 16, 2012. Accessed May 16, 2012. http://online.wsj.com/ article/SB10001424052702303448404577407843978018060.html?mod=googlenews_wsj.

Reuters. "FACTBOX-Top Asian Buyers of Saudi Crude," February 10, 2012. Accessed February 17, 2012. http://sg.news.yahoo.com/factbox-top-asian-buyers-saudi-crude-103606889.html.

Richard Weitz. "Evaluating the Proposed Saudi Arabian Arms Deal," *Second Line Defence*, October 16, 2010. Accessed January 3, 2012. http://www.sldinfo.com/evaluating-the-proposed-saudi-arabian-arms-deal/.

Saudi Arabian Monetary Agency. *47th Annual Report.* (Riyadh: SAMA, December, 2011).

Saudi National Commercial Bank. "Saudi Petrochemical Sector Review," September 2011. Accessed January 22, 2012. *www.menafn.com/updates/research_center/saudi.../ncb180911.pdf.*

Siraj Wahab. "Aramco, Sinopec Sign SR32bn Yanbu Refinery Deal," *Arab News*, January 15, 2012. Accessed January 16, 2012. http://arabnews.com/economy/article563458.ece.

Songying Fang, Amy Myers Jaffe and Ted Temzelides. "New Alignments? The Geopolitics of Gas and Oil Cartels and the Changing Middle East," *James A. Baker III Institute for Public Policy, January* 23, 2012. Accessed January 28, 2012. www.bakerinstitute.org/.../EF-pub-GasOilCartels-012312.pdf.

Stratfor. "Annual Forecast 2012," January 11, 2012. Accessed January 15, 2012. http://www.stratfor. com/forecast/annual-forecast-2012.

The Economist Intelligence Unit. *Country Report: Japan. (*London: EIU, January, 2012)

The Economist. "Oil Prices: Keeping It to Themselves," March 31, 2012. Accessed April 1, 2012. http:// www.economist.com/node/21551484.

_____. "Saudi Arabia and China," December 9, 2010.

Thomas Lippman. "Nuclear Weapons and Saudi Strategy," *The Middle East Institute*, January 2008. Accessed January 13, 2012. http://www.mei.edu/content/nuclear-weapons-and-saudi-strategy.

Tim Niblock. *Saudi Arabia: Power, Legitimacy and Survival* (London: Routledge, 2006)

United Nations. *Global Trends in Renewable Energy Investment 2012. (*Frankfurt: UNEP Collaborating Centre for Climate & Sustainable Energy Finance, 2012)

Wael Mahdi. "Saudi Aramco to Invest $200 Billion in Refining, Exploration," *Bloomberg*, January 16, 2012. Accessed January 17, 2012. http://www.bloomberg.com/news/2012-01-16/saudi-aramco-to-invest-200-billion-in-refining-exploration.html.

Wikileaks. "Saudi Investment Authority Outline Ambitious Plans" January 21, 2010. Accessed January 18, 2012. http://wikileaks.org/cable/2010/01/10RIYADH97.html.

_____. "Scenestter Senator Bond's April 6-8 visit to Saudi Arabia," March 31, 2009. Accessed December 28, 2011. http://cablegate.wikileaks.org/cable/2009/03/09RIYADH496. html.

_____. "SITREP on Saudi Military Operations against Houthis," December 7, 2010. Accessed January 18, 2012. http://wikileaks.ch/cable/2009/12/09RIYADH1687.html.

Yael Yehoshua. "Saudi Arabia Cautiously Navigating Conflict with Iran amid Arab Spring Storm," *The Middle East Media Research Institute*, December 23, 2011. Accessed January 15, 2012. http:// www.memri.org/report/en/0/0/0/0/0/0/0/5946.htm.

Yamada, Makio. "Gulf-Asia Relations as "Post-Rentier" Diversification? The Case of the Petrochemical Industry in Saudi Arabia." *Journal of Arabian Studies* 1:1 (June 2011).

Yoel Guzansky. "Saudi Activism in a Changing Middle East," *Strategic Assessment,* 14:3 (2011).

_____. "Saudi Arabia Nuclear Hedging," *Atlantic Council,* December 13, 2011. Accessed February 15, 2012. http://www.inss.org.il/upload/(FILE)1323850540.pdf.

Chapter Three

Iran's Ties with Asia

Sara Bazoobandi

1. Introduction

Iran's relationship with some of the largest economies in Asia has become stronger over the past two decades. Since the 1970s, when Iran-West interaction (both economically and politically) has become limited as a result of the Islamic Revolution of Iran, the country has been seeking alternative alliances in the East. With the rise of Asia's power, Iran has sought to strengthen its economic and political ties with some of the Asian countries, most importantly China and India. Moreover, Iran-Asia relations have become stronger as Iran has become one of the key suppliers for Asia's growing hydrocarbon demand. By 2011, over 50% of Iran's total crude export was sold to Asia and the country became the provider for nearly one third of the oil demand for the major energy consuming economies of Asia.

From an economic point of view, the recent US and EU economic sanctions, which target Iran's oil sector, have affected the country's relationship with Asia both in terms of trade and investments, and will further limit the economic ties between Iran and major Asian economies. Since late 2011, the United States has been mounting pressure on oil importing countries globally to stop buying Iranian crude in order to force Tehran to end its nuclear energy programme. The latest proposed US sanctions on the Central Bank of Iran (CBI), contained in Section 1245 of the National Defense Authorization Act for fiscal year 2012, was passed by both houses of Congress and signed by President Obama on December 31, 2011. The bill requires foreign financial firms to make a choice between doing business with the CBI and the Iranian oil sector or with the US financial sector. The US sanctions also gained EU support. Following the US sanctions, the EU adopted an oil embargo against Iran and froze the assets of the CBI across EU member states.

From a political point of view, Iran's alliance with Asia, China in particular, has become critical over the past decade. Iran has strongly relied on its political links with the only Asian member of the United Nation's Security Council, while the West has been seeking to isolate Iran internationally in order to bring the Iranian authorities to an agreement over the nuclear negotiations. Despite the US-led political campaign against Iran which has targeted Iran's relationship with China, the Sino-Iranian alliance has remained fairly stable.

Iran's relations with its main Asian partners as well as Russia have reached a critical point. This paper will examine the relations between Iran and its four key Asian economic partners (China, Japan, India and South Korea). The focus of the study will be on three main aspects of Iran-Asia relations, namely: political alliance, trade and investment. The paper seeks to assess the extent to which the US and the EU strategy in dealing with Iran will affect the country's relationship with its major Asian partners. In addition, the study aims to highlight the consequences of a potential downplaying of Asia-Iran relations for both sides.

2. The China-Iran Economic Relationship: "One Step Forward and Two Steps Back"[1]

Iran was one of the first countries in the Gulf region to establish strong economic and political ties with China. The isolating strategies of the West in dealing with Iran, coupled with the rise of Chinese power globally, have prompted Iran to strengthen its strategic alliance with China. China's rising interest in Iran's oil and the growing investment appetite of Chinese state-owned enterprises globally has further reinforced the financial relations between the two countries. Regarding political alliance, the Arab oil-rich countries of the Gulf have maintained close relationships with the US over the past few decades, whilst Iran has sought close ties with China and Russia so as to offset the American influence in the region.

The economic collaboration between the two countries has increased since the early 1990s. China has become one of the major trading partners of Iran and one of the main exports of consumer goods and raw materials to Iran. By 2009, China had become Iran's most important trade partner and the aggregate bilateral trade between the two countries reached $ 21.2 billion. According to *Asia Times*, in 2010, more than 100 Chinese companies were present in Iran and engaged in various projects across the sectors including Tehran's subway, power stations, ferrous metals smelting factories and petrochemical plants.[2]

Despite the growing interest for boosting bilateral economic relations between the two countries, China's investment strategy in Iran has often followed a 'one step forward and two steps backward' trend leading to delays or slow development. Although Western economic sanctions have been partially responsible for the difficulties which Chinese investors have faced in engaging in projects in Iran (without risk to their commercial interests in the West), one cannot ignore the effect of Iran's own legislation. Protective and self-sufficiency measures, aiming to minimize the country's reliance on foreign partners, have been a hindrance to all foreign investors. There are a number of examples which can be given of incomplete and/or delayed Chinese investment projects in Iran. One of the biggest Chinese investment projects in Iran, a $100 billion joint-venture deal to develop the Yadavaran oil field that was to deliver 10 million tons of LNG to China over 25 years, was never really started, and the project is still at the exploration stage 7 years after the deal was signed. Another example of this kind is the China National Offshore Oil Corporation's (CNOOC) $16 billion memorandum of understanding with Tehran, which was cancelled at the last minute just before the signing ceremony in 2008.[3]

China's engagement in investment projects in Iran is not limited to investment in the energy sector. A variety of Chinese construction and engineering consultant companies are also actively operating in Iran which has led to similar results as those in the energy sector. For this research, the writer made contact with a former colleague who is a senior project manager at one of the main government-owned, large scale construction companies in Iran. The company, which is called Melli Sakhteman, over the past two decades has partnered with a number of Chinese construction companies and banks to either build or finance various projects in Iran. He described the current situation between the Iranian construction companies and their Chinese partners as 'rather tense' and added; 'there is a huge lack of trust between both sides as most of the projects have been severely delayed due to either lack of technical capability of the Chinese partners to deliver their commitments, or shortage of capital, or both.'

The development of Sino-Iranian investment projects has also been affected by intense political struggles behind the deals. Given the rising demand for crude oil in China, the country's energy companies have played a crucial role in forming new alliances globally. Chinese energy companies became active agents of the government to create strategic ties with the country's major oil suppliers. At the same time, with the rise of China's economic power, China has become one of the main financiers of the US public debt and the US market has become one of the major destinations for Chinese products. This has led to stronger multi-dimensional dependence between the two countries affecting the strategies of both countries globally. Given the nature of Iran-US relations over the past three decades, it is therefore not surprising for the US government to exercise leverage in its strategic relations with China so as to increase the pressure on Iran. Hence, the investment strategy of the Chinese state-owned enterprises (SOE) in Iran has been no exception to the general rule of China-US international power share.[4]

In the context of China's investment in Iran's energy sector, Iran's vast absorption capacity has presented the Chinese SOEs with unique opportunities, particularly in the absence of other international competitors, which have gradually left Iran as a result of the US economic sanctions. By the end of 2011, almost all the European energy companies, like Shell, Total, Statoil (to name a few), had left Iran. Nevertheless, the commercial interest of the Chinese companies has been restrained by China's foreign policy priorities which seek to maintain the relationship with the US. Given the leading Chinese energy SOEs (China Petro, Sinopec, and CNOOC) have listed their subsidiaries on the US stock exchanges, the American authorities are in a powerful position to influence their investment decisions globally. When a Sudan Divestment and Accountability Act was signed by the former US president George W Bush in 2007, the US government exerted huge pressure on Chinese oil companies to stop them from importing "blood oil" from Sudan.[5] Evidently, the American authorities have shown that they are willing to exercise their power in order to counter China's strategy in the global energy arena. Therefore, if the Chinese SOEs' strategy in Sudan, more than a decade ago, was a reflection of their failure in assessing risks associated with overseas projects, more recent Chinese activities in Iran show a more cautious approach in dealing with regimes without international repute and a better understanding of political risk.

China's 'one step forward and two steps backward' strategy in dealing with Iran may well serve its strategic interest in relation to the West, particularly the US. Nevertheless, it certainly has had negative impacts on the Iranian economy. A quick browse through the job advertisements for the oil and gas sector in Iran on a famous Iranian career website, *Iran Talent* (as of June 2012) shows that the only active foreign energy companies in Iran are four Chinese energy companies (Petro China, China's National Petroleum Corporation, Sinopec, China Petroleum Engineering and Consultation Corporation). With about 12% unemployment officially reported by the Iranian government, Chinese energy SOEs have the potential to create vast employment opportunities in the oil and gas industry, in addition to regenerating the key revenue-earning sector of the Iranian economy. Yet that potential has not been fulfilled.

As noted, Chinese investments in Iran are also partly affected by Iranian government policies. Despite Iran's huge demand for foreign capital, since 2005 the government has promoted the involvement of domestic energy companies, mainly owned by the Islamic Revolutionary Guard Corps (IRGC), in the key economic sectors, including the energy sector. As a result of this strategy, most of the South Pars natural gas production projects, and the shared gas reserve with Qatar, have been either delayed or left incomplete as a result of disputes between the government and the foreign companies, or have produced less than expected due to the poor quality of the infrastructure. Although South Pars Gas Field has brought Qatar double digit annual growth at times, it has not contributed to the Iranian economic growth proportionately.

Chinese SOEs have signed various agreements committing to invest more than $100 billion in Iran's energy sector over the past few years; however, in practice only a small fraction of those funds have been invested. China has substantial surplus reserves and political motivation to engage in projects that are in accordance with its overall strategic and commercial interest. Nevertheless, the Chinese authorities are well aware that their key interest still lies in continued access to Western markets and avoiding long-term damage to China's national and corporate image.

The Western-led economic sanctions imposed on Iran have had an impact on China's activities in Iran, as it has agreed to comply with EU and US trade and finance restrictions in dealing with Iran. In April 2012, a Chinese ship insurance company, the China P&I Club, announced that it would halt coverage for tankers carrying Iranian oil from July 2012 on, making it extremely difficult for ship owners trading with Iran to find sufficient alternative insurance.[6] In the banking sector, too, China has been rather responsive to the Western regulations in dealing with the Iranian financial industry. By March 2012, very few Chinese banks were still willing to process Iranian payments, which must be filtered to ensure that none of the counterparties appear on official sanction lists.[7] Moreover, in compliance with the EU-proposed oil embargo on Iran, China has been cutting oil imports from Iran. In the first quarter of 2012, China cut its purchases of Iranian crude oil to half of the volume in the first quarter of 2011.

Regarding bilateral political relations, the Iran-China alliance is of higher strategic importance for Iran than for China. Iran has benefited from China's support in maintaining its image as a regional power. This is clearly important to Iran's objective in building a so-called "second Safavid Empire"[8] in the region, stretching from Afghanistan to South Lebanon and balancing the power of other regional players like Turkey and Saudi Arabia. At the same time, Iran has underpinned Chinese energy security and enhanced China's power share in the region to counter US influence.

3. Japan at the Crossroads: Loyalty to US Foreign Policy or to Energy Security?

The key aspect of the Iran-Japan relationship to be discussed in this chapter is Japan's crude imports from Iran, which amount to 13% of Iran's total crude exports. Iran's crude exports to Japan increased more than three times between 1990 and 2007 and reached $12.74 billion in 2007, accounting for 12% of total crude oil imports to Japan.[9] However, by January 2012, due to tightened Western sanctions on the Iranian oil sector, Japan along with other Asian major oil importers had been put under significant pressure to limit its oil trade relations with Iran. As a result, Japan announced to be seeking new suppliers of crude oil to lessen the dependence on Iran.

While Japanese officials have frequently expressed their support for the US-led sanctions and promised that Japan would join the campaign against Iran, they repeatedly refer to the difficulties of cutting oil imports from Iran. Japanese officials have argued in the public media that further cuts in oil imports could damage utilities markets in Japan, particularly in the aftermath of the 2011 tsunami-triggered nuclear crisis which heavily affected the country's nuclear power plants. Most of Japan's 54 nuclear power plants have remained offline since the Fukushima nuclear crisis. This has required a substantial increase in the import of crude oil so as to cover the power generation deficit. Therefore, should Japan cut down its import from Iran, an alternative supplier must replace Iranian crude, and this would pose a challenge for the Japanese government.

Japan has already started to find alternatives to supply its high crude demand. The value of the country's total imports from Saudi Arabia almost doubled between 2005 and 2011, from $ 28.3 million to $ 50.3 million. The total value of imports from Iran, however, only increased from $ 10.3 million to $ 12.8 million during the same period which most probably is a result of oil price change, rather than increase of trade volume. While Japan's demand for crude import has increased, therefore, the volume of imports from Iran has probably remained unchanged. Japanese refiners have covered their increased demand for oil over this period mainly with Saudi crude.

Japan's biggest refiner, JX Nippon Oil & Energy, said in January 2012 that it was talking to Saudi Arabia and other countries to find alternative supplies of crude oil.[10] As noted, due to Japan's high demand for crude imports to fill the electricity production gap created by the nuclear power plant crisis, full compliance with the oil embargo against Iran will remain a great challenge for the Japanese policy makers to formulate a position which will avoid controversy amongst the senior policy makers. In January 2012, Japanese finance minister Jun Azumi had an official meeting with U.S. Secretary of the Treasury Timothy Geithner in which Mr. Azumi expressed Japan's commitment to reduce petroleum imports from Iran in line with the American policy. He was contradicted by Prime Minister Yoshihiko Noda, who asserted that Azumi 'was speaking for himself.'[11]

Japan and 10 other EU nations have been exempted by the US government from full compliance with the sanctions because they have significantly cut purchases of Iranian oil. In April 2012, Japan's top buyer of Iranian crude Showa Shell Sekiyu KK, owned by Royal Dutch Shell (35%) and Saudi Aramco (15%), renewed its annual oil purchase deal with Iran while cutting the volume in line with Western sanctions. The contract renewal came after Iran agreed to include a clause in contract terms that releases Japanese buyers from any penalty if international sanctions prevent them from taking delivery of Iranian oil. Showa Shell imported about 100,000 barrels per day (bpd) from Iran in 2011, then cut the import by 60,000 bpd in April 2012. The company had been discussing a cut with the National Iranian Oil Company of around 15% to 20% to its 2011 contract volume of 100,000 bpd, which helped win Japan its waiver to the U.S. sanctions.[12]

The political relationship between Iran and Japan is the next focus of discussion in this study. Iran's political collaboration with Japan has not been as close as it has been with China. During the Khatami administration (1995-2005), the Iranian government tried to push the political ties with Japan as a part of an eastward-looking government strategy. As a result, former Iranian president Khatami visited Japan in 2000 and became the first Iranian head of government to visit the country in 42 years. However, the Japanese government has been reluctant to strengthen the ties with Iran over the past three decades in order to avoid jeopardising the Japan-US relationship. Under US pressure, in December 2011, the Japanese cabinet announced that it would increase the number of Iranian people and organisations subject to Japanese sanctions. The government added 106 organisations, one individual and three Iranian banks to its sanction list, bringing the total number to 267 organisations, 66 individuals and 20 banks.[13]

The next element of the Japan-Iran relationship is that of Japanese investments in Iran. On various occasions discussions over financial collaboration have been held between Iran and Japan at senior official level through official visits and working groups.[14] Nevertheless, the negotiations have not led to close financial collaborations between the two countries, largely as a result of Western pressure. Japanese companies have removed many of their assets from Iran's oil and gas sectors during the past ten years.[15] The cumulative total investment from Japan between 1978 and 2007 has been $ 529 million[16] which is a significantly smaller figure in comparison with Japanese investment in other parts of the world. The Middle East region received $ 4.5 billion investment from Japan between 1995 and 2011, $ 3.8 billion of which has been absorbed by Saudi Arabia.

In 2010, Japan ended its last major investment in Iran. Japanese oil explorer Inpex was put under huge pressure from both Washington and Tokyo to divest its minority interest in the Azadegan oil field in Iran at a considerable loss. The project started in 2000 and was the cornerstone of Japan's 'hinomaru'[17] oil policy to secure energy supplies by investing in Japanese-owned energy deposits in the Middle East. Initially Inpex acquired 75% of an Iranian oil company, NICO, which was a part of a consortium leading the seismographic studies in the oil field, and under Western pressure, by 2006, Inpex cut its stake to 10%, and by 2010 it sold all of its shares in the project.[18]

In addition to investment relations between the two countries, oil trade related financial relations between Iranian and Japanese institutions have been also affected by the Western economic sanctions on Iran. The US government has been leveraging its influence on Japan in order to put more pressure on the Iranian government. In May 2012, Mitsubishi UFJ, a Japanese bank which for many years handled all the transactions for Japan's oil trades with Iran was ordered by an American court to freeze $ 2.6 billion of Iranian assets held at the bank. This was to secure a fund for compensation to be paid to families of victims in the 1983 suicide bombing of a US Marine Corp in Beirut in which Tehran allegedly played a role. The bank filed a petition of objection to the New York State's court.[19] The suit was moved to the federal court and the state court's order was eventually overturned.[20]

As discussed above, the Iran-Japan relationship in the context of the three main streams reviewed in this chapter has been significantly downplayed, with one exception: the oil trade. However, as a result of the Western sanctions the crude inflow to Japan from Iran has been targeted. The Iranian economy is heavily reliant on crude export income, and so the oil trade with Japan (like that with all other major buyers of Iranian crude) will remain of high importance. From Japan's perspective, given the country's high demand for oil, the imports of Iranian crude are likely to remain an important source of supply. Saudi Arabia is, nonetheless, the largest supplier of oil to Japan. The total value of Saudi exports to Japan between 2005 and 2011 came to $267 billion, which was three times greater than the total value of Iranian exports to Japan over that period ($ 85 billion). Whether or not Saudi Arabia is able to fully replace Iranian crude for Japan has been a matter of debate and can only be proven by time. Nevertheless, the current trend shows the importance of the oil trade to both countries and their mutual reliance.

4. Indo-Iranian Relations: a Marriage of Convenience

India, the third largest importer of Iranian oil in Asia, which receives about 12% of Iran's total crude exports, is another important economic and political ally of Iran in Asia. In the context of the three main pillars of the Iran-India relationship (crude trade, investment, and political relations) discussed in this chapter, the crude oil imports from Iran are the key element of the relationship between the two countries (as with other Asian countries). India has joined China in challenging the new EU and US call for sanctions on Iranian oil and the financial sector. The country's officials have expressed their concern that it is not possible for India to take drastic measures to reduce imports from Iran. The political dimension of the Indo-Iranian relationship is also important. With Pakistan, a long term rival of India, located between the two countries, India's political relations with Iran inevitably carry a special strategic significance.

India's reluctance to comply fully with the Western economic sanctions has been interpreted by Iranian officials as a political victory for Iran. It will, however, remain a challenge for Indian companies to make oil payments without the risk of violating the US-led financial regulations against Iran. It is true that India's policy in this respect can jeopardize the country's ties with the US; nevertheless, it can bring great potential and bargaining power for the Indian government in dealing with Iran. Iran has extended offers for discounted prices to sweeten the deals and maintain its crude trade with India – as well as China. This constitutes an attempt by Iran to bypass the US and European sanctions by attracting buyers with highly advantageous credit terms. In April 2012, the *Financial Times* reported that Tehran had been offering some of the potential customers of Iranian crude in Asia, including India, 180 days of free credit. Each month of credit amounts to a discount of roughly \$1.2 to \$1.5 a barrel.[21] India will benefit much more than Iran by importing Iranian oil at discount rates: the price paid by Indian companies through the first and second quarter of 2012 remained below the Iranian government budget breakeven price (\$ 117 per barrel).[22]

Financial transactions for oil payments between Iran and India have become a challenge over the past few years. In December 2010, the Reserve Bank of India (RBI), fearing the US sanctions on India's financial sector, walked out of the Asian Clearing Union that cleared Iran's oil payments. As a result, India began to use one of its small nationalized banks, with little or no exposure to the West, to clear the oil payments with Tehran. Some of the payments were made through intermediaries which over time were also blocked. Germany's EIH Bank and Turkey's Halkbank both stopped handling the oil payment transactions to Iran. Indian companies have had to shuffle the payment options. Some payments go through barter and are offset against Iranian imports, mainly tea, rice and jewelry; some are made in rupees to be utilized in building Indian investments in Iran or vice versa; and some are made in other currencies with transactions going through Turkey. Iran has asked India to be able to use Chinese yuan as a trading currency but this was not approved by Indian officials. It has also offered to route its India payments through its Latin American allies (especially Venezuela and Brazil).[23]

In March 2012, Iran and India agreed to settle 45% of Indian crude oil purchases in rupees.[24] The decision was made in order to facilitate oil payments by India to Iran, but it will leave Iran exposed to the risk of holding large sums of a currency that is only partly convertible. Prior to this decision, in January 2012, Iran exercised another payment method in order to bypass the sanctions when China and India reportedly paid for their crude import from Iran in gold.[25] All the methods mentioned above will increase the cost of the transactions and in practice some of the oil trade income will have to be paid on the operations through which Iran will bring the petrodollars back to the Iranian economy. Despite the arrangements which have been put in place to bypass the sanctions, moreover, India's crude imports from Iran have been declining. There was a substantial drop in early 2012, with imports falling by 35% between March and April (from 410,000 bpd to 260,000 bpd).[26]

Notwithstanding the US effort to block India's economic collaboration with Iran, the Iranian government has become particularly active in promoting economic ties between the two countries through new initiatives such as a liberal business visa regime, direct flights, trade fairs and exhibitions. So far, India's exporters have been positive regarding Iran's initiatives for promoting bilateral trade, particularly in light of the agreements between the two countries over the longstanding payment problem. Being Iran's largest rice supplier, India will naturally focus on increasing exports, particularly agricultural commodities like wheat, rice and sugar. Although agricultural products form a large share of India's export basket to Iran, India also supplies other items including construction equipment, building material and hardware, pharmaceuticals, telecom products, textiles, automobiles and spare parts. As not many countries are willing to trade with Iran, Iran's ability to choose what to import is limited. Even though Indian products are associated with poor quality in the minds of the Iranian consumers, they have little option but to buy them. India is in a highly privileged position from which to benefit from Iran's sizeable market, as long as the trade channels between the two countries remain open.

The investment ties between Iran and India have been affected by the international sanctions. The biggest Indian investment project in the country is led by the Indian state-owned energy company, ONGC Videsh Ltd (OVL). The project is a $ 5 billion project where OVL is committed to developing a gas field in the South of Iran, called Farzad-B. OVL owns a 40% stake in the consortium, state refiner Indian Oil Corp (IOC) also has 40% stake, while Oil India Ltd (OIL) holds the remaining 20%. OVL had been hesitant in delivering its commitments to the project in which it has been a consortium shareholder since 2002. In response to the slow development of the project, Iran in April 2012 gave OVL a one month ultimatum to start the project. The Iranians expressed urgency to develop the project while indicating their intentions to award the contract to some other party, if they were not satisfied with the progress of negotiations. OVL sought the Indian government's advice regarding the project in a letter to the ministry of petroleum. Negotiations have been ongoing since the Iranian government expressed its concern. OVL has faced the risk of Iran's Offshore Oil Company passing the project on to another party, even though it has already invested $ 36 million in the project.[27]

Another case of unsuccessful Indo-Iranian investment relations is the Mashhad-Chabahar railway. The Iranian government has held negotiations with India in order to attract India's engagement in a large railway construction project in the Iranian part of the International North-South Corridor[28] which starts in the port city of Chabahar in the South of Iran and will continue up to the city of Mashhad.[29] Such a trade corridor could connect Indian ships docked at an Iranian port in the Gulf to a railway which crosses Iran leading to Afghanistan and central Asia. The project is an important route to bypass Pakistan, one of India's strategic concerns in the region. Although it is difficult to speculate whether or not this project will materialize within the expected time frame, India's strategy in dealing with Iran is likely to follow the same pattern as China's 'one step forward two step backward' approach if the US does not lift the pressure on Iran.

India's relations with Iran seem to function as a hedge for the Indian government's strategic interests in the region. If the US withdraws its forces from Afghanistan, the Pakistan-sponsored Taliban may regain a powerful situation in the country. Over the past few years, India has supported projects in Iran which could offset Pakistani influence in Afghanistan. One of these is the Chabahar port development which is located in Iran's Sunni-dominated Balochistan province in the South–East.[30]

India, like other Asian countries, has been under pressure by the US government to reduce its collaboration with Iran. The Indian government has taken various initiatives to please the US administration, including the termination of the Asian Customs Union (ACU) arrangement to pay for its oil imports from Iran in December 2010 and issuing open arrest warrants against three Iranian citizens for their suspected involvement in the terror attack against the Israeli embassy vehicle in New Delhi in February 2012. However, from time to time the Indian government has shown resistance to the US pressure over its relations with Iran.[31] The ongoing bilateral trade relations are a good example of such resistance. In addition to the direct influence of the US administration on Indo-Iranian relations, the US campaign for the War on Terror has also affected relations between Iran and India. As the US resuscitated its relationship with Pakistan and dramatically expanded its military footprint in the region by invading Iraq and Afghanistan, Iran and India found their own power both domestically and regionally threatened by the growing presence of the US on their doorstep. As a result, New Delhi and Tehran have sought to strengthen their bilateral relationship: in 2003, through the "New Delhi Declaration," which sets forth a vision for bilateral 'strategic partnership'[32] and seeks to strengthen Indo-Iranian defense cooperation.[33]

5. South Korea: Fourth Biggest Consumer of Iranian Oil in Asia

South Korea is the world's fifth largest oil importer. In 2011, around 10% of South Korea's crude oil consumption was imported from Iran. Like other countries studied in this chapter, the oil trade is a more critical element of the Iran-South Korea relationship than the two other aspects (i.e. investment ties and political relations). Due to the recent Western oil embargo on Iran, South Korea, along with other buyers of Iranian oil, has faced an increasing supply risk for its crude demand. South Korean officials have expressed their concerns over the de-stabilizing effect of sanctions against Iran on international oil markets, which can impose adverse effects on the South Korean economy.[34] As a result, South Korea has been assessing options to cut down on Iranian oil. The US government has increased pressure on South Korea to loosen its ties with Iran. Senior US officials visited South Korea in January 2012 to increase pressure on Seoul to cut imports of Iranian oil.[35] South Korea, however, has been pushing for a waiver from the US to facilitate the country's crude demand imports from Iran.[36]

In order to comply with the Western oil embargo on Iran, South Korea has been evaluating possible sources to replace the Iranian crude. Saudi crude is the main alternative. In 2011, Saudi Arabia supplied over 30% of the country's imports of crude oil. In February 2012, President Lee Myung-bak visited the Gulf oil-producing countries to seek alternative sources for South Korea's energy demand which led to a 20-year deal between South Korea's third largest refiner and Saudi Arabia. The contract is the first long-term commitment to South Korea by Saudi Arabia, and it is highly unusual as one-year supply deals are the norm of the oil markets.[37] The country has also turned to other Gulf producers, including the UAE, Kuwait and Qatar to make up the Iran supply cuts. As a result, shipments to South Korea from Kuwait in January-April 2012 rose 15% to nearly 328,000 bpd; similarly those from UAE increased by 10% to 250,000 bpd; and those from Qatar rose by 10% to more than 288,000 bpd.[38]

South Korea's investment activities have fluctuated over the past few years due to the international sanctions against Iran. In 2010, South Korea's GS Engineering & Construction cancelled a $ 1.2 billion gas project in the South Pars field in Iran.[39] In 2012 an investment project to lay a 1,680-km pipeline to transfer oil from Neka Port in the Caspian Sea in the North of Iran to Jask Port in the Oman Sea was signed between the two countries. The proposed value of the project is between $3 and $4 billion and it is designed to transit one million barrels of oil per day.[40] The Iranian state-owned news agency, *Mehr News*, reported the project had been under negotiation for five years. The investment strategy of South Korea in Iran seems to have more or less followed the same trend as that of China and India. While South Korean companies are not allowed to do business in Iran due to the US unilateral sanctions, they are trying to keep their options open for the time when the sanctions are lifted.

The core of South Korea's relationship with Iran has been focused on economics, whereas political relations have not been as significant as those with some of Iran's other trading partners. As with other Asian partners of Iran, the US has sought to put pressure on South Korea to downplay its relations. However, the South Korean government has often shown resistance to some of the policies which the US government has tried to impose. A good example of such resistance is the controversy over the Mellat Bank, an Iranian Bank in Seoul. In 2010, US officials increased the pressure on South Korean banking regulators to close down the operation of the bank in South Korea which the US suspected was used as a financial channel for Iran's nuclear activities. The bank's activities were suspended for two months.[41] However, it reopened for business following the expiry of the suspension by South Korea's financial regulator.[42] Seoul has officially voiced its support for UN Security Council resolution on the Iranian nuclear program, but at the same time it has tried to draw a line between its position on the nuclear issue and its 'business as usual' activities in Iran.

In addition to the three main elements of the relationship between the two countries, access to the Iranian market is of high importance for South Korean producers. Similarly, South Korean goods are important for Iranian consumers. For over two decades, various South Korean brands of electronic appliances, computers, high tech gadgets, as well as automotive products have been on the top sellers' list of the Iranian consumer goods' market. South Korean industries entered Iran for the first time in the early 1990's, during the country's reconstruction and development phase in the aftermath of the Iran-Iraq war. By 2011, around 2,000 South Korean companies were exporting to Iran, Samsung Electronics and LG Electronics accounted for a combined 30% of Iran's mobile phone market and 57% of the imported cars to Iran are made by South Korean manufacturers (mainly by Kia and Hyundai).[43] According to the Islamic Republic of Iran Customs Administration (IRICA) the total value of direct car imports from South Korea in 2011 was $ 306 million.[44] This figure does not include the UAE re-exports of South Korean cars, which form about 15% of the total imports of Iran from South Korea. In the light of tightened Western sanctions against Iran, there has been speculation that South Korea is considering a reduction in its exports to Iran. The intention would be to reduce the risk of payment defaults as sanctions threaten Iran's oil revenue. A potential interruption of car imports from South Korea could significantly distort the Iranian market which is already suffering from double digit inflation.

According to the American Enterprise Institute (AEI), bilateral trade between Iran and South Korea was valued at roughly $10 billion in 2008.[45] As a major share of the bilateral trade comes from the crude oil trade, it can be expected that Iran would feel the pressure imposed by sanctions more than South Korea would. Nonetheless, the South Korean government announced in 2010 that it would help all South Korean companies which suffer from the termination of their trading with

Iran as a result of the economic sanctions.[46] Furthermore, from October 1, 2010, to compensate for the negative impact of the sanctions, South Korea started using won instead of dollars to clear the payments to Iran through the Industrial Bank of Korea, Woori Bank and the Central Bank of Iran. Additionally, the South Korean government allowed Iran to keep financial resources earned from the export of oil to South Korea inside the country to be used for the import of South Korean products into Iran.[47] As a result of the bilateral trade, Iran has accumulated the equivalent of US$5-6 billion in won accounts in South Korea and further tightening of the South Korean trade regulation is likely to make it more difficult for Iran to transfer its assets to government accounts inside Iran or overseas.

6. Conclusion

For Asia, Iranian oil is crucial for economic growth and it cannot be replaced easily. Nevertheless, in the light of the latest US-led economic sanctions, Iran-Asia ties have become threats to Asia's relationship with the West as the US demands that Asian countries (as well as the rest of the world) choose between maintaining economic relations with Iran and retaining good relations with the US. From Iran's perspective, in the aftermath of the US-led economic sanctions, the country's economic ties with Asia have become particularly important due to the country's heavy reliance on oil revenues. The Iranian government is expected to continue its effort to maintain the crude oil trade at discount rates, even though this will have huge repercussions for the Iranian economy. The major Asian buyers of Iranian oil did not cease to acquire Iranian oil in July 2012, when the EU oil embargo officially took effect. However, various estimates have shown that Iran crude export has fallen significantly.

Iran's Asian oil trade partners have reacted in different ways to the Iran oil embargo. So far, India and China have resisted the US-led sanctions. This will allow Iran's oil exports to continue and will help the Iranian government to sidestep the sanctions. While India and China may be trying to buy time so as to diversify their oil from Iran, their response can nonetheless be interpreted as a lack of full support for the international campaign against Iran. Japan has decreased oil import from Iran significantly over the past years and replaced Iran's crude with Saudi products. South Korea has been seeking an exemption from US sanction regulations along with Japan, but this has not been granted.

Amongst the four major buyers of Iranian crude, China is a strategic partner of Iran. It is not the oil trade alone which is of significance. Given that China holds a veto right in the United Nations Security Council (UNSC), Iran's alliance with China will become more important if the risk of a military attack on Iran increases. As far as Iran's relations with India are concerned, Iran is an important regional player which shares borders with Pakistan, India's antagonistic neighbor. Therefore, maintaining relations with Iran is important. However, given the nuclear dispute, Iran is too troublesome to befriend. So, it is likely that the Indian government will downplay its ties with Iran, every now and then, in order to maintain its relation with the West.

Maintaining investment relations with Asian economic partners has been a challenge for the Iranian government. Iran needs to attract foreign investment in order to overhaul its aged energy sector infrastructures and to ease the high unemployment. Due to the economic sanctions, Iran's Asian foreign investment partners have all shown reluctance in getting too involved with Iran and this has held back the Iranian economy in many respects. Most of the Asian investment partners of Iran have had similar investment strategies in Iran. They have all avoided serious engagements in Iran for the time being whilst trying to keep their name on the list of Iran's investment partners. Such a strategy will allow them to keep a foot in the door for the time when (and if) the sanctions are lifted, without locking large sums of their assets within the Iranian economy. Unless the international sanctions imposed on the Iranian economy ease, significant investment will not be forthcoming.

Endnotes

1   Li, Justin, "Chinese investment in Iran: One step forward and two steps backward." *East Asia Forum*, November 3, 2010. Accessed April 21, 2012. http://www.eastasiaforum.org/2010/11/03/chinese-investment-in-iran-one-step-forward-and-two-steps-backward/.

2   Becker, Antoneta, "Iran sanctions open door wider for China." Asia Times, August 3, 2010. Accessed 3 May, 2012. http://www.atimes.com/atimes/China_Business/LH03Cb01.html.

3   "Iran and Sinopec close to Yadavaran oil field deal." *New York Times*, April 9, 2007. Accessed February 17, 2012. http://www.nytimes.com/2007/04/09/business/worldbusiness/09iht-chioil.4.5201861.html.

4   "New actors shape China's foreign policy." *Stockholm International Peace Research Institute*, September 6, 2010. Accessed February 17, 2012. http://www.sipri.org/media/pressreleases/2010/100906chinaforeignpolicy.

5   Patey. Luke. A. "Against the Asian tide: The Sudan divestment campaign", *Journal of Modern African Studies*. Vol. 47, No. 4, December 2009, p:551-573. Accessed August 2, 2012. http://www.diis.dk/graphics/_staff/lpa/lpatey_againsttheasiantide%20(2).pdf

6   "Key China insurer to stop covering tankers with Iran oil." *Alarabiya*, April 5, 2012. Accessed April 5, 2012. http://english.alarabiya.net/articles/2012/04/05/205553.html.

7   Hornby, Lucy, "New sanctions on Iran constrict trade flows to Asia", *Reuters*, February 7, 2012. Accessed February 7, 2012. http://www.reuters.com/article/2012/02/07/iran-sanctions-trade-idUSL4E8D71VP20120207.

8   The phrase was used by the former Iraqi MP, Iyad Jamal Aldin, in a presentation at the House of Common in London on April 30, 2012.

9   "Japan-Iran Relations," Ministry of Foreign Affairs of Japan, February 2010, http://www.mofa. go.jp/region/middle_e/iran/index.html.

10 "Mixed reactions to new sanctions on Iran." *Xinhua News Agency*, January 20, 2012. Accessed January 20, 2012. http://news.xinhuanet.com/english/world/2012-01/20/c_1313 70485.htm.

11 Crowell, Todd, "Should Japan Say No to Iran Sanctions?", *Real Clear World*, January 26, 2012. Accessed May 17, 2012. http://www.realclearworld.com/articles/2012/01/26/maybe_japan_ should_say_no_to_iran_sanctions.html.

12 Tsukimori, Osamu, "Japan's Showa Shell Renews Deal-Sources with Iran", *Reuters*, April 18, 2012. Accessed May 12, 2012. http://uk.reuters.com/article/2012/04/18/japan-iran-showa-idUKL3E8FI2SL20120418.

13 "Japan extends sanctions against Iran", *Tengri News,* December 11, 2011. Accessed 12 May, 2012. http://en.tengrinews.kz/politics_sub/6086/.

14 "Japan-Iran Relations," Ministry of Foreign Affairs of Japan, February 2010, http://www.mofa. go.jp/region/middle_e/iran/index.html.

15 Pomfret, John; Lynch, Colum, "U.S. criticized on Iran sanctions," The Washington Post, March 5, 2010, http://www.washingtonpost.com/wp-dyn/content/article/2010/03/04/AR2010030404735. html.

16 "Japan-Iran Relations", *Ministry of Foreign Affairs of Japan,* March 2012. Accessed May 17, 2012. http://www.mofa.go.jp/region/middle_e/iran/index.html.

17 Hinomaru in Japanese means "rising sun flag" and the Japanese energy policy was named such because it seeks to secure energy for Japan's future generations.

18 Crowell, Todd, "Should Japan Say No to Iran Sanctions?", *Real Clear World*, January 26, 2012. Accessed May 17, 2012. http://www.realclearworld.com/articles/2012/01/26/maybe_japan_ should_say_no_to_iran_sanctions.html.

19 Okada, Yuji, "Iran Crude to Japan Said to Face Blocks After Court Order", *Bloomberg*, May 17, 2012. Accessed May 17, 2012. http://www.bloomberg.com/news/2012-05-17/iran-oil-cargoes-to-japan-said-to-face-blocks-after-court-ruling.html.

20 "The Bank of Tokyo-Mitsubishi UFJ resumes Iran deals", *The Daily Yomiuri*, May 27, 2012. Accessed May 28, 2012. http://www.yomiuri.co.jp/dy/business/T120526002347.html.

21 Blas, Javier, "Iran woos oil buyers with easy credit." *Financial Times*, April 11, 2012. Accessed April 11, 2012. http://www.ft.com/cms/s/0/4c2f37f6-8322-11e1-9f9a-00144feab49a. html#axzz1tteL8p4L.

22 Ahmed, Masood, "Middle East and Central Asia Regional Economic Outlook Update" *IMF,* April 2012. Accessed 12 June 2012. http://www.imf.org/external/pubs/ft/reo/2012/mcd/eng/pdf/ mena_pp.pdf.

23 Bagchi, Indrani, "Why India's real Iran dilemma isn't oil" *Economic Times*, January 29, 2012. Accessed April 11, 2012. http://articles.economictimes.indiatimes.com/2012-01-29/ news/30674049_1_asian-clearing-union-oil-trades-oil-payments.

24 "India ready to buy Iranian oil with rupees." *RT*, March 28, 2012. Accessed April 28, 2012. http:// rt.com/business/news/india-iran-oil-currency-627/.

25 Nikolas, Katerina, "India to pay for Iranian oil with gold to avoid US sanctions." *Digital Journal*, January 24, 2012. Accessed April 28, 2012. http://digitaljournal.com/article/318404.

26 Rajiv, Samuel "India and the US: Squaring the Circle on Iran" *Institute for Defence Studies and Analyses*, May 10, 2012. Accessed May 11, 2012. http://www.idsa.in/idsacomments/IndiaandtheUSSquaringtheCircleonIran_sscrajiv_100512.

27 Airy, Anupama, "India in a bind on Iran investments" *Hindustan Times*, May 9, 2012. Accessed May 11, 2012. http://www.hindustantimes.com/business-news/WorldEconomy/India-in-a-bind-on-Iran-investments/Article1-853290.aspx.

28 The project envisages a multi-modal transportation network that connects ports on India's West coast to Bandar Abbas in Iran, then overland to Bandar Anzali port on the Caspian Sea; thence through Rasht and Astara on the Azerbaijan border onwards to Kazakhstan, and further onwards towards Russia.

29 "India to invest in building North-South Corridor in Iran" *Press TV*, May 4, 2012. Accessed May 11, 2012. http://www.presstv.ir/detail/239520.html.

30 Bagchi, Indrani, "India to US: Iran curbs will hurt us" *The Times of India*, July 6, 2010. Accessed April 11, 2012. http://articles.timesofindia.indiatimes.com/2010-07-06/india/28298917_1_chahbahar-port-india-iran-energy-sector.

31 Kumaraswamy, P. R. "India's Iran Defiance" *Institute for Defence Studies and Analyses*, March 19, 2012. Accessed March 19, 2012. http://www.idsa.in/idsacomments/IndiasIranDefiance_prkumaraswamy_190312.

32 "Iran-India sign New Delhi Declaration", *The Economic Times*, January 25, 2003. Accessed April 10, 2012. http://articles.economictimes.indiatimes.com/2003-01-25/news/27546023_1_iran-sign-india-and-iran-tehran.

33 Dormandy, Xenia and Desai, Ronak, "India-Iran Relations: Key Security Implications", *Policy Brief Belfer Center for Science and International Affairs*, March 24, 2008. Accessed May 17, 2012. http://belfercenter.ksg.harvard.edu/publication/18176/indiairan_relations.html.

34 Kim, Jack, "South Korea frets as U.S. ups oil pressure on Iran." *Reuters*, January 16, 2012. Accessed January 16, 2012. http://af.reuters.com/article/worldNews/idAFTRE80G0BT20120117.

35 "S. Korea considers reducing oil import dependence on Iran." *Yonhap News Agency*, January 8, 2012. Accessed January 10, 2012. http://english.yonhapnews.co.kr/national/2012/01/08/91/0301000000AEN20120108000700315F.HTML.

36 Jung-a, Song, "S Korea boosts Iran oil imports", *Financial Times*, May 29, 2012. Accessed May 29, 2012. http://www.ft.com/intl/cms/s/0/5da2f57c-a97e-11e1-9972-00144feabdc0.html#axzz1xRvMAf4n.

37 "Oil inks 20-year deal with Aramco to secure oil supplies." Alarabiya, February 9, 2012. Accessed February 12, 2012. http://english.alarabiya.net/articles/2012/02/09/193546.html.

38 "S Korea Iran Crude Imports Rose 42% In April, As May-June Shipments Expedited", *Wall Street Journal*, May 28, 2012. Accessed May 28, 2012. http://online.wsj.com/article/BT-CO-20120528-707692.html.

39 "S.Korea GS E&C says scraps $1.2 bln Iran gas deal", *Reuters*, July 1, 2010. Accessed June 2, 2012. http://af.reuters.com/article/energyOilNews/idAFTOE66007020100701.

40 "South Korea to invest in Iran's cross-country pipeline project", *Tehran Times*, October 7, 2011. Accessed June 5, 2012. http://tehrantimes.com/economy-and-business/3287-south-korea-to-invest-in-irans-cross-country-pipeline-project.

41 "S. Korea to suspend Iranian bank as part of sanctions," AFP, October 7, 2010, Accessed May 28, 2011, http://www.google.com/hostednews/afp/article/ALeqM5hnzUX7JsOejkVQjtmAR67HNjbwOw?docId=CNG.1efa8b21ab6f6757c7e1f6fd1c5ae4e5.401.

42 Vegan, Trond. "South Korean regulator eases off Iranian bank", *Reuters*, December 10, 2010. Accessed June 2, 2012. http://www.complinet.com/global/news/news/article.html?ref=13 9179.

43 *Khabar Online*, September 12, 2011. Accessed June 5, 2012. http://www.khabaronline.ir/news-173038.aspx.

44 "Annual Data Release", *IRICA*. http://www.irica.gov.ir/Portal/Home/ShowPage.aspx?Object= Report&CategoryID=fd61187e-a080-4800-bb4b-0a3d0946cc10&WebPartID=fa961111-0daf-44ac-a4db-6267bbc1fcd5&ID=a3fa5983-b528-491f-9e2f-0e266eefda9e.

45 "South Korea in deal with Iranian Central Bank to revive trade ties," *International Business Times*, October 8, 2010. Accessed June 5, 2012. http://www.ibtimes.com/articles/70022/20101008/iran-south-korea-sanctions-central-bank-woori-ibk.htm.

46 "South Korea in deal with Iranian Central Bank to revive trade ties," *International Business Times*, October 8, 2010. Accessed June 5, 2012. http://www.ibtimes.com/articles/70022/20101008/iran-south-korea-sanctions-central-bank-woori-ibk.htm.

47 "Korea, Iran to open won-based accounts," *Korea Herald,* September 17, 2010. Accessed June 5, 2012. http://view.koreaherald.com/kh/view.php?ud=20100917000703&cpv=0.

Bibliography

Li, Justin, "Chinese investment in Iran: One step forward and two steps backward." *East Asia Forum,* November 3, 2010. Accessed April 21, 2012. http://www.eastasiaforum.org/2010/11/03/chinese-investment-in-iran-one-step-forward-and-two-steps-backward/.

Becker, Antoneta, "Iran sanctions open door wider for China." Asia Times, August 3, 2010. Accessed 3 May, 2012. http://www.atimes.com/atimes/China_Business/LH03Cb01.html.

"Iran and Sinopec close to Yadavaran oil field deal." *New York Times*, April 9, 2007. Accessed February 17, 2012. http://www.nytimes.com/2007/04/09/business/worldbusiness/09iht-chioil.4.5201861.html.

"New actors shape China's foreign policy." *Stockholm International Peace Research Institute*, September 6, 2010. Accessed February 17, 2012. http://www.sipri.org/media/pressreleases/2010/100906chi naforeignpolicy.

Patey. Luke. A. "Against the Asian tide: The Sudan divestment campaign", *Journal of Modern African Studies.* Vol. 47, No. 4, December 2009, p:551-573. Accessed August 2, 2012. http://www.diis.dk/graphics/_staff/lpa/lpatey_againsttheasiantide%20(2).pdf

"Key China insurer to stop covering tankers with Iran oil." *Alarabiya*, April 5, 2012. Accessed April 5, 2012. http://english.alarabiya.net/articles/2012/04/05/205553.html.

Hornby, Lucy, "New sanctions on Iran constrict trade flows to Asia", *Reuters*, February 7, 2012. Accessed February 7, 2012. http://www.reuters.com/article/2012/02/07/iran-sanctions-trade-idUSL4E8D71VP20120207.

"Japan-Iran Relations," Ministry of Foreign Affairs of Japan, February 2010, http://www.mofa.go.jp/region/middle_e/iran/index.html

"Mixed reactions to new sanctions on Iran." *Xinhua News Agency*, January 20, 2012. Accessed January 20, 2012. http://news.xinhuanet.com/english/world/2012-01/20/c_131370485.htm.

Crowell, Todd, "Should Japan Say No to Iran Sanctions?", *Real Clear World*, January 26, 2012. Accessed May 17, 2012. http://www.realclearworld.com/articles/2012/01/26/maybe_japan_should_say_no_to_iran_sanctions.html.

Tsukimori, Osamu, "Japan's Showa Shell Renews Deal-Sources with Iran", *Reuters*, April 18, 2012. Accessed May 12, 2012. http://uk.reuters.com/article/2012/04/18/japan-iran-showa-idUKL3E8FI2SL20120418.

"Japan extends sanctions against Iran", *Tengri News*, December 11, 2011. Accessed 12 May, 2012. http://en.tengrinews.kz/politics_sub/6086/.

"Japan-Iran Relations," Ministry of Foreign Affairs of Japan, February 2010, http://www.mofa.go.jp/region/middle_e/iran/index.html

Pomfret, John; Lynch, Colum, "U.S. criticized on Iran sanctions," The Washington Post, March 5, 2010, http://www.washingtonpost.com/wp-dyn/content/article/2010/03/04/AR2010030 404735.html

"Japan-Iran Relations", *Ministry of Foreign Affairs of Japan*, March 2012. Accessed May 17, 2012. http://www.mofa.go.jp/region/middle_e/iran/index.html.

Crowell, Todd, "Should Japan Say No to Iran Sanctions?", *Real Clear World*, January 26, 2012. Accessed May 17, 2012. http://www.realclearworld.com/articles/2012/01/26/maybe_japan_should_say_no_to_iran_sanctions.html.

Okada, Yuji, "Iran Crude to Japan Said to Face Blocks After Court Order", *Bloomberg*, May 17, 2012. Accessed May 17, 2012. http://www.bloomberg.com/news/2012-05-17/iran-oil-cargoes-to-japan-said-to-face-blocks-after-court-ruling.html.

"The Bank of Tokyo-Mitsubishi UFJ resumes Iran deals", *The Daily Yomiuri*, May 27, 2012. Accessed May 28, 2012. http://www.yomiuri.co.jp/dy/business/T120526002347.html.

Blas, Javier, "Iran woos oil buyers with easy credit." *Financial Times*, April 11, 2012. Accessed April 11, 2012. http://www.ft.com/cms/s/0/4c2f37f6-8322-11e1-9f9a-00144feab49a.html#axzz1tte L8p4L.

Ahmed, Masood, "Middle East and Central Asia Regional Economic Outlook Update" *IMF*, April 2012. Accessed 12 June 2012. http://www.imf.org/external/pubs/ft/reo/2012/mcd/eng/pdf/mena_pp.pdf.

Bagchi, Indrani, "Why India's real Iran dilemma isn't oil" *Economic Times*, January 29, 2012. Accessed April 11, 2012. http://articles.economictimes.indiatimes.com/2012-01-29/news/30674049_1_asian-clearing-union-oil-trades-oil-payments.

"India ready to buy Iranian oil with rupees." *RT*, March 28, 2012. Accessed April 28, 2012. http://rt.com/business/news/india-iran-oil-currency-627/.

Nikolas, Katerina, "India to pay for Iranian oil with gold to avoid US sanctions." *Digital Journal*, January 24, 2012. Accessed April 28, 2012. http://digitaljournal.com/article/318404.

Rajiv, Samuel "India and the US: Squaring the Circle on Iran" *Institute for Defence Studies and Analyses*, May 10, 2012. Accessed May 11, 2012. http://www.idsa.in/idsacomments/IndiaandtheUSSquaringtheCircleonIran_sscrajiv_100512.

Airy, Anupama, "India in a bind on Iran investments" *Hindustan Times*, May 9, 2012. Accessed May 11, 2012. http://www.hindustantimes.com/business-news/WorldEconomy/India-in-a-bind-on-Iran-investments/Article1-853290.aspx.

"India to invest in building North-South Corridor in Iran" *Press TV*, May 4, 2012. Accessed May 11, 2012. http://www.presstv.ir/detail/239520.html.

Bagchi, Indrani, "India to US: Iran curbs will hurt us" *The Times of India*, July 6, 2010. Accessed April 11, 2012. http://articles.timesofindia.indiatimes.com/2010-07-06/india/28298917_1_chahbahar-port-india-iran-energy-sector.

Kumaraswamy, P. R. "India's Iran Defiance" *Institute for Defence Studies and Analyses*, March 19, 2012. Accessed March 19, 2012. http://www.idsa.in/idsacomments/IndiasIranDefiance_prkumaraswamy_190312.

"Iran-India sign New Delhi Declaration", *The Economic Times*, January 25, 2003. Accessed April 10, 2012. http://articles.economictimes.indiatimes.com/2003-01-25/news/27546023_1_iran-sign-india-and-iran-tehran.

Dormandy, Xenia and Desai, Ronak "India-Iran Relations: Key Security Implications", *Policy Brief Belfer Center for Science and International Affairs*, March 24, 2008. Accessed May 17, 2012. http://belfercenter.ksg.harvard.edu/publication/18176/indiairan_relations.html.

Kim, Jack, "South Korea frets as U.S. ups oil pressure on Iran." *Reuters*, January 16, 2012. Accessed January 16, 2012. http://af.reuters.com/article/worldNews/idAFTRE80G0BT20120117.

"S. Korea considers reducing oil import dependence on Iran." *Yonhap News Agency*, January 8, 2012. Accessed January 10, 2012. http://english.yonhapnews.co.kr/national/2012/01/08/91/0301000000AEN20120108000700315F.HTML.

Jung-a, Song, "S Korea boosts Iran oil imports", *Financial Times*, May 29, 2012. Accessed May 29, 2012. http://www.ft.com/intl/cms/s/0/5da2f57c-a97e-11e1-9972-00144feabdc0.html#axzz1xRvMAf4n.

"Oil inks 20-year deal with Aramco to secure oil supplies." Alarabiya, February 9, 2012. Accessed February 12, 2012. http://english.alarabiya.net/articles/2012/02/09/193546.html.

"S Korea Iran Crude Imports Rose 42% In April, As May-June Shipments Expedited", *Wall Street Journal*, May 28, 2012. Accessed May 28, 2012. http://online.wsj.com/article/BT-CO-20120528-707692.html.

"S.Korea GS E&C says scraps $1.2 bln Iran gas deal", *Reuters*, July 1, 2010. Accessed June 2, 2012. http://af.reuters.com/article/energyOilNews/idAFTOE66007020100701.

"South Korea to invest in Iran's cross-country pipeline project", *Tehran Times*, October 7, 2011. Accessed, June 5, 2012. http://tehrantimes.com/economy-and-business/3287-south-korea-to-invest-in-irans-cross-country-pipeline-project.

"Support stepped up for Iran-linked companies," *JoongAng Daily*, August 26, 2010. Accessed June 20, 2012. http://koreajoongangdaily.joinsmsn.com/news/article/article.aspx?aid=2925157.

"S. Korea to suspend Iranian bank as part of sanctions," AFP, October 7, 2010, Accessed on May 28, 2011, http://www.google.com/hostednews/afp/article/ALeqM5hnzUX7JsOejkVQjtmAR67HNjbwOw?docId=CNG.1efa8b21ab6f6757c7e1f6fd1c5ae4e5.401.

Vegan, Trond. "South Korean regulator eases off Iranian bank", *Reuters*, December 10, 2010. Accessed June 2, 2012. http://www.complinet.com/global/news/news/article.html?ref=139179.

Khabar Online, September 12, 2011. Accessed June 5, 2012. http://www.khabaronline.ir/news-173038.aspx.

"Annual Data Release", *IRICA* http://www.irica.gov.ir/Portal/Home/ShowPage.aspx?Object=Report&CategoryID=fd61187e-a080-4800-bb4b-0a3d0946cc10&WebPartID=fa961111-0daf-44ac-a4db-6267bbc1fcd5&ID=a3fa5983-b528-491f-9e2f-0e266eefda9e.

"South Korea in deal with Iranian Central Bank to revive trade ties," *International Business Times*, October 8, 2010. Accessed June 5, 2012. http://www.ibtimes.com/articles/70022/20101008/iran-south-korea-sanctions-central-bank-woori-ibk.htm.

"Korea, Iran to open won-based accounts," *Korea Herald*, September 17, 2010. Accessed June 5, 2012. http://view.koreaherald.com/kh/view.php?ud=20100917000703&cpv=0.

Chapter Four

Turkey and the Gulf:
an Evolving Economic Partnership

Özlem Tür

1. Introduction

After a decade of conflict and tension with Middle Eastern countries during the 1990s, Turkey's relations with the region began to change at the end of the decade. Improvement in the political relationship was coupled with greater economic activity between the two sides. Economic relations, therefore, grew within the shadow of political developments and political objectives. This is not surprising as politics, rather than economics, generally drives regional developments. As Turkey's political relations with the Middle East began to normalize by the end of the 1990s, economic relations also improved in a short time. This chapter looks at the growing economic relations with the Gulf region and builds on a previous article by the author analyzing Turkey's growing economic relations with the Middle East in general.[1] The article argues that, as with the rest of the region, there have been two factors which have brought about the intensification of Turkey's economic relations with the Gulf region – in addition to contingent political developments. The first factor is the structural change which has occurred in the Turkish economy, with its integration into global markets and a high level of economic growth; and the second is the coming to power of the AKP, its vision of foreign policy and the increasing importance of business communities in foreign policy making since then.[2] The first factor emphasizes Turkey's emerging need to trade more with this region due to its economic growth and the transformation of its economy and how the Gulf, with its oil wealth, became one of the major regions in this regard. The second factor emphasizes that the Turkish state under the AKP has started to act in line with its role as a "trading state"[3] and underlines the influence the business communities have on Turkish foreign policy and the pressure from these groups to strengthen relations with the Middle East in general and the Gulf region in particular.

2. Turkish Economic Growth and Trade

The Turkish government embarked on an economic liberalization program on 24 January 1980 and since then has transformed its economy from a state-led developmentalist model to an export-led growth strategy. The results of this policy bore its fruits by the end of the 1990s and Turkey has gone a long way towards integrating with the world economy through trade and investment. One of the most important developments regarding the changes that came with the reform package was the emergence of small-scale businesses in Anatolia, called the 'Anatolian Tigers', that were dynamic, well equipped to adapt to the flexible production patterns and actively competing in the international markets. The creation of the Independent Industrialists and Businessmen Association (MUSIAD) in 1990 as the representative of this newly emerging business group has been very significant. Until the 1990s, the interests of the business community in Turkey were mainly represented by the Turkish Industrialists and Businessmen Association (TUSIAD), founded in 1971, which represented large firms and holdings, based on the European model of organization, concentrating mainly in the Western cities, especially around Istanbul and having Western orientation both economically and politically. From 1990 onwards, with the creation of MUSIAD, small to medium-size businesses from cities around Anatolia that adopted mainly an Eastern-looking strategy where Middle Eastern countries emerged as an important market, began to be active. MUSIAD brought Islamic values and conduct into the business community and has become especially important during the Welfare Party government in the mid-1990s and later with the AKP in the 2000s.

While the 1990s witnessed the integration of the Turkish economy with global markets and the growth of the Anatolian bourgeoisie, they also witnessed a series of economic crises. The 2001 economic crisis has been especially important in changing the structure of the economy. The crisis led to a huge drop in the growth rate in 2001, which has been -9.4 per cent compared to the 6.3 per cent in 2000. The manufacturing industry shrank by nine per cent and the number of businesses closed during the first five months of 2001 reached 15,317.[4] The stabilization program that was adopted as a result of the crisis prioritized market economy and minimum intervention by the state. Besides, the crisis led to the transformation of industrial and financial capital in Turkey from the dominant capital accumulation strategy resting on "rentier profits extracted from the state apparatus" to a "dynamic accumulation" model, based on internationalization and competition on a global scale.[5] This had far-reaching results. First, it led to the bankruptcy of the companies that were using the old model and were dependent on state funds. Second, the companies that managed to shift their strategies to the new model, dynamic accumulation, had turned to new regions and new sectors. Kutlay underlines that this process has encouraged further the economic actors that were excluded from the state mechanisms beforehand (Anatolian Tigers) to 'go and invest abroad.' This was a period in which "the Turkish business elite started to explore the economic and financial opportunities in the neighboring countries and backed the state in its efforts to stabilize the region for the sake of their interests, *inter alia*".[6] The AKP came to power at a time when the 2001 stabilization program was at work and the demand for more integration with the global markets and the neighboring countries was very high.

3. The AKP, the Turkish Economy and the Business Community

Since it came to power in 2002, the AKP has shown that it is a party of business with its emphasis on macro-economic stability, economic growth and expansion of private investment. The party adopted a program that encouraged more trade and investment especially in Turkey's surrounding regions. The idea of carrying the wealth of the region to Turkey was emphasized. In his book *Strategic Depth* (2001), Foreign Minister Ahmet Davutoğlu wrote, "in the relations with our neighbors, we need to increase the mobilization of individuals. What is needed is a policy that will ensure the flow of values and relations of the surrounding regions to Turkey."[7] The Middle East in general (and the Gulf region in particular) stands out as an important region in this thinking with its oil wealth, as increased business with oil-rich economies of the region would promote growth in Turkey's economy. The importance of business in foreign policy was made clear, as Davutoğlu underlined in an interview in 2004 how the business community became one of the drivers of Turkish foreign policy.[8] Kirişçi states that this was a period in which Turkey was becoming a "trading state", where "foreign policy becomes increasingly shaped by economic consideration" and foreign trade constitutes an important part of the GNP.[9] Within the business community, the relationship of MUSIAD members with the AKP was critical as MUSIAD had supported the AKP since its creation, and in return the AKP supported MUSIAD and its economic activities.

Under the AKP, most of the state visits began to be organized by the business community and many businessmen accompanied the state leaders on their official visits. Until 2005, it was mainly DEIK, formed by the state in the mid-1980s and charged with coordinating the business community's foreign economic relations that provided information, organized official visits and facilitated foreign economic relations through bilateral cooperation councils. The creation of TUSKON (Confederation of Businessmen and Industrialists of Turkey) in 2005 as a private, voluntary umbrella organization with a large number of businesses mainly of small and medium size has been important in this context, reaching 33.260 entrepreneurs by 2011.[10] TUSKON, despite having many other functions, shares with DEIK a responsibility in Turkey's foreign business relations and, although not formed by the state, works closely with the state institutions. What is important is that TUSKON's statements and line of action are in full conformity with those of the AKP, "always supporting and never challenging the government's position."[11] Some writers underline that it was TUSKON's pro-government stance that gave it such a privileged position in its relations with the government.[12] TUSKON annually organizes the Turkey-Middle East Trade Bridge, a business forum bringing together businessmen from the region in Istanbul. It was not only the MUSIAD organization that supported the AKP government and formed its backbone; now through TUSKON the government also has an organization through which to support its foreign economic activities.

3.1 The AKP and the Gulf Markets

The performance of the Turkish economy has been impressive since the 2001 reform package. The economic policy of the AKP government, resting on and reaping the benefits of the stabilization program, was successful in generating economic growth, reaching 7.8 per cent in 2010. The growth in the economy caused an increasing hunger for new markets. Turkey's total foreign trade volume increased from $72 billion in 2001 to $333 billion in 2008 and it is important to note that in 2009, 59.8 per cent of exports were from small and medium-size businesses.[13] Turkey became the 16th largest economy of the world with a GDP of approximately USD

736 billion in 2010[14] and became a member of G-20. In 2009, Turkey produced half of the entire output of the Middle East and North Africa combined including Saudi Arabia, Iran, Egypt and Israel.[15]

Looking at Turkey's foreign trade structure, the increasing share of the Middle East in general can be seen. In 2003, Turkey's trade figures showed the share of Europe at 53.6 per cent and the Middle East at 8.49 per cent. The figure for 2007 was 46.5 per cent for Europe and 10 per cent for the Middle East. In 2010, although the figures are still not final, trade decreased to 41.6 per cent for Europe and increased to 17.16 per cent for the Middle East.[16]

In this context, the reason why the Middle East has emerged as the main new route for trade and business becomes an important question. The significant reason lies in the new foreign policy vision put forward by Davutoğlu. In facilitating Turkey's economic relations with the Middle East countries, a "zero problems with neighbors" policy was applied and through establishing economic interdependence the vision of bringing peace to the region was put forward. By arguing that "order in the Middle East cannot be achieved in an atmosphere of isolated economies," Davutoğlu aimed to achieve peace in the region through creating interdependencies.[17] Not only intense economic relations but also human interaction was seen as key to this. Increasing trade figures, growing investments and the movement of people through the lifting of visas have been important in this framework. One should underline that unlike the European model of interdependencies, which developed as a result of cooperation in key economic areas – steel and coal – and later had a spill-over effect on other segments leading to political interdependencies and integration, Turkey's trade with the region has developed under the shadow of political developments and the cooperation at the political level was then reflected later at the economic level. This model of economic cooperation carries the risk of being weakened as a result of political change in either of the sides and needs institutionalization to make economic activities immune to possible turmoil at the political level.

Apart from the reasons related to Davutoğlu's 'new foreign policy vision', there are some other important factors which complement the 'vision' in increasing economic relations with the Middle East. The obvious factor is the proximity of the region and its attractiveness with its oil-rich economy. Second, the relations with the EU have led Turkey to search for new markets and the Middle East emerged as an alternative. The Customs Union agreement signed in 1996 had disappointing results for the development of trade with the EU countries, as this agreement was not followed by a free trade agreement with the EU. As the accession negotiations also got stuck, Turkey had to turn to alternative markets and the Gulf emerged as one of the most important venues.[18] The shift away from Western markets is in line with the general trend in world economy as global economic activity is shifting towards the East. This has been so especially since the 2008 economic crisis hit the Western economies and trade and business relations have been shifting to the East where capital transfers between the Eastern economies have been increasing.[19] Turkey is following that trend.[20] Thirdly, the Middle East has become an important market and an economic partner as most of the MUSIAD and TUSKON members feel ideologically close to the Muslim nations of the Middle East. Pertinent to this argument is the fact that on both the Turkish and the Arab sides the changing of stereotypical images of each other that had been dominant for years played a role in bringing the two communities closer. Parallel to Turkey's increasing soft power and the impact of Turkish soap operas, the attractiveness of Turkish goods in the Arab market has increased.[21] As Turkey's and Erdoğan's popularity increased in the Arab streets, Turkish goods and investments also became more popular. This was also reflected in the number of tourists coming to Turkey from the Gulf. As Turkey's Culture and Information attaché in Dubai Sedat Gönüllüoğlu underlines, there has been an increase in Arab tourists to Turkey, the number having grown by 98 per cent over the past five years. Notably, tourism from Qatar, Kuwait, UAE and Bahrain has increased according to Gönüllüoğlu. He underlined not only the importance of growing political and economic ties between the two sides but also Turkish soap operas in facilitating tourism.[22]

Table 4.1: Turkish Exports to its Four Main GCC Trading Partners $ million

	2000	2001	2002	2003	2004	2005	2006	2007	2008	2009	2010
Saudi Arabia	386.5	500.6	554.6	741.4	768.5	962.1	983.2	1486	2201	1768	2217
Kuwait	73.4	104.7	139	165.9	266	210.3	219	221.2	493	211.2	395
Qatar	9.9	8.4	15.5	15.6	35	82	342.1	499.9	1074	289.3	162.5
UAE	315.9	380.1	457.3	702.9	1143.7	1675.1	1985.6	3240.9	7975.4	2896.5	3332.8

Source: Directorate of Foreign Trade

Table 4.2: Turkish Imports from its Four Main GCC Trading Partners $ million

	2000	2001	2002	2003	2004	2005	2006	2007	2008	2009	2010
Saudi Arabia	961.6	729.6	120.8	208.5	353.9	587.1	623	735.7	908.9	775.7	1380.6
Kuwait	161.3	123.3	26.5	15.9	25.6	41.6	56	90.4	80.6	184.2	214.5
Qatar	11.3	5.7	10.6	8.3	17.7	50.7	66.643	29.6	159.3	85.6	177
UAE	39.7	65.1	100.8	113.5	183.4	205.4	352.2	470	691	667.8	698.4

Source: Directorate of Foreign Trade

Table 4.3: Turkish Trade Volume with Iran and Iraq $ billion

	2000	2001	2002	2003	2004	2005	2006	2007	2008	2009	2010
Iran	1.051	1.200	1.254	2.394	2.775	4.382	6.693	8.056	10.229	5.430	10.687
Iraq	-	-	-	941	2.288	3.208	2.965	3.490	5.238	6.078	7.398

Source: Directorate of Foreign Trade

Looking at the trade figures it is possible to see that there is an increase in the volume of trade with the Gulf Cooperation Council countries, especially from 2007 onwards – AKP's second term in office. Exports have grown much more than imports, which reflects the arguments put forward above. There was a decrease in 2009 parallel to the world economic crisis but trade increased again in 2010. Still, it is also important to note that when compared to the trade figures with Iran and Iraq, trade with the GCC remains very limited. The State Minister responsible for Foreign Trade, Zafer Çağlayan, said they were determined to pursue "zero problems, limitless trade." State visits continued to include large number of businessmen. Minister Çağlayan underlined that business worth $247 million was settled during state visits to Kuwait and Qatar held at the beginning of 2011.[23] This is just an example showing how state visits have become influential in settling business deals and the growing amount of interaction and trade.

3.2 The Arab Spring

Although it is still early to talk about the impact of the 'Arab Spring' on Turkish trade with the region, the initial figures give us ideas as to how the trade and investment with the region are affected. Although economic relations with Tunisia and Egypt seem to have been recovering, the picture with Libya and Syria has been severe. The President of the Turkish Exporters Assembly, Mehmet Büyükekşi, argued that the developments in the Middle East and North Africa were very important for Turkey "because trade with this region constituted 27 per cent of Turkey's exports, 11 per cent of its imports and 17 per cent of its overall trade." Büyükekşi said that despite the developments, there has been no radical change because the losses in some of the countries are made up for by the increase in others. Büyükekşi gives examples of this by looking at the exports in the first two months of 2011, when there were decreases of 21 per cent with Egypt, 38 per cent with Tunisia, 6 per cent with Libya but increases of 61 per cent with Iran, 40 per cent with Iraq, 33 per cent with Saudi Arabia and 144 per cent with the UAE.[24] Data support the arguments that while investments from major Gulf investment companies like Abraaj Capital, Investcorp and NBK Capital in Egypt and Bahrain have been declining, Turkey's attractiveness has been on the rise.[25] The head of Şahinler Holding in Turkey, Kemal Şahin, argued along similar lines. Şahin claimed that as a result of the regional developments, the capitalists of the Middle East will be shifting their investments to Turkey, which will make Turkey "a castle of construction and investment in other service sectors."[26] Growing relations seem to confirm this optimism. In the past two years there has been a common belief that the Gulf countries have found a safe haven in Turkey. Turkey is keen to attract Gulf capital, which has played an important role in Western economies in the past decade. While there was no investment from the Gulf region in Turkey in 2003, in 2006 it reached $1.78 billion.[27] However, this figure remains very small, only 0.1 per cent of total Gulf investment abroad. It is believed that there will be Gulf interest especially in the construction, energy, health and industry sectors.[28] The possibility of Turkey attracting over $30 billion in the coming three to five years has been given attention.[29] The CEO of Noor Islamic Development Bank El-Qemzi, for example, argues that in the coming two years around 4 billion dollars will be invested in Turkey, and that in five years, these investments will diversify to include many different sectors.[30] There is great hope that such a scenario could be realized easily, especially in the case of new regulations being introduced in Turkey regarding Islamic bonds (*sukuk*). If *sukuk* become available in Turkey, there is an expectation that it will be easier to attract Gulf investment. Vice Prime Minister Ali Babacan announced that the regulations for *sukuk* would be ready within 2012.[31]

While attracting the oil money of the Gulf countries remains an important aspect of the relationship, oil itself is also very significant. Turkey sees the Gulf as an important supplier for its increasing energy needs. The growing economic ties are thought to lead to increasing and favorable oil deals with the regional countries also. However, to what extent Turkey's dependence on Russia regarding oil and gas supplies could be diversified as a result of closer ties with the Gulf region remains questionable according to some observers. Han argues that despite calls from the Turkish side, the Gulf countries do not seem very interested in providing Turkey with a strategic advantage in becoming an "energy corridor" and the direction of most of the trade from the Gulf region will be flowing towards the East and Far East rather than to Europe via Nabucco.[32] Still, the Turkish side in its attempt to diversify its supplies hopes that closer relations with the Gulf could help it to meet its oil and gas needs and to become an energy hub.

4. The Free Trade Agreement – Where are We?

Although the Free Trade Agreement with the GCC has been on the table since 2005, it has not been signed yet. Calls for the signing of the Agreement have been made especially by the Turkish side on many occasions. The first Turkey-GCC Business forum held in Istanbul in February 2012 became one of these platforms.

In the opening ceremony, the Turkish Minister of Economy called for more trade and investment with the GCC countries and justified such a call on a *hadith* of the Prophet Muhammad. Minister Çağlayan said: "Prophet Muhammad told [us] to eat together. There is no doubt that the meal of one person is enough for two. The meal of two will be enough for five-six. There is no doubt plenty/bounty *(bereket)* comes with the community. If we come together, our trade will increase and will be plentiful." Çağlayan continued by arguing how important such cooperation becomes at a time when European and Western economies in general are in crisis. Proposing ways of how to increase the trade volume, Çağlayan calls for the lifting of visa requirements with the countries of the region and the approval of the Free Trade Agreement (FTA).[33] Minister of Customs and Trade Hayati Yazici also emphasized the need to increase "the mobility of goods, individuals and capital with the region."[34]

While the Turkish side has been emphasizing the need to lift the visa requirements and the signing and approval of the FTA, the GCC countries in general complained about the high customs taxes (around five per cent) on the Turkish side. For example, the General Secretary of Qatar's Industrialists and Trade Chambers Muhammed bin Ahmed el Obaidli was complaining about these high customs taxes,[35] as was the President of the Board of directors of Saudi Arabia's Alrabiah Consulting firm, Abdurrahman Alrabiah. Alrabiah emphasized the need to sign the FTA between the two parties.[36] He said that Saudi businessmen wanted this for their benefit. Obaidli stated that the sectors which would be prominent for collaboration were construction, petrochemicals, energy, tourism and agriculture. He stressed that in Qatar alone, Turkish construction firms' investment has reached 11.5 billion dollars. Obaidli argues that what they want is a long-term relationship with these companies. He said, "We do not want companies that will come to Qatar and go back to Turkey once the project finishes. This is good neither for us nor for them. What we need is a long term unity... It is not enough to talk anymore, we need action."[37] The president of the Board of the International Emirates Business Group in the UAE, Badriya el Mulla, stressed the need to increase cooperation and be very effective and swift in doing. El Mulla said that Gulf countries had mainly traded with the EU before, "but now Turkey's worth is understood by everyone. ... The market here is developing. Besides, there are a lot of commonalities regarding the values, understanding and warm feelings of our people".[38] El Mulla argued that Turkey should be a model not only for the UAE but for the whole Arab region in general.

Mehmet Karagözlü, the head of the Trade and Industrialists Board in Tarsus in Mersin, said in a meeting in April 2012 (where he discussed the results of the 1st Business meeting), that the places of production and sources of wealth were changing their traditional places in the world. The world's production was shifting to Turkey's east while the consumption was in the West. In this new shift, Turkey and the Gulf region presented many opportunities according to Karagözlü.[39] The Head of the Turkish Chambers of Commerce, Rifat Hisarcıklıoğlu was reported to have said in this meeting, "There is no one country that has become rich because of natural resources. For a population to become rich, production, investment and trade is necessary. Because of this the young and the female entrepreneurs must be encouraged to be investors."[40]

Karagözlü went on to argue that the US makes 30 per cent of its trade with its neighbors Mexico and Canada; while Turkey's trade with the GCC region is only 3 per cent of its overall trade. Considering the whole Middle East, the number increases to 10 per cent. Karagözlü argued that the impediments to further trade were the visa requirements and high customs barriers. Hisarcıklıoğlu argued that in five years, Turkey will need energy investments of 100 million dollars and any investor in this sector will be profiting. However only one in thousand investments in the Gulf region has been coming to Turkey and in this context the willingness on the Turkish side to increase the investments coming to Turkey from the Gulf is once more underlined. The amount of money invested out of the Gulf region is 2.5 billion dollars – Turkey receives 30 billion dollars – which is miniscule according to Turkish policy-makers and tradespeople in general. He stated that:

> Allah has given all kinds of treasures to the territories of this region – above and below its soils. Turkey is the ninth largest cultivable land in the world; it has very fertile lands. We have four seasons in our lands. There is no agricultural commodity that cannot be cultivated here. Turkey has a potential to feed the whole region. It has underground resources. The Gulf region is the richest in terms of energy resources. It has half of the world's oil reserves. Beyond everything else, we have immense human resources. The only missing thing is the limited cooperation between us. We are saying we are the wealthiest of the Islamic world. Despite our vast foreign trade, 1.3 trillion dollars in total, Turkey and GCC trade is only 12 billion dollars – only one per cent of the total. We will increase this.[41]

The signing of the FTA will no doubt contribute to the increase of these figures, yet there still seem to be barriers, especially on the GCC side, to sign the agreement.

5. Conclusion

Turkey's economic relations with the Gulf countries have come a long way especially since 2007. As argued, this is mainly related to the economic developments in Turkey as well as AKP's political vision. The Gulf region is seen as an attractive venue for Turkish trade and investments and there is great willingness on the Turkish side to attract oil-rich Gulf economies especially at a time when the European markets are going through a deep economic crisis. However, there is still an important potential which has not been fulfilled. Considering that politics drives economics in the region in general and in Turkish-GCC relations, it is normal to expect a further increase in the relations in the following years.

Looking at the political developments, cooperation regarding the region is deepening. The uprising in Syria has brought Turkey closer to Saudi Arabia and Qatar and positive economic results could be expected. However, much needs to be done still. The signing of the FTA seems to hold the key for furthering economic cooperation. On the Turkish side, the importance of new regulations regarding Islamic bonds (*sukuk*) will definitely increase the attractiveness of the country for Gulf money.

Endnotes

1 Özlem Tür, "Economic Relations with the Middle East under the AKP – Trade, Business Community and the Reintegration with Neighbouring Zones", Turkish Studies, Vol. 12, No.4, December 2011, pp. 589-602.

2 Ibid.

3 Kemal Kirişçi, "The Transformation of Turkish Foreign Policy: The Rise of the Trading State", *New Perspectives on Turkey*, No. 40, (2009), pp. 29-56.

4 Meliha Altunışık and Özlem Tür, *Turkey – Challenges of Continuity and Change*, (London: Routledge, 2005), pp. 85-86.

5 Mustafa Kutlay, "Economy as the 'Practical Hand' of 'New Turkish Foreign Policy': a Political Economy Explanation", *Insight Turkey*, Vo. 13, No.1, (2011), p. 71.

6 Kutlay, (2011), p. 77.

7 Ahmet Davutoğlu, *Stratejik Derinlik*, (İstanbul: Küre, 2001), p. 414.

8 See Ahmet Han's interview with Ahmet Davutoğlu, "İş Dünyası Artık Dış Politikanın Öncülerinden", *Turkishtime*, (April-May 2004).

9 Kemal Kirişçi, Turkey's "Demonstrative Effect" and the Transformation of the Middle East", *Insight Turkey*, Vol. 13, No. 2, 2011, p. 37.

10 See TUSKON's website, www.tuskon.org.tr.

11 Altay Atlı, "Businessmen as Diplomats: The Role of Business Associations in Turkey's Foreign Economic Policy", *Insight Turkey*, Vol. 13, No. 1, (2011), p. 124.

12 Ibid.

13 See *Türkiye İstatistik Kurumu Haber Bülteni*, No. 7, (11 January 2011).

14 Economist, 2010, 228.

15 International Crisis Group, p. 9.

16 See TUIK, www.tuik.gov.tr

17 Ahmet Davutoğlu, Insight Turkey.

18 Stephen Larrabee, "Turkey and the Gulf Cooperation Council, Turkish Studies, Vol. 12, No. 4, p. 692.

19 "WSJ: Körfez Ülkeleri Türkiye'ye Yoğun Yatırım Yapıyor", Milliyet, 4 June 2012.

20 Mehmet Babacan argues that "it is quite evident that a slow but a gradual 'axis shift' towards the East is in place on a global scale". Mehmet Babacan, "Whither an Axis Shift: A Perspective from Turkey's Foreign Trade", *Insight Turkey*, vol. 13, No. 1, 2011, p. 135.

21 "Türk Dizileri Ortadoğu'da Ticareti Patlattı", *Doğan Haber Ajansı*, 11 December 2011. http://www.dha.com.tr/haberdetay.asp?tarih=14.05.2011&NEWSid=128666&Categoryid=5

22 "Körfez Ülkelerinden Türkiye'ye ilgi Artıyor", HaberTürk, 22 July 2012.

23 *Yeni Şafak*, 16 January 2011.

24 "Başkandan - Ortadoğu Pazarı Önemini Koruyor", Timreport, 2011 – 74, p. 4.

25 "WSJ: Körfez ÜlkeleriTürkiye'ye Yoğun Yatırım Yapıyor", Milliyet, 4 June 2012.

26 Ekonomik Ayrıntı, (5 May 2011), http://www.ekoayrinti.com/news_detail.php?id=62364).

27 Larrabee, "Turkey and the Gulf Cooperation Council", p. 692.

28 Hürriyet Ekonomi, "Körfez'den Türkiye'ye Para Yağacak", 6 February 2012.

29 İbid.

30 Songül Hatısaru, "Avrupa Kurudu, Sukuk Çıkarsa Körfez Parası Türkiye'ye akar", Milliyet, 28 May 2012.

31 "İlk Sukuk'lar bu yıl Çıkıyor", Vatan Ekonomi, 31 January 2012.

32 Ahmet K. Han, "Turkey's Energy Strategy and the Middle East: Between a Rock and a Hard Place", Turkish Studies, Vol. 12, No. 4, 2011, p. 610.

33 "Bakan Çağlayan'dan Körfez Ülkelerine: Vizeleri Kaldıralım", http://www.haberler.com/bakan-caglayan-dan-korfez-ulkelerine-vizeleri-3337004-haberi/.

34 See the full speech delivered by Minister Yazıcı. "Bakan Yazıcı: Türkiye ile Körfez İşbirliği Konseyi arasında Serbest Ticaret Anlaşması En Kısa Sürede İmzalanacaktır", 6 February 2012 at http://www.hayatiyazici.com.tr/haberler/bakan-yazici-turkiye-ile-korfez-is-birligi-konseyi-arasinda-serbest-ticaret-anlasmasi-en-kisa-surede-imzalacaktir/.

35 "Türkiye ile Körfez Ülkeleri Arasındaki Ticari İlişkiler Gelişiyor", Ses Türkiye, 10 February 2012. http://turkey.setimes.com/tr/articles/ses/articles/features/departments/economy/2012/02/10/feature-01.

36 Ibid.

37 Ibid.

38 Ibid.

39 "Türkiye körfez işbirliği konseyi 1. iş forumu'nun ardından", http://mersin.haber.pro/haber-Turkiye-korfez-isbirligi-konseyi-i-is-forumunun-ardindan-37517.html.

40 Ibid.

41 Ibid.

Bibliography

Altunışık, Meliha and Özlem Tür, *Turkey – Challenges of Continuity and Change*, (London: Routledge, 2005).

Atlı, Altay, "Businessmen as Diplomats: The Role of Business Associations in Turkey's Foreign Economic Policy", *Insight Turkey*, Vol. 13, No. 1, 2011.

Babacan, Mehmet, "Whither an Axis Shift: A Perspective from Turkey's Foreign Trade", *Insight Turkey*, Vol. 13, No. 1, 2011.

"Bakan Çağlayan'dan Körfez Ülkelerine: Vizeleri Kaldıralım", http://www.haberler.com/bakan-caglayan-dan-korfez-ulkelerine-vizeleri-3337004-haberi/

Bakan Yazıcı: Türkiye ile Körfez İşbirliği Konseyi arasında Serbest Ticaret Anlaşması En Kısa Sürede İmzalanacaktır", 6 February 2012 at http://www.hayatiyazici.com.tr/haberler/bakan-yazici-turkiye-ile-korfez-is-birligi-konseyi-arasinda-serbest-ticaret-anlasmasi-en-kisa-surede-imzalacaktir/

"Başkandan - Ortadoğu Pazarı Önemini Koruyor", *Timreport*, 2011 – 74.

Davutoğlu, Ahmet, *Stratejik Derinlik* (İstanbul: Küre, 2001).

Han, Ahmet K., "Turkey's Energy Strategy and the Middle East: Between a Rock and a Hard Place", *Turkish Studies*, Vol. 12, No. 4, 2011, pp. 603-617

Hatısaru, Songül, "Avrupa Kurudu, Sukuk Çıkarsa Körfez Parası Türkiye'ye akar", *Milliyet*, 28 May 2012.

"İlk Sukuk'lar bu yıl Çıkıyor", *Vatan Ekonomi*, 31 January 2012.

Kemal Kirişçi, The Trasformation of Turkish Foreign Policy: The Rise of the Trading State", *New Perspectives on Turkey*, No. 40, (2009), pp. 29-56.

_____, "Turkey's "Demonstrative Effect" and the Transformation of the Middle East", *Insight Turkey*, Vol. 13, No. 2, 2011.

"Körfez'den Türkiye'ye Para Yağacak", *Hürriyet Ekonomi*, 6 February 2012.

"Körfez Ülkelerinden Türkiye'ye ilgi Artıyor", *HaberTürk*, 22 July 2012.

Kutlay, Mustafa, "Economy as the 'Practical Hand' of 'New Turkish Foreign Policy': a Political Economy Explanation", *Insight Turkey*, Vol. 13, No.1, (2011).

Larrabee, Stephen, "Turkey and the Gulf Cooperation Council, *Turkish Studies*, Vol. 12, No. 4, 2011, pp.689-698.

Tür, Özlem, "Economic Relations with the Middle East Under the AKP – Trade, Business Community and the Reintegration with Neighbouring Zones", *Turkish Studies*, Vol. 12, No.4, December 2011, pp. 589-602.

"Türk Dizileri Ortadoğu'da Ticareti Patlattı", *Doğan Haber Ajansı*, 11 December 2011. http://www. dha.com.tr/haberdetay.asp?tarih=14.05.2011&NEWSid=128666&Categoryid=5

"Türkiye körfez işbirliği konseyi 1. iş forumu'nun ardından", http://mersin.haber.pro/haber-Turkiye-korfez-isbirligi-konseyi-i-is-forumunun-ardindan-37517.html

"WSJ: Körfez Ülkeleri Türkiye'ye Yoğun Yatırım Yapıyor", *Milliyet*, 4 June 2012.

Chapter Five

Russia and the Gulf: the Main Principles of the Political and Economic Dialogue

Nikolay Kozhanov

1. Introduction

The twists in Russian relations with the countries of the Gulf often confuse those Western and Russian experts who try to understand the place of the Gulf region in global Russian foreign policy. The task of these researchers would be easier if they could identify a comprehensive Russian strategy on Iran, Iraq and the members of the Gulf Cooperation Council (GCC), as well as a clear vision of who is responsible for its formulation. It is, however, almost impossible to find any signs of such a general strategy or to identify a decision-making centre involved in its formulation and implementation.

Currently, there are a number of different Russian institutions which deal with the Gulf region. Their range is wide and their interests and activities are diverse. Among these are the Presidential Administration, the Ministry of Foreign Affairs, the Ministry of Trade and Economic Development, the Russian Chamber of Commerce and Industry, NGOs as well as governmental, semi-governmental and private commercial companies. It is also obvious that a certain role is played by military structures and special services. At the same time, almost all of these (apart, probably, from the Administration of the Russian president), deal with a certain set of issues, and their area of responsibility is limited. As a result, whenever troubles occur, these structures justify their mistakes or passivity by saying that they "are simple executors of the government will."[1] However, they always have difficulties explaining who exactly or what exact body in the Russian government was the source of this will. Some of these simply refer to the Administration of the President whereas more informed people name the aide to the President of the Russian Federation, Sergei Prikhodko.[2]

2. Russian Global Foreign Policy and the Region of the Gulf

According to the Constitution of the Russian Federation, the President defines the main guidelines of Russian foreign policy, and the government is responsible for the implementation of his decisions. It is, however, hard to find a document clearly stating the Russian strategy towards the region of the Gulf written either by the Presidential Administration or the government. This, in turn, poses a question about the very existence of such a doctrine, especially one which could be used by Russian private companies and public structures as a beacon in their activities in the Gulf.

All in all, the vectors of Russian foreign policy are generally defined by a number of official documents usually named Concepts, Doctrines or Strategies. Among these, only the following three to a certain extent deal with the Gulf: *The Foreign Policy Concept of the Russian Federation* (adopted 12 July 2008); Annex I to the Russian Foreign Policy Concept, *The Main Directions of Russian Federation Policy in the Field of International Cultural and Humanitarian Cooperation* (adopted 18 December 2010); and *The Russian Federation Concept of International Scientific and Technological Cooperation* (adopted 20 January 2000). However, none of the three give a clear understanding of Russian intentions towards the Gulf.

2.1 The Foreign Policy Concept of the Russian Federation and the Gulf

The Foreign Policy Concept of the Russian Federation document does not mention the GCC among the vectors of Russian diplomacy. It only states Moscow's intention "to further develop its relations with Turkey, Egypt, Algeria, Iran, Saudi Arabia, Syria, Libya, Pakistan and other leading regional states in bilateral and multilateral formats."[3] However, this passage leaves more questions than gives answers. For instance, it is unclear why Iran and Saudi Arabia were included in a list with the other countries: each of them has a different importance for Russian foreign policy and requires specific approaches. Even the geographical principle is inapplicable here: according to Russian geographical traditions, the states mentioned above are related to, at least, five geographical regions. In each region Russia pursues a different set of goals. It is also unclear in what way and with what purpose Russia is going "to further develop its relations" with Iran and Saudi Arabia.

Iran is again mentioned in the *Foreign Policy Concept* in relation to the non-proliferation problem existing in the Middle East. The document states that:

> Russia will fully contribute to finding political and diplomatic ways of solving the situation regarding the nuclear programme of the Islamic Republic of Iran based on the recognition of the right of all States Parties to the Nuclear Non-Proliferation Treaty (NPT) to the peaceful use of nuclear energy as well as upon strict compliance with the requirements of nuclear non-proliferation regime.[4]

Again, it is hard to find sense in this statement. There is no actual explanation as to which parameters Moscow is going to use to judge that the nuclear problem is settled. For instance, it is not only by creating a nuclear weapon that Iran may endanger the NPT regime. As stated by some experts, Iran may, in order to ensure its national security, limit itself to developing the capacity to create a bomb in a six-month period, if necessary.[5] Technically, this will not be a violation of the NPT, but the consequences for the non-proliferation regime in the Middle East could be disastrous: it could provoke other countries to start or, in some cases, to resume their own nuclear programmes.[6]

Little is also said about Russian goals in Iraq. The official document only states that:

> ..the Russian Federation is in favour of increasing collective efforts, on the basis of mutual respect, to contribute to ending violence and to reach a political settlement in Iraq through national reconciliation and full restoration of the country's statehood and economy.[7]

2.2. *The Russian Federation Concept of International Scientific and Technological Cooperation and the Gulf*

The Russian Concept of International Scientific and Technological Cooperation declares "the commercialization of Russian technologies abroad" as one of the main tasks of the Russian government.[8] The document stresses that cooperation with solvent developing countries could be very promising in terms of the achievement of this purpose. As stated by the authors of the Concept, these states may serve as a testing area for the approbation of different forms of international scientific and technological cooperation with the participation of Russian companies. The latter are expected to offer high technologies and necessary knowledge to developing countries, whereas developing states are supposed to provide them with necessary investments and infrastructure. The Russian government, for its part, makes a commitment to stimulate the interest of Russian companies to export high technologies and engineering services to developing countries, including Iran.[9]

It is necessary to note that Iran is the only Gulf country mentioned in the document. However, even the IRI was not distinguished in the separate direction of the Russian foreign policy in this field. On the contrary, Iran is usually mentioned among the other developing countries such as Brazil, Egypt, India, Mexico and South Africa.[10] This, in turn, shows that the importance of the IRI even within this aspect of the Russian foreign policy is relative: Iran is one of the possible, but not the only potential partner of the Russian government in its attempt to stimulate the exports of Russian high technologies abroad.

It is also notable that Iran as well as other developing countries are considered to be "testing areas" for the prospective schemes of international cooperation with the participation of Russian companies (mostly, in the form of venture projects and joint ventures). It is reasonable to suppose that in the case of success, these schemes are expected to be implemented mainly in other (possibly, more developed) states. As a result, Iran and other developing countries named as prospective partners for Russian companies should not be considered as the main direction for Russian exports of high technologies. It is also arguable to what extent the export of high technologies is important for the current government of Russia. The five-year period stated as the time framework for the implementation of the majority of tasks stipulated in the document expired in 2005. Nevertheless, no updates have since been made in this obviously outdated Concept.[11]

2.3. Annex 1 to the Russian Foreign Policy Concept and the Gulf

The Russian authorities have recently intensified their activities in another sphere of international relations. This, in turn, has inevitably had an impact upon the Middle Eastern direction of Moscow's foreign policy. In 2010, the Russian government adopted Annex I to the Russian Foreign Policy Concept determining the main vectors of Russian diplomacy in the field of cultural and humanitarian cooperation. This document states the necessity to strengthen cooperation with the Middle East and to increase the Russian cultural presence in this region.[12] Iran, Iraq and the UAE are named among the Middle Eastern and Asian countries with which cultural and humanitarian contacts should be intensified in the first round.[13] However, it is highly possible that the overall importance of these countries for Moscow were not the first choice in the selection process. It is more likely that the Russian authorities saw the above-mentioned states as the easiest targets for Russian cultural penetration.

It is necessary to remember that "soft power" as effective diplomatic leverage has been neglected by the Russian authorities for the last two decades. Consequently, by 2010, Moscow's previously strong influence in humanitarian and cultural spheres as well as in the international media had been seriously weakened (if not shattered).[14] Under these circumstances, Moscow probably considered that it would be easier to begin the restoration of its positions in those countries which either have a tangible Russian speaking community or experienced serious Russian cultural presence during the Soviet era. These factors were obviously supposed to assist the spread of Moscow's soft influence. As a result, Iran, Iraq and the UAE were chosen as priority targets for Russian cultural diplomacy in the Middle East. However, these calculations of Moscow did not take into account the political and economic importance of the Gulf region for Russia.

2.4. Russian Foreign Policy in the Absence of Clearly-Stated Top Priorities in the Region

All in all, existing concepts, doctrines and strategies outlining the main principles of Russian foreign policy are unable to give a picture of Russian strategy and top priorities in the Gulf. The absence of any clear guidance for Russian working-level officials about Moscow's strategy vis-à-vis the Gulf suggest that Russia simply does not have any lucid and applicable foreign policy strategy towards the countries of this region. If asked, Russian politicians are unanimous that close engagement with the Gulf countries is necessary, but none of these are able to answer what the strategic purposes of this engagement are. In general, this situation is unprecedented in the history of Russian foreign policy of the Middle East. Both the Russian Empire and the USSR always possessed a clear vision of their tasks in the region whereby the establishment of an influential Russian presence in the Gulf was always considered as their top priority.

In the absence of well-articulated top priorities, there is no main decision-making centre on the Gulf in Russia which would be responsible for the formulation and implementation of the government's strategy towards the region, its correction according to emerging challenges and coordination between the Russian government and non-governmental structures dealing with Iran, Iraq and the GCC. On the one hand, the lack of such a centre leads to a situation where Russia has different organisations acting discordantly in the Gulf on different levels, with sometimes mutually exclusive goals. Moreover, in some cases, there is even no clear understanding of the hierarchy between them. This, subsequently, brings additional disorder in Russo-Gulf relations.

On the other hand, the lack of a general strategy as well as a centre supervising its implementation is compensated for by the existence of a number of smaller decision-making centres, which emerged in almost every organisation or structure dealing with the Gulf. Steps made by these centres eventually form what is called the Russian foreign policy in Iran. However, decisions made by these bodies are tactical, not strategic: they are mostly made on the basis of situational judgements and according to current requirements. It is also notable that the method of making decisions on the Gulf solely from a short-range perspective is typical for decision-making centres in Russia, irrespective of their level and status. As a result, Russian foreign policy towards the region is not only inconsistent and contradictory but also extremely practical and opportunistic. In other words, almost all decisions are made on the basis of a cost-benefit approach. Moscow will never take a decision which is currently politically and economically unprofitable, even if this decision can bring tangible benefits from a long-distance perspective.[15]

However, it is wrong to think that the development of Russian relations with the Gulf is completely unpredictable and that they do not comply with certain rules: Russia lacks a unified plan of action and a clear perception of the top priorities of Russian foreign policy towards the countries of the region, but the Russian Federation has certain national interests and its foreign policy is based on these. The most important national interests shaping Russian foreign policy towards the Gulf are: evading tensions with the US which could seriously spoil a Russo-American dialogue; ensuring national security; securing Russian dominance in the ex-Soviet territories (such as Central Asia, the Caucasus and Caspian region); preventing nuclear proliferation and protecting the economic interests of the Russian political elite.

3. Russia's Political Dialogue with the Countries of the Gulf

Russia does not have one universal approach towards the Gulf region. Moscow clearly distinguishes the following three independent targets for its diplomacy in the region: Iran, the GCC, and Iraq.

3.1. Iran

Russian approaches towards the IRI are relatively well-articulated in comparison with approaches to other Gulf states. The absence of a unified strategy determining Russian activities in the region has led to the emergence of the phenomenon of Russia dealing with the IRI on a case-by-case basis. In other words, the current dialogue between Tehran and Moscow is nothing but a result of the intersection of Russian and Iranian interest in different issues. Given the geographical proximity of Iran and Russia, Moscow has considerably more issues to discuss with the IRI than with the GCC members. However, the attitude of the Russian government towards Tehran depends on the importance of each particular case for Russia and the Russian approach in handling it. For instance, when discussing the issue of the presence of third countries in the Central Asian or Caspian regions, Moscow can position itself as a close and reliable partner for Tehran. At the same time, both countries see each other as potential rivals in the European gas market. The importance of each case also determines the persistence of the Russian government in securing its interests as well as Russian flexibility. Thus, the Russian position on the legal status of the Caspian Sea is well articulated and difficult to change, whereas either in the economic sphere or in cultural relations Moscow is less active and its goals are not clearly determined.

Under these circumstances, the only possible task which both countries can declare as the main priority of their relations is the general intention to continue all-embracing dialogue without stating specific tasks. It is notable that according to the Treaty on the Basic Principles of Cooperation between the Russian Federation and the Islamic Republic of Iran (signed in 2001 by the former presidents of these countries, Vladimir Putin and Mohammad Khatami), the dialogue between Moscow and Tehran is described as neither strategic, nor partnership, but "corresponding to the basic interests of both states."[16] Such a formulation is not widely spread in international documents. This, in turn, symbolizes the specific nature of the Russian perception of Iran and relations with this country. On the one hand, taking into account the importance of the IRI as a neighbouring state, it is essential for Moscow to underline the special character of the bilateral relations. On the other hand, the Russian authorities do not seem interested in raising Russo-Iranian relations to the level of partner status. First of all, the level of dialogue between the two countries (either by economic, political or any other parameters) does not correspond to this status.[17] Apart from that, Moscow considers Iran more as a tool of its foreign diplomacy than as a partner. Thus, Iran plays the role of a lever used by the Russian Federation (RF) in its political dialogue with Washington. It is notable that the Russian authorities played this card during both the periods of Russo-American rapprochement and during the times of intense tensions between the two countries by either freezing their cooperation with Tehran or boosting it. For instance, experts argue that, in 2010, the "reload" in the Russo-American dialogue initiated by the administration of Barack Obama partly guaranteed Moscow's refusal to export S-300 surface-to-air missile systems to the IRI and the imposition of unilateral sanctions against the IRI by Dmitry Medvedev. However, in 2011, the situation changed. The US persistence in unfolding the anti-missile umbrella compelled Russia to look for asymmetric answers. Among other measures, this implied the new revival of friendship with Tehran and the supplies of equipment for electronic warfare to the IRI.[18]

Russo-Iranian relations are influenced not only by the development of the Russian contacts with Washington, but by Iranian attempts to open contacts with the US. Under these circumstances, both the Russian authorities and analysts have a clear idea that a rapprochement between the IRI and the United States would constitute a serious threat to the presence of the RF in Iran. As a result, any signs of US-Iranian reconciliation cause an immediate intensification of the dialogue between Russia and Iran. For instance, active official and semi-official contacts between Washington and Tehran during the period 1998 – 2000 led to the signing of the Treaty on the Basic Principles of Cooperation between the Russian Federation and the Islamic Republic of Iran in 2001.[19]

The Russian authorities also believe that the establishment of a dialogue between Washington and Tehran will inevitably lead to the formation of another generally anti-Russian coalition with substantial capabilities to influence the situation in Central Asia and the Caucasus. The latter is not an acceptable option to Moscow: traditionally neighbouring countries seriously influence political, emigrational, drug and criminal situations in the RF itself. In order to ensure its national security, Russia is compelled to attentively control the development of the situation in bordering regions and, if necessary, to get involved in it. Since the fall of the USSR, Moscow has been trying to play the role of a leading power in the ex-Soviet territories. It was and still is extremely jealous of any attempts by third powers to penetrate these regions. Iran's geo-strategic position allows it to influence the development of the situation in the Caspian, Caucasian, Central Asian, Middle Eastern and Gulf regions. This inevitably prompts Moscow into discussions with Tehran about a large range of foreign policy issues.

In general, Russian policy aimed at ensuring national security in the bordering regions is based on the following four principles: prevention of possible conflicts in bordering regions and the settlement of currently existing tensions; prevention of bordering states from acquiring nuclear weapons or any other type of weapons of mass destruction (WMD); counterbalancing the growing presence of the non-regional forces and military blocks in bordering countries; and strengthening cooperation with bordering countries in the counteraction of terrorist threats and drug-trafficking.

These principles have dual implications for the IRI. On the one hand, due to similarities in approaches towards a number of regional issues, Moscow considers Tehran as an important partner in the Caucasus, Central Asia and the Caspian region. For instance, the Russian political elite remembers that, as opposed to Turkey, the IRI did not use the fall of the Soviet Union for the aggressive spread of its influence in the Caucasus and Central Asia by propagating the ideas of the Islamic revolution or by funding local nationalistic and religious movements. On the other hand, the Russian authorities do not completely trust Iran: Moscow is still cautious about some of its regional activities and concerned that the IRI may be a possible starting point for another conflict. As a result, the Russian government opposes the acquisition of WMD by Tehran. It believes that Iran's acquisition of WMD would drastically change the balance of power in the region in a manner not favourable to Moscow: a nuclear-armed Islamic regime on the Southern flank of Russia could be far less cooperative in Central Asia and the Caspian basin and could undermine Moscow's influence in these ex-Soviet regions. Furthermore, a nuclear-armed Iran could destabilize the situation in the Middle East.[20]

At the same time, Russian politicians and experts argue that the simmering dispute between the IRI and the West over the Iranian nuclear programme has not only negative, but also positive implications for the RF. On the one hand, it limits the Western economic presence in the IRI and, thus, creates additional opportunities for Russian companies to penetrate the Iranian economy. On the other hand, the unsettled nuclear issue is considered to be an ironclad guarantee against US-Iranian rapprochement. As a result, some Russian analysts even state the necessity to freeze the situation and, thus, sustain the simmering dispute between the US and the IRI for as long as possible.[21]

As a result, the Russian position on the nuclear issue could not be called either pro-Iranian or pro-Western (namely, pro-American). Moscow balances between the US, Europe and Israel, on the one side, and the IRI, on the other, without any attempts to join either of them. Russia insists that the nuclear issue be settled diplomatically, because it wants to prevent the emergence of a new zone of conflict and instability near the Russian borders. In addition to that, currently, the Russian government and experts do not have ironclad proof that the authorities of the IRI made a decision to create nuclear WMD.[22] Moreover, they believe that, from a mid-range perspective, Tehran is incapable of achieving this status, and all statements by Iranian officials are considered nothing but bravado to bargain for better conditions in its dispute with the West. Under these circumstances, the authorities of the RF only occasionally demonstrate their dissatisfaction with continuing nuclear research in Iran (and only when Tehran demonstrates excessive stubbornness). The extreme pressure on Iran is considered harmful to other aspects of the Russo-Iranian dialogue where Moscow badly needs Tehran's support, or at least its neutrality.

3.2. GCC States

Russian foreign policy approaches towards the GCC substantially differ from those towards Iran. First of all, direct diplomatic relations with these countries have been established relatively recently: in most countries, Russian (or USSR) embassies were opened during the last decade of the Soviet era or immediately after the fall of the USSR. Thus, the Russian diplomatic mission in Saudi Arabia was opened in 1991, in Oman in 1987, in the UAE in 1986, in Bahrain in 1993, and in Qatar in 1989 (the only exception is Kuwait: its diplomatic relations with the USSR were established in 1963). Moreover, until the 2000s, the level of cooperation between Moscow and the GCC remained extremely low. This could be explained by domestic political and economic turmoil in the RF during the 1990s and by the Western orientation of Russian diplomacy under President Boris Yeltsin (1991–1999). However, this time was not completely wasted: during these years, the Russian government and its Gulf partners signed a number of official agreements and memorandums of understanding which formed the judicial base for economic cooperation and political dialogue between them. The latter helped to boost bilateral relations after the election of Vladimir Putin as Russian president in 2000.

The Arab countries of the Gulf were literally opened for Russia by Yeltsin's successor Putin, who tried to implement the Russian doctrine of a multipolar world by establishing close and friendly ties with non-European and non-Western countries. Thus, in 2003, during his visit to Malaysia, Putin stated that Russia was going to closely cooperate with the Islamic world. Later, he declared the Arab countries one of the main vectors of Russian diplomacy. In 2007, Putin supported this statement by official visits to Saudi Arabia, Qatar and the UAE. These trips were not the mere demonstration of the Russian interest in dialogue with the countries of the Gulf. On the contrary, Moscow made an attempt to become deeply involved in the situation in the region. Thus, in 2007, the Russian government increased its focus on the region with a document entitled *The Concept for Ensuring Security in the Region of the Persian Gulf.* The main principles proposed in the document implied the settlement of conflict situations solely by diplomatic means; the conduct of peacekeeping military operations only in accordance with UN resolutions; the participation of all sides involved in emerging issues in a decision-making process, and the implementation of agreements achieved by the regional countries in strict compliance with international documents regulating relations in the region of the Gulf.[23]

The settlement of the issue of the Iranian nuclear programme and the stabilisation of the situation in Iraq were named as the first stage of the practical implementation of the Russian initiative. These steps were aimed at the creation of mutual trust between the countries of the region. It was also supposed that the Gulf states would confirm their loyalty to their international legal obligations by being transparent in the development of their military capacities, banning the use of force for the settlement of conflicts, adopting multilateral treaties on arms control, paying attention to the observation of the non-proliferation regime, creating a WMD-free zone in the Middle East, and signing agreements on counteracting terrorism, criminal activities, drug, human and arms trafficking. The second stage implied the creation of an organisation for security and cooperation in the Gulf which would become an element of a new multilateral security system in the Middle East.[24]

This idealistic and probably naïve initiative aroused some interest among the smaller GCC members, but mostly as an eloquent theoretical speculation. Its practical implementation was obviously hampered by mounting Arab concerns over the Iranian nuclear programme, the continuing instability in Iraq and US hegemony in the Gulf. However, this concept has achieved one of its main goals: it has demonstrated the Russian intention to come to the region and to try to stay there for the long term.[25] Putin's trips to the Gulf also served as a signal for Russian officials and the private sector that the members of the GCC were worth dealing with: since 2007, both economic and political Russian relations with the members of the GCC have substantially intensified.

However, Moscow failed to keep up with the initial high tempo. The personal influence of Russian leaders on the foreign policy of the country appeared to be a crucial factor for the dialogue between the RF and the Gulf countries.

Putin's decision to establish close relations with Arab countries and to declare this vector of Russian diplomacy as important, remained spoken only and was not added as an amendment to any of the official concepts to determine the general long-term strategy of the foreign policy of the RF. Subsequently, when, in 2008, Dmitry Medvedev, who is famous for his pro-Western orientation, took the presidential office, he probably considered the development of a dialogue with Arab countries as Putin's personal idea and never supported it. As a result, under Medvedev, Russian activities in the region were less intensive.

In addition to that, during the period 2009–2012, Russian relations with the Arab monarchies of the Gulf were challenged by a number of confusing political incidents. For example, in 2009, the ex-commander of the Russian Military Special Battalion "Vostok", Sulim Yamadayev, was killed in Dubai. Although, this murder was probably a result of a personal blood feud between Yamadayev and the clan of the current president of the Chechen Republic, Ramzan Kadyrov, it reminded the UAE authorities of the assassination of Chechen terrorist Zelimkhan Yandarbiyev in Doha in 2004. He was allegedly killed by a member of the Russian secret services. Under these circumstances, the probable political background of Yamadayev's killing caused serious concerns in the government of Dubai and the UAE. Another unfortunate incident took place in 2011 when the security forces of Doha airport attacked and seriously injured the Russian ambassador to Doha, Vladimir Titorenko, while he was accompanying diplomatic mail bags. This incident seriously aggravated Russian relations with Qatar: Moscow even threatened to downgrade relations.

Nevertheless, the push given by Putin to the Russian dialogue with the GCC in 2007 prevented Russian-Arab contacts from returning to the low level of the 1990s. Instead, the development of relations continued. Moreover, on 1 November 2011, the Russian minister of foreign affairs met with his counterparts from the Gulf Cooperation Council for the first time in a summit. This so-called GCC-Russia strategic dialogue meeting allowed Moscow to state and to discuss its strategic interests in the Gulf with the Arab monarchies, outlining the direction of future partnership. During this meeting, Moscow clearly demonstrated that Russian positions on the majority of regional and international issues are relatively close to those of the GCC members. Thus, Russia insists on the necessity to create an independent Palestinian state and strives to support peace and stability in the region. Russian authorities also emphasise that they stick to an "open doors" policy: the RF is ready to conduct a dialogue with any country of the region as long as this dialogue corresponds to Russian national interests.[26]

However, the practical outcomes of the 2011 meeting appeared to be less impressive than initially expected. No tangible agreements were achieved. Moreover, in 2012, differences in Russian and GCC views on the current political situation in the Middle East caused certain tensions between Moscow and the Gulf Arabs (at first, between Russia and Qatar). This, in turn, put the continuation of the Russia-GCC strategic dialogue under question. Yet this does not mean its end. Being seriously disappointed by the decision of some Arab monarchies to finance the military activities of Syrian rebels, their unwillingness to continue the dialogue with Assad's regime in order to find a peaceful solution, the GCC's unofficial support of the foreign military intervention in Syria and the Arab persistence in evading a dialogue with Moscow on the issue, the Russian authorities have difficulty in finding a common language with the Gulf Cooperation Council members and preserving the current level of cooperation with them.

3.3. Iraq

Since Saddam Hussein's fall in 2003, there has not been much clarity concerning Russian goals in Iraq. Officially, Moscow supports the process of stabilisation and ethnic reconciliation in this war-torn country. Russian officials also make frequent statements on the necessity to boost the process of economic reconstruction in Iraq. At the same time, it is obvious that the authorities of the RF have a narrow set of options for influencing the situation inside the country. As a result, most of the actions taken by Russia are limited to support for UN Security Council measures and seldom involve bilateral contacts.[27]

Some experts argue that the peace process in Iraq is less important for Moscow than the issue of Iraqi refugees and the problem of ambitious contracts signed by Russian energy companies with Saddam Hussein which were frozen after 2003. Russia has achieved some success on the former by tightening border controls, but the second issue is still unresolved. It is also notable that Moscow indirectly supported Iraqi federalism in 2007 by establishing a Consulate General in Erbil, with the obvious purpose of building relations with the Kurdish Regional Government.

4. Russian Economic Relations with the Countries of the Gulf

The beginning of the gradual economic recovery of the Russian economy from 2000 on led to a rise in the general capacity of Russian producers to export their products abroad. As a result, since 2000, the volume of trade between Russia and the countries of the Gulf has been gradually increasing with a slight downfall in 2009 which could be explained by the general negative influence of the economic crisis of 2008–2009 (see Table 5.1). During the last decade, the structure of the trade between Russia and the Gulf countries has remained relatively the same. Russian exports have consisted of ferrous metals and metallurgical products, wood, pulp and paper, fuel and energy resources, machinery, food products, cereals and fertilizers. The Gulf countries, in turn, are mainly selling textiles, food and agricultural products, chemical products and automobiles.

At the same time, in spite of existing positive trends, bilateral economic relations between Russia and the Gulf countries remain underdeveloped. By 2011, even Iran who is Russia's main trade partner in the Gulf region, occupied only the 29th place among the trade partners of the RF. Its share in Russian external trade was constantly decreasing. By 2011, this figure accounted only for 0.6% (according to other sources, 0.4%). In 2010, the IRI was only the 26th importer of Russian products and the 61st exporter of goods to the Federation. The situation of Russian trade with the GCC members is even worse. In 2010, the volume of trade between Russia and the members of the GCC comprised less than 1.5 billion dollars versus 3.65 billion dollars of Russo-Iranian trade.[28] The Russian share in the volume of trade of Asian countries with the Gulf region is also minimal. The statistical data mentioned in Chapter One of this book shows that, in terms of trade with Iran, Iraq and GCC, Russia is not only far behind the leading Asian economies (such as China, South Korea and Japan), but is challenged by the economically less powerful Indonesia, Malaysia and Thailand.

The low level of economic relations with the Gulf could be partly explained by the fact that the Middle Eastern region is generally of little interest to the business circles of the RF. The latter mainly orientate themselves towards European and Far Eastern markets. Moreover, the Gulf countries are not seen by Moscow as a priority market for Russian goods, even within the Middle East. Thus, the IRI is occasionally challenged by Syria and Israel whose volume of trade with Russia, in 2008, peaked at 2 and 3 billion dollars respectively (versus 3.69 billion dollars of Russo-Iranian trade).[29] From a mid-range perspective, it is also doubtful that Iran and the GCC members will be capable of competing with another Middle Eastern country – Turkey. In 2010, the volume of trade between Ankara and Moscow achieved 25 billion dollars (according to the other sources, 26).[30]

Table 5.1: Volume of Russian Trade with the Countries of the Gulf, 2006 – 2011. $ million

Year Country	2006	2007	2008	2009	2010	2011
Iran	2144.5	3314.7	3690.3	3059.9	3651.1	3750.0
Iraq	113.5	51.8	102.4	n/a	n/a	n/a
Saudi Arabia	272.7	426.5	466.0	264.5 (Jan.– Sept.)	366.4	192.4 (Jan. – June)
Kuwait	n/a	n/a	n/a	n/a	80.0	n/a
Bahrain	10.8	15.0	3.6	1.9	2.4	n/a
UAE	648.4	821.3	846.4	670.6	950.0	n/a
Oman	n/a	n/a	n/a	24.2	13.2	n/a
Qatar	n/a	n/a	n/a	8.7	14.6	n/a

Source: Ministry of Economic Development of the Russian Federation (http://www.economy.gov.ru/ Last accessed on 2 February 2012); and Ministry of Foreign Affairs of the Russian Federation (http://www.mid.ru/ Last accessed on 29 March 2012).

The situation with investments is slightly different. The volume of accumulated Russian investments in the Iranian economy is insignificant (27.3 million dollars in 2010), whereas the volume of Russian investments in the economy of the GCC countries is substantial for Russia (about 4.5 billion dollars). Oil, gas, petrochemical and the high-technological (primarily, space and nuclear energy) sectors as well as the banking sphere are considered to be the most interesting for Russian investors.[31]

4.1. The Main Driver: Support by the Russian State

Links between government and business which exist in every country are especially evident in Russia. Existing close connections between the Putin administration and major Russian governmental and semi-governmental corporations make the lobbying of the economic interests of these companies one of the main goals of the foreign policy of the RF. The situation with Russian business in the Gulf could serve as an example: it is not a mere coincidence that the majority of the success stories of Russian business in Iran and the GCC are related to corporations affiliated with the government.

Russian governmental and semi-governmental companies actively penetrate the oil, gas and petrochemical sectors of the Gulf economy. Setting it apart from many other foreign investors, Russia is self-sufficient in energy resources. However, as will be shown below, Moscow has its own reasons to support the active penetration of its companies into the energy sector of the Gulf economies. Lukoil and Gazprom should probably be considered as the main driving force of the Russian penetration.[32] For instance, in 2008, head of Gazprom Alexey Miller visited Iran three times. According to agreements achieved during his visits, the Russian company was expected to participate in the organisation of swap deals with Turkmen, Russian and Iranian gas; in the development of the North and South Pars gas fields; in the construction and exploitation of the Neka-Jask pipeline in order to organise the transit of hydrocarbons from the Caspian region to the Oman Gulf (by 2011, the talks were halted);[33] in the creation of the LNG producing capacities in South Iran (with the possible participation of Qatar) and in the building of the Caspian oil refinery (project "Caspian") in the Golestan province of the IRI. In 2008, special working groups were created by Gazprom and the National Iranian Oil Company (NIOC) to control the implementation of these decisions.[34] In addition to the projects mentioned above, Gazprom and its Iranian counterparts are actively discussing the options for the implementation of regional projects and projects in the third countries (such as Qatar, Turkmenistan and Pakistan). For instance, Gazprom periodically discusses the possibilities of its participation in the construction of a gas pipeline between Iran, Pakistan and India.[35]

During the period 2008–2009, Gazprom was active in establishing contacts with Bahrain. Thus, this Russian company signed a memorandum of understanding with the National Oil and Gas Authority of Bahrain and studied options for participating in geological studies of the Awali field. The management of the Russian company is also discussing the possibilities for the implementation of joint projects in the field of LNG production and for the organisation of gas swap deals with Qatar. Apart from that, Gazprom and its Qatari partners have been studying options for cooperation on the regional level within the framework of existing and perspective hydrocarbon exploration and extraction projects in Russia (project Yamal LNG) and the Middle East.

In 2004, Lukoil Overseas also signed a contract with Saudi Arabia. According to the document, the company was granted a 40-year long concession on the exploration and development of the gas field in the Rub-al-Khali desert. For the implementation of this project, Lukoil Overseas and Saudi Aramco established the joint company Lukoil Saudi Arabia Energy Ltd. (LUKSAR). The share of the Russian company is 80%. In 2006, the exploration works of LUKSAR resulted in the discovery of a new hydrocarbon field with estimated resources of

85 million tonnes in equivalent fuel. Currently, LUKSAR is making an assessment of discovered reserves in order to begin the development of the field. By August 2011, accumulated investments of the Russian company had achieved 300 million dollars.[36]

The document *The Energy Strategy of Russia until 2030*, which was adopted in 2009, implies that Russian foreign policy in securing the safety and profitability of governmental and semi-governmental oil and gas corporations is supposed to be relatively aggressive and expansionist. The document states that Moscow's ultimate goal should be the preservation of the necessary level of supplies of energy resources to the European market and the manifold increase in exports to the East. These aims are expected to be achieved not only by raising the output of domestic gas and oil fields, but also through active intervention in the energy sectors of other countries (both hydrocarbon producers and consumers) and the establishment of Russian control over most of Eurasia's gas and oil transportation infrastructure. Russia's 2009 Energy Strategy had controversial outcomes for the Gulf.

On the one hand, being the keepers of large gas and oil reserves, Gulf countries are inevitably interested in the coordination of price and marketing policies on consumer markets. As a result, the Russian government can always count on Iran and some Gulf countries in negotiating common market policy on the international arena and within the framework of economic organisations (such as the Gas Exporting Countries Forum). On the other hand, Tehran's periodic attempts to join the Nabucco project as well as to position itself as an alternative to the Russian supply of gas to the European market (as is Qatar) has made Moscow consider Iran a potential rival.[37] However, this perception of the IRI and Qatar as possible opponents in the international gas market leads to closer Russian cooperation with them. Moscow tries to intensify its interaction with both countries in international projects and, thus, to re-direct the existing and potential export flows of Iranian and Qatari gas to non-European markets. For instance, as believed by some experts, the Russo-Iranian deal on the swap operations with natural gas and oil (as well as the discussion of swap deals with Qatar) serves this goal.[38]

Oil, gas and petrochemical companies are not the only Russian firms penetrating the Gulf. Nuclear and electric energy corporations, such as Rosatom State Corporation and its subsidiary company Atomstroyexport are able to compete with the oil and gas giants in receiving government assistance. The construction of the Bushehr nuclear plant in Iran is one of the most notorious illustrations of this. From the very beginning, this project has raised serious concerns in the West. As a result, the Russian contractor of the project, Atomstroyexport, its subcontractors and suppliers were and still are under pressure from the US and its Western partners. Under these circumstances, the Russian authorities were compelled to protect the interests of the corporation, whose profits, during the 1990s, were among the few stable sources of foreign exchange for Moscow. Indeed the government of the RF demonstrated its resolution and consistency in securing the Bushehr project from multilateral and unilateral sanctions as well as in helping Atomstroyexport to evade them. The Russian companies became so assured in the capabilities of Moscow to protect them from US pressure that, currently, they intend to bid for the construction of any other nuclear projects in Iran.[39] The Russian progress with the construction of the Bushehr nuclear station encouraged the Arabs to discuss joint projects in the nuclear sphere. For instance, in 2010, Rosatom and the UAE authorities were discussing options for cooperation.

Moscow also promotes the interests of the Russian space industry in the Gulf. Thus, the RF and the IRI are discussing possibilities to launch Iranian earth remote sensing satellites (project Sepehr) with Russian carrier rockets from Baykonur or Plesetsk, as well as options to provide Iran with high resolution photographs of its territory received from Russian satellites. Under these conditions, in February 2007, Russia successfully launched the first Emirates' satellite for the earth distance sensing Dubaisat-1 from Baykonur. Since 2000, the Russian federal space Roscosmos agency has launched 14 telecommunication and distance sensing satellites for Saudi Arabia. In 2008, Moscow and Riyadh started discussing further Russo-Saudi cooperation in the space field (including the usage of the Russian GLONASS satellite navigation system).

4.2. Obstacles

However, Russian economic relations with the Gulf face a number of serious problems. Economic sanctions imposed against Tehran by the international community are one of them. The Russian government is compelled to comply with the requirements of UN resolutions and to limit some exports to the IRI. For instance, since 2010, when Moscow decided to suspend its sales of the S-300 air defence systems to Iran, the amount of Russian weapon exports has been gradually decreasing.[40] Moreover, the Russian authorities applied additional measures of export control which make the sales of dual-use products to Iran harder.[41] The exterritorial nature of the US sanctions as well as the fact that these punitive measures were supported by a large number of countries (such as the UAE, Japan, Canada, Australia, the members of the EU and others), also have a negative influence on Russo-Iranian economic relations. As stated by Russian officials, after the imposition of sanctions in 2010, the volume of machinery exports from Russia to the IRI has drastically decreased. Russian exporters appear to be scared to deal with Iran in order not to be punished by the US authorities.[42] Apart from that, almost all joint projects with the participation of third countries were frozen. For instance, all talks on trilateral cooperation between Russia, Qatar and Iran in the gas field were suspended.

The close ties of the Russian economic elite with American, European and Israeli business circles as well as the financial and technological dependence of Russian companies on the West also do not allow Moscow to use all the opportunities provided by the sanctions adopted against the IRI. For example, during the period 2009–2011, a number of private and semi-governmental companies with strong economic interests in the US and EU (such as the oil and petrochemical corporation Lukoil) took a decision to leave Iran. Analysts argue that, since 2010, even oil and gas companies enjoying the support of the Russian government have been compelled to slow down the pace of their cooperation with the IRI by trying not to go beyond the level of general and technical discussion of possible projects. This could be the reason for the current suspension of the practical implementation of such joint projects as the construction of the Neka-Jask pipeline and the establishment of a joint Russo-Iranian hydrocarbon company.[43]

However, it is not only sanctions that prevent Russia from cooperating with Iran and the Gulf. It is also necessary to admit that the political and economic realities of modern Russia are unfavourable for the development of Russo-Gulf economic relations. Russian statism seriously restrains options for cooperation between the RF and the Gulf. In modern Russia, government support became one of the main (if not the only) factors boosting the penetration of Russian business of foreign markets. In spite of the above-mentioned advantages provided by state protection to government and semi-government corporations, this patronage has the following substantial disadvantages. Firstly, it limits the initiative of Russian corporations which often act upon the direct order of Moscow. Secondly, the excessive protectionism leads to the artificial closure of the Russian domestic market for Iranian producers. Thirdly, existing government support is selective and provided only to business connected with the political elite of Russia. As a result, medium and small businesses as well as private corporations with insufficiently close connections to the state usually face difficulties in dealing with the Gulf by themselves. The lack of government support in certain areas, in turn, weakens the Russian position in a number of fields and creates serious problems for the development of Russo-Gulf economic ties.[44]

Problems with the development of Russian economic relations with the Gulf are also related to the specifics of the economy of the Russian Federation. In spite of the proclaimed attempts of the authorities of the RF to accelerate economic growth, Russia is still heavily dependent on the exports of raw materials (minerals, hydrocarbons and wood). The policy of diversification and modernisation declared by President Medvedev is implemented at a slow pace, and it has obviously failed to reach initially projected goals. The Russian Federation demonstrates signs of a country with a rentier economy, and increasing technological backwardness in certain fields only makes these signs more obvious. As a result, apart from its ferrous metals, wood and petrochemical products, Moscow has a very limited range of products to offer the Gulf. Moreover, this range is gradually shrinking. As stated by the officials of the Chamber of Commerce and Industry of the RF, it is mere technological backwardness which prevents Russian companies from dealing with Iran and the Gulf. Currently, Iran is lacking engineering and technological support as well as equipment for the upgrade and construction of oil refineries and LNG producing plants. However, Russia is unable to provide the IRI with all the required assistance, equipment and technologies. Moreover, Moscow is itself badly in need of them.[45]

5. Conclusion

All in all, the dialogue between the countries of the Gulf and Russia has a certain potential in both the political and economic spheres. Moscow is unable to challenge US dominance in the region as well as China's growing influence (and that of other Asian countries). Yet, Russia is probably capable of finding its own niche in the Gulf system of political and economic relations. Nevertheless, the Russian government should demonstrate considerable patience, vigilance and courtesy in developing its relations with the Gulf. Thus, on the one hand, Moscow is supposed to carefully watch over the development of its relations with Tehran in order to prevent them from exceeding the level at which they endanger the Russian dialogue with the West. On the other hand, the established ties with the GCC members are still young and fragile as well as exposed to the negative influence of external factors such as the unstable situation in the Middle East, the changeable attitude of the Russian leaders to the Russo-Arab dialogue, and confusing political incidents.

Under these circumstances, Moscow should probably concentrate its attention on the creation of a well-articulated long-term strategy towards the Gulf. Clearly stated strategic goals would allow the Russian administration to avoid extreme opportunism, inconsistency and multiple miscalculations which are currently typical of Moscow's diplomacy in the Gulf. A well-articulated strategy would also make Russian behaviour in the region more predictable for other players, and this, in turn, would assure the Gulf countries of the seriousness of Russian plans and intentions.

Endnotes

1 During his civil service at the Russian Ministry of Foreign Affairs, the author encountered this explanation many times.

2 Interview with a Russian expert on Iran. The Institute of Oriental Studies of the Russian Academy of Science. Moscow, October 2011; Aleksy Mukhin, Piterskoye Okruzhaniye Prezidenta (Moscow: TsPI, 2003).

3 Ministry of Foreign Affairs of the Russian Federation, The Foreign Policy Concept of the Russian Federation (adopted 12 July 2008). Accessed November 14, 2011, http://www.mid.ru/ns-osndoc.nsf/osndd.

4 Ibid.

5 Interview with a Russian expert on Iran. The Institute of the Middle East. Moscow, October 2011.

6 Tariq Khaitous, Arab Reactions to a Nuclear Armed Iran (Washington: Washington Institute for Near East Policy, 2009).

7 Ministry of Foreign Affairs of the Russian Federation, The Foreign Policy Concept of the Russian Federation.

8 Ministry of Foreign Affairs of the Russian Federation, The Russian Federation Concept of International Scientific and Technological Cooperation (adopted 20 January 2000). Accessed November 14, 2011, http://www.mid.ru/ns-osndoc.nsf/osndd.

9 Ibid.

10 Ibid.

11 Ibid.

12 Ministry of Foreign Affairs of the Russian Federation, Annex I to the Russian Foreign Policy Concept, "The Main Directions of the Russian Federation Policy in the Field of International Cultural and Humanitarian Cooperation" (adopted 18 December 2010). Accessed November 14, 2011, http://www.mid.ru/ns-osndoc.nsf/osndd.

13 Ibid.

14 Farit Mukhametshin, "Vystupleniye Rukovoditelya Rossotrudnichestva F.M.Mukhametshina na Moskovskom Forume Kul'tury", Persona PLUS, №1, 2011. Accessed October 23, 2011, http://persona-plus.net/nomer.php?id=3496.

15 Brandon Fite, U.S. and Iranian Strategic Competition: Competition Involving China and Russia (Washington: Center for Strategic & International Studies, 2011).

16 Ministry of Foreign Affairs of the Russian Federation, The Treaty on the Basic Principles of Cooperation between the Russian Federation and the Islamic Republic of Iran (signed on 12 March 2001). Accessed on October 23, 2011, http://www.iran.ru/rus/dogovorobosnovnixvzaimootnosheniiax.php.

17 Interview with a Russian expert on Iran. Institute of the Oriental Studies of the Russian Academy of Science. Moscow, 14 October 2011.

18 Stephen Blank, "A New Rapprochement between Moscow and Tehran", Eurasia Daily Monitor, November 16, 2011, Volume 8, Issue 212.

19 Vladimir Evseev, "Rossiysko-Iranskoye Nastorozhennoye Partnerstvo", Vestnik Kavkaza, 5 July 2010. Accessed March 10, 2012, http://www.vestikavkaza.ru/analytics/politika/22111.html.

20 Ministry of Foreign Affairs of the Russian Federation, The Military Doctrine of the Russian Federation (adopted on 5 February 2010). Accessed November 14, 2011, http://www.mid.ru/ns-osndoc.nsf/osndd.

21 Interview with the Russian expert on Iran. Institute of Oriental Studies of the Russian Academy of Science. Moscow. October, 2011; Interview with a Russian expert on Iran. Rasht, 22 December 2011.

22 Vladimir Evseev, Voenno-politichekiye Aspekty Iranskoy Yadernoy Problemy (Moscow: IPRAN, 2010), 129.

23 A. Potserob, K Voprosu Obespecheniya Bezopasnosti v Zone Persidskogo Zaliva. Accessed April 25, 2012, http://www.iimes.ru/rus/stat/2010/31-10-10b.htm.

24 Ibid.

25 Ibid.

26 Vladimir Isaev, Aleksandr Filonik, "Rossiya – Arabskiye Strany: Politicheskiye Imperativy i Ekonomicheskoye Sotrudnichestvo", Novoye Vostochnoye Obozreniye, 3 September 2010. Accessed April 25, 2012, http://journal-neo.com/?q=ru/node/1154.

27 Ibid.

28 Ministerstvo Ekonomicheskogo Razvitiya Rossiyskoy Fedratsii, Torgovo-ekonomicheskoye Sotrudnichestvo Rossiyskoy Federatsii s Islamskoy Respublikoy Iran. Accessed February 2, 2012, http://www.economy.gov.ru/minec/activity/sections/foreigneconomicactivity/cooperation/economicaa/doc20110318_5.

29 Ibid.

30 Ministerstvo Insotrannikh Del Rossiyskoy Federatsii, Torgovo-Ekonomicheskiye Svyazi Mezhdu Rossiyey I Turtsiyey. Accessed March 29, 2012, http://www.mid.ru/bdomp/ns-rasia.nsf/1083b79 37ae580ae432569e7004199c2/432569d80021985fc325744f002b5bb8!OpenDocument.

31 Ludmila Shkvarya, "Rossiya i Strany Zaliva: Investitsionnoye Sotrudnichestvo", Aziya i Afrika Segodnya, №5, 2011, 21.

32 Apart from Gazprom and Lukoil, Russian oil, gas and petrochemical companies in the Gulf are also represented by Rosneft (exploration works in Sharjah, strategic partnership treaty with Emirates' Crescent Petroleum), Zarubezhneft, Sibur Holding, Stroytransgaz (construction of pipeline Tavila-Fujairah, development projects in Saudi Arabia), Tatneft, Gazprom Neft, Kriogennoe Mashinostroeniye, REP Holding and others.

33 Interview with a Russian expert on Iran. Moscow, 17 October 2011.

34 Interview with the expert of the Russian Trade Mission in Tehran. Tehran, 19 August 2009.

35 VOA, Ministr Nefti Irana i Ministr Energetiki Rossii Podpisali Zayavleniye o Sotrudnichestve. Accessed February 2, 2012, http://www.voanews.com/russian/news/russia-iran-2010-07-14-98435184.html.

36 Ludmila Shkvarya, "Rossiya i Strany Zaliva: Investitsionnoye Sotrudnichestvo", 18 – 23.

37 Nikolay Kozhanov, Ekonomicheskiye Sanktsii Protiv Irana: Tseli, Masshtabi, Vozmozhniye Posledstviya Vvedeniya (Moscow: Institut Blizhnego Vostoka, 2011).

38 Interview with a Russian expert on Iran. Moscow, 17 October 2011.

39 Interview with the research fellow of the Institute of Oriental Studies of the Russian Academy of Science. Moscow, 10 October 2011.

40 Evseev Vladimir, Rossiysko-Iranskoye Nastorozhennoye Partnerstvo.

41 Interview with the Russian diplomat. Moscow, 7 October 2011.

42 Ministerstvo Ekonomicheskogo Razvitiya Rossiyskoy Fedratsii, Torgovo-ekonomicheskoye Sotrudnichestvo Rossiyskoy Federatsii s Islamskoy Respublikoy Iran.

43 Interview with the Russian expert on the energy sector of the Russian economy. Moscow, October 25, 2011.

44 Interview with the Russian expert on Iran. Rasht. 24 December 2011; Interview with the expert of the Chamber of Commerce and Industry of Gilan. Rasht. 25 December 2011.

45 Interview with an expert of the Chamber of Commerce and Industry of the Russian Federation. Moscow, 11 December 2011.

Bibliography

Stephen Blank, "A New Rapprochement between Moscow and Tehran", Eurasia Daily Monitor, November 16, 2011, Volume 8, Issue 212.

Vladimir Evseev, "Rossiysko-Iranskoye Nastorozhennoye Partnerstvo", Vestnik Kavkaza, July 5, 2010. Accessed March 10, 2012: http://www.vestikavkaza.ru/analytics/politika/22111.html

Vladimir Evseev, Voenno-politichekiye Aspekty Iranskoy Yadernoy Problemy (Moscow: IPRAN, 2010).

Brandon Fite, U.S. and Iranian Strategic Competition: Competition Involving China and Russia. (Washington: Center for Strategic & International Studies, 2011).

Vladimir Isaev, Aleksandr Filonik, "Rossiya – Arabskiye Strany: Politicheskiye Imperativy i Ekonomicheskoye Sotrudnichestvo", Novoye Vostochnoye Obozreniye, 3 September 2010. Accessed April 25, 2012. http://journal-neo.com/?q=ru/node/1154

Tariq Khaitous, Arab Reactions to a Nuclear Armed Iran (Washington: Washington Institute for Near East Policy, 2009).

Nikolay Kozhanov, Ekonomicheskiye Sanktsii Protiv Irana: Tseli, Masshtabi, Vozmozhniye Posledstviya Vvedeniya (Moscow: Institut Blizhnego Vostoka, 2011).

Ministerstvo Ekonomicheskogo Razvitiya Rossiyskoy Fedratsii, Torgovo-ekonomicheskoye Sotrudnichestvo Rossiyskoy Federatsii s Islamskoy Respublikoy Iran. Accessed February 2, 2012. http://www.economy.gov.ru/minec/activity/sections/foreigneconomicactivity/coopera-tion/economicaa/doc20110318_5

Ministerstvo Insotrannikh Del Rossiyskoy Federatsii, Torgovo-Ekonomicheskiye Svyazi Mezhdu Rossiyey I Turtsiyey. Accessed March 29, 2012 http://www.mid.ru/bdomp/ns-rasia.nsf/

Ministry of Foreign Affairs of the Russian Federation, Annex I to the Russian Foreign Policy Concept "The Main Directions of the Russian Federation Policy in the Field of International Cultural and Humanitarian Cooperation" (adopted 18 December 2010). Accessed November 14, 2011. http://www.mid.ru/ns-osndoc.nsf/osndd

Ministry of Foreign Affairs of the Russian Federation, The Foreign Policy Concept of the Russian Federation (adopted 12 July 2008). Accessed November 14, 2011. http://www.mid.ru/ns-osndoc.nsf/osndd

Ministry of Foreign Affairs of the Russian Federation, The Military Doctrine of the Russian Federation (adopted on 5 February 2010). Accessed November 14, 2011. http://www.mid.ru/ns-osndoc.nsf/osndd

Ministry of Foreign Affairs of the Russian Federation, The Russian Federation Concept of International Scientific and Technological Cooperation (adopted 20 January 2000). Accessed November 14, 2011. http://www.mid.ru/ns-osndoc.nsf/osndd

Ministry of Foreign Affairs of the Russian Federation, The Treaty on the Basic Principles of Cooperation between the Russian Federation and the Islamic Republic of Iran (signed on 12 March 2001). Accessed October 23, 2011. http://www.iran.ru/rus/dogovorobosnovni‾xvzaimootnosheniiax.php

Farit Mukhametshin, "Vystupleniye Rukovoditelya Rossotrudnichestva F.M.Mukhametshina na Moskovskom Forume Kul'tury" in Persona PLUS, №1, 2011. Accessed October 23, 2011. http://persona-plus.net/nomer.php?id=3496

Aleksey Mukhin, Piterskoye Okruzhaniye Prezidenta (Moscow: TsPI, 2003).

Aleksey Potserob, "K Voprosu Obespecheniya Bezopasnosti v Zone Persidskogo Zaliva". Accessed April 25, 2012. http://www.iimes.ru/rus/stat/2010/31-10-10b.htm

Ludmila Shkvarya, "Rossiya i Strany Zaliva: Investitsionnoye Sotrudnichestvo", Aziya i Afrika Segodnya, №5, 2011, 18 – 23.

VOA, Ministr Nefti Irana i Ministr Energetiki Rossii Podpisali Zayavleniye o Sotrudnichestve. Accessed February 2, 2012. http://www.voanews.com/russian/news/russia-iran-2010-07-14-98435184.html

Interviews

Interview with an expert of the Russian Trade Mission in Tehran. Tehran, 19 August 2009.

Interview with a Russian expert on Iran. The Institute of the Middle East. Moscow, October 2011.

Interview with a Russian diplomat. Moscow, 7 October 2011.

Interview with a research fellow of the Institute of the Oriental Studies of the Russian Academy of Science. Moscow, 10 October 2011.

Interview with a Russian expert on Iran. Institute of the Oriental Studies of the Russian Academy of Science. Moscow, 14 October 2011.

Interview with a Russian expert on Iran. Moscow, 17 October 2011.

Interview with a Russian expert on the energy sector of the Russian economy. Moscow, 25 October 2011.

Interview with an expert of the Chamber of Commerce and Industry of the Russian Federation. Moscow, 11 December 2011.

Interview with a Russian expert on Iran. Rasht, 22 December 2011.

Interview with a Russian expert on Iran. Rasht. 24 December 2011

Interview with an expert of the Chamber of Commerce and Industry of Gilan. Rasht. 25 December 2011

Chapter Six

Situating the Gulf in India's Engagement with Emerging Asia

Girijesh Pant

1. Introduction

India, the third largest economy in terms of purchasing power parity (at $44.46 trillion), is treading a growth trajectory that demands greater integration into the globalizing world economy. Since the global economy is gravitating towards Asia, it is natural that India's economic relations with other Asian countries are undergoing a quantitative and qualitative shift. India and China are the leading players in the Asian growth story, and despite the huge gap separating them, the interface between the two nations is vital in defining Asian economic resurgence. In addition to being a growing market, the democratic quotient provides India with a distinct leverage in projecting its strategic salience. The central thesis of this chapter is that India needs wider Asian resurgence to promote its economy to the high end of the global production chain. Its engagement with emerging Asia aims at accelerating this process by forging economic relations leading to strategic convergence. It intends to use leverage in these relationships on the strength of the knowledge economy. To reap the advantages, India needs a comprehensive Asia policy which promotes the furthering of Asian interdependence, and one part of this is the integration of the Gulf region into the Asian framework. On its Eastern flank, India has articulated its position through its Look East Policy. On the Western Asian flank, a corresponding formulation remains to be spelled out, though the region blips prominently on its radar. It is argued in this paper that the growing dynamic relations between India and the Gulf countries have reached a threshold where a strategic leap can be made. The Gulf region provides India with the critical geo-economic space to augment its global reach; a slippage could therefore be detrimental to its positioning.

2. Emerging Asia: the Geo-economic Shift

A report from the Asian Development Bank (ADB) states:

> Asia is in the midst of a truly historic transformation. If it continues to grow on its recent trajectory, it could, by 2050, account for more than half of global Gross Domestic Product (GDP), trade and investment, and enjoy widespread affluence. Its per capita income could rise sixfold to reach the global average and be similar to European levels today (though Europe and North America will remain much richer in per capita terms). It thus holds the promise of making some 3 billion additional Asians, hitherto commonly associated with poverty and deprivation, affluent by today's standards. By nearly doubling its share of global GDP (at market exchange rates) from 27 percent in 2010 to 51 percent by 2050, Asia would regain the dominant global economic position it held some 250 year (sic!) ago, before the Industrial Revolution." [1]

"From wealth to power" could have been the logical corollary for emerging Asia to position itself in the global system but for the fact that power in the globalizing world is more diffuse than before.[2] It is no longer located exclusively with the state, the market or in a defined territorial construct. Consequently, rising economic Asia cannot visualize an imperial or neocolonial trajectory to define its role. Asia is emerging essentially as part of the global supply chain. It is well-documented that during the last three decades East and Southeast Asia have increasingly evolved as key elements in global production processes: a regional platform, promoting inter- and intra-regional investment and trade. As stated in a United Nations Economic and Social Commission for Asia and the Pacific (UNESCAP) report, "Rapid growth of production networks has dramatically transformed patterns of production and international trade in the region, with a notable expansion of intra-regional trade 'through multiple border crossing of parts and components'".[3] Thus, emerging Asia, as part of a global construct, does not enjoy a high degree of autonomy.

Significantly, the logic of Asia's global economic position is increasingly defying the geopolitical mapping defined by the power dynamics of the Cold War and post-Cold War periods.[4] Since economic factors are reshaping the geography, the power quotient of the political is going to witness a relative decline. The rise of Asia is therefore bound to be more a geo-economic than a geo-political phenomenon. Unlike Europe where regional impulses, though driven by economic imperatives, evolved in the context of Cold War politics to provide a rationale for strategic convergence, in Asia it is the unfolding dynamics of geo-economics contesting the logic of territorialization that is going to be the raison d'être for convergence. It is the hypothesis here that the dynamics for Asian strategic convergence lie in economic interdependence, not in geopolitical strategies of domination.

According to the ADB, seven Asian players are critical to the developing Asian economic order: China, India, Indonesia, Japan, Korea, Malaysia and Thailand. According to ADB estimates,

> In 2010 these seven economies had a combined total population of 3.1 billion (78 percent of Asia) and a GDP of $14.2 trillion (87 percent of Asia). By 2050 their share in population is expected to fall to 73 percent of Asia, while the share of GDP rises to 90 percent. These seven economies alone will account for 45 percent of global GDP. Their average per capita income of $45,800 (PPP) would be 25 percent higher than the global average of $36,600.[5]

Clearly Asia is emerging as a multipolar space with its own ramifications. Simultaneous growth has widened the canvas and enhanced the competition, as well as ensuring resilience. Furthermore, growth is hugely mutually interdependent. The Chinese and the Association of Southeast Asian Nations' (ASEAN) economies are very closely linked. What is significant is that the growing economic expanse is shaping the totality of their mutual exchanges. Consequently, the rising powers of the region are renegotiating their mutual engagements and relations. Moreover, with larger economic flows between Asian countries, a new interdependence is unfolding which is compelling them to interact on the larger canvas with strategic understanding. The India-China template illustrates this. Being the key drivers of Asian growth, both China and India loom large on the overall Asian economic scene, and it is precisely their stature that is sharpening the geopolitical tension. Yet their mutual trade is booming and both see their economic future in their respective growth. Something similar is happening between India and Pakistan. As India's Security Advisor has observed, "The new equilibrium in Asia is likely to be as much a result of production chains and regional and global market integration as of purely security driven alliances or structures."[6]

However, while the imperatives of the Asian production network are reshaping Asian economic geography, the high stakes of external players are reinforcing the political territoriality according to the geopolitical matrix present during the Cold War. What is more disturbing is that the spillover of this has a crucial bearing on the unfolding relations among the countries of the region. The Security Advisor states:

> ...Asia as a whole is and will remain dependent upon the rest of the world for its own continued growth and security, whether in terms of energy security, food security or, in the more conventional calculation of the sources and providers of security capabilities and technologies. In several respects that matter (concepts, technology, security, energy etc), Asia is still and will remain a net global consumer for some time to come. With younger populations, and the task of maintaining the growth necessary to generate jobs for new entrants to the labor force, this will remain true of the major Asian developing economies for the foreseeable future. (Historically speaking, this is very different from the situation before the mid-eighteenth century when Asia last enjoyed relative global pre-eminence. Then Asia depended on itself for its needs and markets. Again, the contrast with the Soviet Union's autonomy from others could not be greater. So expect different behavior from Asian powers.)[7]

3. Emerging Asia: the Strategic Salience of Inclusive Interdependence

To appreciate the dynamics of interdependence among Asian countries, a clear distinction needs to be drawn with the interdependence which exists between developed and developing countries. In the context of North-South transactions, the interdependence has been largely asymmetrical even though it has evolved away from the earlier unequal exchange and core-periphery relationship (articulated by Prebisch, Singer, Samir Amin and Frank), as a result of the technological breakthrough which has reduced transaction and transport costs.[8] The move from dependence to interdependence marked a definite departure, and the terms of engagement did witness a change towards enhanced mutual sensitivity between developed and developing economies. However, as Nye and Koehne have underlined, sensitivity and vulnerability are two distinct attributes of interdependence, and the vulnerability of developing economies remains. The power has remained located with the North despite interdependence.[9]

In contrast, the nature of interdependence among the Asian countries does not indicate the leverage of power because the nature of their economic transaction is more horizontal than vertical in the global value chain. It is not hegemonic. The larger economies do enjoy advantages of scale, yet their growth targets compel them to be sensitive to the concerns of other Asian economies. This is not due to any short-term utilitarian concerns, but because of the structural dynamics. Asian economies have to respect the mutuality of sensitivity because their high growth regime has sharpened the internal contradictions of neoliberal policies. A holistic view of interdependence requires that transactions among nations do not promote internal inequalities which create discontent and disrupt growth. Therefore, Asian interdependence has to be inclusive in nature. This may constitute a significant development in transforming trade and foreign investment into instruments of empowerment.

The titanic shift of the global economy towards Asia needs to be appreciated in the context of the evolving dynamics of globalization. The global economy is evolving by deconstructing the territoriality of markets, in conformity with the principle of enhancing surplus value. It is encouraging regionalization of economies by promoting trans-border engagement. Thus, Asian interdependence is induced by the processes of globalization. It is emerging as a result of the changing dynamics of the division of labor. With dispersal of production processes to cheaper sites, Asia has joined the global production network. Furthermore, globalization is now moving to the dispersal of knowledge at different geographical sites, with associated networks of innovation. A new geography is emerging, giving Asia a distinct position.

However the dispersal of production and knowledge sites does not negate the hierarchical nature of the global knowledge network. The high-end economies remain the high spenders on research and development (R&D). Ernst Dieter argues that:

> ...innovation still remains geographically concentrated, because tacit knowledge is exchanged through social networks embedded in local institutions (universities, R&D, patents, start-ups, venture capitalists, legal and other knowledge-intensive support services). For the time being, established centers in the USA, Europe and Japan retain their dominance. All 15 leading companies with the best record on patent citations are based in the USA (9 in the IT industry). The 700 largest R&D spenders (mostly large US firms) account for 50% of the world's total R&D expenditures and more than two-thirds of the world's business R&D. More than 80% of the 700 largest R&D spenders come

from only five countries (USA, followed by Japan, Germany, UK and France).[10]

Although globalizing Asia is making every attempt to move up the global innovation network, it will not be able to change world Gross National Income (GNI) rankings and, unless it breaks the barrier to reach the top echelon of the innovation hierarchy, Asia's power will be limited by its GNI status. Dieter argues that the new geography of knowledge is "shaped by intense competition between multiple and hierarchically ordered innovation hubs." He classifies these hubs in terms of hierarchy as follows:[11]

- global centres of excellence (in the United States, Japan, and the EU)
- advanced locations (e.g. Israel, Ireland, Taiwan, and Korea)
- Catching-up locations (e.g. Beijing, the Yangtze River Delta, and the Pearl River Delta in China; and Bangalore, Chennai, Hyderabad, and Delhi in India)
- "new frontier" locations (e.g., lower-tier cities in China and India, plus Romania, Armenia, Bulgaria, Vietnam, and others)

The point made here is that emerging Asia's position in the global manufacturing and knowledge network rests simply on the strength of its comparative cost advantage. In this sense Asian economic power is partial in nature. What Asia needs now is to go beyond the current structures, moving up the hierarchy and developing new components of power (including hard military power). In this manner it would sensitize the whole global order to its interests. However, the projection necessitated by this economic logic has a potential to promote rivalries which in turn could be detrimental to the very processes of interdependence. Moreover, it could strengthen the geopolitical fault lines inherited from the Cold War. There could be situations where one Asian country might seek to block another Asian country by collaborating with an external player. The framework of Asian resurgence assumes that a cooperative approach will be pursued, and there is a wide perception that this is necessary, but the particular interests of Asian countries may conflict.

The uneven dispersal of Asian growth, both across the national boundaries and within the boundaries, has positioned countries in an asymmetrical setting, leading to apprehension and suspicion. This can be seen most clearly in the case of China. China is emerging as the second largest economy of the world and its growth is casting a shadow on Southeast Asia and on India. Significantly, while rising China creates tremors among its neighbors in Southeast Asia, its presence is appreciated in West Asia, particularly in the Gulf region. China shares its border with India and the border between the two is still to be defined. China is also impinging upon those Asian spaces which India had assumed to be within its zone of influence. Southeast Asia is keen for an Indian presence as a countervailing player, and also on India's Western flank there are countries wanting India to play a larger role. Tensions arising from the interplay of interdependence and power disparity are a distinct feature of the emerging Asia. Interdependence may not remain sustainable if its tendency to create skewed power dynamics is not mediated. This is the challenge before the Asian leadership.

4. India's Engagement with Emerging Asia

In the Indian imagination Asia, from Suez to the Pacific, is a wide and inclusive construct. The Indian civilizational imprint continues to be visible on many parts of the Asian tapestry. What is important is that India recognizes the co-existence of diversities in Asian cultures and civilizations as a source of strength and resilience. The first Prime minister of India, Nehru, who was the architect of Indian foreign policy in the formative years, was very clear about the civilizational and strategic depth that India gained from its Asian identity. Spelling out the Indian vision of Asia at the Asian Relations Conference in New Delhi, Nehru said:

> We are of Asia and the peoples of Asia are nearer and closer to us than others. India is so situated that she is the pivot of Western, Southern and South-East Asia. In the past her culture flowed to all these countries and they came to her in many ways. Those contacts are being renewed and the future is bound to see a closer union between India and Southeast Asia on the one side and Afghanistan, Iran and the Arab world on the other. To the furtherance of that close association of free countries we must devote ourselves.[12]

The Asian factor, however, receded in Indian foreign policy formulations, although at a bilateral level India continued to build ties with countries of the continent.

In the 1990s the shift in the orientation of the economic regime made India redefine its foreign policy correspondingly. Consequently India revisited its Asian engagement, transcending the civilizational dimension. As observed by the Indian Foreign Minister:

> This foreign policy initiative had a domestic dimension based in the economic restructuring and reform program that we had commenced in July 1991 where- in we placed emphasis on reducing licensing, giving greater play to private initiative and entrepreneurship and in

general making it easier to do business in India. One aspect of this course correction was the relative emphasis given to trade and foreign investment. As a result, economic diplomacy became an integral part of foreign policy formulation and implementation.[13]

With Asia on India's Eastern and Southeastern flank becoming economically cohesive, India recognized the need to reconceptualize its Asian approach. The rise of China further mobilized India to be in the Asian orbit. The possibilities of the Asian Century have added new momentum to Indian initiatives. The pressure of growth on the economic frontier has been making India renegotiate its external relations both at global and at regional levels. In interdependent global relations the multiple levels of exchanges rule out any disjuncture between the two, yet the nature of exchange has its bearing on content and style of engagement, reflecting in foreign policy postures. Apparently India needs an external environment that contributes to promoting its growth momentum. Furthermore, it needs a friendly neighborhood to sustain its high growth regime. Asia is India's neighborhood. The strategic salience of neighborhood lies in its potential to contribute or jeopardize the growth process. Obviously India needs a vibrant Asia but it also needs an Asia that is responsive to its growth momentum.

Apparently the Indian foreign policy establishment, recognizing the Indian stakes in Asia, has been recrafting the emerging engagements institutionally. The Ministry of External Affairs is moving beyond the territorial divide drawn largely from the Western Cold War perspective. Asia is perceived as a composite entity with a diversity of stakes. Initiatives are taken to blur the geopolitical constructs, thus South Asia is split into two divisions with: Bangladesh, Sri Lanka and the Maldives as one cluster, and Pakistan, Iran and Afghanistan as another, clearly demonstrating a distinctive nature of concerns and engagement. The trio (Pakistan, Iran and Afghanistan) is not part of the emerging economies. Pakistan, Iran and Afghanistan are predominantly the victims of a Cold War "clash of civilizations" mindset. Their economic potentialities are caged by global geopolitics. It can be argued that Asia in general and India in particular cannot be confident of its growth without enabling those countries which are not currently part of it. This means that Asian countries need to work towards a framework and action plan. This would require a common assessment and understanding among the leading Asian players. No Asian country alone could provide the alternative wherewithal.

The Bangladeshi and Sri Lankan efforts to transform ties on the strength of economic stakes are becoming more visible. This was eloquently demonstrated by the fact that the Indian Prime Minister in his crucial visit to Bangladesh was accompanied by the Chief Ministers of four neighboring Indian states, namely Assam, Meghalaya, Tripura and Mizoram. Indian economic frontiers are being stretched to accommodate understanding and endorsement of both local and national affairs. This corroborates the contention that the geo-economic is pushing relations beyond geopolitics.[14] Significantly the gains from the new economic geography are perceived and acknowledged by Bangladesh also.

> We believe that three very important factors have helped in influencing Bangladesh's relations with India. First, the formidable growth of India in recent years. India is no longer just an emerging economic power. It has, indeed, emerged as a major economic power. So, it makes sense for a country like Bangladesh, as a next door neighbor which shares over 4000 km of border, to benefit from this growth, whether it's through trade, investment, technical and scientific cooperation or education cooperation. Second, for most thinking Bangladeshis, it's now patently clear that the geopolitics of the past where we had our own version of the Cold War in South Asia, is over. … India's foreign policy has evolved and is a demonstration to countries like Bangladesh that they could benefit enormously from the changes taking place in the South Asian landscape. Third, there is the turnaround in India's thinking in terms of both regional and sub-regional cooperation. … A new relationship between the North-East and Bangladesh could do wonders for the North-East economy. Thousands of Bangladeshi tourists, who travel to Bangkok and other parts of India, would, given a chance, happily visit the North-East. … We can now move towards a deeper relationship between India and Bangladesh, particularly in terms of India's North-East and West Bengal, and also explore greater connectivity, including transit and access to the Chittagong Port. Energy cooperation is an area where there are enormous opportunities, both at the bilateral as well as the regional levels.[15]

The emerging interface between the growing Indian economy and global production processes is shifting and defining the contours of India's Asia Policy and can be further observed in its endeavor to regionalize South Asian economies by pushing the region towards economic union.[16] South Asia is the least integrated region in Asia. The mutual trust deficit among the countries, especially India and Pakistan, has been restricting forward movement despite the fact that the South

Asian Association for Regional Cooperation (SAARC) has been in existence for nearly thirty years. However with India breaking the growth barrier, the region is recognizing the rationale for economic cooperation. It was the endorsement of India's growth story that made the Pakistani President suggest that long term historical issues need not restrict the potential of economic gains. Apparently the border will lose sanctity only if economies interact despite it. India needs the trans-border links so as to have access to energy and transit routes at minimal cost. Moreover, uneven growth among neighboring countries could pose security issues like illegal migration towards economic growth poles in India.

It was natural that globalizing India's Asian re-engagement began with the emerging East. Therefore, the Look East Policy can be seen as the initial articulation of its Asia policy, which is still unfolding. Opinions are divided over the coherence of Indian policy. It is clear that in two decades, the Look East Policy has given India a unique strategic position in its engagement with the region. Although the initial trigger for looking East was the ASEAN economic miracle, the current terms and reference of the policy have moved beyond that. In the words of Yashwant Sinha:

> The first phase of India's Look East policy was ASEAN-centered and focused primarily on trade and investment linkages. The new phase of this policy is characterized by an expanded definition of 'East,' extending from Australia to East Asia, with ASEAN at its core. The new phase also marks a shift from trade to wider economic and security issues including joint efforts to protect the sea lanes and coordinate counter-terrorism activities.[17]

A closer scrutiny of India's Look East Policy reveals that it assigns differential weightings to different regions. Broadly the policy has four facets: one around China and its orbit; the second around the Japan-Australian sphere; the third around ASEAN and the fourth Myanmar and the Indian Ocean trade routes. Even within ASEAN it is observed that two distinct shades can be discerned between the old ASEAN (namely Indonesia, Malaysia, Thailand, Philippines and Singapore), and the latecomers (Vietnam, Myanmar, Laos and Cambodia).[18] With the advantage of hindsight, it can be argued that although the policy is driven by economic engagement, it is gradually acquiring a strategic dimension. India does not seek to contain China, in fact it does not possess the power, but Chinese moves have caused some apprehension, affecting the relationship between the two. The "String of Pearls" and the South China Sea oil explorations illustrate this. The Chinese quite often view the Indian response in the context of the shifting position of the US on the region. Since economics weighs heavily on both sides, however, it can be used to soften an initially aggressive rhetoric. The Japan-Australia focus of India's Look East Policy is driven by both strategic interdependence and shared economic interests, but it is the latter which provides the main rationale. Australia and Japan, for their part, clearly endorse Indian regional initiatives on the basis of their compatibility with shared US-Australia-Japan strategic objectives.[19]

India enjoys strong cultural ties with the new ASEAN members but economically these are latecomers, hence the nature of economic engagement is not so much about the market matrix as about empowerment processes. These countries have a strong tradition of a central command economy. Recognizing the importance of building a solid relationship with these countries, the Indian state has created a separate division within the foreign policy establishment, called the Cambodia, Laos, Myanmar and Vietnam (CLMV) department. In the regional framework of ASEAN, the slower progress of these countries has received special attention. A collective for reducing regional disparities was formed in the fourth ASEAN Informal Summit held on the 22-25th November 2000 to launch the ASEAN Integration Initiative (IAI). Under the work plan of the IAI, the areas of priority identified for the CLMV countries included: infrastructure development (transport and energy); human resource development (public sector capacity building, labor & employment and higher education); information and communication technology and promoting economic integration (trade in goods and services, custom standards and investment).[20] Taking cognizance of the regional (IAI) spirit, India also focused on the capacity-building processes in these countries. It dovetailed its ITEC (Indian Technical Economic Cooperation Program) with the other programs of the MEA under the Bilateral Assistance Program.[21]

India's economic engagement with the old ASEAN members has expanded multi-dimensionally. In January 1992, India became the Sectoral Dialogue Partner with ASEAN and in 1995, it became full Dialogue Partner. In 2002, a further elevation of relationship led India to become a summit partner in ASEAN + 4. Significantly, in August 2009, the Free Trade Agreement was concluded and became operational from January 2010. India and the ASEAN countries are defining a Vision 2020 to create shared prosperity. As was reported:

This Vision 2020 of ASEAN-India Partnership proposes a long-term strategic roadmap that will enable them to exploit the synergies to foster a comity of nations integrated at the commercial, cultural, political, and social spheres and to achieve their respective long-term developmental goals.

Given the complementarities between ASEAN and India, a greater integration will help them join the ranks of developed economies. It will also enable them to address the common challenges to comprehensive security. The eventual vision of the ASEAN-India Partnership is to promote Asian economic integration as a new engine of growth along with other East Asian countries (Japan, China and Korea).[22]

The emerging regional dynamics point towards the possibility of India as a new promoter of the Asian International Production Network as part of the global value chain. South Asia is a huge market and India could be the regional promoter, forging diverse production assembly lines as part of Asian emergence as a center of global economic prosperity. It has been observed that its "status as Asia's tertiary super power is enabling India to play a kind of avuncular strategic role, giving it a platform on which to team with the Southeast Asians on their military development without bringing any of the perceived strategic baggage that comes with dealing with the Chinese or the Americans."[23]

The changing economic frontiers are making countries visible in spaces where they were previously absent. Thus, Chinese expansion is perceived by the Southeast Asians with apprehension. Indian economic frontiers too are changing. India is also moving out to sustain its growth momentum. Such outward expansion can put countries into conflict situations. India and China, for example, do face such situations. The challenge before the Asian leadership is to address these unprecedented situations in a way that such conflicts are resolved by mutual engagement.

Asian economic resurgence is expanding to South and West Asia. Here India does enjoy advantages comparable to China in Southeast Asia. Recognizing the role that it has to play in the wider context of the Asian Century, India has to reconfigure the nature of its engagement with South and West Asia. The Indian imagination of West Asia is that of Afghanistan to Egypt. In fact Asian economic resurgence will not only remain incomplete but might become unsustainable if South and West Asia are not made part of it. The epicenter of a possible backlash is in this region, and backlashes can be highly migratory in nature and do not recognize borders. Though largely perceived as a security issue it is essentially a response to a construct that is based upon alienation and marginalization. Asian key players have to make a strategic choice to engage South and West Asia economically in the Asian growth orbit.

Cold War geopolitics pushed West Asia from the Asian space. The rise of oil monarchies further distanced the region from Asia and consolidated ties with oil customers who promised security as a trade-off. Oil-centered strategic relations with the West bolstered a new identity: the Gulf. The six oil exporters of the Arabian peninsula countries, namely Saudi Arabia, Kuwait, the UAE, Oman, Qatar and Bahrain, decided to forge a regional identity in order to negotiate with their big neighbors, namely Iraq and Iran. The Gulf Cooperation Council was formed in 1981 after the Islamic revolution in Iran. Three decades after that, the Council has not yielded any substantive results (particularly in the economic domain), despite regular meetings, summits and reaffirmation of intent and commitments. The economies, however, have been evolving around the oil revenue popularly called the "Rent". Oil rent indeed brought prosperity to the region but at the cost of the natural processes of economic, social and even political evolution. The oil-based economy redefined the economic exchange of the Gulf countries with some Asian countries as exporters of manpower, such as India, Pakistan, Korea, Sri Lanka, Bangladesh and the Philippines. It cannot be denied that remittances from the Gulf countries contributed critically to balancing the payment accounts of all these countries. Gulf investment too has been flowing to these countries but these economic exchanges could never acquire strategic salience until recently when Asia started consuming the bulk of the oil from the Gulf. Today, China is the largest oil importer from the region, and India, Japan and Korea also figure prominently. Oil continues to define external ties. Can the Gulf economies sustain their resilience on the narrowly defined premise of development or would they like to be part of Asian resurgence, thereby part of the global economy? It is argued that for natural evolution, the Gulf needs to reintegrate with the wider Asian production network and India could be the key player in this process. The GCC could be a meaningful economic entity if it follows the ASEAN rather than the European model. The GCC as a group could grow faster if it joined the Asian production network. The economic geography of the region is changing[24] and is reaching a threshold where political borders will have to yield, otherwise the distortions could jeopardize the stability and security of the region.

5. Visioning India's Gulf Policy

India's relations with the Gulf countries are fairly robust and dynamic, and they have grown. The Gulf countries are India's largest trading partners, accounting for $130 billion worth of trade in 2010-11 with over six million Indians living and working there. In 2011, India gained nearly $64 billion from remittances globally, and of this about $19-20 billion came from the Gulf. The Gulf states also supply more than 60 per cent of the oil imports of India. India with an oil import dependent economy, needs more than 75 per cent of its oil from overseas sources. Despite high stakes India has yet to formulate a regional perspective in terms of Gulf policy. It can be argued that given the regional context India could better pursue its interest in a bilateral frame than in a regional matrix. The argument made here is that with Asia becoming the prime mover of the global economy, India as an Asian player needs to have Asian vision and by extension a regional vision, hence a Gulf policy. No wonder sentiments have been expressed, drawing parallels from the Look East Policy. Indian Prime Minister Manmohan Singh observed that, "The Gulf region, like South-East and South Asia, is part of our natural economic hinterland. We must pursue closer economic relations with all our neighbors in our wider Asian neighborhood. India has successfully pursued a 'Look East' policy to come closer to the countries of South-East Asia. We must, similarly, come closer to our western neighbors in the Gulf."[25] Indian Vice President Hamid Ansari reiterated this idea, saying, "For us in India, a 'Look West' policy towards this part of West Asia would be as relevant for safeguarding and promoting India's interests as its Look-East Policy aimed at East Asia … The strategic relevance of the sub-region to India has to be located in geographic and economic terms."[26] In the annual reports of the Ministry of External Affairs, the Gulf takes precedence in the region.[27]

In defining its Gulf policy, India needs to locate the region in the wider canvas of West Asian and North African countries. The Gulf countries being part of the Arab and Islamic world draw heavily from the wider regional background in formulating their world view and foreign policy vision. It is no wonder that their governments are sensitive to the unfolding logic of the Arab Spring and the undercurrents in the *ummah*. Yet this approach tends to overlook the reality that the Gulf region has carved out its own identity and all efforts are made by the six countries to consolidate this profile. However, unlike East Asia, the Gulf region still remains heavily influenced by the effects of Cold War geopolitics. It is not regionalized despite regional entities. In fact, in recent years, after the US invasion of Iraq and the escalation of sanctions against Iran, the region is witnessing a deepening of geopolitical fault lines which might sharpen the contradictions of the rentier system. The region may not be able to withstand the fall-out from the unfolding dynamics of regional geopolitics, despite surging sovereign funds. Certainly this will hamper organic links with emerging Asia. Being the largest depository of oil and gas, the region will continue to be the major supplier of hydrocarbon to growing Asian economies and the latter will endeavour to strengthen hydrocarbon ties. However, the nature of engagement will not contribute to interdependence as envisaged earlier in this paper. On the contrary, it might escalate tension with many new players rushing for energy in the region. China has overtaken traditional consumers of hydrocarbons from the region. Sino-Gulf economic exchange has grown dramatically. The increased Chinese presence is viewed with apprehension by countries such as India. More critical however is the fact that the escalation of tension in the region would not be in the interest of Asian consumers, be it China or India. Not only would the oil prices and supply security have an adverse impact upon growth prospects, it would further encourage extremist movements, including escalating the scale of terrorism. The security bar of the region would increase and Asian countries would be forced to be part of a binary matrix which would have an adverse bearing upon their global positioning.

From the Asian and Indian perspective, the Gulf countries need to be embedded in a Gulf orbit, which itself is conceived as an organic part of the whole of Asia. This transformation is possible only if the region moves gradually and permanently away from the geopolitics mode to geo-economics. The GCC, Iran and Iraq are three critical dimensions of this transition. All three could pose a threat to each other on different scales and delay development prospects leading to a backlash from within. The experience of the last three decades has demonstrated that none of them has the individual capacity to define the region on their own terms. The huge expenditure on arms and the aspiration to acquire nuclear weapons to obtain a sense of security is going to be belied not by external invasions but by the people from within. All three entities are fragile internally because institutions are becoming dysfunctional and unable to meet the popular aspirations. If the people were able to assert themselves against autocracy, the royal families could only survive by accepting structures of popular participation. All three states could empower each other if their engagement moves onto the geo-economic axis. Therefore, Asian players must define their engagement to integrate the Gulf region into an Asian production network, beyond the trading of hydrocarbon.

India as a key Asian player can play a strategic role to promote Pan-Asian knowledge production processes by creating a regional knowledge architecture on the Western flank, with the Gulf as a vital component. India-Gulf interaction would be more substantive in promoting Asian resurgence by elevating their respective economies to the high end of the global value chain. The driver for this move is the knowledge economy. During the last two decades India has developed a knowledge platform as leverage for its future growth. India intends to reap the advantage of its demographic dividend by promoting a knowledge-based economy as the prime mover of its growth. It is looking for partnership. The GCC countries also recognize that the transformation of their oil-based economy can take place through research and innovation. The GCC needs to move to a high knowledge-based economy because low-end jobs are not acceptable to its people. An IMF study points out that between 2000 and 2010 about 7 million jobs were created, but only 2 million nationals accepted them.[28] In other words, the economy needs to create high-skill jobs, and this means developing the knowledge sector. Paradoxically, the local human resources pool is not trained to be employable in the high-end sector. Thus, along with moving the economy to the high-end knowledge sector, the region also needs to reorientate its education system. This again could be an area that India can look at with the Gulf region in order to promote interdependence, by creating a regional knowledge architecture which could have knowledge clusters and hubs. In the words of H. D. Evers, "a knowledge cluster is a local innovation system organized by universities, research institutions and firms which intend to drive innovations and create new industries. Knowledge hubs are localities with a knowledge architecture of high internal and external networking and knowledge sharing capabilities."[29] Such transnational clusters and hubs could be dedicated to a specific industry. It is emphasized that a wider rather than a restricted search for innovation links could help Asia to be part of a value chain at a high level. It is clear from Competitiveness Reports issued by the World Economic Forum that there is a huge gap, and without breaking the glass ceiling of productivity Asia would not be able to set the global agenda. The high capital intensity has been restricting Indian endeavor to advance in terms of innovation indices. The Gulf lacks human resources, as well as the infrastructure to become a partner with other Asia countries in creating a regional knowledge hub.

Youth engagement and economic diversification are going to be the key drivers of the geo-economic transition of the GCC countries. The oil revenue could be seen as the facilitator to this transition. Estimates suggest that youth under 25 years of age account for as high as one-third to one-half of the total population, constituting more than 50 per cent in Oman and Saudi Arabia, around 40 per cent in Bahrain and Kuwait and more than 30 per cent in Qatar and the UAE. Significantly, the literacy level in the GCC countries is very high as the governments have been investing heavily in education. Consequently, participating actively in cyberspace, the awareness and aspiration level of this generation is very high. Although the state has been the prime employer, the oil-based economy has a low propensity in generating employment. While the education regime has increased the literacy rate, work skills have remained undeveloped and the region is facing unemployment.[30] The next generation is therefore facing a unique situation of being co-opted into the system without participating in it. Recognizing its limitations, the governments are reforming the education system, but the solution for unemployment lies in the diversification of the economy and sustainable development. The GCC countries have been attempting to move beyond the rent-based economy but the pace needs to be accelerated. Though small size constraints could be addressed by the GCC integration processes, it is equally important that regional integration be conceived as part of the globalization process. GCC diversification needs to be driven by the external sector. The investment and trade links with emerging Asian economies could replicate the story of Southeast Asia. India's market size and its service sector could be leveraged with growing GCC diversification processes. The Indian experience is relevant to the Gulf because its factor endowment and geo-strategic location are shaping the country's comparative advantage around the knowledge-based service sector. According to a recent study:

> Over the last several years, India has been able to capitalize on its strong capabilities in IT-enabled service sectors to increase its share of services exports to the GCC countries. According to industry estimates, India's IT products and services exports to the GCC countries have been increasing at a growth rate of above 30% annually. Lower costs and English language skills remain the prime advantage for the Indian IT sector. India continues to offer skill-based services at a 50–80% lower cost than their source locations and 10–30% cheaper than other low-cost destinations. Consequently, IT sector revenues from exports have risen at a CAGR of 25% over the last 10 years in India.[31]

The emerging structural links between India and the Gulf countries, when measured in terms of investment flows, indicate that there is a huge potential still to be materialized. The above-mentioned study notes four characteristics: first, the pace of investment is growing but it accounts for only 3 per cent of trade; second, the scale of investment is very small in proportion to the global investments of the GCC; third, most of the investment is done by expatriate Indians; and finally, it is highly skewed towards the UAE and Oman which account for more than 85 per cent of GCC investment in India. Importantly, Indian companies of late are investing in the GCC market. The study states:

> Indian business houses have developed a larger footprint in the GCC compared to the GCC business community in India. An increasing number of establishments, JVs and branch or representative offices have

been set up in the region by India-based companies. This has largely been facilitated by GCC's liberalization and diversification efforts, rising Indian expatriate population and growing preferences for Indian products in the region. By far, UAE is the most favoured and popular nation in the GCC, encouraging a lot of Indian businesses and traders to establish a base in the emirate.[32]

The study contends that, apart from hydrocarbons, the service sector is the growing market for India in the Gulf and it is developing exponentially due to an expanding population and its diversifying demands and reforms.

> We estimate demand for healthcare in the region to grow due to a rapidly growing population, rising income levels and increased insurance penetration. The change in disease mix with an increased prevalence of lifestyle-related diseases is also expected to drive per capita spending on healthcare ... With soaring healthcare costs and the consequent additional burden on state finances, the GCC governments are actively pursuing reforms and policy measures to promote private sector participation. ... The GCC healthcare sector offers attractive opportunities as reforms gather pace and the market opens up further.[33]

With a view to strategies in India-GCC economic relations, the idea of a Free Trade Agreement was mooted in 2004. The potential areas identified included: information technology, telecommunication, education, health care services, tourism and the hotel industry, banking and financial services etc. In the past eight years, negotiations have reportedly been moving on, but there is yet to be a breakthrough. In the first round of negotiations held in Riyadh in March 2006 it was agreed that Free Trade agreement between the two would include services and investment in addition to trade. An India-based report on this states:

> Four working groups, on Trade in Goods, Trade in Services, Investment and Economic Cooperation and Rules of Origin and Customs Cooperation were established. The 2nd round of negotiations took place in Riyadh on September 9-10, 2008. The third round of India-GCC FTA negotiations were held in January 2009 at Riyadh. It opened up the position of the two sides on various issues. India is examining the GCC proposal on the tariff liberalization schedule with reference to Category A, B & C goods; finalization of initial offer list; GCC request to conduct negotiations on trade in goods at 8 digit level; GCC text; and the GCC

proposal to base ROO on change in tariff classification at 4-digit level or value addition (35% to 40%).[34]

The negotiations have been encountering a few difficulties such as over the need to agree on terms of engagement with the six countries simultaneously.[35] Similarly there have been differences over including petroleum and petroleum products on the negative list.[36] It has been reported that Saudi Arabia and the UAE refused the Indian demands. India has been seeking protection of its petrochemical industry. At the level of platitude the sentiments are high and the expectations are that by the end of 2012 there will be progress.[37]

With a view to arriving at a shared perspective, the India-GCC countries decided to have an annual political dialogue held alongside the United Nations General Assembly (UNGA) in New York. The September 26, 2003 initiative came from the GCC as observed by the Indian External Affairs Ministry: "The GCC decision regarding this dialogue constituted a clear political signal from the GCC to engage pro-actively, on a regular basis with India. Both sides recognized the significance of this dialogue, which marked 'a new era' in the India-GCC relationship."[38] The 6th round was held on 2 September 2011. The Indian side was led by the External Affairs Minister and the GCC was represented by the UAE Foreign Minister, (presently the Chairman of the GCC), the Deputy Foreign Minister of Saudi Arabia and the Secretary General of the GCC.[39] Presumably in these dialogues the GCC might have expressed its expectation for India to be a stake holder in their security regime. In bilateral meetings they have been asking the new Asian oil consumer to come forward. Even in America there is a view that the US should not bear the burden of ensuring oil supplies to Asian oil consumers.

High security salience has not only been undermining the growth of local institutions but is delaying the future evolution of the GCC beyond the rentier stage. This is detrimental to the interest of Asian stake holders including India. The present security architecture, heavily reliant on American support, is running out of steam both in terms of legitimacy and delivery. Consequently the region is looking for alternatives which need not necessarily be exclusive of the US. The new stakeholders, however, do not possess the wherewithal to replace present players. However, if the Asian players venture to move the goal posts in the security game, the regional security ambiance could contribute in the transition of the Gulf region into Asian space. The rules of the new game would demand strategic understanding among the leading Asian players to view their Asian engagement not as rivalry but as collaboration to optimize gains. The collaboration, however, is not in terms of supplier and consumer but in terms of Asian inclusive interdependence. Viewed within a holistic perspective, Gulf security becomes part of Asian interdependence. The framework of Asian interdependence would mean production networking from West to South, Southeast and East Asia. Correspondingly, the Pan-Asian security architecture will subsume the sub-regional security architecture including the Gulf security. This bold vision will assume bolder initiatives. In the context of the Gulf region, it means an Asian initiative to include Iran as a legitimate player in the regional ambiance, as well as providing a sense of collective security to Iran, thereby enabling the scaling down of the Iranian nuclear project. This would provide the GCC states with space to downgrade their security links with external countries and the reduction of the external military presence in the region. If this is accomplished in the first stage, the Asian initiative could be directed to facilitate Iranian engagement with Western withdrawal of sanctions and the recognition of Israel by Iran.

6. Conclusion

Along the axis of de-securitization, the incremental economic engagement would ensure that the Asian economies could facilitate trans-border projects, particularly the infrastructure of road, rail, pipe lines and power grids. Ensuring access to resources and the market, the cooperative endeavor of trans-border initiatives will rule out the possibility of being seen as power projection. Spelling out a strategic framework for realizing the Asian Century, an Asian Development Bank (ADB) study entitled *Asia 2050: Realizing the Asian Century* makes a strong case that leading Asian players have to recognize their positioning beyond the nationally defined agenda. The future growth of the national economies has to be seen within the Pan-Asian frame, more so when the West is facing its own structural crisis. A buoyant Asia will also contribute to the recovery of the West. The Asian growth story needs to move beyond being the manufacturing or service providing platforms. Asia needs to be the source of knowledge-generating processes. This requires huge investment in R&D across the Asian platform. A pan-Asian R&D infrastructure and networking along the production line could trigger it.

The major contention of this paper is that globalizing India's interests would be better served by Asia moving from its present location of a globally-defined geopolitical matrix to a regionally constructed geo-economic space. Since the latter is derived from globalization processes, these will not be mutually antagonistic. On the contrary, this will facilitate the evolutionary processes of globalization.

Being a leading Asian player, China is navigating Southeast Asia towards an Asian production network. India can visualize a similar role in West Asia, piloting the region towards an Asian regional knowledge network by situating research and development centrally in the Indo-Gulf space as the mover of India's engagement with emerging Asia.

Endnotes

1   *Asia 2050: Realizing the Asian Century* (Manila: Asian Development Bank, 2011), 1.

2   Joseph Nye, *Power in the Global Information Age* (Routledge, 2004).

3   India: A New Player in Asian Production Networks? UNESCAP http://www.unescap.org/tid/publication/tipub2624.asp

4   World Development Report 2009: Reshaping Economic Geography. World Bank 2009.

5   Asia 2050: Realising the Asian Century, 2.

6   Ambassador Shivshankar Menon, Closing Remarks at the 13th Asian Security Conference, IDSA. http://www.idsa.in/keyspeeches/AmbShivshankarMenon_13ASC

7   Ibid.

8   Paul Krugman, The Increasing Returns Revolution in Trade and Geography http://www.nobelprize.org/nobel_prizes/economics/laureates/2008/krugman_lecture.pdf

9   R. O. Koehne and J. S. Nye, Power and Interdependence. Third Edition. (Longman 2001).

10 E. Dieter, Innovation Offshoring and Asia's Electronics Industry: The New Dynamics of Global Networks. http://dieterernst.files.wordpress.com/2010/06/pdf42.pdf

11 Ibid.

12 Jawaharlal Nehru, Speeches, Vol. 1 (1946-49) and Vol. 2 (1949-53), Publications Division, Government of India (Delhi: Government of India, 1949 and 1953). Quoted in S. D. Muni, India's 'Look East' Policy: The Strategic Dimension. ISAS Working Paper No. 121, 1 February 2011, p. 5.

13 Speech by Foreign Secretary on India's Look East Policy at the10th meeting of the BMIC (Bangladesh, China, India, Myanmar) Cooperation Forum. http://mea.gov.in/mystart.php?id=530119048

14 http://mea.gov.in/mystart.php?id=50042439

15 Farooq Sobhan, India-Bangladesh Relations: Past, Present and Future. ORF Discourse Issue No 3, May 2008. Observer Research Foundation, New Delhi, p. 4-5.

16 http://www.thedailystar.net/newDesign/news-details.php?nid=220604

17 Yashwant Sinha's Speech at Harvard University, Cambridge, 23 September 2003. Quoted in S. D. Muni, Asean-India Relations: Future Directions. ISAS Special Reports, 25 May 2012. http://www.isas.nus.edu.sg/Attachments/PublisherAttachment/ISAS_Special_Report_05__-Asean-India_Relations_-_Future_Directions_New_25052012172612.pdf

18 Ibid.

19 "The joint statement, issued after the meeting of the US-Australia Ministerial Consultations in San Francisco, said "it Welcome (sic!) India's engagement with East Asia as part of its 'Look East' policy. Deepen strategic ties with India. Identify areas of potential cooperation between the US, Australia and India, including maritime security, disaster risk management and regional architecture."" http://articles.economictimes.indiatimes.com/2011-09-16/news/30165421_1_strategic-ties-trilateral-strategic-dialogue-maritime-security

20 http://www.aseansec.org/pdf/IAI_doc1_6904.pdf

21 The Government of India provided assistance for establishing the Lao-India Entrepreneurship Development Centre (LIEDC) at Vientiane, Lao PDR, in 2004. The establishment of the centres was facilitated by India with initial funding for necessary infrastructure and training for development. This initiative became the epicentre for similar centres in the CLMV region. Subsequently, similar Entrepreneurship Development Centers (EDCs) came up at Hanoi, Vietnam (in 2005), Cambodia (in 2006) and Myanmar (in 2009). These centres have not only helped creating a conducive environment for entrepreneurship development in their respective countries, but also helped each other in several different ways in introducing entrepreneurship training programmes for specific niche areas. http://www.southcases.info/casestudies/csasia05.php

22 http://newasiaforum.org/book_ASEAN_India_Vision_2020.htm

23 http://www.globalpost.com/dispatches/globalpost-blogs/india/india-look-east-policy-southeast-asia

24 Trade & The New Economic Geography of The Middle East. DIFC. http://www.difc.ae/difc/sites/default/files/DIFC_Economic%20Note10%20Final_1.pdf

25 Sanjaya Baru, 08 Mar 2010, Business Standard - Look West Policy. IISS The International Institute for Strategic Studies. http://www.iiss.org/whats-new/iiss-experts-commentary/look-west-policy/

26 India Needs New Look-West Policy: Vice President. http://www.thaindian.com/newsportal/business/india-needs-new-look-west-policy-vice-president_100462783.html

27 The report sectional heading reads: Gulf, West Asia and North Africa.

28 Gulf Cooperation Council Countries: Enhancing Economic Outcomes in an Uncertain Global Economy IMF 2011.

29 H. D. Evers, Knowledge Hubs and Knowledge Clusters: Designing a Knowledge Architecture for Development. ZEF Working Paper Series, 27. Department of Political and Cultural Change, Center for Development Research, University of Bonn, p. 4.

30 "According to the latest available official national data, unemployment rates among people age 15 to 24 between 2001 and 2009 were highest in Bahrain, 31 percent in 2001, followed by Saudi Arabia, 29.9 percent in 2009. Kuwait suffered 18.4 percent youth unemployment in 2005. In 2008, Qatar reported 7 percent unemployment among its youth. And the UAE indicated in 2005 that its youth unemployment rate was 8 percent. However, a labor force survey conducted in the UAE in 2009 revealed that the unemployment rate in the age group 15 to 19 reached 36.1 percent; among those age 20 to 24, it was 11.3 percent." Youth in GCC Countries: Meeting the Challenge. http://www.booz.com/media/uploads/BoozCo-GCC-Youth-Challenge.pdf

31 Trade and Capital Flows – GCC and India. May 02, 2012, p. 13. http://www.alpencapital.com/downloads/Trade%20and%20Capital%20Flows%20-%20GCC%20and%20India_Final_May%2002%202012.pdf

32 Ibid., p. 18.

33 GCC Healthcare sector projected to grow steadily, says Alpen Capital's latest GCC Healthcare industry report. 13 December 2011. http://www.alpencapital.com/news-article-2011-13-12.htm

34 http://meaindia.nic.in/staticfile/GulfCooperationCouncil.pdf

35 India-GCC to Ink Free Trade Agreement within a Year: CII. http://articles.economictimes.indiatimes.com/2012-06-27

36 India-GCC FTA hangs fire as UAE, Sarabia oppose petro product list.

37 GCC, India seen to sign FTA within a year. www.saudigazette.com Thursday, 28 June 2012.

38 "The political dialogue added a new dimension to the GCC India relations, and provided an institutional mechanism for a structured exchange of views on a regular basis for addressing issues of mutual concern. In fact, the very first dialogue focused on topical issues like Iraq, Middle East, terrorism, UN reforms etc. It also touched on multilateralism, NAM and OIC. The GCC Chairman's statement that UN Security Council should be expanded and India should be a member of the Security Council, constituted the first GCC expression and concrete outcome of the political dialogue process." http://mea.gov.in/staticfile/gccmarch2011.pdf

39 Ibid.

Bibliography

Books

Nye, Joseph. *Power in the Global Information Age*. Routledge 2004.

Koehne, R. O. and Nye, J. S. *Power and Interdependence*. Longman 2001.

Documents

Asian Development Bank. *Asia 2050: Realising the Asian Century*. Manila 2011.

Evers, H. D. *Knowledge Hubs and Knowledge Clusters: Designing a Knowledge Architecture for Development*. ZEF Working Paper Series, 27. Department of Political and Cultural Change Center for Development Research, University of Bonn.

ESCAP, India: A New Player in Asian Production Networks? http://www.unescap.org

World Bank. World Development Report 2009: Reshaping Economic Geography. Washington, D.C. 2009.

Journals:

Krugman, Paul. The Increasing Returns Revolution in Trade and Geography. *American Economic Review*, 99 no 3 (1999): 561–7.

Sobhan, Farooq. India-Bangladesh Relations: Past, Present and Future. *ORF Discourse*. Issue No 3. May 2008 p1-5

Electronic sources

Asian Development Bank. Emerging Asian Regionalism: A Partnership or Shared Prosperity. http://aric.adb.org.

ASEAN-India Vision 2020: Working together for Shared Prosperity. http://newasiaforum.org.

Baru, Sanjaya. 08 Mar 2010, Business Standard - Look West Policy. IISS The International Institute for Strategic Studies. http://www.iiss.org/whats-new/iiss-experts-commentary/look-west-policy/

Dieter, E. *Innovation Offshoring and Asia's Electronics Industry: The New Dynamics of Global Networks*. http://dieterernst.files.wordpress.com/2010/06/pdf42.pdf

DIFC. Trade & The New Economic Geography of the Middle East. http://www.difc.ae/difc/sites/default/files/DIFC_Economic%20Note10%20Final_1.pdf

Foreign Secretary Speech, *India's Look East Policy at the 10th meeting of the BMIC (Bangladesh, China, India, Myanmar) Cooperation* Forum. http://mea.gov.in/mystart.php?id=530119048

GCC, India seen to sign FTA within a year. **http://www.saudigazette.com.**

Gulf Cooperation Council. http://meaindia.nic.in/staticfile/GulfCooperationCouncil.pdf

Gulf Cooperation Council. http://meaindia.nic.in/staticfile/GulfCooperationCouncil.pdf

GCC Health Care Industry. www.alpencapital.com

IMF. Gulf Cooperation Council Countries: Enhancing Economic Outcomes in an Uncertain Global Economy. 2011

India - Bangladesh Relations. http://meaindia.nic.in

India-GCC FTA hangs fire as UAE, S Arabia oppose petro product list. http://www.financialexpress.com

India's Look East Policy Looking Good? http://www.globalpost.com

India needs new look west policy vice president, http://www.indiavideo.org

Initiative for ASEAN (IAI), Work Plan for the CLMV Countries http://www.aseansec.org

ITEC Programme for Entrepreneurship Development in CLMV Region http://www.southsouthcases.inf

Menon, Shivshankar, *Closing Remarks at the 13th Asian Security Conference*. IDSA New Delhi. http://www.idsa.in

Nehru, Jawaharlal, *Speeches Vol.1 and Vol. 2,* Publications Division, Government of India (Delhi: Government of India, 1949 and 1953). Quoted in Muni, S. D., India's 'Look East' Policy: The Strategic Dimension. ISAS Working Paper. February 2011

Saarc moves ahead for economic union. http://www.thedailystar.net

Sinha, Yashwant, Speech at Harvard University. Quoted in Muni, S. D., Asean-India Relations: Future Directions. ISAS Special Reports, 25 May 2012. http://www.isas.nus.edu.sg/Attachments/PublisherAttachment/ISAS_Special_Report_05__-Asean-India_Relations_-_Future_Directions_New_25052012172612.pdf

Trade and Capital Flows – GCC and India. www.alpencapital.com

US, Australia decide to deepen strategic ties with India. http://articles.economictimes.indiatimes.com

Youth in GCC Countries: Meeting the Challenge. http://www.booz.com.

Chapter Seven

India and the Emerging Gulf: Between "Strategic Balancing" and "Soft Power" Options

K. M. Seethi

1. Introduction

India's engagement with the Gulf region has become a subject of debates today in the context of the role and dynamics of the emerging economies (China in particular) in the region, as well as that of the long-term strategic and economic interests of the Unites States, Israel, Pakistan and Iran in the security architecture of the region. India's short-term economic strategies and soft-power options in the region have resulted in multi-level interactions. Yet, its medium and long-term strategy towards the Gulf as well as towards individual Gulf countries is unclear, perhaps due to the uncertain implications of the global recession and the changes underway following the Arab Spring. Thus, India's Gulf policy, as it has been evolving for the last decade, calls for an in-depth analysis of the relationship, against the backdrop of its foreign policy changes in the post-liberalization phase.

2. Trans-regionalism and India's Foreign Policy

During the last two decades, there has been a remarkable shift in India's foreign policy orientation following the change in the country's development paradigm in the 1990s. A notable feature of this shift has followed from the increasing openness on issues of trade and commerce. This has been evident in its engagements with all major regions in the world, including the Gulf.[1] The globalized world economy has obviously created a favorable environment for India which is marked by increased mobility of capital and technology, more competition, structural changes in manufacturing, and a proliferation of trade agreements.[2]

One of the striking characteristics of India's foreign policy engagements in the post-cold war period is its increasing commitment to trans-regionalism, a critical area of interaction in the world today.[3] Trans-regionalism is a dynamic process that involves the development and maintenance of common, yet flexible, links across regions where individual countries, communities and organizations operate and have close associate ties with each other in a defined mode. Trans-regionalism fosters expansion beyond the bounds of regionalism, responding to the changing trends of the world economy. This 'new wave' of international relations manifests itself in diverse forms of trading arrangements, such as in common markets, free trade areas, economic unions, and preferential trade agreements. Trans-regional arrangements are gaining ground in the present-day international system, prompting different levels of integration. They have significance across and within their respective continents. In many such groupings, India is a key player, such as in the BRICS forum (comprising Brazil, Russia, India, China and South Africa), the IBSA forum (India, Brazil and South Africa), the BIMST-EC forum (Bay of Bengal Initiative for Multi-Sectoral Technical and Economic Co-operation), and the IOR-ARC (Indian Ocean Rim Association for Regional Co-operation). India's signing of a free trade agreement with the Association of Southeast Asian Nations (ASEAN) and negotiations for a similar agreement with the European Union (EU) and the Gulf Cooperation Council (GCC) are other instances of trans-regional engagements.

Over the last two decades, India's trans-South Asian engagement has been promoted by policy planners and business stakeholders, with a view to examining the role and prospects of Indian capital and the Indian service sector beyond the traditional home region of South Asia. The notion of trans-regionalism in the Indian context has several implications. India has now acknowledged that the South Asian market is not only inadequate for the expansion of its capital, technology, trade and services, but also that the region does not provide a flexible political climate within which New Delhi can comfortably carry forward its economic and commercial transactions. Intra-regional trade in South Asia is too small (India's share is also very small) even after the establishment of the South Asian Free Trade Association (SAFTA). A strong case exists for more worthwhile trans-regional ties. New Delhi seems determined to reorient its development and foreign policy strategies so that these accord with changing global dynamics.[4] Under this new framework, India seeks to avoid conflict even with its traditional rival China, which is a key partner in BRICS, India's biggest trans-regional engagement today.[5] The relevance of trans-regionalism in India's emerging Gulf policy is thus obvious. India sees the GCC as yet another major regional grouping with which it needs to expand its trade and commercial ties.

3. Global Recession: India's Policy Responses

It is worth noting how the Indian government has responded to the challenges posed by the global financial crisis and the ensuing recession. It has seen the crisis as constituting an opportunity for exploring alternative channels of economic engagement, especially with emerging economies.[6]

The Indian government recognized that as long as the underlying structural problem of the world economy persisted, the economic situation would remain weak and unemployment might, in the words of the Indian Ministry of Finance, worsen to "politically unacceptable levels" adding to "social tensions and adversely affecting productivity and growth in the medium to long-term."[7] The Indian economy had already experienced a fall in the growth rate due to the slowdown in the world economy, intensification of the euro zone crisis and hardening of crude oil prices in the global market.[8] However, India appeared to be "reasonably confident" that its "underlying growth fundamentals remain firm."[9] According to the Government of India's Mid-Year Analysis 2011-12, "while India's and other emerging markets' growth prospects are undoubtedly still connected to the developed world, the setting has changed, dramatically. It is the developing world that is now driving world growth, from largely its own savings and domestic resources, and trading and growing with each other."[10] Thus, the Indian government sees the crisis as an opportunity to build new coalitions in international relations with the help of emerging nations such as China and Brazil.

The trans-regional grouping BRICS is seen as having great potential to harmonize the interests of the leading emerging nations. The government's *BRICS Report* of 2012 points out that the BRICS countries account for nearly 40 per cent of the world population, almost 30 per cent of the landmass, and a share in global GDP that shot up from 16 per cent in 2000 to around 25 per cent in 2010. As per the estimates of GDP in terms of PPP, China holds the second position and India the third among the G20 top ten in 2012.[11] The report says that in the post-global crisis world, the BRICS countries have a remarkable opportunity to coordinate their strategies to enhance their position as a grouping in the international economic and financial system.[12] It indicates that India, China and other countries in the grouping are expected to "increasingly harmonize and coordinate their policies with a view to sustaining their growth momentum and capacity to weather global turbulence," and further points out that the "real GDP growth in India and China remained impressive." The report notes that notwithstanding differences in macroeconomic parameters, there is optimism about their emergence based on their "respective durable comparative advantages."[13] The implication of this trans-regional grouping is obvious. India no longer considers China as a rival in its engagements across the world and the Gulf region is not an exception.

4. India's Gulf Policy

Currently, according to the *Annual Report 2011-12* of the Ministry of External Affairs, India's engagement with the globalized world seeks "to ensure an appropriate role for India in the international environment," "to maintain an atmosphere of peace, security and stability in the extended neighborhood," and "to enhance India's economic and technological development by leveraging external linkages." Situated as it is in "an extremely complex neighborhood," India considers "the promotion of a politically stable and economically secure periphery" as its "foremost priority."[14] The Gulf is certainly a critical factor in India's extended neighborhood and trans-regional engagements. In the wake of the global recession transcending across regions, as well as in the background of the uprisings in the Arab world such as Tunisia, Egypt, Libya, Syria, Yemen and Bahrain, India sees the Gulf within the perspective of its expanding geo-economic interests with the help of its 'soft power' assets in the region. The adherents of India's 'Look West' policy feel that India has not yet made the best of its soft power assets in the region and can do much more on this front.

The Gulf plays an important role in India's global links for a variety of reasons. The countries of the region constitute India's largest trading partner group in the world with a total trade exceeding $140 billion. The Gulf is also vital for India's energy security with more than 50 per cent of its crude oil needs met by a few countries in the region.[15] Having recognized the growing importance of energy security issues in the present-day world, and given India's burgeoning dependence on energy imports, the Government of India decided to upgrade the Energy

Security Unit in the Ministry of External Affairs to a full-fledged Division in 2009. This decision was taken with a view to making "sustained diplomatic interventions on energy security issues overseas, assisting the government's efforts to further diversify India's supply base for oil, gas and coal as well as other energy resources." The Energy Security Division is also expected to provide vital inputs "to articulate India's position on energy and food security matters in various multilateral forums like G-20, NAM, BRICS, IBSA etc."[16] The Gulf region is further significant for India due to the presence of more than six million Indian expatriates, whose contributions are seen not only through the looking glass of remittances and financial flows, but also from the angle of serving "as an important bridge to access knowledge, expertise, resources, and markets for the development" of India.[17]

The Gulf is considered to be a vital link in India's strategic chains. According to the Ministry of Defence, India's geo-strategic location, trade links and its exclusive economic zone (EEZ) connect its security environment directly with its extensive neighborhood and the regions such as the Gulf and the Indian Ocean. In an extremely globalized milieu, "these factors involve concomitant security concerns, responsibilities, and challenges."[18] The reference, obviously, is to the new challenges from piracy and terrorism which transgress regional boundaries and high seas. Added to these geo-strategic and geo-economic imperatives is the geo-cultural significance of the Gulf for India. The region is home to one of the world's great religions and for India, Islam is certainly a factor to be reckoned with, both at the domestic level and in its engagements with the Gulf and other West Asian countries. India is keen on ensuring that Pakistan does not take undue advantage of its Islamic identity in its dealings with the Gulf. Kashmir being a sensitive issue, India is well aware of the imperative of sustaining friendship with all countries in the region, given the history of Pakistan's campaign in the Organization of Islamic Conference (OIC). The long years of the Afghan war and the eventual rise of Taliban forces further reminded India of the need to be cautious on questions involving religion and ethnicity. India's guarded approach could, at best, be characterized as strategic balancing vis-à-vis the countries promoting/propagating different strands of Islam. It is within these challenges and opportunities that we need to analyze the different dimensions of India's engagements with the Gulf.

5. India and the Gulf: Emerging Trends in Economic Ties

India's relations with the Gulf states have assumed a trans-regional dimension today in the context of its fast expanding economic and trade ties, as well as due to pressing energy requirements. The countries of the region from Saudi Arabia to Qatar have varied socio-economic experiences and development trajectories. The vast resource base of the region had attracted the major powers and business firms long before the current spell of globalization. It had also intensified international migration, technology transfer, trade and investment. Thus each country in the Gulf is important for emerging economies like India and China which are dependent on the region for energy security and trade.

Saudi Arabia is the world's leading crude oil exporter and it has a resilient oil-based economy which is highly integrated into the global capitalist system. It holds substantial public assets abroad in the form of liquid reserves and other investments. Saudi Arabia is already India's fourth largest trading partner, besides being the largest supplier of crude oil to the country. India currently imports almost 23 per cent of its crude oil from Saudi Arabia. India's bilateral trade with Saudi Arabia exceeded $26.5 billion during 2011-12.[19] According to official sources, Saudi Arabia is the 11th largest market for Indian exports, accounting for 5.51 per cent of these exports.[20] When Saudi Arabia agreed to double its crude oil exports to India in 2011, it was predicted that this was "the first big step towards a strategic energy partnership" between the two countries.[21] For India, the strategic energy partnership as highlighted in the 2010 Riyadh Declaration (signed during the Indian Prime Minister's visit to Saudi Arabia in February-March 2010) was the beginning of an increased level of interaction in areas ranging from oil and natural gas, science and technology to banking and investment. Bilateral investment has also been growing substantially over the years, and there is a good synergy between Indian and Saudi firms. During the last decade, many Indian companies established joint venture projects, or fully owned subsidiaries facilitated by the new laws in place in Saudi Arabia. By the end of the last decade, hundreds of Indian companies secured licenses for launching joint ventures in sectors such as management and consultancy services, construction projects, telecommunications, information technology, software development, pharmaceuticals etc. In India too, there are several Indo-Saudi joint ventures or Saudi-owned firms in fields such as paper manufacture, chemicals, computer software, granite processing, industrial products and machinery, cement, metallurgical industries etc. The two countries also cooperate through institutions such as the India-GCC Industrial Conference, and processes such as the India-GCC Free Trade Agreement negotiations.[22] In the emerging scenario of economic uncertainty in Europe, the US and Japan, there is tremendous scope for diversification and deepening of Indo-Saudi economic ties, particularly in the field of investment. There are positive indications of Saudi investors looking seriously at enhancing the levels of investment in India in sectors such as infrastructure, tourism and real estate.[23]

Among all the GCC countries, India maintained the strongest politico-economic ties with the UAE over the last 40 years. The bilateral relations, which saw an additional upswing recently, cover the full range of economic, technical, social and cultural fields that are mutually beneficial for both. India and the UAE are each other's largest trade partners. During 2010-11, the trade between them crossed $67 billion and India and the UAE are currently making robust efforts to strengthen their ties further.[24] The relationship has evolved into a major partnership in the economic and commercial sphere with the UAE becoming the second largest market globally for Indian goods. Indian firms have become important investors in the UAE, and India is a significant export destination for UAE-manufactured goods. A part of India's exports to the UAE is also transshipped to other countries such as Saudi Arabia, Yemen, Iran, Pakistan, Afghanistan and Iraq, thereby opening up a regional market for Indian products.[25]

In tune with the emerging global realities, the relations between India and the UAE are gathering momentum today. The two countries have forged partnerships in the field of commerce and trade which are expanding, diversifying and emerging into a strategic partnership with emphasis on cooperation in defense, energy etc.[26] There is much scope for cooperation in technology transfer, R&D and for joint ventures, given the fact that India is set to become a major power in IT, space, pharmaceuticals, agriculture, and biotechnology. The UAE is also focusing on knowledge-based industries. Besides, the UAE is keen on investing in the tourism sector in India, one of the areas that has tremendous potential for future growth. It may be noted that India has recently taken further initiatives to promote trade and tourism, and signed agreements ending double taxation and boosting consular services—some of the issues that have long remained unsettled.[27] The UAE investors have already registered their presence in India with a substantial amount of money being pumped into areas ranging from energy, computer services and programming to construction and tourism, making the country the 10th largest foreign investor in India. During his visit to the UAE in April 2012, India's Foreign Minister S.M. Krishna said that given "the trajectory of India's annual growth of 7-8 per cent, India has to expand the imports of oil and gas sourced from countries like UAE with whom we enjoy extraordinary ties." [28]

Bahrain, an oil-producing island of about one million inhabitants that serves as a banking hub, has strategic importance in the Gulf region. Since February 2011, Bahrain has witnessed a series of uprisings triggered off by the movements in

Tunisia and Egypt. The Shiite-led opposition and demonstrators grew to such strength that Saudi Arabia felt compelled to send troops to support the conservative bulwark of the ruling Sunni minority in Bahrain. Meanwhile, Iran's declared support to the Shiite uprising in Bahrain generated different levels of response. While India preferred to maintain silence on the question, except in regard to issues related to the Indian expatriates, the US, Saudi Arabia and Pakistan viewed the events from the perspective of Iran's alleged ambitions in the region. However, the new policy regime in India and Bahrain's industrial diversification efforts are steadily increasing the momentum for economic cooperation between the two countries. India's bilateral trade with Bahrain reached $1.5 billion in 2010-11.[29]

India sees Oman as a 'strategic partner' and an entry point for wider commercial operations in the Gulf. The trade between the two countries, which has spanned centuries, saw a new dynamism in the context of globalization. Oman has enormous potential to work as a base for the greater involvement of Indian business activities in the GCC. The bilateral trade was $5.2 billion during 2010-2011.[30] At the end of last decade, India was the fifth largest source of imports into Oman after the UAE, Japan, the US and China. In 2010, India ranked second as a destination for Omani non-oil exports, after the UAE, and third as a destination for Omani crude oil exports. The balance of trade is in Oman's favor. In the case of FDI, there are around 1,500 Indian-Omani joint ventures with a total investment of $7.53 billion in which Indian participation was estimated to be $4.52 billion. Under the Indian Technical and Economic Cooperation (ITEC) program, India provides 50 slots annually for Omani nationals, to avail of training facilities in diverse areas. During 2011-12, 30 additional slots have been offered to Oman. There is also a vital Indian presence in sectors like oil and gas, mining, manufacturing, IT and telecom, power and water, construction, real estate and consultancy, warehousing, logistics, railway and steel. [31]

India and Kuwait have always maintained close and friendly relations and, over the years, the two countries have sustained shared perceptions on various regional and global issues. India has consistently been amongst Kuwait's top ten trading partners. As an important partner of India's energy security agenda, Kuwait provides 10-11 per cent of India's crude oil imports. The trade between the two countries has been increasing steadily and reached $12.27 billion in 2010-11.[32] Exports from India to Kuwait jumped by 150 per cent (to over $1.95 billion) in 2010-11. Many Indian and private sector companies are working in the petroleum and power sectors in Kuwait. Kuwait investment in India has been mainly indirect through portfolio managers—international investment companies or through Mauritius, Singapore or other countries providing tax breaks.

India and Qatar have a long-term relationship marked by commercial ties and people-to-people contacts. A few years ago, the two countries decided to upgrade the relationship to a strategic level. The areas of cooperation include energy, trade and investment, defense and security, civil aviation, human resource development etc. India's bilateral trade with Qatar increased from $1.2 billion in 2005 to $7.2 billion in 2010-11—an almost six-fold increase within a short period.[33] India has also emerged as the fourth largest export market for Qatar after Japan, South Korea and Singapore. India occupies the tenth position in Qatar's imports.

India's relations with Iraq have witnessed many phases of change and continuity during the last few decades. After long years of support for the Saddam regime, India eventually shifted to a policy of "supporting a free, democratic, pluralistic, federal and united Iraq." While actively supporting the ongoing reconstruction efforts underway in Iraq, India has been making efforts to enhance and diversify economic and commercial relations with the war-torn country. Bilateral trade with Iraq stood at $9.75 billion during 2010-11.[34] Iraq possesses the second highest reserves of oil and is also the third largest exporter of crude oil to India, after Saudi Arabia and Iran. Iraqi exports of 250,000 barrels per day of crude oil to India constitute one eighth of its total oil exports. Iraq is working hard to strengthen its revenues in the context of fluctuating oil prices by inviting global firms to extract its oil and gas. Iraq is now very much involved in rehabilitating its war-ravaged economy, oil refineries, power plants, telecommunications, hospitals, roads, railways, bridges etc. The country is also in need of food, medicine, and other essential commodities. Indian firms are well placed to take care of the opportunities that exist in Iraq today. The Iraqi government also invited Indian investments and sought diversification of the trade basket to enhance economic cooperation in areas such as food, construction, minerals, IT, pharmaceuticals, energy and automobiles. India is the preferred destination for Iraqis looking for medical treatment, higher studies and tourism. Under the ITEC program, India provides training to a large number of Iraqi civil servants. India also helped strengthen Iraq's healthcare system and a number of Iraqi doctors are now undergoing training in India. [35]

India's relations with Iran also saw a significant improvement during the last decade. However, there was apprehension in Tehran when India decided to support the Western-sponsored resolution in the International Atomic Energy Agency (IAEA) against Iran's nuclear program in 2005. India sought to convince the Iranian leadership about India's helplessness on the issue in the background of New Delhi's negotiations for a civil nuclear agreement with the US. However, over the next few years, India-Iran relations were strengthened through a series of high-level interactions and exchanges. Bilateral trade between the two countries shows a growth trajectory, registering 2.07 per cent growth during 2010-11. The total volume of trade stands at $14 billion. India's exports to Iran showed a 48 per cent increase during the same year. India is also dependent on Iran for 10-12 per cent of its oil imports.[36]

6. Indian Expatriates in the Gulf: Critical Challenges

Indian expatriates in the Gulf have a long history going back to the oil exploration days in the early part of the twentieth century. The character of the migration, however, has changed significantly since the 1970s when there was a substantial increase in the oil revenues of the Gulf states. The 'new' diaspora represented by highly skilled professionals moved to the Western world and semi-skilled and contract workers moved to the Gulf and other regions such as Southeast Asia.[37] However, expatriates in the Gulf have always been "in constant flux" due to "upgradation of the skill composition of the workforce," and the "continuous 'circulation' of migrants."[38]

Among all the Gulf states, the largest number of Indian expatriates is found in Saudi Arabia. There are about 2 million Indians in Saudi Arabia, constituting the largest single expatriate community in the country.[39] Over 70 per cent of the Indian expatriates are in the blue-collar category. Of Saudi Arabia's total migrant labor force, construction, wholesale and retail sectors account for 40 per cent and 25 per cent of the labor employed, whereas services account for 11 per cent. Of the Indian migrant labor force, 75 per cent are of the unskilled and semi-skilled category, mostly employed in construction and healthcare, maintenance and retail. A study conducted to assess the impact of the global recession on Indian migrant workers in GCC countries and Malaysia by ICOE concludes that "the impact of recession on the overall Saudi economy is negligible despite the impact on the retail and steel industries, primarily because the construction and the health-care sectors have remained unaffected—these two sectors account for the bulk of the employment of the Indian workforce."[40] The ICOE study says that construction and real estate projects are mainly state-controlled (as much as 90 per cent) and they remained unaffected as there was no shortage of state funds. It also noted that demands for residential and real estate have not been affected and there are large-scale infrastructure projects like economic cities, universities and real estate projects. The study, quoting a Saudi source, projected that as many as 11 million jobs would be generated by 2014. However, it acknowledged that a "perceptible impact of recession" has been seen in the steel sector, where of 15,000 workers employed, 7000 happen to be Indians, of which about 500 would have lost their jobs.[41]

While the global recession may have some impact on certain sectors in Saudi Arabia, the future of the Indian expatriate community in the country is also uncertain given the anxieties in the ruling circles over the tempo of events unfolding since the Arab Spring in other West Asian countries. The overall feeling is that the local people (particularly the emerging middle class) have become restive and are more aware of the challenges of the economic downturn in their daily lives. This has obviously put increasing pressure on the government to accommodate native people not only in the state-run sector but also in the private sector. As unemployment among the native population has been growing, the Saudi government has already decided to bring reforms into the labor market. The introduction of the "Saudization Policy" sought to create adequate employment opportunities for residents as well as reducing dependence on expatriate labor. The policy of Saudization seeks to encourage employment of Saudi natives in the private sector, which has been dominated by expatriates from South and Southeast Asia. However, the employment scenario in Saudi Arabia, shaped by the introduction of the Saudization policy, might remain complex given the comparative advantage in having expatriates in the labor market insofar as the employment of natives would cost more. Yet, the socio-political factors may favor the long-term employment of more indigenous labor and a reduced dependence on expatriates.[42]

The close links between the people of India and the UAE can be understood from the fact that the Indians constitute the largest single expatriate community in the UAE, numbering about 1.75 million.[43] According to official sources, the global recession has "served to strengthen the shift away from purely speculative activity without having a significant impact on the principal energy, infrastructure and real estate projects" being pursued in the country as "finance is available readily for such national development-related projects."[44] Although it was claimed that the crisis would be "unlikely to have any significant impact on the recruitment of Indians," reports have already appeared that many companies have started downsizing their budgets, having a significant impact on the employment scenario in the UAE. The ICOE study concludes that the impact has been "relatively limited" to some parts of some regions. While Dubai has been more affected, Abu Dhabi is in a relatively better position. The study noted that thousands of Indian migrant workers have gone back and the figure is likely to cross 200,000 in the near future.[45]

India-Bahrain relations are often characterized as "cordial" and "excellent." The presence of a 400,000 strong Indian expatriate community in Bahrain (which accounts for over a third of the total population) is an important factor in India's bilateral relations with the country.[46] The ICOE study says that the global recession had some impact on the construction sector. It was estimated that approximately 20,000 Indian migrant workers would lose their jobs, mainly from the construction sector. The study forewarned that Bahrain's economy would continue to worsen in the coming months. It also noted that there has been a significant reduction in the flow of Indian workers to Bahrain, a trend that would be likely to continue for some time.[47]

Over 700,000 Indians constitute the largest single expatriate community in Oman out of the total population of 3.2 million.[48] Of the 700,000 expatriates, there are 581,000 legally registered workers in Oman. Indian expatriates play a significant role in the realm of health and education in Oman. ICOE study says that of the 581,000 Indian workers in Oman, 75 per cent belong to the unskilled category, the majority of whom are in the construction sector. It says that the impact of the recession on construction was 'mild' and "no major retrenchment of Indians has been reported." However, the study says that the new inflow of workforce to this sector has been reduced. There has also been some impact on Indian workers in the automotive industry, whereas there has been no impact on the healthcare and education sectors. According to the study, the impact of recession on Oman has been "restricted to those projects which involved foreign/private investment. The construction sector was not hit as the majority of the projects were state-funded and they were "progressing normally."[49]

Numbering around 640,000, Indians constitute the largest single expatriate community in Kuwait.[50] They are working in all sectors of Kuwaiti society and make a significant contribution to the country's development. The total remittance from Kuwait to India is estimated to be around $3.5 billion annually. The ICOE study says that there has been a reduction in the pace of growth of Kuwait's economy since the beginning of the slowdown and the first few months were the worst affected due to the cancellation of refinery contracts and a reduction in the number of government tenders. Civil construction and financial services were the worst affected areas. It was anticipated that about 10,000 Indian migrants would lose their jobs and there could be further reduction in the flow of migrants to Kuwait in the ensuing months.[51]

The Indian community in Qatar is estimated to be around 500,000, the largest single expatriate community.[52] Indian professionals constitute a significant section of the expatriates. The annual remittance from Qatar to India is estimated to be over $1 billion. The ICOE study says that the impact of recession on Qatar's economy was limited. While some housing projects have slowed down, infrastructure, by and large, remained unaffected. The oil and gas sector also witnessed no significant impact. The study says that 90 per cent of the Indian community in Qatar is part of the workforce, 70 per cent of which is unskilled. Around 30 per cent of the Indian workforce belongs to the oil and gas sector, whereas the construction sector employs another 30 per cent. The study says that only 1,000 Indian workers were retrenched due to recession and there was no impact on remittances to India. However, it noted that "fresh inflow of Indian migrants to Qatar has been consistently declining since September 2008," and the report attributed the situation to the guarded approach followed by the local companies in employing workers.[53]

In short, the future of the Indian expatriates in the Gulf is contingent upon many factors, given the policy changes underway in the Gulf states as part of the indigenization drive. This is crucial in the emerging scenario given the fact that the number of Indian expatriates in the Gulf is above 6 million and the remittances are quite substantial. Currently, remittances account for about 4 per cent of India's GDP. Remittances to India as a percentage of GDP have also increased over time, and with the liberalization of India's economy (from 1.1 per cent in 1985, 2.8 per cent in 2000 to about 4 per cent in 2008). By the end of the last decade, the Gulf was the largest source of remittances to India—at about 40 per cent, which was estimated to be around $60 billion.[54]

7. The Gulf and India's Emerging Strategic Concerns

In the politico-security architecture of the Gulf, India's policy options are determined by a number of factors. India's geo-political setting connects directly to the security environment with its extended neighborhood, particularly the region of the Gulf and the Indian Ocean. India's maritime concerns are quite evident considering its 7,600 kilometers coastline and an EEZ of over 2.2. million sq.km. The Mumbai terror attacks obviously came as a wakeup call and, since then, India has been augmenting its coastal and maritime security. Added to these is India's location astride major commercial routes and energy lifelines in the Indian Ocean, namely, the Malacca Strait and the Gulf. Annually, $200 billion worth of oil passes through the Strait of Hormuz and $60 billion through the Malacca Strait.[55] Increasing piracy in this location surely calls for cooperation and collaboration between India and the Gulf states, given India's military infrastructure and naval capability.

The role of Pakistan and Iran in the Gulf states (such as Saudi Arabia and Bahrain) is also a major factor in India's security concerns. New Delhi perceives

Pakistan as the preferred choice of Saudi Arabia and Bahrain, given its geo-strategic and geo-cultural advantages, alongside Washington's approval of its role and capability. However, on the question of Iran, particularly its possible rise in the Gulf, India does not seem to share the concerns of the West. In the emerging scenario, India's policy option would be some sort of strategic balancing, seeking to ensure relative autonomy in its engagements with the Gulf states as well as with other extra-regional actors. India also tries to develop a strategic relationship with some countries in the Gulf (like Saudi Arabia and UAE) with a view to expanding its influence in the region.

India's relations with Saudi Arabia, which witnessed many facets of interaction in the past, have been making headway in the emerging politico-security situation in the Gulf. Though influenced critically by the US and Pakistan factors over the years, Saudi Arabia now recognizes that India could be a potential strategic partner, particularly in the context of Iran's ambitions in the region. Saudi Arabia does not approve of Iran's active role in the region for both religio-cultural and strategic reasons. It has reacted against Iran's alleged role in the unrest in Bahrain, and also against Tehran's nuclear ambition, which the West views with great concern. On the other hand, observers argue, the traditionally warm ties between Pakistan and Saudi Arabia are also poised for change ever since Osama bin Laden was killed by the US Special Forces in Pakistan. Saudi Arabia has reservations about Islamabad's role in the war against terror, especially in the background of the grenade attack at the Saudi Consulate in Karachi after bin Laden's death.[56] Saudi Arabia also knows that Pakistan's strategic ties with Washington have undergone changes during the last decade.

India views all these developments from a strategic perspective and within the framework of expanding its 'Look West' policy. Perhaps the most important development in India-Saudi Arabia relations during the last few years was the decision by the two countries to form a joint committee on defense cooperation to work out "the contours of the relationship." The decision was taken at a high-level delegation meeting held in Riyadh in February 2012 when the Indian Defence Minister A. K. Antony visited Saudi Arabia. The joint committee is expected to evolve plans for cooperation in numerous areas, including defense cooperation, signing of a memorandum of understanding on cooperation in hydrography, increased participation of both sides in training programs, joint military exercises, and the possibility of cooperation in defense industries.[57] Against the background of increasing incidences of piracy in the Indian Ocean region, the navies of the two countries agreed to cooperate in the high seas with a view to ensuring the safety and security of ships passing through the Arabian Sea and the Indian Ocean. Though it is too early to predict any major push in the Indo-Saudi strategic relationship, it is possible that the two countries may work out plans for defense cooperation given India's increasing capability in both conventional and nuclear spheres.

India and the UAE are also collaborating bilaterally and regionally in defense and security issues. Defense cooperation reached a new level with the first ever India-UAE air exercise and the India-UAE Joint Defense Cooperation Committee deliberations. It may be noted that the UAE had extended support to India on the issue of terrorism, particularly after the Mumbai terror attacks. Major areas of India-UAE bilateral cooperation identified in the defense field are: the production and development of defense equipment; joint exercises of armed forces, particularly naval exercises; sharing of information on strategy and doctrines; technical cooperation in respect of the Intermediate Jet Trainer etc. In recent years, bilateral Defense cooperation has been strengthened, notably in the field of defense training and the supply of defense inventory, besides regular exchange programs.[58]

Oman was the first GCC country with which India had developed defense ties. India-Oman bilateral defense cooperation has been growing over the years. The navies and air forces of both countries have conducted joint exercises from time to time. There is also an India-Oman Joint Military Cooperation Committee which meets periodically. India and Oman share concerns relating to regional and maritime security, particularly when incidents of piracy were taking place close to the Oman coast and had been spreading close to the Lakshadweep Islands. On the anti-piracy front, Oman has also extended the Indian naval ships berthing facilities for its operations. India has also entered into defense collaborations with Qatar and Kuwait. In most cases, all the Gulf countries have now recognized that India is capable of playing a significant role in the maritime security of the region.

8. India and the Iranian Dimension

India's ties with Iran have been rendered complex due to the Western dimension today because of concerns over Tehran's nuclear program as well as its solidarity with the Shiite uprising in Bahrain. The two issues involve the role and interests of regional and extra-regional actors such as the US, Israel, Saudi Arabia and Pakistan. While the US and Israel see a possible 'rise' of Iran in the context of their geo-strategic interests, Pakistan and Saudi Arabia perceive threats from Iran in terms of a possible geo-cultural and geo-economic shift, potentially leading to regime change. However, China does not seem to consider Iran as a potential threat given its economic and strategic links with the country. It is within these conflictual settings and perceptional differences that India is called upon to weigh its options. Many observers say that India's Iran policy reflects an element of autonomy, even defying the diktat of its strategic partners in the West.[59] Admittedly, on the Iranian question, India tries to maintain strategic balance given its energy dependence on the country.

It may be noted that under the US sanctions, India had to discard the Asian Customs Union arrangements to pay for its oil imports from Iran. It was reported that the alternative payment arrangement through Germany, Turkey and the UAE was not working well and hence India and Iran sought to settle for partial rupee payment for oil imports. Still, the rupee payment mode covers only 45 per cent of the oil bill and the balance of trade is basically in favor of Iran. In early 2012, the US was obviously angered by Indian Finance Minister Pranab Mukherjee's statement that India "will not decrease imports from Iran."[60] This was followed by reports that India was short circuiting the sanctions imposed by the West by paying for 45 per cent of its oil imports in rupees and seeking alternative ways to facilitate shipping lines transporting Iranian crude. Moreover, in March 2012, a trade delegation led by India's Commerce Minister Anand Sharma visited Iran and sought to strengthen business ties with the country. The proposal of the North-South Corridor, which seeks to convert Iran into a key transit hub for India's trade with Eurasia, has also been revived in this context.[61]

American officials and political leaders have already expressed their reservations about India's unwillingness to toe the US line on Iran. Nicolas Burns, former US Under Secretary of State and the principal negotiator on the nuclear deal, openly criticized India for its Iran policy. He said that India was "now actively impeding the construction of the strategic relationship it says it wants with the US." Burns also said that India's reluctance to go with the American-led sanction amounted to a failure "to meet its obvious potential to lead globally," thereby, in Bharat Karnad's words, "equating, in a spurious sort of way, India's leadership ambitions with toeing the American line."[62]

The situation, as it is, calls for a realistic understanding of India's compulsion in engaging Iran. As oil prices go up, India is much more constrained by the refineries set up specifically for Iranian crude. The Indian officials in Washington had already indicated that an "automatic replacement of all Iranian oil imports is not a simple matter of selection or a realistic option." If India is forced to find alternative sources of supply, this would require a major investment, in terms of setting up new refineries to process alternative types of crude oil. This is not feasible under the present economic conditions when India is facing an increasing budget deficit, high inflation, fluctuating GDP growth and FDI fall. Besides this, it is not all that easy for New Delhi to find adequate alternative sources of crude oil to make up for the possible loss of Iranian supply if the situation turns against India. Arguably, Saudi Arabia could be a potential source which could offer additional supply, but its capacity to go for a major push is doubtful given its existing commitment to global supply, the rising demand in countries like China and the supply gap arising from Libya's oil exports.

Under such circumstances, India's policy option is very clear—maintain strategic balance by sustaining its energy ties with Iran, without undermining its economic and security engagements with the US, Israel and Saudi Arabia. Iran also knows that India's vote on the nuclear question in the IAEA in 2005 was under pressure from Washington in the context of its own negotiations for a civil nuclear agreement with the US and that New Delhi cannot afford to alienate Tehran in the long-run. Though characterized as a "slap on the face of the US" or 'defiance' of the unilateral US oil sanction,[63] India's policy agenda has been set to ensure its energy security through short-term and long-term adjustments.

9. Conclusion

In summary, India's engagement with the Gulf has assumed multi-level significance in a trans-regional setting. New Delhi is extremely confident that at the politico-strategic level, India can do well with its strategic balancing, ensuring relative autonomy in its engagements with the Gulf states as well as with other extra-regional powers. Though the possibility of China emerging as a major player in the region is viewed with concern in some circles in India, it is highly unlikely that any single major Asian power can dominate the security architecture of the region given the Gulf states' monopoly in energy trade and their multi-level interactions. The role of Pakistan and China in the Gulf region could be seen as challenging (and therefore conflictual), but the fact is that all the stakeholders in India and the Gulf seek to explore more avenues of cooperation, and thereby sustain synergies of collaboration in diverse areas. China is increasingly seen (by the Gulf states as well as India) as a potential partner rather than a rival. Here trans-regionalism necessarily provides the framework of cooperation and collaboration.

Thus, India, in partnership with the countries in the Gulf, is well placed to explore the possibilities of expanding its economic engagement with the rest of Asia and the world. During the last few years, there has been an increasing tempo of events unfolding India's economic and strategic relationship with the Gulf at various levels and diversified ties in conformity with its 'Look West' policy. In fact, high-level interactions by way of mutual visits and signing of agreements contributed to strengthening India's engagement with the Gulf. It is also important to note that India's soft power assets can contribute immensely to the development of the Gulf region. India's soft power potential lies, among other things, in its democratic credentials, secular values, pluralistic society, considerable pool of skilled professionals, varied culture and, most importantly, comparative advantage in health, education, tourism etc. India's sectoral strengths, no doubt, appeal to the Gulf, which is looking for trade and investment opportunities in the services sector. The Gulf states have found India strong in information technology, services, construction, fishery, food processing, resources, capital, technology, manpower, knowledge and tourism. Many of the Gulf economies, including Saudi Arabia, the UAE, Qatar and Kuwait have abundant savings and find investment opportunities in India promising.

However, India will have to address some issues in the coming years, such as: shrinking opportunities in overseas employment; stringent immigration rules; an increase in the exploitation of migrant labor; job losses in the construction, manufacturing, finance and service sectors; a reduction in migrant earnings due to reduced overtime opportunities; an increase in working hours; an increase in illegal migrants and a lack of assistance on return etc. Considering all these, India will have to work out a detailed plan of action for both short-term and long-term requirements. It is very important to have the necessary mechanisms in place to identify countries and areas in the Gulf which have the greatest employment potential such as IT, hospitality, travel and tourism, healthcare, education etc.—the areas where India has tremendous soft power assets. Once identified, the government must formulate the necessary capacity building measures for these sectors. For instance, the UAE is seeking alternative sources of energy and is promoting wind, solar and nuclear energy projects. Similarly, Saudi Arabia is in the process of developing several economic cities and other major infrastructure projects, such as those in railways and transport. These are certainly some of the areas where India has comparative advantage and enormous potential to invest in and contribute to the development of the region. The government also needs to develop a comprehensive plan of action at home to meet any situation arising out of large scale job losses due to the unforeseen consequences of global recession and the policies favoring local citizens in these countries.

Endnotes

1   Hamid Ansari, "India and West Asia in the Era of Globalisation," in *India and West Asia in the Era of Globalisation,* ed. Anwar Alam (New Delhi: New Century Publications, 2008), 3-9.

2   Government of India, Ministry of Finance, "Text of the Intervention Made by the Union Finance Minister Pranab Mukherjee in the First Session of the G-20 Finance Ministers' and Central Bank Governors' Meeting in Washington DC," 19 April 2012 (23 April 2012). <http://finmin.nic.in/press_room/2012/FM_G20_FMs_CBGs_WashingtonDC.pdf (April 23, 2012)

3   K. M. Seethi. "Beyond Regions: Political Economy of India's Trans-South Asian Engagements," *South Asian Journal of Diplomacy*, 1(1) 2010:130-144.

4   K. M. Seethi and Vijayan P., "The Political Economy of India's Third World Policy," in *Engaging with the World: Critical Reflections on India's Foreign Policy,* ed. Rajen Harshe and K. M. Seethi (New Delhi: Orient Longman, 2005).

5   K. M. Seethi, "Emerging India and China: Potentials and Constraints," in *The Rise of China and India: A New Asian Drama,* ed. Lam Peng Er and Lim Tai Wei (Singapore: World Scientific Press, 2009).

6   Jayati Ghosh, "Global Financial Crisis and the Developing world," *Indian Journal of Politics and International Relations*, 2, no. 1 (January-June 2009): 76-95; also see C. P. Chandrasekhar, "Crisis as Opportunity: New Directions for Regulating Finance," *Indian Journal of Politics and International Relations* 2, no. 1 (January-June 2009):56-74.

7   India, Ministry of Finance, "Text of the Intervention."

8   Government of India, Ministry of Finance, *Mid-Year Analysis,* 2011-2012 (New Delhi: Department of Economic Affairs, Economic Division), <http://finmin.nic.in/reports/MYR 201112English.pdf>

9   India, Ministry of Finance, "Text of the Intervention."

10   India, Ministry of Finance, *Mid-Year Analysis.*

11   As per the 2012 estimates, India has overtaken Japan to become the third largest economy in PPP. The Economic Times, April, 19, 2012. The figures for 2010 are available in Government of India, Ministry of Finance, *The BRICS Report: Study of Brazil, Russia, India, China and South Africa,* New Delhi: Oxford University Press, 2012), <http://finmin.nic.in/reports/BRICS_Report.pdf>

12   India, Ministry of Finance, *The BRICS Report.*

13   India, Ministry of Finance, *The BRICS Report.*

14   Government of India, Ministry of External Affairs, *Annual Report 2011-12* (New Delhi: Policy Planning and Research Division, 2012), 1.

15   India, Ministry of External Affairs, *Annual Report 2011-12,*1

16   India, Ministry of External Affairs, *Annual Report 2011-12,*135.

17   Government of India, Ministry of Overseas Indian Affairs, *Annual Report 2010-11* (New Delhi: MOIA, 2011), 2, <http://moia.gov.in/writereaddata/pdf/Annual_Report_2010-2011.pdf>

18   Government of India, Ministry of Defence, *Annual Report 2010-11* (New Delhi: MoD, 2011), 2.

19   India, Ministry of External Affairs, *Annual Report 2011-12,* 44.

20   Government of India, Embassy of India, "India-Saudi Arabia Business Relations," January 18, 2012 <http://www.indianembassy.org.sa/Content.aspx?ID=784>

21   Rajeev Sharma, "India Gets Close to Saudi Arabia," *The Diplomat*, 27 June 2011, <http://the-diplomat.com/indian-decade/2011/06/27/india-gets-closer-to-saudi-arabia/>

22   Embassy of India, "India-Saudi Arabia Business Relations."

23   India, Ministry of External Affairs, *Annual Report 2011-12,* 44.

24 Government of India, Ministry of Commerce and Industry, *India's Foreign Trade: February 2012* (New Delhi: Economic Division), F. No. 1(7)/2011-EPL); also see India, Ministry of External Affairs, *Annual Report 2011-12*, 44.

25 UAE, Embassy of UAE in New Delhi, "UAE-India Relations," <http://www.uaeembassy-newdelhi.com/uae-indiarelations_index.asp> (April 24, 2012)

26 Embassy of UAE, "UAE-India Relations."

27 Joseph Mayton, "For the UAE, India is the World's Economic Powerhouse" Medialine, April 23, 2012, <http://themedialine.org/news/news_detail.asp?NewsID=34986>

28 Government of India, Ministry of External Affairs, "Visit of External Affairs Minister to United Arab Emirates," 14 April 2012, <http://www.mea.gov.in/mystart.php?id=530219220>

29 India, Ministry of External Affairs, *Annual Report 2011-12*, 41.

30 India, Ministry of External Affairs, *Annual Report 2011-12*, 43.

31 Government of India, Ministry of External Affairs, "India and Oman Bilateral Relations," <http://www.mea.gov.in/mystart.php?id=50044507>

32 India, Ministry of External Affairs, *Annual Report 2011-12*, 44.

33 India, Ministry of External Affairs, *Annual Report 2011-12*, 43-44.

34 India, Ministry of Commerce and Industry, *India's Foreign Trade*; also see India, Ministry of External Affairs, *Annual Report 2011-12*, 42-43.

35 India, Ministry of External Affairs, *Annual Report 2011-12*, 42-43.

36 India, Ministry of External Affairs, *Annual Report 2011-12*, 41-42.

37 Government of India, Ministry of Overseas Indian Affairs, *Annual Report 2010-11* (New Delhi: MOIA, 2011), 1, <http://moia.gov.in/writereaddata/pdf/Annual_Report_2010-2011.pdf>

38 Prakash C. Jain, "Globalization and Indian Diaspora in West Asia and North Africa: Some Policy Implications," in *India and West Asia in the Era of Globalisation*, ed. Anwar Alam, 171.

39 India, Ministry of External Affairs, *Annual Report 2011-12*, 42.

40 Government of India, Ministry of Overseas Indian Affairs, *Salient Points of the Study Conducted by ICOE through Dloitte Touche Tohmatsu India Pvt Ltd to Assess the Impact of Global Recession on Indian Migrant Workers in GCC Countries and Malaysia* <http://moia.gov.in/writereaddata/pdf/deloitte_study.pdf>

41 India, Ministry of Overseas Indian Affairs, *ICOE Study.*

42 It has already been noted by many that Saudi Arabia may prefer to hire the expatriate labour for the development process because of the higher salary that the natives might demand. Politically also, expatriates are more reliable because they cannot participate in any political activity, thereby escaping from the burden of handling labour unrest or unionisation. See Tim Niblock and Monica Malik, *The Political Economy of Saudi Arabia* (London: Taylor & Francis Group, 2007); Andrzej Kapiszewski, "Arab Versus Asian Migrant workers in the GCC Countries," *United Nations Expert Group Meeting on the International Migration and Development in the Arab Region* (Beirut: UN Secretariat, Department of Economic and Social Affairs, 15-19, May 2006), 1-20, <http://www.un.org/esa/population/meetings/EGM_Ittmig_Arab/P02_Kapiszewski.pdf>; Rodney Wilson et al., *Economic Development in Saudi Arabia*, (London: Routledge Taylor and Francis Group, 2004).

43 India, Ministry of External Affairs, *Annual Report 2011-12*, 44.

44 Embassy of UAE, "UAE-India Relations."

45 India, Ministry of Overseas Indian Affairs, *ICOE Study.*

46 India, Ministry of External Affairs, *Annual Report 2011-12*, 41; also see Government of India, Ministry of External, Affairs," India - Bahrain Relations," <http://www.indianembassybahrain.com/india_bahrain_bilateral_relations.html>

47   India, Ministry of Overseas Indian Affairs, *ICOE Study*.
48   India, Ministry of External Affairs, *Annual Report 2011-12*, 43.
49   India, Ministry of Overseas Indian Affairs, *ICOE Study*.
50   India, Ministry of External Affairs, *Annual Report 2011-12*, 43.
51   India, Ministry of Overseas Indian Affairs, *ICOE Study*.
52   India, Ministry of External Affairs, *Annual Report 2011-12*, 44.
53   India, Ministry of Overseas Indian Affairs, *ICOE Study*.
54   India, Reserve Bank of India, *RBI Bulletin*, 13 April 2010, <http://www.rbi.org.in/scripts/BS_ViewBulletin.aspx?Id=11116#S3?
55   India, Ministry of Defence, *Annual Report 2010-11*, 7.
56   Rajeev Sharma, "India Gets Close to Saudi Arabia."
57   "India, Saudi Arabia to set up joint defence panel, says Indian Defence Minister AK Antony," *The Economic Times*, February 15, 2012.
58   India, Ministry of External Affairs, "India-UAE Relations," http://www.mea.gov.in/mystart.php?id=50044537
59   P. R. Kumaraswamy, "India's Iran Defiance," *IDSA Comments*, March 19, 2012., Accessed April 28, 2012 <http://www.idsa.in/idsacomments/IndiasIranDefiance_prkumaraswamy_190312>
60   Jeff M. Smith and Sarah McKeever, "Iran: A test for U.S.-India relations," CNN World. Accessed April 29, 2012. <http://globalpublicsquare.blogs.cnn.com/2012/03/22/iran-a-test-for-u-s-india-relations/>
61   Smith and McKeever, "Iran: A test for U.S.-India relations."
62   Bharat Karnad "U.S. Wrong on India's Iran Policy," *The Diplomat*, March 19, 2012. Accessed April 29, 2012. <http://the-diplomat.com/2012/03/19/u-s-wrong-on-india%E2%80%99s-iran-policy/>
63   Kumaraswamy, "India's Iran Defiance."

Bibliography

Ansari, Hamid. "India and West Asia in the Era of Globalisation." In *India and West Asia in the Era of Globalisation*, edited by Anwar Alam, New Delhi: New Century Publications, 2008.

Chandrasekhar, C.P. "Crisis as Opportunity: New Directions for Regulating Finance." *Indian Journal of Politics and International Relations* 2(1) (January-June 2009): 56-74.

Cohen, Stephen Philip. *The Idea of Pakistan*. Washington: The Brookings Institute, 2004.

Ghosh, Jayati. "Global Financial Crisis and the Developing world." *Indian Journal of Politics and International Relations*, 2(1) (January-June 2009): 76-95.

Government of India, Ministry of Commerce and Industry. *India's Foreign Trade: February 2012*. New Delhi: Economic Division, F. No. 1(7)/2011-EPL.

Government of India, Ministry of Defence. *Annual Report 2010-11*. New Delhi: MoD, 2011.

Government of India, Embassy of India. "India-Saudi Arabia Business Relations." January 18, 2012. Accessed April 23, 2012. Accessed April 25, 2012. <http://www.indianembassy.org.sa/Content.aspx?ID=784>

Government of India, Ministry of External Affairs. *Annual Report 2011-12*, New Delhi: Policy Planning and Research Division, 2012.

Government of India, Ministry of External Affairs. "Visit of External Affairs Minister to United Arab Emirates." Accessed April 28, 2012. <http://www.mea.gov.in/mystart.php?id=530219220>

Government of India, Ministry of External Affairs. "India and Oman Bilateral Relations." Accessed April 29, 2012.<http://www.mea.gov.in/mystart.php?id=50044507>

Government of India, Ministry of External, Affairs. "India - Bahrain Relations." Accessed April 28, 2012. <http://www.indianembassybahrain.com/india_bahrain_bilateral_relations.html>

Government of India, Ministry of Finance. "Text of the Intervention Made by the Union Finance Minister Pranab Mukherjee in the First Session of the G-20 Finance Ministers' and Central Bank Governors' Meeting in Washington DC." April 19, 2012. Accessed April 23, 2012. <http://finmin.nic.in/press_room/2012/FM_G20_FMs_CBGs_WashingtonDC.pdf.

Government of India, Ministry of Finance. *Mid-Year Analysis,* 2011-2012. New Delhi: Department of Economic Affairs, Economic Division. Accessed April 23, 2012. <http://finmin.nic.in/reports/MYR201112English.pdf>

Government of India, Ministry of Finance. *The BRICS Report: Study of Brazil, Russia, India, China and South Africa.* New Delhi: Oxford University Press, 2012.

Government of India, Ministry of Overseas Indian Affairs. *Annual Report 2010-11.* New Delhi: MOIA, 2011.

Government of India, Ministry of Overseas Indian Affairs. *Salient Points of the Study Conducted by ICOE through Dloitte Touche Tohmatsu India Pvt Ltd to Assess the Impact of Global Recession on Indian Migrant Workers in GCC Countries and Malaysia.* Accessed April 29, 2012. <http://moia.gov.in/writereaddata/pdf/deloitte_study.pdf>

Jain, Prakash C. "Globalization and Indian Diaspora in West Asia and North Africa: Some Policy Implications." In *India and West Asia in the Era of Globalisation,* edited by Anwar Alam, New Delhi: New Century Publications, 2008.

Kapiszewski, Andrzej. "Arab Versus Asian Migrant workers in the GCC Countries." *United Nations Expert Group Meeting on the International Migration and Development in the Arab Region.* Beirut: UN Secretariat, Department of Economic and Social Affairs, May 2006. Accessed April 28, 2012. <http://www.un.org/esa/population/meetings/EGM_Ittmig_Arab/P02_Kapiszewski.pdf>;

Karnad, Bharat. "U.S. Wrong on India's Iran Policy." *The Diplomat* March 19, 2012. Accessed April 29, 2012. <http://the-diplomat.com/2012/03/19/u-s-wrong-on-india%E2%80%99s-iran-policy/

Kumaraswamy, P. R. "India's Iran Defiance." *IDSA Comments,* March 19, 2012. Accessed April 28, 2012. <http://www.idsa.in/idsacomments/IndiasIranDefiance_prkumaraswamy_190312>

Leghari, Faryal. "The Soft Security Threat: Linkages between Pakistan and the Gulf State." In *Gulf-Pakistan Strategic Relations,* edited by Faryal Leghari. Dubai: The Gulf Research Centre, 2008.

Mayton, Joseph. "For the UAE, India is the World's Economic Powerhouse." Medialine, April 23, 2012. Accessed April 28, 2012. http://themedialine.org/news/news_detail.asp?NewsID=34986

Meyer, Henry. "China and Saudi Arabia Form Stronger Trade Ties." *New York Times,* April 20, 2010. Accessed April 20, 2012. <http://www.nytimes.com/2010/04/21/business/global/21energy.html>

Niblock, Tim and Monica Malik. *The Political Economy of Saudi Arabia.* London: Taylor & Francis Group, 2007.

Seethi, K.M. "Beyond Regions: Political Economy of India's Trans-South Asian Engagements." *South Asian Journal of Diplomacy* 1(1) 2010:130-144.

Seethi K.M. "Emerging India and China: Potentials and Constraints." In *The Rise of China and India: A New Asian Drama,* edited by Lam Peng Er and Lim Tai Wei. Singapore: World Scientific Press, 2009.

Seethi K.M. and Vijayan P. "The Political Economy of India's Third World Policy." In *Engaging with the World: Critical Reflections on India's Foreign Policy,* edited by Rajen Harshe and K.M.Seethi. New Delhi: Orient Longman, 2005.

Sharma, Rajeev. "India Gets Close to Saudi Arabia." *The Diplomat*, June 27, 2011. Accessed April 25, 2012. <http://the-diplomat.com/indian-decade/2011/06/27/india-gets-closer-to-saudi-arabia/>

Smith, Jeff M. and Sarah McKeever. "Iran: A test for US-India relations." CNN World. Accessed April 29, 2012. <http://globalpublicsquare.blogs.cnn.com/2012/03/22/iran-a-test-for-u-s-india-relations/>

UAE, Embassy of UAE in New Delhi. "UAE-India Relations." Accessed April 28, 2012. <http://www.uaeembassy-newdelhi.com/uae-indiarelations_index.asp>

UAE, Ministry of Foreign Trade. "Ministry of Foreign Trade discusses ways to enhance cooperation with the Chinese Ministry of Commerce." March 23, 2012. Accessed April 28, 2012. <http://www.moft.gov.ae/en/det.aspx?detid=413&resourceid=30>

Wilson, Rodney et al. *Economic Development in Saudi Arabia.* London: Routledge Taylor and Francis Group, 2004.

Chapter Eight

The Economic Relations Between China and the GCC Countries Since 2008

Chen Mo

1. Impact of the Global Financial Crisis on the Economic Relations Between China and the GCC Countries

The global financial crisis started in September 2008 and originated from the United States of America, dragging down the world economy. It hurt the economies of the Gulf Cooperation Council (GCC) and China, and it influenced the economic relations between China and the GCC countries.

The crisis affected the GCC countries' economies in three different ways. First, it had a big impact on the GCC countries' financial sectors, decreasing foreign investment, depressing the stock market and bursting the real estate bubble. The fall in the assets of the sovereign wealth funds, for example, triggered the Dubai debt crisis. Second, the oil price declined, which reduced the exports of almost all of the GCC countries, except those of Bahrain. Third, the recession dragged down the pace of economic growth, contracting the market, reducing exports and imports, negatively affecting the construction engineering market, and causing several business failures.

The impact on the economic relations between China and the GCC countries came through the effects of the crisis not only on the economies of the

GCC countries but also that of China, where the trading and financial sectors were affected. The economic growth of the Chinese economy in 2009 was 8.7%, compared to 9.6%[1] in 2008. Trade between China and the GCC countries was reduced, engineering contracts were cut off, and investment decreased after the crisis. Despite the impact, the underlying trends in the economic relationship between China and the GCC countries are strongly positive and it is clear that their relationship rebounded after the crisis.

2. The Rebounding of Economic Relations between China and the GCC Countries in the Post-Crisis Era

The period since 2009 has seen an increase in demand in the global energy market and a rise of the oil price, resulting in a resumption of economic growth in the GCC countries. This has been positive for China-GCC economic relations. Four factors have underpinned the rebounding of the relationship: increasing demand for GCC countries' oil due to the rapid growth of the Chinese economy; the recovery of the GCC countries' economies; the complementary economic structures of the two sides; and the development of a strategic partnership between China and the Gulf Cooperation Council. These factors are covered in the section which follows.

2.1 China's Rapid Economic Development Increases Its Demand for Oil from GCC Countries

The rapid growth of the Chinese economy and its increasing energy demand has played an important role in the mutual economic relations between China and the GCC countries. As a developing nation, China has set economic development and the improvement of living standards as its long-term goals, resulting in a rapid pace of economic growth. The continuing economic growth has in turn pushed up the energy demand.

There are several factors which account for China's remarkable growth pace. First, China has a very strong manufacturing industrial sector which generates the major part of its wealth. Large-scale infrastructural construction in the energy, transportation and communication sectors has enabled the manufacturing sector to become one of the most significant components of China's economic growth. Second, China's economy has been significantly changed by another important component: trade. The low cost of labor and the relatively good market conditions have attracted a substantial amount of foreign investment, boosting the production of manufactured goods. This has led to a steady increase in Chinese exports.

Meanwhile, there has also been an expansion in high energy consuming industries such as steel, non-ferrous metal, building materials and chemical engineering. Currently, Chinese industrial energy consumption constitutes 70% of domestic energy consumption, and other domestic uses of energy have increased because of the change in living and heating conditions. Third, as the largest developing country in the world, China enjoys a natural momentum in economic development. With the world gradually returning to the track of economic recovery, China has seen an increasing growth rate. China's GDP increased by 10.4% in 2010 and 9.2% in 2011. It is clear that in the post-crisis era, China still has a fast pace of growth.

The sustained and rapid growth of the Chinese economy has led to an increasing demand for oil and oil products. The development of the automobile industry, at the same time, makes the same call. Because of the relatively limited oil production capacity in China, the increase in its own production of oil is not able to satisfy the increase in oil consumption, which has resulted in a huge supply and demand gap and an increase in oil imports. In 1990, China's oil import came to only 2.92 million tons, whereas in 2010 the total was 239.3 million tons. China has now become the world's second largest oil consuming country, which exposes it to security issues over its oil supply. In order to maintain its economic security, China requires a stable, long-term oil supply.

For two reasons, the Middle East countries currently account for the lion's share of China's oil imports and will continue to be the major source of China's oil imports for the foreseeable future. One reason for this is the size of their oil reserves and their capacity for exporting. This puts them at the center of global oil supply, and hence also of China's oil supply. In 2010, China imported 130 million tons of oil from the Middle East region (mainly the GCC countries), accounting for 47.1% of its total oil imports. The second reason is that China benefits from good political and economic relations with all GCC countries, providing a good basis for long-term supply. The Chinese government's growing concern for energy security has promoted the search for a stable long-term source of oil supply. (See Figure 8.1: 2008-2010 China's Total Value of Oil Imports, and Oil Imports from GCC Countries[2])

2.2 GCC Countries Put Themselves on the Track of Economic Recovery in the Post-Crisis Era

The economic recovery of the Gulf Cooperation Council countries has also played an important role in the mutual economic relations between China and the GCC. The recovery was not caused by the rising oil price alone, but nonetheless that was clearly the most important factor. The dynamics of the global oil market have been very favorable for the Gulf states. The marginal cost of global oil exploration, especially in newly explored oil fields, is climbing up to $70 per barrel, but production costs in the Gulf states remain relatively low. The GCC countries naturally earn higher rent revenues or profits when the global oil price is soaring. The high population growth rate in the GCC is also worth mentioning as it boosts economic growth by increasing the demand for commodities. (See Figure 8.3: GDP Growth Rates of GCC Countries[3]) This in turn provides more opportunity for trade between China and the GCC countries.

2.3 The Economic Complementarities Between China and GCC Countries Promote Bilateral Economic Development.

China and the GCC economies are complementary in the following three fields: trade, project contracting and bilateral investment. These are covered in the sub-sections which follow.

2.3.1 Complementarity of Trade

China and the GCC countries have considerable complementarity in international trade. In the light of the expansion in its oil imports from GCC countries, China has sought to balance its trade by boosting its exports to GCC countries. GCC countries' national economies depend critically on imports because of their relatively weak agricultural and manufacturing sectors. Typically, GCC countries import electromechanical products, transport equipment, financial derivatives, metal products, foods and fabrics, all areas in which China enjoys comparative advantages in production and export. The proportion of GCC imports accounted for by developed countries has plunged in recent times. For instance, the shares of the European Union, Japan and the US in the total trade of the GCC countries declined from 18.2%, 19.2% and 11.3% in 2000 to 15.5%, 12.4% and 8.0% in 2009. The shares of China and India meanwhile climbed from 4.1% and 2.5% in 2000 to 9.0% and 8.5% in 2009.

China-GCC trade has registered rapid development in the post-crisis era. From 2008 to 2011, the value of the bilateral trade increased from $92.5 billion to $133.8 billion, maintaining a high compound annual growth rate. China's exports to the GCC climbed in value from $38.7 billion to $46.9 billion, and imports from the GCC jumped from $53.7 billion to $86.8 billion.[4] In 2009, China became the GCC's third largest goods trade partner, remaining the largest source of imports and becoming the third largest export market of the GCC countries. Meanwhile, the Gulf Cooperation Council became China's sixth largest goods trade partner, remaining the sixth largest source of imports and becoming the eighth largest destination of exports.[5]

Oil has always been considered as the most crucial product China imports from GCC countries, and in 2009 oil accounted for 75% of the value of China's total imports from the GCC countries. Besides oil, petrochemical products are also significant products imported by China from the GCC countries. In terms of Chinese exports to the GCC, garments, textiles and electromechanical products are predominant. Electromechanical exports have grown particularly rapidly, constituting 30.4% of the total value of China's exports to the GCC countries in 2008, compared to 18.8% in 2000. Garments and textiles exports have grown more slowly, such that the proportion of exports to the GCC contracted from 41.8% in 2000 to 24.2% in 2008. In addition, the trade value of steel, transportation products, furniture and furniture parts and assembly, which China exports to GCC countries, is growing with a rising proportion in the total value of Chinese exports to the GCC.

Looking to the future, it can be predicted that little change will occur in the composition of the goods trade between China and the GCC countries. In the import sector, oil and oil products will still remain predominant in China-GCC goods trade, and in the export sector, garments, textiles and electromechanical products are also likely to retain the lead. China will maintain a promising, long-term trading economic relationship with the Gulf Cooperation Council due to the complementarity of their economic structures.

2.3.2 Complementarity of Project Contracting

The complementarity of project contracting between China and GCC countries is also evident. Due to the increase in GCC oil income and national plans for economic development, the market for project contracting has been enlarged. GCC project contracting is currently China's predominant market in foreign project contracting.

There are five factors underpinning development on the GCC side. The first factor is the increase in oil income. Oil income ensures the prosperity of the GCC countries' project contracting market, enabling large scale economic development. The soaring oil income has not only increased GCC countries' government expenditure, but also that of the royal family and businesses, so the economic foundations for project contracting are secure. The second factor is population growth and urban modernization. In the post-crisis era, the population of GCC countries, including both foreign and native residents, has continued to grow rapidly. Correspondingly, demand for services such as housing, transportation, hydropower, communications, education, or medical treatment has increased, as also demand for facilities for work, worship, leisure, entertainment, sports and shopping. Along with the growing population and increasing income comes a growing desire for high-grade residences, stylish architecture, landmark architecture, luxury office buildings, and new forms of transportation. The biggest GCC country, Saudi Arabia, for example, has 29 million permanent residents, and a significant portion of these are young people, who have an urgent need for housing. The populations of the UAE and Qatar have similar needs, and in these cases the lack of suitable land resources and the concentration of the population in coastal areas, have led governments to reclaim land from the sea for the construction of high-grade residences, providing ample opportunities for project contracting.

The third factor is the change in the economic development strategy. Although still setting economic diversification as their main strategy for economic development, the smaller GCC countries have in particular come to realize that the service industry is a critical area where they enjoy comparative advantage. In consequence, these countries have been seeking to develop as air and sea transportation centers, financial and trade centers, international exhibition centers and centers of Islamic culture. For such purposes, they have needed to build airports, high-ways, railways, pavilions, tourist sites, luxury hotels and office buildings, shopping malls, recreation facilities, and high-grade residences. They have also needed supporting facilities such as electrical and water plants. Saudi Arabia, meanwhile, has focused more on industrialization, making use of its abundant oil and natural gas reserves. For all these purposes, the project contracting market has expanded.

The fourth factor is the acceleration of economic integration. In 2003, GCC countries formed their own customs union, in which there was to be free trade. However, the lack of infrastructure and flow of production factors were a problem. Vast transportation projects were needed so as to enable benefit to be drawn from economic integration. In order to solve the problem of soaring electricity consumption and power shortage in some countries, the GCC countries initiated the Gulf Electrical Network in 2004. The railway project connecting Kuwait, Saudi Arabia, the UAE and Oman and the national railway projects of Saudi Arabia and the UAE are also critical to economic integration among GCC countries. All this has offered new opportunities in project engineering.

The fifth factor is the positive effect of policy changes in foreign investment, usually linked to accession to the World Trade Organization (WTO).

Foreign investments had previously been highly restricted by regulations and it was difficult for foreign contractors to enter the GCC market. After GCC countries had acceded to the WTO, however, the situation radically changed and this has enhanced the market for project contracting. Many barriers in the construction and contracting sectors were cleared so as to accelerate infrastructure development. Saudi Arabia, while negotiating WTO access, abolished the requirement for foreign contractors to have local agents and opened up the market for project contracting. Most of the unfavorable regulations which prevented foreign companies from coming into project contracting have now been cleared.

In project contracting, four factors have contributed to the development of a profitable market in the GCC countries. First, China's investment in the GCC countries has become the new growth point of its overseas project contracting. China's total contract value in the GCC has grown from $340 million in 2000 to $11.74 billion in 2008, with an average annual growth rate of 66%. Turnover also grew, from $100 million to $5.29 billion over the same period, at an average annual growth rate of 76%, exceeding the average annual growth rate of China's total overseas project contracting value (37%) and China's total overseas turnover (31%). In 2008, China was the fifth largest investor globally, with 6.5% of the top 225 project contracting enterprises of the Middle East.[6] Second, China is able to take on large projects in the GCC countries, due to improvements in design capability, construction and installation capacity. China's average contract value in the GCC countries rose from $4.72 million in 2000 to $527.0 million in 2008. China has invested in large rail projects in Saudi Arabia such as the Mega Light-Rail and the North-South Railway. PetroChina signed a $3.29 billion EPC (engineering, procurement and construction) contract in Abu Dhabi in 2008. Third, Chinese contracts have changed from mainly labor-intensive civil engineering and sub-contracted projects to capital-intensive projects such as petrochemical and water power. In such projects, China is now more likely to be the general contractor. Finally, Chinese enterprises are very competitive and therefore offer many advantages for the Gulf Cooperation Council's construction and engineering contract market.

In the competitive contract market, there are four factors which account for China's success. First, China has the advantage of being able to offer low-cost skilled and professional labor in labor-intensive industries in the GCC countries. Despite Saudi Arabia's labor localization regulations, native workers are not able to compete with the educational background and the motivation of the Chinese labor force. Chinese enterprises also have the advantage of a reputation for efficiency and for producing goods of outstanding quality.

Second, Chinese enterprises are able to offer advanced manufacturing, design and construction technology. This, coupled with lower production costs is advantageous for those industries with large infrastructures such as electricity and water supply, power transmission, port machinery, telecommunication and smelting, oil, highway equipment, hydraulic engineering, hydropower station and ports. China is a leader in large high-tech projects, especially electronic communication projects, due to accumulated knowledge and experience in these areas. China has made full use of its technical expertise in communications, electricity supply, power transmission and smelting on the international project contracting market. It is well placed to compete for large projects, and has the technical capability and know-how in new energy technologies, such as nuclear power, solar and wind energy.

Third, China, having started as a sub-contractor, has now progressed to adopting EPC contracting methods, assuming the role of the general contractor in designing, purchasing and construction. In Saudi Arabia most Chinese enterprises have adopted EPC, while a small number use subcontract, "package-workers" or rendering of services. Chinese contractors have already entered the field of oil exploration and development, natural gas exploration and development, development of petrochemical engineering, infrastructure construction, industrial and civil architecture, and road and bridge construction.

Finally, complete sets of equipment manufacturing are an advantage for China in the GCC's project contracting market. China is building its industrial chain in large-tonnage mechanical produce and complete sets of equipment manufacturing. Strong manufacturing capacity and reasonable prices contributed to China's ability to take charge of international contracting projects. In short, GCC countries have a healthy project contracting market and China is in a good position to realize its aim to expand its overseas project-contracting sector.

2.3.3 Complementarity of Bilateral Investment

China and the GCC countries have many economic complementarities in bilateral investment. From the perspectives of the GCC countries, there is an increasing demand for foreign direct investment. In practice, because of the economic recovery and soaring prices of energy and primary products in the post-crisis era, GCC countries' energy markets and resources have attracted a considerable amount of foreign direct investment. Improvement of the business environment and infrastructure and the commencement of energy and construction projects, have facilitated this increased investment in the GCC countries. In 2008, foreign direct investment in GCC countries reached $63.4 billion.

Capital inflow to the GCC countries is concentrated in the following sectors: the service industry, finance, transport, communication, real-estate, hydraulic engineering, petrochemical products and refining. The GCC countries require capital inflow for technological management. However, in the energy industry, there are strict prohibitions in foreign direct investment, especially in oil and natural gas exploration and development, so most foreign investment here takes place in the oil refining and petrochemical industries. Yet there are exceptions to this pattern: in Saudi Arabia and Qatar foreign investment is being attracted to the natural gas industry.

In general, it is evident that GCC countries have a positive attitude towards capital inflow, hence the encouragement of foreign direct investment. Countries that are open to foreign direct investment (FDI) have a relatively lighter market regulation and a relatively higher market demand, in order to encourage foreign investment. The economic diversification policy of the GCC countries is beneficial to Chinese enterprises. China has established a Foreign Investment Promotion Board, encouraging foreign investment in infrastructure development and construction projects, and this plays a role in GCC developments.

Under a relatively free market, the FDI of the GCC countries increased from $2.3 billion in 2001 to $63.4 billion in 2008, accounting for 32.5% of the FDI in West Asia in 2001, and increasing to 70.3% in 2008. Although the FDI of the GCC countries is a relatively small part of global FDI, it increased from 0.27% of global FDI in 2001 to 4.56% in 2008. This increase can be explained in several ways. First, the increasing demand for oil and natural gas products, with consequent investment needs. Second, the high oil price has boosted the GCC countries' economic development, therefore providing assurance and encouragement for investors. Finally, the privatization policy of industries in some GCC countries has created opportunities for foreign capital merger and acquisition.

Bilateral investment between China and the GCC countries has increased year by year in the post-crisis era. The relatively relaxed market regulation in GCC countries encourages foreign direct investments and therefore increases capital inflow. Although initially the proportion of China's investment in GCC countries was relatively small - under 1% per year of total Chinese investment overseas - it has continued to increase every year. Based on a mutually beneficial strategy, China's investment in the GCC countries concentrates mainly on the traditional energy exploration and development sectors and on the services industry. The GCC countries' investment in China has grown since 2003, increasing from

$790 million in 2003 to $7.76 billion in 2010. Saudi Arabia and the UAE remain the first and second largest investors. GCC countries' investments in China are mostly allocated through Sovereign Wealth Funds (SWF) and located in joint ventures. Since China has become the predominant country for foreign investment in GCC countries, the investment relationship with China has become more of a concern for the GCC.

GCC involvement in China has been enhanced as a result of Western policies in the Arab world after 9/11. The US and some European countries introduced new constraints on the inflow of capital and people from the Arab world, with the result that some petrodollars were then diverted towards other countries. The GCC countries looked to the East for new markets, particularly to China, which had undergone economic reform and had just joined the World Trade Organization. GCC investors, then, began to pay close attention to the finance, real-estate and petrochemical industry in China. Simultaneously, as the progress of China's market economy and financial system reforms deepened and opportunities for foreign investment increased, China became an important partner in the capital market.

Economic relations and cooperation between China and GCC countries, then, have continued to develop and strengthen. In summary, the mutually beneficial economic relations between China and the GCC countries in the post-crisis era have been significantly strengthened. Economic development in China and GCC countries has benefited through bilateral trade, project contracting and bilateral investment. Economic relations are likely to expand with the implementation of China's LNG development plan.

2.4 Development of the Strategic Partnership

The post crisis-era has seen economic recovery and growth in China and an increase in its demand for oil from GCC countries. Strategic and economic cooperation has strengthened market growth in both China and the GCC countries, creating a foundation for further development in trade. However, there are non-economic as well as economic reasons which have been furthering cooperation between China and the GCC countries. These will be outlined in the following sections.

2.4.1 China's Strategic Dependence on GCC Countries in Terms of Oil Imports

China depends on the Gulf Cooperation Council for the provision of most of its oil imports. This dependence is strategic as the oil is needed to supply China's growing energy demand. China's energy dependency on the GCC can be explained in two ways. First, the GCC countries are leading oil exporters in the global market. Sixty per cent of the oil fields around the world are located in the Gulf region, capable of producing more than 5 billion barrels. The GCC countries are renowned for their high reserves, high production, good quality oil, low cost oil export and easy accessibility for oil transfer. Up until 2010, 50% of oil consumed globally came from the Middle East—mainly from the Gulf Coast countries. In 2008, Saudi Arabia, the UAE and Kuwait were among the top 10 oil-producing countries, ranked as the first, seventh and eighth largest respectively. Saudi Arabia accounted for 13.5%, the UAE for 3.6% and Kuwait for 3.5% of the world's oil production.[7] Qatar, Saudi Arabia and the UAE were among the countries with the top 5 natural gas reserves. Qatar remains in the top 5 and is the largest exporter of liquefied natural gas (LNG). The US New Energy Plan states that the global economy depends on GCC countries, in which Saudi Arabia remains the key factor in maintaining a stable oil market. Reliance on overseas oil is 50% in the US, 60% in Western Europe and 99% in Japan, whose oil imports from the Gulf region (mainly from GCC countries) are over 25%, over 60% and over 80% respectively.[8] The Asian-Pacific region's reliance on imported oil is over 94%. Global demand for oil will increase with the global economic recovery; therefore, oil producers in the Gulf region—especially the GCC countries—will become even more significant in the international supply of oil and gas.

Second, it is very difficult for China to fulfill its demand for oil without imports from other countries. Since 1990, the soaring national oil consumption has widened the supply and demand gap. China became a net importer of oil in 1996 and has remained the world's second largest oil consuming country. Onshore oil, considered predominant in China's oil industry, accounts for 90% of the national crude oil output, of which 75% comes from eastern China. However, output in east China will not rise due to the depletion of oil fields. Although the West China region could be developed, there are factors which would make this very difficult, such as complex geology, an unfavorable natural environment and higher production costs in comparison to other local and global sources. Although China's oil and natural gas resources prospects are quite considerable in the East China Sea and the South China Sea, it is difficult for China to acquire offshore oil and natural gas because of unresolved territorial disputes with neighboring countries. Offshore oil extraction presents further challenges, as it needs high technology and is high risk. China faces difficulties importing enough oil from countries outside the Gulf Cooperation Council. Oil imports from Russia, Central Asia and Africa would not be sufficient to meet China's needs. Imports from Russia and Kazakhstan, furthermore, are restricted by limited production and/or transportation capacities. China's oil imports from Russia made up only 10.8% of total oil imports in 2010, far below the 47.1% from Middle Eastern countries.[9] Oil imports from Africa do not present a viable alternative, because of fierce competition and the dominance of Western oil corporations in the region. Therefore, China is fundamentally and strategically dependent on the Gulf Cooperation Council for oil imports in the longer term.

2.4.2 GCC Countries' Strategic Dependence on China in Terms of Oil Exports

A stable export market is essential for the GCC countries, as the oil industry is their main asset. They are strategically dependent on China for their oil exports. Although the US and European countries constitute significant oil export markets, these countries have been trying to reduce their reliance on Middle East oil since the 1970s, pursuing oil diversification policies. This has resulted in a decline in Western imports of oil from the Middle East. In 2002, for example, US oil imports from the Middle East countries made up only 22.9% of its total oil imports, and that of European countries only 32.2%. In 2010, US and European oil imports from the Middle East declined to 14.9% and 19.6%.[10] The main sources of US oil imports are now Latin America, Canada and Africa.

The international oil market is competitive in that new oil discoveries have been made in both Latin America and Africa. Despite having great potential in oil exploitation, GCC countries need to consider oil export markets other than the US and Europe in order to take advantage of opportunities. Although Japan is seen as an important export target country by the GCC, China as the world's second largest energy consumer has assumed greater importance. It is believed that China provides a safe haven for the investment of petrodollars and potentially as a market for petrochemical products. China's good record in project contracting in GCC countries has strengthened its reputation as a valued trade partner.

This mutual dependence between the GCC countries and China is beneficial for both. The establishment of a stable and cooperative relationship has improved the bilateral economy and trade between the two. The GCC countries rely on China and Asia for the continued stabilization of their oil export market.

2.4.3 China and GCC Countries Are Both Developing Nations

As developing nations, both China and the GCC countries face similar problems for which they both seek support. For example, China needs the support of the GCC in addressing the Taiwan Question, and GCC countries hope that China can play an important role in Middle East issues, especially the Arab-Israeli conflict and the dilemma over Iran's nuclear issue. Both China and the GCC countries need to adjust in order to resist the impact of financial crisis and climatic change. As developing nations in the G-20 major economies, China and Saudi Arabia have a common interest in the progress of global governance and protection of the interests of developing countries.

In conclusion, despite the global financial crisis, economic relations between China and GCC countries in the post-crisis era can still be viewed as promising. Energy and political security form the foundation of cooperation between China and the Gulf Cooperation Council. With common interests, governments on both sides will support and propel the development of links in politics, economy and culture. Economic complementarity and strategic partnership will underpin the improvement of economic relations between China and the GCC countries.

3. The Economic Relations between China and the GCC Countries Face Challenges

Although the economic relationship between China and GCC countries is growing, it nonetheless faces challenges which stand in the way of further development. First, China has an interest in the expansion of the range of investment in GCC countries, yet there are potentially lucrative areas which Chinese investors have difficulty in accessing such as the upstream industry and the financial sector.

Second, there are difficulties for foreign investors in some GCC countries, such as the guarantee system (which prevents the expansion of China's project contracting) and the complex processes involved in the development of exclusively foreign-owned enterprises. The bilateral investment stock and flow represents a relatively small part of foreign direct investment, which needs to be addressed in the development of economic relations between China and GCC countries.

Third, although the negotiations for a China-GCC free trade area agreement began years ago and has made remarkable progress, the China-GCC Free Trade Agreement (FTA) has still not been signed. The main Chinese reservation is that once market access is established, GCC petrochemical products may dominate the market with a detrimental effect on the Chinese petrochemical industry. This would lead to severe unemployment in China. The establishment of a free trade area is essential for the development of economic relations between China and the GCC countries, but pending this, good relations could help in creating solutions to such problems as arise.

Finally, there is competition in trade and project contracting between China and other oil importers, such as Japan, South Korea and India, all major trade partners of the GCC countries. In 2012, for example, South Korea began negotiations regarding oil field development with the Abu Dhabi National Oil Company (ADNOC) and also signed an oil supply deal with Saudi Arabia. In 2009, the GCC countries' most important trade partners were Japan (12.4%), South Korea (9.5%), China (9.0%), India (8.5%) and the US (8.0%). Their main export flows were Japan (17.0%), South Korea (13.1%), India (7.8%), China (7.7) and the US (6.5%).[11] (See Figure 8.4: GCC countries' major trade partners). As the EU countries are taken individually, the EU does not figure in this listing as a trading partner.

Economic relations between China and the GCC countries were influenced greatly by the financial crisis, which led to the contraction of bilateral trade, project contracting and investment. However, mutual dependence in oil trading between them has led to a deepening of economic complementarity. Although challenges remain, economic relations between China and the GCC countries continue to grow and have great potential for expansion.

Figure 8.1: 2008-2010 China's Total Value of Oil Imports, and Oil Imports from GCC Countries ($billions)[12]

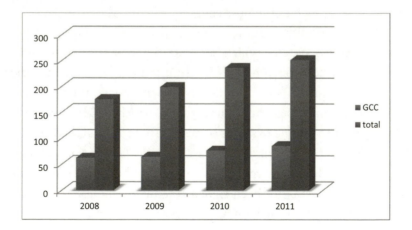

Figure 8.2: 2008-2011 Average Prices of Major Crude Oils [13]

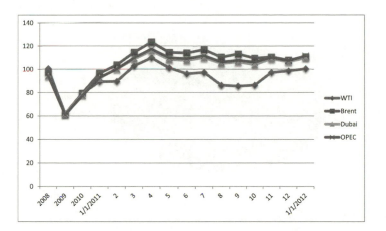

Figure 8.3: GDP Growth Rates of GCC Countries[14]

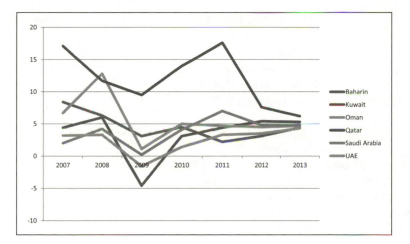

Figure 8.4: GCC Countries' Major Trade Partners

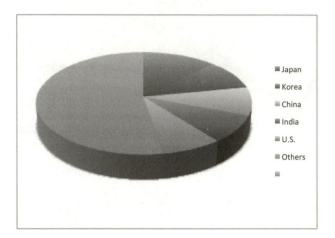

Endnotes

1 IMF World Economic Outlook, New Data, April 2010, p. 2.
2 China Customs Statistics Yearbook, 2010.
3 EIU Country Report, March 2012.
4 China Customs Statistics Yearbooks, 2008-2011.
5 IMF, Direction of Trade Database, July 17, 2010.
6 The Engineering News-Record, August 2009.
7 BP Statistical Review of World Energy 2009, p. 9.
8 US Energy Information Administration (EIA), Persian Gulf fact sheet, 2001.
9 China Customs Statistics Yearbook, 2010.
10 BP Statistical Review of World Energy, June 2011, p. 18.
11 IMF Direction of Trade database, July 17, 2010.
12 China Customs Statistics Yearbook, 2010.
13 Platt's Energy Price from Reuters.
14 EIU Country Report, March 2012.

Bibliography

1 Ahmad, Ehtisham, and Faris Abdulrazak. Al. *Fiscal Reforms in the Middle East: VAT in the Gulf Cooperation Council.* Cheltenham: Edward Elgar, 2009.
2 Yang, Guang. *The Report for development of Middle East and Africa.* China Social Science Documentation Publishing House. 2007-2011.
3 An, Weihua. *The New theory on the Gulf Oil, 2001.* China Social Science Documentation Publishing House. 2000.
4 Li, Yi. *The Security Situation in the Arab Gulf and China's Strategic Choices.* The world knowledge press. 2010.

5   Qian, Xuewen. *Study on the Development of Gulf Countries' Trade and Economy*. Shanghai: Shanghai Foreign Language Education Press. 2000.

6   Yang, Yanhong. *Gulf Countries' Petroleum and Gas Resources and China's Energy Security*. China's foreign economic and trade university press. 2010.

7   http://www.mofcom.gov.cn

8   http://www.stats.gov.cn

9   http://www.fmprc.gov.cn/chn/gxh/tyb/

10   http://www.bp.com/

11   http://unctad.org/en/Pages/Home.aspx

12   http://www.opec.org/opec_web/en/

13   http://www.imf.org/external/index.htm

14   http://www.cei.gov.cn

15   http://www.iea.org

16   http://www.eia.doe.gov/

17   http://www.amf.org.c\ae/

18   http://www.people.com.cn

19   http://www.oilnews.com.cn

Chapter Nine

China and Iran: Special Economic Partners

Huang Minxing and Ji Kaiyun

1. Background to Sino-Iranian Economic Relations

Iran is an economically important and politically significant Gulf oil-producing country. The character of its overall relationship with China is bound to carry weight for both countries, but also to have an impact on the wider region of the Middle East. However, it is the economic relationship which is fundamental. This chapter will focus on how this relationship has developed since 1979, and especially since 1990.

There are three aspects of the relationship which are worth highlighting at this stage. The first aspect is the manner in which market size and complementary structures provide a good basis for cooperation. On the one hand, Iran produces a good range of agricultural products and is a significant oil-producer with the world's second largest known oil reserves. Since the Islamic Revolution, it has suffered from Western sanctions of one kind or another, led by the US. It needs consumer goods of all kinds, in addition to capital goods, capital and technology. After long years of war with Iraq and the end of low oil prices on the world market, Iran has ample petrol-dollars but needs help in building up its weak infrastructure and improving its inefficient oil and gas industry. On the other hand, China is an emerging market, known as "the world's factory," and is an ideal supplier of commodities, equipment, technology and capital for Iran.

The second aspect is that the economic relationship benefits from a political convergence, given that both countries pursue a policy of "no interference in internal affairs" in relation to the other. Each respects the core interests and the development road of the other party. However, it is only in the last two decades that the relationship has been able to develop properly. After the end of the Cultural Revolution in China in 1976, economic development became the focal point of national policy, and China wanted to have good political and economic relations with all the countries in the world, including Iran. In the early years of the Islamic Republic, however, Tehran gave China the cold shoulder due to the latter's good relations with the Pahlavi regime before 1978. With the end of the Iran-Iraq War in 1988, Tehran tried to establish good relations with Europe, but these efforts ran into trouble over such issues as human rights and weapons of mass destruction. This led to the emergence of Iran's "Look Eastwards" policy. After being frustrated in trying to develop relations with Japan, Iran turned to China. As will be clear, political developments have determined the course of the economic relationship between the two. China has always resolutely opposed the US sanctions policy.

The exchange of high-level visits helped to promote the economic relationship. The visit of President Hojateslam Ali Akbar Hashimi Rafsanjani to China in 1992 was important, and even more so were the visits of President Seyyed Mohammad Khatami to China in 2000, and that of President Jiang Zemin's visit to Iran in 2002. In Khatami's visit, the two sides decided to establish "a 21st century-oriented long-term and wide-ranging relationship of friendship and cooperation in the strategic interests of the two countries on the basis of mutual respect for sovereignty and territorial integrity, equality and mutual benefit, and peaceful coexistence".[1] And during President Jiang's visit to Iran in 2002, a number of economic agreements were signed between the two governments.

The most important economy-related treaties and agreements concluded since 1979 have been in the following fields, activities and initiatives[2]:

1. Culture, science and technology cooperation (1983)
2. Establishment of a Joint Committee on Cooperation in Economy, Trade, Science and Technology (1985)
3. Reciprocal promotion and protection of investments (2000)
4. Cooperation in the oil sector (2002)
5. Long-term agreement on crude oil trade (2002)
6. Cooperation on plant protection and quarantine (2002)

7. Avoidance of double taxation and prevention of tax evasion (2002)

8. Maritime merchant shipping (2002)

9. Cooperation in telecommunications and IT technology (2002)

10. Establishment of the Iran-China Joint Trade Council (2002)

11. Aerospace (2004)

12. Chinese group travel in Iran (2006)

The third aspect, perhaps surprisingly, is that the developing role of women in the Iranian economy makes investment more beneficial than in some other regional countries. In the early years after the Islamic revolution in Iran, the new regime took a conservative attitude to women's employment. However, prior to 1978 women's overall social and economic level in Iran had been more developed than was the case in some other Gulf states, and in time the Islamic government began to adopt a softer approach. The Iran-Iraq war also played its role in this process of the relaxation of societal constraints, due to the need for manpower in wartime. As a result of this, Iranian women now work relatively freely, and this suits the interests of foreign companies in Iran, which are now free to employ female staff.[3]

2. Trade Relations between China and Iran

Trade is the main field of economic interaction between China and Iran. The main characteristics of Sino-Iranian trade since 1980 are covered in the sub-sections which follow.

2.1. Rapid long-term increase in trade

The past 30 years has witnessed both the rapid increase of Sino-Iranian bilateral trade and a general rise in the percentage of Sino-Iranian trade in the total value of China's foreign trade, as indicated in Chinese statistical data (Table 9.1). In 1980, the total value of Sino-Iranian bilateral trade was only $179.11 million. It rose to $361.97 million in 1990, and $29,391.08 billion in 2010, showing a 163-fold increase during the period.[4] To illustrate the nature of this long-term trend, we can divide the Sino-Iranian bilateral trade since 1980 into three periods.

The first period was from 1980 to 1991 and covers the early years of "Opening and Reform" in China. It was characterized by a low level of bilateral trade, fluctuations in the rate of annual increase, changing balances of surplus/deficit, and fluctuations in the percentage of China's total foreign trade accounted for by Iran.

All these characteristics are connected with the economic situation of China during this period.

The second period was from 1991 to 1999 and covers the most important years of the "Opening and Reform" period. It was characterized by the rapid growth of bilateral trade, frequently surpassing 50% per annum (but also registering decreases in two years).[5] A further characteristic was the substantial trade surplus which China enjoyed in this trade in the early part of the period, with this turning to a deficit in the final two years. These characteristics stem mainly from the changes which China's economy was undergoing at the time. China was now the new center of industry in the world, and an importer of oil after 1993. Iran, for its part, needed to import heavily in the aftermath of the Iran-Iraq war and ran a substantial deficit in its external trade in the early part of the 1990s.

The third period was from 2000 to the present and is characterized by an intensified growth of bilateral trade in most years. The percentage of the value of Sino-Iranian trade in the total value of China's foreign trade rose to 1 percent, with exports from Iran to China substantially exceeding imports from China. China, therefore, was now running a large deficit in its trade with Iran. Overall, it was clear that China and Iran had established close and complementary economic relations. Statements made by Chinese and Iranian government officials suggested that trade would increase (from $29.4 billion in 2010) to $50 billion in 2015, and then to $80 billion in 2030.[6] China has become an economic superpower, and this has had significant implications for its relationship with Iran. In 2002, China was Iran's 3rd largest foreign trade partner, and by 2011 had overtaken even the EU to become Iran's largest trading partner (See Table 1.9 in Chapter 1 of this book). In 2007, Iran became China's 2nd largest trade partner in the Middle East, and remained firmly in that position in 2011.[7]

2.2. Composition of Sino-Iranian Trade

Iran has been one of the main exporters of oil and other hydrocarbon materials to China, and a significant importer of Chinese manufactured goods.

In 1998, the percentage of manufactured goods exported to Iran was over 88 percent; declining in 2002 to 66.1%. The main elements of this were construction machinery and fully-assembled equipment (see Table 9.2). The most important products exported to Iran were: tractors, iron and steel products, motor vehicles, power generators, electric motors, building equipment, mechanical equipment, drilling equipment, tubing, phosphate, insecticide, clocks and watches, household appliances, articles for daily use, etc.

Oil is the most important commodity that China imports from Iran, and it has raised the importance of trade with Iran in China's total foreign trade, changing China's balance with Iran from surplus to deficit. In the 1980s, China was able to meet its own oil needs domestically and the small amount of oil imported from Iran was re-exported. After 1993 when China became a net oil importer, it was unable to handle the high sulphur content of Iranian oil, due to the limitations of its refining capacity. This changed after 1997 when many oil refineries with desulphurisation equipment were set up in China, and from 2000 onwards oil began to dominate China's trade with Iran. In 2000, the volume of oil imported from Iran was 7 million tons, making up 10 percent of China's oil imports; but in 2004, the volume of oil imported amounted to 13.2 million tons, raising the proportionate share slightly to 10.8 percent of total oil imports (Table 9.3). In 2001, Iran had surpassed Oman to become the leading Middle Eastern oil exporter to China for that year. Saudi Arabia, however, was also increasing its oil exports to China, and for most subsequent years China imported more oil from Saudi Arabia than from Iran. Nonetheless, in 2006 Iran was the world's leading oil exporter to China, ahead of both Saudi Arabia and Angola. In 2010, the volume of raw oil Iran exported to China stood at an annual figure of 27 million tons, placing it third in the ranking of oil exporters to China.[8] In the same year, China ranked first among the importers of Iranian oil.[9] Further evidence of the long-term strength of the oil-based relationship was the opening of a branch office of the National Iranian Oil Company(NIOC) in March 2009, and the Iranian plan to establish oil reserve bases in China.[10]

The key Chinese company involved in oil trading with Iran is the Zhuhai Zhen Rong Company, established in 1994. It is one of the four state-owned oil importers of China authorised by the government, and it began the import of crude oil from Iran after 1995. It is also one of the major importers of Iranian refined oil. In December 2002, Zhen Rong reached an agreement on the regular supply of crude oil with NIOC, and in March 2004, it reached a framework agreement with the National Iranian Gas Exports Company (NIGEC) on the cooperation of the import of liquefied natural gas (LNG).[11] In recent years, it has imported about 12 million tons of oil annually from Iran. It is also one of the major importers of Iranian refined oil.

There are, nonetheless, some other Iranian exports going to China – although in relatively limited quantities. These non-oil exports come mainly from the agricultural and mineral sectors. Among the products are sulphur, copper ore, refined copper, iron ore, bleach, chromium ore, zinc ore, building stones, raw cotton, raisins and pistachios. The only manufactured goods of importance are carbinol, vinyl chloride, polymers, and synthal.

2.3. Changing Actors and Forms of Sino-Iranian trade

In the bilateral trade between China and Iran, the government institutions have played a prominent role. Exhibitions have been one of the main channels for expanding non-oil trade. Since 2006, the Trade Development Bureau of the Ministry of Commerce of the People's Republic of China (PRC) held the annual Chinese Industry Expo-Iran. There have been 6 exhibitions to date.[12] In addition, Chinese companies take part in different exhibitions of special commodities, such as the Iran HVACR (Iran International Exhibition of Heating, Cooling, Ventilation, Air Conditioning, and Refrigerating Systems).

Research and discussion about bilateral trade by both governments and non-official institutions are an important force pushing for the sustained development of bilateral trade and economic cooperation. In January 2007, SUNTV, the Tidetime Group and the Iranian-Chinese Chamber of Commerce in Iran held the China-Iran Commercial Cooperation Forum in Tehran, to discuss the theories and the legal base for the development of bilateral trade and economic cooperation and to strengthen influence on the media. In Shanghai in May 2008, the Consulate General of Iran, the Centre for the Promotion of International Trade (Shanghai) and the Chamber of International Commerce (Shanghai) held a gathering entitled "Introduction to Opportunities of Trade and Investment in Iran". The purpose of this new platform established by both the Chinese and Iranian governments, was to introduce Iranian investment policies and opportunities of investment to Chinese business circles Laws and regulations on privatization in Iran were discussed with a view to advancing bilateral trade and investment between the two countries. As an example of the cooperation between Iran and local governments of China, the value of trade between Iran and Shanghai was estimated to have reached $480 million in 2007, an increase of 33 percent over the year before.[13]

Although China has an important position in the Iranian market, it also faces competition from other countries. It is difficult to document this in ongoing statistics, but lessons can be drawn from an analysis of trading developments between 1998 and 2002. Over these years there was a decrease in China's export of the following goods to Iran: mechanical and electrical products and meters, grain and product oil. The export of chemical, mineral and metal products remained unchanged and the export of textiles increased.[14] This is a pattern which has been replicated at other times, although not always quite so clearly. The decrease of mechanical and electrical products and meters was an indication that China had and continues to have strong rivals in trade with Iran; most household appliances sold in Iran, especially high end products, are imported from Korea and Japan, and most cars sold are from France or are produced in French-Iranian joint ventures locally. However, China's shares rose in goods such as textiles, as well as in agricultural products (see Table 9.2).

3. Investment and the Services Trade between China and Iran

In contrast to the trading relationship between the two countries, China is a much bigger investor in Iran than Iran is in China. Both governments, however, have given much attention to mutual investment. This has been done through a variety of channels. The two countries signed a Memorandum of Understanding on Cooperation between Cooperatives of the Peoples' Republic of China and the Islamic Republic of Iran on March 10th, 2009.[15] Among other items, this included aspects of investment. Trade fairs have also been used to promote investment. In May 2009, a China-Iran Trade Fair was held in Tehran, and nearly 500 enterprises (representing 300 or more Chinese and Iranian companies) were present.[16] In August 2009, a China-Iranian Kurdistan Trade Fair was held in Beijing, and nearly 40 Chinese and Iranian enterprises were present.[17]

Chinese investment in Iran has been expanding since the 1980s and has covered a number of different fields and industries, with a concentration on infrastructure and industry, spread across different regions of Iran. The most complete picture of how the investment has developed comes from the 2000-2007 period, although it is significant that even here information coming from different sources does not cohere. According to a Reuters report, based on information from the American Enterprise Institute, China was the biggest foreign investor in Iran during the 2000-2007 period, with a total FDI of $101.74 billion. The total Chinese FDI during the seven years included: $96.7 billion in the oil, gas and petrochemical industries, $620 million in the banking and exporting sectors, $3.38 billion in power, energy and construction and $1.08 billion in the transportation sector. France and Germany followed China in investment ranking in Iran.[18] Figures from China have been rather more modest, although still substantial. According to information recently acquired from the Economic and Commercial Counselor's Office of the Embassy of the PRC in Iran, China has had 31 major investment projects in Iran since the 1990s, with a total contract value of $23.83 billion.[19] In 2006, more than 70 Chinese companies were conducting economic and trade activities in Iran, and nearly 2,000 Chinese people were working in the construction projects connected with them.[20] In 2010, it was reported that there were more than 100 Chinese state companies operating in Iran.[21]

Iran's industry is becoming a new important field for Chinese investment, in a number of different categories, including petrochemical processing, machinery manufacture, the consumer industry and transportation. Chinese investment has also appeared in Iran's agriculture and tourism sectors. Such investment has covered transfer of skills, project contracts, training of manpower, purchase of the rights for resource mining, supply of investment-related equipment, and the establishment of production plants.[22] The main investors are state companies, which have established joint ventures in Iran.

China's engineering contracts and technical cooperation began in Iran after 1982. Currently, Iran is the country with the largest number of Chinese engineering contracts in the Middle East. In 2007, the turnover of these engineering contracts was $1,041.22 million, and it rose to $1,860.68 million in 2010. In the Middle East, only Saudi Arabia and the UAE had a larger number of Chinese engineering contracts in that year. Contracts were signed for 62 engineering projects with a total value of $11,474.36 million in 2009. This rose to 178 in 2010, but the total value of the contracts was only $1,293.55 million. There were 1,258 Chinese people working on the engineering contracts in Iran in 2007, rising to 2,246 in 2010. Only Saudi Arabia, the UAE and Qatar had larger numbers of Chinese workers on engineering projects in the Middle East.[23]

China's engineering contracts in Iran are mainly in the following areas:

1. Energy, including oil and gas development, refining and servicing oil and gas supply, thermal power stations and hydropower projects
2. Transportation, such as, construction of railways, subways, electrified railway and highway projects
3. The chemical industry, including petrochemical and chemical construction projects
4. Communications, including transmission machines, switches, and GSM digital communication equipments, etc.
5. Non-ferrous metals, such as construction and renovation projects for aluminum plants, zinc plants and copper plants
6. Shipbuilding - cargo ships, large tankers, LNG carriers, multipurpose vessels, bulk carriers, dredgers, etc.
7. Water conservancy, such as dam projects
8. Metallurgy, as in that involved in the construction and renovation projects of coking and steel plants
9. Building materials, including cement production lines.

Other contracts are connected with transport vehicles, home appliances, and the assembly and manufacturing of cars, motorcycles and home appliances, etc.

Some examples of the specific projects where China has been involved, in investment and contracts, are given below.

Yadavaran oil field. In October 2004, the Iranian Oil Minister Bijan Namdar Zanganeh and Chinese officials signed a memorandum of understanding with the total value of $70 billion. Under the memorandum, the state-owned SINOPEC Group would buy 250 million tons of LNG over 30 years from Iran and develop the giant Yadavaran oil field. Iran was also committed to exporting 150,000 barrels per day (bpd) of crude oil to China for 25 years at market prices after commissioning of the field.[24] Other Chinese companies like CNPC, Sinochem and CNOOC are also partners of the deal. On completion of the 2004 memorandum, SINOPEC and Iran signed a $2 billion agreement on developing the Yadavaran oil field, on December 9th, 2007. The field would produce 85,000 bpd in four years and a further 100,000 bpd in the following three years. Under the agreement, China would pay Iran as much as $100 billion over 25 years for LNG and oil and have a 51 percent stake in Yadavaran. The Iranian Constitution bars the sale of equity in the nation's oil and gas fields, and so SINOPEC will be compensated for its spending on the oil field, by a method known as "buyback."[25]

Azadegan oil field. This is one of the biggest oilfields to have been discovered anywhere in the world in the last 30 years. It has a 42 billion barrel reserve. Iran and Japan signed a contract worth $2 billion for the development of the Azadegan oil field in February 2004 and the field was projected to yield 260,000 bpd of crude oil by 2013. However, the Japanese company INPEX (International Petroleum Exploration Corporation), was reluctant to invest heavily because of the pressures exerted by the US, and in October 2006, the share of the company was reduced from 75 percent to 10 percent and 90 percent of the plan was given to the National Iranian Oil Company (NIOC). In January 2009, the China National Petroleum Corporation (CNPC) signed a 12-year $2 billion deal with the NIOC to develop the north Azadegan oil field. Under phase 1, capacity is expected to reach 75,000 bpd and phase 2 should double production to 150,000 bpd. [26] In August 2009, CNPC signed a new memorandum with the NIOC to invest $2.5 billion in the South Azadegan oil field on Iran's side of the Iraqi border. The field currently produces 55,000 bpd and it is expected to increase output to 320,000 bpd after the completion of the first phase of the project. The completion of the second phase will boost output to 600,000 bpd.[27] Currently, NIOC holds a 90 percent share in the project and INPEX holds the remaining 10 percent. Under the memorandum, CNPC will buy 70 percent of NIOC's share.[28]

Pars gas fields. These include the North and South Pars fields. The latter is the world's largest reservoir of gas and is shared by Iran and Qatar. SINOC signed a $16 billion contract in 2007 to develop both the upstream and downstream sections of the North Pars gas field, and in 2009, NIOC and CNPC signed a $5 billion contract for the development of phase 2 of the South Pars gas field, replacing the French company, Total.[29]

The Caspian Sea Republic's Oil Swap Project (CROS). The contract for this was signed in March 2000 between NIOC and three contractors: SINOPEC Engineering Incorporation(SEI), Vitol and Federal Asia of Hong Kong. The total investment was $150 million and the project has various sections including: the Neka oil terminal, Rey Blending Facilities, Tehran refinery and its expansion and Tabriz refinery. It was inaugurated in January 2001.[30]

Aras Khodro Diesel Automobile Assembling Factory. The project began in July 2004, and the China National Heavy Duty Truck Group (Sinotruk), in cooperation with Amico of Iran, would set up the Aras Khodro Diesel Assembling Factory in Tabliz. Later, Sinotruk signed another contract worth $350 million. According to the contract, it would provide 10,000 heavy duty trucks to the Iran Khodro Company (IKCO) in 2006, of which 8,000 would be Semi Knocked Down (SKD) for assembling. During this 10-year contract, Sinotruk will provide more trucks and help Iran to establish local marketing and an after-sale service network for its heavy duty trucks. [31]

Taleghan hydropower and water conservancy project. Sinohydro Corporation won the $150 million contract. The project included the construction of the dam and subsequent power generation work. It has a clay core rock-filled dam with a height of 101m and a length of 1,090 m. The underground powerhouse is 28.9 MW in installed capacity. Its functions are: the regulation of surface water of the Shahroud River, to meet the needs for irrigation, cities, hydropower and tourism. The project commenced in March 2002 and terminated in August 2006.

Tehran Metro. The metro consists of 4 operational lines. China's International Trust and Investment Corporation group (CITIC) was the overall contractor; China's North Industries Corporation (NORINCO) was responsible for the construction of the mechanical and electrical sections, and the Iranian companies the civil engineering etc. The project commenced in 1995 and in March 1999, an overland express electric train started a limited service. From 2000 onwards, commercial operation began on Lines 1 and 2. The Tehran Metro is now transporting about 2.5 million passengers daily through its 4 operational lines.

Iran's China Town of Commerce. This is a big shopping centre located in Anzali Free Trade-Industrial Zone near the Caspian Sea, and the contract value was worth 0.6 billion RMB yuan, with Zhejiang traders from China as investors. The work started in December 2006.[32]

China and Iran also have some agricultural cooperation projects, connected with: liquid pesticide, fruit and potato improvement, the production and packing of fruit, dried fruit, Chinese medicinal herbs and mushrooms, transformation of aquatic production, deep processing of agricultural and livestock products, papermaking from bagasse and straw, agricultural mechanisation, etc.[33]

In 2005, China listed Iran as a group travel destination for Chinese citizens. The Iranian government agreed to grant Chinese tourists a two-week landing visa preference. Since then, China Southern Airlines has opened flights between the two countries. In 2006, 16,000 Iranian tourists visited China.[34]

Iran also has some investment in China, which is relatively small. By the end of 2010, the total number and investment of registered enterprises with Iranian capital in China were respectively 207 and $731.95 million; and the number and FDI of utilised Iranian investment contracts in China in 2010 were respectively 61 and $17.86 million.[35] An interesting investment plan was the production of the Iran Khodro Company's (IKCO) Saymand car in China, and it, in cooperation with the China Youngman Automobile Group Co., Ltd., registered a joint car company in Shandong in 2006, with 30 percent of the funds of the new company.[36]

4. Overview

As mentioned above, close economic relations have developed between China and Iran in recent years, and such relations have played important roles on both sides. For China, Iran is a key provider of energy (oil and gas) and a significant market for Chinese goods and investment. Such relations have political effects, but it is wrong to think that China wants to make use of the relations to defy the position of the USA either in the Middle East or in the world.

For Iran, China has played a much greater role, particularly in the following areas:

1. Chinese goods have met the basic needs of Iranians. Unlike the commodities from Europe, Japan and Korea, many of the Chinese goods sold in Iran are cheap articles of everyday use. In practice, one effect of this has been Chinese commodities have played a role in reducing prices for Chinese consumers.

2. China is an important investor in the Iranian economy. This has been of increased importance as the sanctions imposed by the West have become harsher. As shown above, Chinese investment in infrastructure, energy and industry has been in sectors which are important for the development of the Iranian economy. There has had a generally positive effect on the development of these sectors, and has helped the industrialisation, urbanisation and improvement of the environment of Iran.

3. Trade and investment from China has had financial benefits for Iran. Firstly, the export of oil and gas is the most important source of financial income for Iran. Secondly, China provides loans to fund its exports to Iran and for engineering projects in Iran. Problems which Iran has encountered with obtaining hard currency to cover immediate importing needs have been overcome in this manner. China has at times, reduced Iranian debts in exchange for crude oil. Iran now accepts RMB as payment for some oil exported to China.[37]

4. China's exports to Iran, nonetheless, can also have a negative influence on small Iranian businesses. According to the Iranian media, one high-level official of the Ministry of Industries and Mines has said that the import of large quantities of Chinese textiles has been problematic for Iran's textile industry. The Iranian government therefore provided $200 million to transform its textile industry.[38] Other industries, such as the manufacture of televisions, have faced similar problems.

The difficulties which Chinese business has faced in Iran have in fact been substantial. International sanctions constitute a major problem for China in seeking to develop its relationship, although this is not entirely without benefit for China. Some Chinese companies have been sanctioned, for example, the Zhen Rong Company in January 2012. Other companies have problems in obtaining credit when banks are threatened by the West. This has led some companies like ZTE, the second largest supplier of communication equipment in China, to begin to reduce their business in Iran.[39] Another example is SINOC, which signed a $16 billion contract in 2007 to develop the North Pars gas field, but then took no action to start the project. After waiting for five years, Iran announced that SINOC's contract would be cancelled. However, SINOC has insisted that it wants to develop the field. Meanwhile, the fate of Phase 2 of Iran's joint South Pars oil and gas field, which is to be developed by CNPC, is still unknown.[40]

Problems are created by the shortfalls of, and chaotic competition between, Chinese companies and by cultural and language differences. For example, many

Chinese companies have little experience of overseas projects, and some have provided low quality goods to Iranian businessmen. Further problems are caused by factors specific to Iran, such as: inflation, weather conditions, public order, efficiency of staff, customs in negotiation and execution of contracts, corporate culture, technical norms, construction specification, limits on visas, subcontracting and the import of equipment.[41] Some Chinese scholars claim that this is the main reason for the failure to advance some of the Iran-China projects mentioned earlier.

To conclude, the Sino-Iranian economic relationship is a special and interesting case of South-South cooperation, and the two countries follow the principle of equality and mutual benefit. It is obvious that such a relationship has political meaning and has been influenced deeply by international politics. On the other hand, the EU, Japan, Korea, Russia and some Third World countries like India are also active economic partners with Iran, thus forming a delicate balance there. Compared with the economic relations maintained by these powers, China's relations with Iran are more comprehensive.

Table 9.1 Change in Total Value of Sino-Iranian Trade, 1980-2010   ($ million)

Year	Total value	Annual growth rate	China's exports to Iran	China's imports from Iran	The balance	% in China's foreign trade
1980	179.11		120.56	58.55	62.01	0.47
1985	191.50	1.3 [a]	87.62	103.88	-16.26	0.28
1990	361.97	13.6 [a]	318.43	43.54	274.89	0.31
1991	313.69	-13.3	293.18	20.51	272.67	0.23
1992	436.60	39.2	335.00	101.60	233.40	0.26
1993	712.71	63.2	402.69	310.02	92.67	0.36
1994	447.28	-37.2	265.75	181.53	84.22	0.19
1995	504.45	6.7	277.89	226.56	43.54	0.18
1996	780.00	54.6	394.00	386.00	8.00	0.27
1997	1,032.00	32.3	496.00	536.00	-40.00	0.32
1998	1,215.00	17.7	657.00	558.00	99.00	0.38
1999	1,347.46	10.9	662.74	684.72	-21.98	0.37
2000	2,485.47	84.5	713.41	1,773.06	-1059.55	0.52
2001	3,312.89	33.3	888.98	2,423.91	-1534.93	0.65
2002	3,742.05	13.0	1,395.63	2,346.42	-950.79	0.60

Year	Total value	Annual growth rate	China's exports to Iran	China's imports from Iran	The balance	% in China's foreign trade
2003	5,623.31	50.3	2,315.54	3,307.78	-992.24	0.66
2004	7,045.46	25.3	2,554.76	4,490.69	-1,935.93	0.61
2005	10,083.27	43.1	3,296.59	6,786.68	-3,490.09	0.71
2006	14,447.41	43.5	4,488.95	9,958.46	-5,469.51	0.82
2007	20,589.65	42.5	7,284.05	13,305.60	-6,021.55	0.95
2008	27,757.62	34.8	8,163.43	19,594.20	-11,430.77	1.1
2009	21,219.09	-23.6	7,919.11	13,299.97	-5,380.86	0.96
2010	29,391.08	38.5	11,091.99	18,299.08	-7,207.09	1.0

a. Average annual growth rate for 5 years.

Source: for data before 1996, see "Total Volume of China's Foreign Trade and Sino-Iranian Trade, 1950-95" (Chinese), Economic and Commercial Counselor's Office of the Embassy of PRC in Iran, last modified March 31st, 2003. Accessed at http://ir.mofcom.gov.cn/aarticle/zxhz/tjsj/200303/20030300078818.html; data for 1996-2010 are from the website of the National Bureau of Statistics of PRC, http://www.stats.gov.cn.

Table 9.2 The Proportion of Commodities China exports to Iran, 1998-2002 (%)

Year	Machinery and instruments products	Chemical products	Metal products	Minerals	raw materials of Textiles	Food	Refined oil	Others	Total value ($ 100 million)
1998	70.0 Product 28.0 Project 42.0	11.9	6.57	2.6	1.8	4.3		2.83	6.57
1999	58.0 Product 27.0 Project 31.0	17.4	5.55	4.0	1.05	3.49	9.2	1.2	6.627
2000	58.4 Product 33.0 Project 25.4	16.8	5.7	4.1	2.4	1.6	4.1	6.5	7.134
2001	49.5 Product 27.6 Project 21.9	17.1	9.1	6.0	8.8		2.5	7.0	8.89
2002	47.5 Product 20.1 Project 27.4	11.8	6.8	3.0	21.7		1.6	7.6	13.96

Source: "The Proportion of Commodities China Exports to Iran (a total of five years)" (in Chinese), Economic and Commercial Counselor's Office of the Embassy of PRC in Iran, last modified March 29th, 2003. Accessed at http://ir.mofcom.gov.cn/aarticle/zxhz/tjsj/200303/20030300078753.html.

Table 9.3 Oil Imported by China from Iran, 2000-2004

Year	Total Volume		Total Value	
	million tons	% of China's total oil imported	$ million	% of China's total oil imported
2000	7.0005	9.96	1,773	14.64
2001	10.847	18.00	2,424	20.69
2002	11.107	15.76	2,346	20.40
2003	12.390	13.60	3,008	22.76
2004	13.237	10.78	4,000	24.32

Source: "Sino-Chinese Trade Statistics, 1996-2004" (Chinese), Economic and Commercial Counselor's Office of the Embassy of PRC in Iran. Cited from Han Shaoqing, "Study on Iran's Investment Environment in the New Era and China's Investment Strategies in Iran" (Chinese, MA diss., Southwest University, China, 2008), 31.

Table 9.4 Iran's Top Oil Export Destinations, 2010

Countries	1,000 bbl/d	% of total
China	426	20
Japan	362	17
India	345	16
Italy	208	10
South Korea	203	9
Others	610	28
Total Exports	2,154	100

Source: "EIA Country Analysis Briefs: Iran", EIA, last modified Feb. 17th, 2012. Accessed at http://www.eia.gov/EMEU/cabs/Iran/pdf.pdf.

Table 9.5 China's Recent Business Activity with Iran (current dollar value)

Contractor*	Project Name	Amount	Last Action	Status
CNPC	CNPC to Develop North Azadegan Oilfield	$2 billion	01/16/09	Contracted
SINOPEC	SINOPEC - Gasoline Shipment to Iran	----	06/30/10	----
CNOOC	CNOOC -NIOC North Pars Oil and Gas Field Development	$16 billion	08/22/09	In Progress
CPTDC	China-Iran, North Drilling Company Oil Rig Deal	$143 million	03/06/10	----

Contractor*	Project Name	Amount	Last Action	Status
MCC	MCC to Build Steel Mill in Ardakan, Yazd	$203 million	08/01/09	Contracted
MCC	MCC, Iran Investment	----	01/18/10	----
SINOPEC	SINOPEC Upstream Operations Garmsar Block	$20 million	06/19/09	----
----	National Iranian Tanker Company - Chinese Firms, 12 VLCC Deal	$1 billion	08/26/09	----
SINOPEC	SINOPEC - NIGEC South Pars Phases 13 and 14 LNG Minority Stake Discussions	$2 billion	04/27/09	Discussed
----	Chinese Consortium in South Pars Phase 12 LNG Partnership	$3.39 billion	03/15/09	----
CNPC	CNPC Upstream Activities - Kuhdasht Block	$18 million	12/31/09	----
SINOPEC	SINOPEC - NIOC, Yadavaran Oil Field	$2 billion	12/10/07	----
SINOPEC	SINOPEC - NIORDC Abadan Refinery Expansion	$3.76 billion	07/24/09	Discussed
SINOPEC	SINOPEC Refinery MoU	$6.5 billion	11/30/09	----
Zhenhua	Zhenhua Heavy - Spain›s ADHK Provide Equipment for NIOC	$2.2 billion	07/29/09	Contracted
CNPC	SINOPEC, CNPC, Crude Oil Imports	----	11/11/09	----
CNPC	CNPC - NIOC South Azadegan Field Development	$2.5 billion	09/28/09	In Progress
CNPC	NIOC - CNPC, South Pars Phase 11	$4.7 billion	02/10/10	----

* CPNC (China National Petroleum Corporation); SINOPEC (China Petrochemical Corporation); CNOOC (China National Offshore Oil Corporation); CPTDC (China Petroleum Technology & Development Corporation); MCC (China Metallurgical Group Corporation; Zhenhua (Shanghai Zhenhua Heavy Industry Co., Ltd)

Note: all information here is drawn from the media reports cited on project pages, the database is representative rather than comprehensive.

Source: "Global Business in Iran Database", Irantracker, last modified May 10th, 2012. Accessed athttp://www.Irantracker.org/global-business-in-Iran.

Table 9.6 China's FDI to Iran, 2003-2010 ($ thousands)

2003	2004	2005	2006	2007	2008	2009	2010
782	1,755	1,160	6,578	1,142	-3,453	12,483	51,100

Note: Data in 2003-6 exclude financial investment.

Source: Ministry of Commerce of PRC, National Bureau of Statistics of PRC, and State Administration of Foreign Exchange, 2010 Statistical Bulletin of China's Outward Foreign Development Investment (Beijing: China Statistics Press, 2011), 36.

Endnotes

1   "Joint Communiqué Between The People's Republic of China and the Islamic Republic of Iran", Ministry of Foreign Affairs of the PRC, last modified June 5, 2002, http://www.fmprc.gov.cn/eng/wjb/zzjg/xybfs/gjlb/2818/2819/t16315.htm.

2   Information on the items listed here have been taken from Chinese official sources.

3   Interview with one staff member of Chinese company in Iran, December 16, 2011.

4   These figures come from Chinese government sources. The figures provided in IMF publications are slightly different, but show a similar scale of increase. For the IMF figures see Table 1.3, 1.8 and 1.9 in Chapter 1 of this book.

5   For the overall trend, see Tables 1.3 and 1.4 in Chapter 1 of this book.

6   In practice, the development of trade since 2010 has shown that such targets may be easily attainable. Table 1.9 in Chapter 1 of this book shows that, according to IMF figures, China-Iran trade had already reached $43.8 billion in 2011.

7   National Bureau of Statistics of PRC, China Statistics Annual 2007 (in Chinese), Beijing: China Statistics Press, 2007, 17, 18. See also Table 1.9 in Chapter 1 of this book. In practice China's trade with Iran is understated in the IMF statistics, given that part of China's trade with the UAE consists of goods which are then transhipped to Iran.

8   Hua Liming, "Sixty years of relations between the New China and Iran" (Chinese), *West Asia and Africa*, no.4, 2010.

9   "EIA Country Analysis Briefs: Iran", EIA, last modified Feb. 17, 2012, 4, http://www.eia.gov/EMEU/cabs/Iran/pdf.pdf.

10 The Iranian Oil Minister mentioned this in 2007, see "Iran hopes to have strategic oil reserve in China for oil export channel" (in Chinese), SOHU, last modified June 12, 2007, http://news.sohu.com/20070612/n250522282.shtml.

11 Shanghai University for Finance and Economics, Research Center for Top 500 Enterprises, "Zhuhai Zhen Rong Company" (in Chinese), last modified 2 September 2009, accessed at http://top500.shufe.edu.cn/upload/_info/50top/29862_0909020656061.doc

12 2012 China Industry Expo-Iran, "Review of the Previous Exhibitions" (in Chinese), last modified April 29, 2012, accessed at http://www.tdb.org.cn/exhibition/view.do?exhb_id=661924&id=124565

13 Report from Islamic Republic News Agency, Beijing, Saturday May 2, 2009.

14 "The proportion of commodities China exports to Iran (a total of five years)" (Chinese), Economic and Commercial Counselor's Office of the Embassy of PRC in Iran, last modified March 29, 2003, http://ir.mofcom.gov.cn/aarticle/zxhz/tjsj/200303/20030300078753.html.

15 "All China Federation of Supply and Marketing Cooperatives signed a memorandum of understanding on cooperation with the Ministry of Cooperatives of Iran", Jiangsu Supply and Marketing General Cooperative, last modified March 15, 2009, http://www.jsco-op.gov.cn/gxhzs/showinfo/showinfo.aspx?infoid=bcfbb5e8-481d-4c11-86ad-e7a6f30543d4&siteid=1.

16 Central Peoples' Government of the PRC, "China-Iran Trade Fair held in Tehran the Capital of Iran on 10th" (in Chinese), last modified May 10, 2009, Accessed at http://www.gov.cn/jrzg/2009-05/10/content_1309992.htm.

17 China Council for the Promotion of International Trade", "China-Iranian Kurdistan Trade Fair held in Beijing" (in Chinese), last modified August 18, 2009, Accessed at http://www.ccpit.org/Contents/Channel_67/2009/0818/201619/content_201619.htm.

18 "China tops Iran investor list", Payyand.com, last modified Dec. 13, 2007, http://www.payvand.com/news/07/dec/1127.html.

19 Arranged according to the data from the Economic and Commercial Counselor's Office of the Embassy of PRC in Iran.

20 "Domestic Situation is Stable, People don't believe in the Possibility of War" (inChinese), Tencent, last modified Feb. 8, 2007. Accessed at http://news.qq.com/a/20070208/002156.htm.

21 Ariel Farrar-Wellman, Robert Frasco, "China-Iran Foreign Relations", Irantracker, last modified July 13, 2010. Accessed at http://www.Irantracker.org/foreign-relations/China-Iran-foreign-relations.

22 Euro Asia Economic Forum and University of International Business and Economics "Chinese Enterprises Investment Rrport in Eurasian Countries, 2009-2011" (in Chinese), Beijing: UIBE,, 2011, p.303.

23 Ministry of Commerce of the PRC, National Bureau of Statistics, and State Administration of Foreign Exchange, *2010 Statistical Bulletin of China's Outward Foreign Development Investment*. Beijing: China Statistics Press, 2011. 667, 660, 679 and 675.

24 "China, Iran sign biggest oil & gas deal", *China Daily*, last modified Oct. 31, 2004. Accessed at http://www.Chinadaily.com.cn/english/doc/2004-10/31/content_387140.htm.

25 "Sinopec to develop oil field in Iran", *The New York Times*, last modified December 10, 2007. Accessed at http://www.nytimes.com/2007/12/10/business/worldbusiness/10iht-chioil.4.8675286.html.

26 "CNPC to Develop North Azadegan Oilfield", Irantracker, accessed May 23, 2012, at http://www.Irantracker.org/global-business-in-Iran/projects/cnpc-develop-north-azadegan-oilfield. The total value was $1.76 billion according to other sources.

27 "China to invest $2.5b in Iran's Azadegan oilfield", Payyand.com, last modified Nov. 26, 2002. Accesssed at http://www.payvand.com/news/11/feb/1257.html.

28 "CNPC signs pact to develop South Azadegan oilfield", *China Daily*, August 1, 2009.

29 "CNPC begins phase 11 of South Pars gas field", Emran Hussain, last modified Oct 18, 2010, http://www.arabianoilandgas.com/article-7951-cnpc-begins-phase-11-of-south-pars-gas-field/.

30 Wang Yi, "A Summary of the Work Process of the Overall Project of Transformation of Refineries in Iran" (in Chinese), Project Manager Union, last modified Nov. 28, 2007. Accessed at http://www.mypm.net/articles/show_article_content.asp?articleID=12128&pageNO=1.

31 "Sinotruk signed a big deal of 350 $ million with Iran Khodro Company", Ministry of Commerce of PRC, last modified March 13, 2006. Accessed at http://www.mofcom.gov.cn/aarticle/ztzzn/200603/20060301678729.html.

32 For the webpage of the company, see "Iran Anzali International I & T CO (LTD)" (in Chinese), accessed February 20, 2012, at http://www.iaci88.com/.

33 Han Shaoqing, "Study on Iran's Investment Environment in the New Era and China's Investment Strategies in Iran" (in Chinese), MA diss., Southwest University, China, 2008. 36.

34 The Embassy of the Islamic Republic of Iran in China, "Entering Iran" (in Chinese), no.2, 2007.24-26.

35 Ministry of Commerce of PRC, National Bureau of Statistics of PRC, and State Administration of Foreign Exchange, 2010 Statistical Bulletin of China's Outward Foreign Development Investment. Beijing: China Statistics Press, 2011. 646 and 638.

36 "Expose the 'Track' of No.1 Iranian Automobile Producer in China", Gasgoo Global Auto Sources, last modified May 21, 2008. Accessed at http://auto.gasgoo.com/AutoDetail.aspx?Idx=cdce18b8-813a-4db6-a032-dc1408a7672d&page=2.

37 "China buying oil from Iran — paying with RMB", Eideard, last modified May 10, 2012. Accessed at http://eideard.com/2012/05/10/China-buying-oil-from-Iran-paying-with-rmb/.

38 "Iran Plans to Increase Investment to Textile Industry to Improve its Power of Competition with China" (Chinese), Zhongguo Diyi Fangzhi Wang, last modified July 6, 2004. Accessed at http://news.webtex.cn/info/2004-7-6@51908_1.htm.

39 "ZTE corporation will reduce its business in Iran" (Chinese), Reuters (in Chinese), last modified March 26, 2012. Accessed at http://cn.reuters.com/article/ChinaNews/idCNCNE82P02L20120326.

40 "China Returns to Iranian North Pars While Problems Remain at South Pars", CIPE, last modified May 15, 2012. Accessed at http://www.cipe.com.cn/2013/en/News/IndustrialNews/524.html.

41 Xue Hua, "Opening and Development Tactics in the Market of Engineering Contract of Iran" (Chinese), International Economic Cooperation, no.10, 2006.

Bibliography

China Daily. "China, Iran sign biggest oil & gas deal." Last modified Oct. 31, 2004. http://www.Chinadaily.com.cn/english/doc/2004-10/31/content_387140.htm.

China Daily. "CNPC signs pact to develop South Azadegan oilfield." August 1, 2009.

CIPE. "China Returns to Iranian North Pars While Problems Remain at South Pars." Last modified May 15, 2012. http://www.cipe.com.cn/2013/en/News/IndustrialNews/524.html.

Economic and Commercial Counselor's Office of the Embassy of PRC in Iran. "The proportion of commodities China exports to Iran (a total of five years)" (Chinese). Last modified March 29, 2003. http://ir.mofcom.gov.cn/aarticle/zxhz/tjsj/200303/20030300078753.html.

EIA. "EIA Country Analysis Briefs: Iran." Last modified Feb. 17, 2012. http://www.eia.gov/EMEU/cabs/Iran/pdf.pdf.

Eideard. "China buying oil from Iran — paying with RMB." Last modified May 10, 2012. http://eideard.com/2012/05/10/China-buying-oil-from-Iran-paying-with-rmb/.

Farrar-Wellman, Ariel, and Robert Frasco. "China-Iran Foreign Relations." Irantracker. Last modified July 13, 2010. http://www.Irantracker.org/foreign-relations/China-Iran-foreign-relations.

Gasgoo Global Auto Sources. "Expose the 'Track' of No.1 Iranian Automobile Producer in China." Last modified May 21, 2008. http://auto.gasgoo.com/AutoDetail.aspx?Idx=cdce18b8-813a-4db6-a032-dc1408a7672d&page=2.

Han Shaoqing, "Study on Iran's Investment Environment in the New Era and China's Investment Strategies in Iran." (Chinese, MA diss., Southwest University, China, 2008).

Hua Liming. "Sixty years of relations between the New China and Iran" (Chinese). West Asia and Africa, no.4, 2010.

Irantracker. "CNPC to Develop North Azadegan Oilfield." Accessed May 23, 2012. http://www. Irantracker.org/global-business-in-Iran/projects/cnpc-develop-north-azadegan-oilfield.

Jiangsu Supply and Marketing General Cooperative. "All China Federation of Supply and Marketing Cooperatives signed a memorandum of understanding on cooperation with the Ministry of Cooperatives of Iran." Last modified March 15, 2009. http://www.jsco-op.gov.cn/gxhzs/ showinfo/showinfo.aspx?infoid=bcfbb5e8-481d-4c11-86ad-e7a6f30543d4&siteid=1.

Ministry of Foreign Affairs of the PRC. "Joint Communiqué Between The People's Republic of China and the Islamic Republic of Iran." Last modified June 5, 2002. http://www.fmprc.gov.cn/eng/ wjb/zzjg/xybfs/gjlb/2818/2819/t16315.htm.

Ministry of Commerce of PRC, National Bureau of Statistics of PRC, State Administration of Foreign Exchange. 2010 Statistical Bulletin of China's Outward Foreign Development Investment. Beijing: China Statistics Press, 2011.

Ministry of Commerce of PRC. "Sinotruk signed a big deal of 350 $ million with Iran Khodro Company." Last modified March 13, 2006. http://www.mofcom.gov.cn/aarticle/ ztzzn/200603/20060301678729.html.

Muslim Herald. "The trade volume between Iran and China will amount to $ 30 billion in 2009." Last modified May 9, 2009. http://www.muslimherald.com/news/China/22504076.htm.

National Bureau of Statistics of PRC. China Statistics Annual 2006 (Chinese). Beijing: China Statistics Press, 2006.

Payyand.com. "China to invest $2.5b in Iran's Azadegan oilfield". Last modified Nov. 26, 2002. http:// www.payvand.com/news/11/feb/1257.html.

Payyand.com. "China tops Iran investor list." Last modified Dec. 13, 2007. http://www.payvand.com/ news/07/dec/1127.html.

Reuters (in Chinese). "ZTE corporation will reduce its business in Iran" (Chinese). Last modified March 26, 2012. http://cn.reuters.com/article/ChinaNews/idCNCNE82P02L20120326.

SOHU. "Iran hopes to have strategic oil reserve in China for oil export channel" (in Chinese). Last modified June 12, 2007. http://news.sohu.com/20070612/n250522282.shtml.

Tencent. "Domestic Situation is Stable, People don't believe in the Possibility of War" (Chinese). Last modified Feb. 8, 2007. http://news.qq.com/a/20070208/002156.htm.

The Embassy of the Islamic Republic of Iran in China. "Entering Iran" (Chinese). No.2, 2007.

The New York Times. "Sinopec to develop oil field in Iran." Last modified December 10, 2007. http:// www.nytimes.com/2007/12/10/business/worldbusiness/10iht-chioil.4.8675286.html.

Top 500 Enterprises Research Center. "Zhuhai Zhen Rong Company" (Chinese). Last modified Sep. 2, 2009. http://top500.shufe.edu.cn/upload/_info/500top/29862_0909020656061.doc.

Wang Yi. "A Summary of the Work Process of the Overall Project of Transformation of Refineries in Iran" (Chinese). Project Manager Union. Last modified Nov. 28, 2007. http://www.mypm.net/ articles/show_article_content.asp?articleID=12128&pageNO=1.

Xue Hua. "Opening and Development Tactics in the Market of Engineering Contract of Iran" (Chinese). International Economic Cooperation. No.10, 2006.

Zhongguo Diyi Fangzhi Wang. "Iran Plans to Increase Investment to Textile Industry to Improve its Power of Competition with China" (Chinese). Last modified July 6, 2004. http://news.webtex. cn/info/2004-7-6@51908_1.htm.

Chapter Ten

Mobilizing the Muslim Minority, Targeting Arab Trade: China's Ningxia as the Islamic Hub for China-Arab Connections

Ho Wai-Yip

1. Introduction: the China Model in the Arab World

In the midst of China's rise, China's developmental model of economic success without political reform in the past thirty years posed a challenge to the Western modernization model, by which economic development and political democratization are seen as interrelated and inseparable. The 'China Model' emphasizes the possibility of a free market economy and an authoritarian regime co-existing (Zhao 2010). The developmental path of the China Model, now upgraded to the 'Beijing Consensus', is set against the 'Washington Consensus'. In Africa and the Middle East, China's increasing influence and presence have raised the question whether China will become the next colonizer in exploiting local energy and natural resources, thereby replicating the Western imperial legacy. Whether or not China is becoming the next hegemonic power in Africa and the Middle East requires extensive research and analysis. This chapter suggests, however, that China has been developing its own logic in engaging with the Middle East. In forging a closer link with the Middle East, the Chinese government has necessarily become more aware of Islam as a monotheistic belief which defines the cultural identity of Arab Muslims, provides an ethical norm for the social structure of Arab societies and shapes national behavior and foreign policy. While China's current outward-looking policy puts emphasis on China 'going global', this chapter argues that China's deepening engagement in the Muslim world has also unintentionally driven an inward-looking or 'going local' process within the country. Dialectically, the Chinese government has come to recognize the importance of the cultural heritage of its own Muslim minorities in order to build stronger China-Middle East relations. Take, for example, Chinese companies' recent involvement in building the Al-Mashaaer Al-Mugaddassah Metro (Mecca Metro). This railway project facilitates the annual Hajj pilgrimage of Muslims worldwide to the holy places in Mecca. Non-Muslims are not allowed to access the holy places[1], bringing the Chinese Railway Construction Corporation a serious problem in recruiting quality Muslim railway engineers and workers. The Chinese government and the Corporation were inevitably forced to recruit Muslim workers in China; a news source even reported that China simply converted hundreds of workers to Islam to access the holy areas in order to finish the Mecca Metro project.[2]

In this sense, local Muslim minorities weigh strongly in China's diplomatic and outreach mission to the Muslim world. In forging a stronger China-Arab economic ties and re-imagining the primordial Silk Road trade route, China's own Muslim minorities are essential in building the bridge. In view of the flourishing connections between China and the Muslim world, this chapter argues that the Chinese government has strategically deployed Muslim minorities within China and expanded alliances with Southeast Asia to foster Sino-Islamic collaboration. Compared to the successful story of Yiwu in the Zhejiang province – which attracts thousands of Arab traders to its wholesale market for cheap consumer goods and small business (Simpfendorfer 2011) – large-scale investments in the areas where most Muslims live have been more limited.[3] Nonetheless, in contrast with the bottom-up Arab business formation process of Yiwu, Sino-Arab business connections in Ningxia (which has a strong Muslim community) enjoy governmental encouragement. This is seen as a national project, blessed by the Chinese state.

Uyghur Muslims in Northwest China have in the past often been seen as disruptive to national unity, due to the Han-Uyghur confrontations over the years. To address this, the PRC imposed a heavy-handed 'hard-strike' policy to crack down on the Uyghur separatist movement. However, this chapter points out that the PRC policy in treating local Muslim minorities has become more sophisticated since it has been fostering a closer trading partnership with the Middle East. The growing dependence on oil supply from the Middle East makes this particularly important. The Muslims in China are not monolithic in nature; the PRC has a differentiated policy in treating Muslim minorities and the regions they live in. The Uyghurs in Xinjiang have been under extremely tight political control while the state has been combating the 'three evil forces' of 'terrorism, extremism and separatism'. Hui Muslims in Ningxia, on the other hand, have been given much freedom and flexibility in practicing their faith (Congressional-Executive Commission on China 2004).

On this basis, this chapter argues that China has skillfully selected the city of Yinchuan in Ningxia Hui Autonomous Region as an Islamic hub in promoting China-Arab trade. The novelty of the state's management of the Muslim Hui peoples in Ningxia, and the use of them to strengthen foreign relations and trading links with the Arab world, deserves attention. In this chapter, I describe this approach as the 'Ningxia model'. This is contrary to the 'Xinjiang model' where antithetical relations between the state and the Uyghurs has resulted in a zero-sum game, with the state's interest in national unity running counter to Uyghur separatism. First, this chapter explains these two models and how they relate to the growth of Chinese links with the Muslim world. Then, the chapter argues that the tradition of Hui entrepreneurialism distinguishes Hui Muslims from other Muslim groupings in China, and assesses the advantages and the challenges of the Ningxia model in promoting China-Arab trade and other relations.

2. Hui and Uyghurs: Divergence in the Treatments of Muslim Minorities

The termination of Manchu rule after the success of the 1911 Republic revolution in China raised the issue of the role of ethnic groupings in national integration. Dr. Sun Yat-sen's proposal of a republic of ethnic groups in common harmony gave recognition to the Hui as one of the five ethnic groups in China (Han, Manchus, Mongols, Hui and Tibetans). In fact, the term Hui was being used here to refer to all the 'Mohammedans' in China, just as today also it is sometimes used to refer to Turkic Muslims as well as Muslims of mixed Chinese and Central Asian ancestry (Dillon 1999, pp. 82). Dr. Sun's strategy of including ethnic minorities was important in preventing modern China from disintegrating and enabling the state to quell unrest and resolve grievances among Muslims in China. Historically, the relations between Muslims and the Chinese authorities had been strained for centuries (Dillon 1996, pp. 65). In the Qing Dynasty, the conquests of the Turkic-speaking Muslims in Northwest China (Kim 2004) and the heavy-handed suppression of the Hui Muslims and Sufi orders in Southwest China (Atwill 2006) created hostility among Muslims towards the sovereign rulers of the Han Chinese. The confrontations created a negative cultural stereotype among Han Chinese towards Muslims in China. Until now, Muslims have been widely viewed as inherently rebellious and not wholeheartedly loyal to the Chinese state (Israeli 2002). The perception is ambivalent: Muslims are the 'familiar strangers' in China (Lipman 1997). The historical memory forms a deep-seated cause of mutual suspicion and distrust between Muslims and Han Chinese.

According to a statement issued by the Chinese Islamic Association in 2009, there are twenty-two million Muslims living in China. The Hui people are the largest of the ten official Muslim nationalities (*minzu*) in China (overall there are 56 nationalities which are recognized in the country). The other nine Muslim nationalities are Uyghur, Kazakh, Dongxiang, Kyrgyz, Salar, Tajik, Uzbek, Bonan, and Tatar. Language is the key dividing line among the various Muslim ethnic groups. Unlike the Chinese-speaking Hui, the nine other Muslim nationalities use Turkic, Turkic-Mongolian and Indo-Persian languages. Chinese is not their native language.

Among the ten Muslim nationalities, the Uyghurs have been the most problematic to the Chinese state since the Qing era when the Uyghur-populated Xinjiang region was conquered. Following the collapse of the Qing dynasty, the Republic of China took control of the Xinjiang region. There was an attempt to create an independent "East Turkestan", but this was suppressed. The region later became an autonomous region of the People's Republic of China. Uyghurs have, however, still not integrated well in the Chinese state and have complained that the autonomous status of the Xinjiang region is not authentic. In addition to the wave of Han Chinese migration to Xinjiang, the widening social inequality in education and employment, the state's containment of terrorism by tightening restrictions on the *madrasah*s and access to Mosques in the post-9/11 era, have all contributed to the deterioration of Han-Uyghur relations since the 1990s (Dillon 2009; Mackerras 2009).

If Uyghur Muslims have been perceived as a threat to the national unity in China, then Hui Muslims are the most assimilated ethnic Muslim minority within the Han Chinese culture. Unlike other Muslim nationalities having their own languages, Hui Muslims do not have their own ethnic language but speak Chinese. The Hui people are widely distributed all over China and are the largest Muslim community. They are the second-largest minority group in China. In comparison, Hui Muslims have traditionally been understood as politically loyal and patriotic in supporting Chinese rule (Matsumoto 2006). In addition to speaking the same language and having close cultural affinity with the Han Chinese, they have benefited from the PRC government allowing relatively free expression of Hui identity with reference to Islam. Not wanting to offend the international Muslim community, the PRC's generally lenient policy has encouraged the ethno-genesis of Hui ethnic identity; Hui people are allowed to build a stronger solidarity with the Islamic world (Gladney 2004, pp. 167; Jankowiak 2008, pp. 106). The contrasting historical experience and cultural expression of the Hui and Uyghurs explain why the PRC deliberately puts its bet on Hui Muslims as the bridge-builder between the revitalized China-Arab ties, rather than the Uyghurs located in the unstable Xinjiang region.

2.1. Hui Urban Entrepreneurialism: Middlemen between Han Chinese and Arab Traders

Among the Muslims living in China, the Hui Muslims or 'Sino-Muslims'[4] are the largest of the ten official Muslim nationalities in China. Contrary to the dominant Chinese perception of Muslims (which focus on those of Xinjiang), Hui Muslims have been very active in urban Chinese life and have been playing a vital role in business. Rather than rejecting this-worldly behaviour, Hui Muslims in China have been actively involved in business. In his insightful fieldwork in Beijing, anthropologist Dru Gladney even argues that trade and entrepreneurialism define the Hui Muslim identity in China. They are in fact the most urban ethnic group in China (Gladney 1993, pp. 278, 282). Gladney observes that this is an outcome of their unique historical position as marginal middlemen between foreigners and Han Chinese in many Chinese cities and not due to any inherent talent in doing business. The ethno-religious traditions of avoiding pork, belief in one God (Allah), doing small business, ethnic social practices and Islamic rituals have distinguished Hui Muslims culturally, religiously and economically from the Han majority Chinese (Gladney 1993, pp. 279). Hui Muslims' ethnic traditions and marginalized trading activities have constituted their survival strategies to maintain their unique identity in China.

In 2009, the first China-Arab Business Forum was hosted in Ningxia Province, the only Hui Muslim Autonomous Region in China. The links between their tradition of entrepreneurship and the outgoing role associated with this were clearly being revived. In fact, the tradition of Hui Muslim entrepreneurship had its history over a thousand and three hundred years in China. Ma Ping and Ding Ke Jia, leading scholars of the Institute of Hui People and Islamic Studies in the

Ningxia Academy of Social Sciences, pointed out that Hui Muslims have enjoyed a long legacy of entrepreneurship in China's history. Hui Muslims have for a long time contributed to economic development with their pioneering spirit. In the Republican period of modern China, a prominent group of Hui Muslim traders from Wuzhong of Ningxia, whose business ethics were widely praised as honest and reliable, delivered regional goods (e.g. licorice, hair-like seaweed, Chinese wolfberry, soap and towels) to Inner Mongolia, Zhangiakou, Tianjin and Beijing. Later, they brought silks and other precious products from Beijing and Tianjin to Baotou (Wang 2009; Wang 2009). Similarly, the Hui now play a significant role as effective middlemen facilitating the growing business between China and the Arab world (Ma 2010; Ding 2008). From 26 to 30 September 2010, the First China-Arab States Economic and Trade Forum and the Ningxia Economic and Trade Fair was held in Yinchuan, the regional capital of Ningxia Hui Autonomous Region. Chen Deming, the Chinese Minister of Commerce, proclaimed in his inaugural speech that the purpose of the Sino-Arab trade forum was to "pass on friendship, push forward cooperation and seek common development" between China and the Arab states, as well as the Muslim regions. The PRC State Council has officially released a guideline for the development of China's Western regions, and Ningxia as one of these is encouraged to deepen the economic, educational, technical, and cultural ties with the countries in the Arab world.

3. Ningxia's Advantages: Making a China's Islamic Hub for Sino-Arab Trade

This section examines the various aspects which underpin Ningxia's role in the development of Sino-Arab relations.

3.1. Ningxia as Muslim Legacy: Islamic Heritage and Hui Muslim Leadership

Traditionally, Ningxia hosts the largest Hui Muslim community in China and is home to at least one-tenth of China's more than twenty million Muslims. Today, Ningxia has a total population of 6.3 million and the number of Hui Muslims comprises 35 percent of the total population of the province, at 2.1 million. In the past, Ningxia was hesitant in asserting its Islamic heritage and connections with the Muslim *ummah*. Today, Ningxia is boldly reasserting this heritage and seeking to rebuild the disconnected link with the Muslim world. Ningxia's Islamic turn was spurred by the global financial crisis of 2008 which resulted in a fall in its trade with the developed world. The Ningxia authorities reassessed the region's economic strategy and shifted their attention away from the West and towards the emerging Muslim economies.[5]

Located in the interior of Western China and adjoining the Gobi Desert, Ningxia has been one of the most impoverished and mostly desert regions in China. Compared with the vibrant Arab trading hub of Yiwu (Simpfendorfer 2011), Yinchuan in Ningxia has never been the primary choice for Arab traders coming to China for trade. Set beside the huge economic output of Guangdong province ($580 billion in 2009), Ningxia region's output is small ($20 billion in 2009).[6] Ningxia, however, has advantages. Wang Zhengwei, Chairman of the PRC of Ningxia Hui Autonomous Region has stated that, besides having a cultural empathy with the Arab and Muslim worlds, Ningxia has two further positive aspects. First, it is situated in the central part of China, enjoying geographical proximity with all of China's provincial capitals as well as neighboring major cities in Southeast Asia. Air-flights between Yinchuan and Dubai have been convenient in connecting Ningxia with all Gulf and Arab states. Second, Ningxia has hosted five international Muslim foods and products expositions and has reached cooperation agreements in these fields with some Southeast Asian and Arab countries.[7] Furthermore, autonomous status granted to Ningxia by the PRC has enabled the governorship of the Ningxia region to be entrusted to a Hui Muslim. Wang Zhengwei, the official leader of the Ningxia region, is a Hui Muslim born in Tongxin. He has considerable expertise in developing projects which revitalize the local Hui Muslim heritage. This is done within the wider contexts of 'opening the West' and 'going global'. The strengthening of relations with the Arab States clearly fits well with this strategy.

3.2. Ningxia as a Business Hub: China–Arab Forum, Free Trade Zone and Arabic Translation

Authorized by the PRC State Council, Ningxia Autonomous Region has been the host to both the First and Second China-Arab States Economic and Trade Forums in 2010 and 2011. Chairman Wang Zhengwei declared that the Ningxia region was not only a channel for promoting the image of China, but also a platform for fostering China-Arab trade – with mutual benefits for both the Arab states and China.[8] The First and the Second China-Arab States Economic and Trade Forum attracted thousands of Chinese enterprises and over sixty countries from around the world. The Forum created opportunities for Arab manufacturers and purchasers to meet counterparts in China and enhance mutual understanding and trade cooperation. In these two Forums, contracts worth a total of 170 billion yuan ($ 26.94 billion) were signed. Hoping to take trade and economic linkages with the Muslim nations further, Ningxia is now planning to set up a free trade zone to expand bilateral trade with the Muslim world, covering activities in manufacturing, design, certification, skills and logistics.[9]

In addition to the Free Trade Zone, Ningxia has been developed overall as a platform for cooperation and open trade among Muslim countries. Since the objective is to build a "World Muslim City" center, more than ten Muslim countries have made donations to cover the cost of infrastructure. Projects associated with Ningxia's Muslim identification include the Islamic History Museum, the Qur'an Mosque, the World Muslim Country Expo Hall, the Folk Cultural Street and Friendship Square, and an Arabian Nights theme park displaying the world of Arab customs, culture and artistic achievements. Apart from honoring the legacy of world Islamic civilization, the city also features local Muslim culture including the Ningxia Muslim Orphanage, the Ningxia Muslim International Language College, and the tombs of local Sufi saints.[10] According to locals, Ningxia has deliberately fashioned itself as 'China's Mecca', attracting Muslim visitors from around the world.

In facilitating China-Arab trade, sufficient well-trained translators are essential. In South China (Guangdong and Shenzhen), Arabic translators are highly in demand, and Yiwu alone already has five thousand Arabic interpreters.[11] Viewing the importance of bilingual interpreters of Arabic and Chinese, the PRC has made Ningxia an important training centre and the supplier of Arabic translators to other regions of China which have business connections in the Arab world.

3.3 Ningxia as Halal Food Centre: Developing the Halal Food Industry

Among all business options, Ningxia has given particular attention to promoting Qingzhen food - halal food with Chinese Muslim characteristics. Though the industries producing Qingzhen food have developed rapidly in Ningxia, the lack of international recognition and branding of halal food has hindered its export. Nonetheless, Ningxia is seeking to remedy this. In 2009, Ningxia Hui Autonomous Region issued an official document entitled 'Certifying Guideline of the Ningxia Hui Autonomous Region' to provide standardized terminologies and normative procedures for Qingzhen food production. To date, Ningxia cooperates with the halal certification organizations of Malaysia and Thailand to speed up the export of Qingzhen food abroad and its reintegration in the global Muslim community market (Hong & Liu 2010, pp. 108-109). Analyzing the historical and geographical advantages, then, the regional government officials of Ningxia appropriated the region's Islamic heritage so as to improve the impoverished domestic economy. They created a new market.[12] Under the eleventh five-year national planning, Ningxia invested heavily in the halal food industry. More than fifty kinds of Muslim original foods from Ningxia have been marketed in the major mainland coastal cities. Internationally, producers of Ningxia halal food have been seeking new markets and distribution centers in United Arab Emirates, Kuwait, Thailand and Malaysia.[13] In the 2011 China-Arab Trade Forum, China highlighted some business projects to be developed in the future, and among these was the Ningxia halal food business. In the context of the world's five hundred billion dollar halal food business, China's hundred million dollar halal food export business constitutes an insignificant portion of the global halal trade. Looking at the figure, Sha Pengcheng, honorary director of the China Islamic Research Centre sees a huge business potential for Ningxia to tap into.[14] In the fall of 2011, it was reported that the Halal Food Certification Centre in Ningxia had signed agreements with Saudi Arabia, Egypt and Qatar to grant mutual recognition of their certifications. China has already signed similar mutual halal recognition agreements with authorities in Malaysia, Australia and New Zealand.[15] According to the PRC strategic plan, the Ningxia Hui Autonomous Region has been targeted to develop as an international manufacturing base of halal food and products for the Arab world. Preferential taxation policies will be implemented to attract Arab investors, developing Ningxia itself into a design, manufacturing, exposition and logistics center catering for Arab markets.

3.4. Ningxia as Southeast Asia Node: Asian Muslims as Strategic Partner

Another Chinese strategy which links to developments in Ningxia is to align Southeast and South Asian neighbors with it in pursuing common business interests in the Middle East. Given the huge population of Muslims in South and Southeast Asia, it is clear that a higher credibility of recognition and strict halal certification is needed generally in these countries. One noted strategy in the development of Ningxia's Islamic halal food center has been to see the Southeast and South Asian Muslim countries as partners in this process, and not competitors. With the strategy of 'going global', the delegation from Yinchuan in China was tasked to reach out and invite Brunei entrepreneurs to participate in the China-Arab States Economics and Trade Forum. The Deputy Director of the Expo Bureau of Ningxia Hui Autonomous Region, Hou Hongguang, stated:

> "We hope that Brunei entrepreneurs can form a delegation to participate in our activities lined up for the fair and forum that is coming up in Ningxia."[16]

While India has been viewed as China's competitor in the strategic interest of the Arab world, China's recent strategic move has been to turn the competition into a strategic alignment with Asian nations where there are substantial Muslim populations. Changing the mode of competition to cooperation, China's national policy is not to exclude but to include India by inviting India to the China-Arab States Economic and Trade Forum. The rationale is that India has a substantial Muslim population. Inviting India to China's strategic business partnership of targeting common business interest in the Arab world could eventually result in strengthening China's economic ties with the Islamic world.[17] Malaysia, another important business partner of China's halal food, was the first invited partner in the First Forum of China-Arab Trade. With thirty companies and government agencies represented, including the Halal Industry Development Corporation and the Kelantan State Economic Development Corporation (KEDC), halal food was displayed. Apart from concentrating on countries having substantial Muslim populations, China has also developed an alignment with countries where Muslims are the minority. The Ningxia government, for example, opened contacts with five South Thailand provinces (Yala, Pattani, Narathiwat, Songkhla and Satun) where Muslims constitute a significant part of the population. As a result of this, China and Thailand have joined together in developing the halal food market for exports and brand-building.[18]

4. Ningxia's Challenges: Jasmine Revolution, Islamism and Inter-Ethnic Rivalry

Despite what has been said so far, challenges do exist in the strategy which has been adopted in Ningxia. There are factors which could limit Ningxia's attempt to develop as a stable and mature hub between China and the Arab world.

In evaluating the impact of the Arab revolutions and revolts in the Gulf region and in North Africa, it is worth noting that the Chinese government has no intention of halting the growth of business with the Arab world, despite the possible impact of the social unrest in China. Without a record of involvement in wars in the Middle East, and without a colonial history, the PRC considers that no matter what new governments come to rule, China's longstanding friendship with the Middle East will remain unchanged. Arab trust has enabled China to pursue its investments in the Middle East (Ma 2011). In response to a journalist's question on the volatile situation following the Arab revolts in 2011, Wang Zhengwei resolutely replied that the uncertainties of political change in the Middle East will not affect

Ningxia's engagement in the Arab world.[19] Against the background of the United States and its Western allies pressuring for regime change in the Arab world, Premier Wen Jiabao's visit to the Arabian Peninsula in 2012 reaffirmed the strength of the China-Arab friendship and the continuation of bilateral cooperation. China now imports more than 55% of its crude oil needs, and 47% come from Middle East. Saudi Arabia and Qatar are the largest suppliers of oil and natural gas, respectively. Rather than downgrading Sino-Arab ties in the uncertain political chaos of the 'Arab Spring', China has been cementing political mutual trust and charting the future partnership with the new political order in the Arab world.[20]

Though it is true that China-Arab ties keep growing, the PRC has no hesitation in guarding itself against the infiltration of extremism and the domino effect of the Arab Spring. It can be observed that state policies on Islam and ethnic Muslims have needed continual attention since the 9/11 attack (Gladney 2009), especially in the region of Xinjiang. The PRC's management of Islam is no longer totalistic. Tight control of ethnic minority issues still exists, but at the same time civil society is developing and there is more room for autonomy. The Ningxia Hui Autonomous Region is rediscovering Islam as its local heritage, with a link to the wider Muslim world. However, the PRC is also cautious about the infiltration of Islamic radicalism through these revived links:

> The Chinese government keeps a close eye on these developments, though. Mosques must be licensed, foreign *imams* are not allowed to preach in them, and youngsters are not allowed to pray in mosques. "The government supports economic links, which it hopes will increase, but has a cautious attitude to cultural and religious links with the Middle East," explains Professor Ma. For the sake of trade, however, "they have put their concerns on the backburner," he believes. "The Ningxia authorities are confident they can minimize negative cultural influences and maximize economic influences."[21]

Another threat to the success of the Ningxia model comes from the nature of Ningxia as a region. Ningxia is a small province with six million people located in remote central China. Its facilities are not competitive compared to those of Beijing, Shanghai and Guangzhou in terms of trading infrastructure and logistics. In addition, other Muslim-populated provinces such as Gansu are emerging to compete with Ningxia. Most importantly, the inter-ethnic rivalry between the Han-dominated local government and the Hui-majority population in Ningxia has posed problems. In January 2012, the local government authorities demolished a newly renovated mosque (built in 1987). This caused social conflicts and political tension in the region. A Hui Muslim expressed sadness and discontent to a journalist, stating:

> "We refurbished this mosque with our hard work and blood. It is so sad to see it demolished … We don't understand what happened. We never had any interference with our religious life before. We love our country. We love the party."[22]

Though the Central Government of the PRC is supportive to Ningxia's initiative in forging trade links with the Muslim world, whenever local government officials or Han Chinese individuals show disrespect for the Islamic tradition of the Muslim minority, conflicts break out. With riots in Xinjiang and the uprising in Tibet creating social disorder, the relatively stable Ningxia model will not be sustainable if the Islamic traditions of China's Muslim community are not respected and Islamic culture is not honored. There is also danger that the ethnic conflicts in Xinjiang and Tibet, and the strict monitoring of mosques and Muslim communities in provinces like Ningxia and Gansu[23] will damage the free business environment and harm the prospect of the Ningxia model.

Conclusion: Mobilizing Hui Muslims, Welcoming Arab Traders

Without a doubt, China's global rise and the Arab world's policy of 'looking East' will lead to closer ties between China and the Arab world. While many focus on China's outward-looking policy of 'going global', this chapter argues that China's interest in the Middle East unintentionally drives an inward-looking search for domestic cultural resources with which to legitimize China's growing presence in the Middle East. China is rediscovering and appropriating the legacy of local Muslim minorities to use as a soft power in promoting its involvement in the Arab world.

In terms of cultural and political identity, the Muslim Uyghur community has been viewed as either a burden towards national development or a direct threat to the sovereign rule of the PRC. On the other hand, the PRC appropriates the Muslim faith of Hui Muslims, the Hui tradition of entrepreneurialism, and the Ningxia Hui Autonomous Region, to promote China–Arab economic ties. As the managing director of Silk Road Associates, Ben Simpfendorfer, concisely pointed out, "the rise of China–Middle East trade is also about the rise of Islamic economies."[24] The Ningxia Hui Autonomous Region is now positively treasured as an important asset, containing loyal citizens of the PRC who play an ambassadorial role in welcoming Arab traders doing business in China. Mobilizing Hui Muslims for the nation's diplomatic strategy, Ningxia doubtlessly helps to secure China's needs in the importing of oil and gas from Arab countries. But with the broadening of bilateral cooperation, the future development of the Ningxia model may go beyond energy diplomacy and embrace a wider business vision with the Arab countries.[25]

Apart from importing non-oil products, China's current exports to Arab countries tend to be low-end, low valued-added and labor-intensive products. The vision for China's export is to move to high-end, high valued-added, high-tech products and also technological transfer to the Arab world, as explained by a board member of the Amman Chamber of Industry:

> "To reduce the technology gap with advanced industries at the international level, we look forward to benefiting from the distinguished Chinese experience through development of industrial technology cooperation plans between Arab and Chinese companies, in a manner that targets integration and contributes to mutual benefit."[26]

In conclusion, the next stage in ensuring that China's Ningxia model does not follow the Western colonial legacy is to develop China-Arab connections away from petro-dependency and towards the real mutual benefit of boosting China's multidimensional investment and promoting Arab technological progress.

Endnotes

1   "China Railway Construction Meets Mecca." *China Economic Review*, June 1, 2010. Accessed June 2, 2010. http://www.chinaeconomicreview.com/node/26623.

2   "Looking East: The Saudis are Hedging Their Bets." *The Economist*, December 9, 2010. Accessed December 10, 2010. http://www.economist.com/node/17680668.

3   Bardsley, Daniel. "The New Silk Road is Slowly Becoming a Two-Way Street for Emirates." *The National*, May 16, 2011. Accessed May 17, 2011. http://www.thenational.ae/thenationalconversation/industry-insights/energy/the-new-silk-road-is-slowly-becoming-a-two-way-street-for-emirates.

4   Instead of using a generalized term 'Hui' in differentiating other Muslim ethnic groups in China, Jonathan N. Lipman adopts the term 'Sino-Muslim', depicting their hyphenated culture and distinguishing those Muslims from the non-Chinese speaking ethnic Muslims. In this article, 'Hui', 'Muslim Chinese', 'Sino-Muslim' are, however, used interchangeably to refer to the designated Muslim nationality in China. See Jonathan N. Lipman (1997).

5   "Ningxia To Boost Free Trade With Muslim nations." *China Daily*, August 28, 2010. Accessed August 29, 2010. http://www.chinadaily.com.cn/cndy/2010-08/28/content_11217848.htm.

6   Simpfendorfer, Ben. "What Next For Ningxia." *Silk Road Associates*, October 1, 2010. Accessed May 1, 2012. http://www.silkroadassoc.com/blog/2010/10/01/what-next-for-ningxia/

7   Yang, Lina. "Ningxia Officials Briefs Reporters on China-Arab States Economic and Trade Forum." English. *Xinhuanet.com*, September 16, 2011. Accessed May 1, 2012. http://news.xinhuanet.com/english2010/china/2011-09/16/c_131142727.htm.

8   Tang, Hong and Zhang Hong. "The Second China-Arab States Economic and Trade Forum: A Fruitful Event." *China Today* 60, no. 11 (2011): 72-75. Accessed May 1, 2012. http://www.chinatoday.com.cn/ctenglish/se/txt/2011-11/17/content_406469.htm.

9   Wen, Ya. "Muslim Ningxia Seeks Arab Trade." *Global Times*, March 7, 2012. Accessed May 1, 2012. http://www.globaltimes.cn/NEWS/tabid/99/ID/698933/Muslim-Ningxia-seeks-Arab-trade.aspx.

10 "Separate and Unequal: The Hui of Ningxia and the Uyghurs of Xinjiang." *Xinjiang Review*, February 8, 2011. Accessed January 29, 2012. http://xingjiangreview.wordpress.com/2011/02/08/why-xinjianguyghur-and-ningxiahui-are-treated-diffently-a-comparison/

11 "Ningxia Forum Seals China-Arab Ties." *China.org.cn*, September 21, 2011. Accessed May 15, 2012. http://www.china.org.cn/travel/Ningxia/2011-09/21/content_23465136.htm.

12 Ningxia Expects to Open a New Market in the Islamic States.". *China-Arab States Economic and Trade Forum*. Accessed March 11, 2011. http://en.casetf.org/zjnj/dzmy/252005.shtml

13 "Ningxia, Prominent Exchange Platform Between China, Arab World." English. *Xinhuanet.com*, September 20, 2011. Accessed May 15,2012. http://news.xinhuanet.com/english/china/2011-09/20/c_131148750.htm

14 "China Hopes to Broaden Halal Food Exports." *People's Daily*, September 24, 2011.

15 "China's Halal Food to Get Free Access to Arab States." *China.org.cn*, September 22,2011. Accessed November 29, 2011. http://www.china.org.cn/travel/Ningxia/2011-09/22/content_23473528.htm.

16 Goh, De No and Bandar Seri Begawan. "Entrepreneurs Invited to Ningxia Halal Fair." *The Brunei Times*, June 28, 2011. http://www.bt.com.bn/business-national/2011/06/28/entrepreneurs-invited-ningxia-halal-fair

17 "China Plans to Invite India to Major Islamic Trade Forum." *Financial Chronicle*, September 21, 2011. http://wrd.mydigitalfc.com/economy/china-plans-invite-india-major-islamic-trade-forum-339

18 "China's Ningxia Looks for Thai Halal Partners." *McClatchy –Tribune Business News*, December 3, 2007.

19 "Ningxia Official Briefs Reporters on China-Arab States Economic and Trade Forum." English. *Xinhuanet.com*, September 16, 2010. Accessed May 1, 2012. http://news.xinhuanet.com/english2010/china/2011-09/16/c_131142727.htm

20 Wang, Hui. "Cementing Ties with Arab World" *China Daily*, January 14, 2012. http://www.chinadaily.com.cn/cndy/2012-01/14/content_14444843.htm

21 Ford, Peter. "Chinese Muslims Join Global Islamic Market." *The Christian Science Monitor*, September 16, 2008. http://www.csmonitor.com/World/Asia-Pacific/2008/0916/p06s04-woap.html

22 Demick, Barbara. "China Mosque Demolition Heightens Ethnic Tensions." *Los Angeles Time*, January 3, 2012. http://latimesblogs.latimes.com/world_now/2012/01/china-mosque-demolition-hui-ethnic-tensions.html

23 "Muslims Clash with Chinese Police Who Destroyed Mosque." *The Telegraph*, January 2, 2012. http://www.telegraph.co.uk/news/worldnews/asia/china/8988205/Muslims-clash-with-Chinese-police-who-destroyed-mosque.html

24 Hook, Leslie. "China: Red Carpet Treatment to Foster Closer Business Ties." *Financial Times*. September 28, 2011. http://www.ft.com/cms/s/0/dcb9ab04-e5f1-11e0-b196-00144feabdc0. html#axzz28OztxdHz
25 Ibid.
26 Li, Jiabao and Ding Qingfen. "Boost High-Tech Exports to Arabs, Trade official Says." *China Daily*, September 29, 2011. http://www.chinadaily.com.cn/bizchina/2011-09/29/content_13814876. htm

Bibliography

Atwill, David G. *The Chinese Sultanate: Islam, Ethnicity, and the Panthay Rebellion in Southeast China*, 1856-1873. Stanford: Stanford University Press, 2006.

Congressional-Executive Commission on China. "Practicing Islam in Today's China: Differing Realities For the Uighurs and the Hui." *Congressional-Executive Commission's Roundtable Document*, U.S. Government: Washington, 2004.

Dillon, Michael. *China's Muslims*. Hong Kong: Oxford University Press, 1996.

Dillon, Michael. *China's Muslim Hui Community: Migration, Settlement and Sects*. Surrey: Curzon Press, 1999.

Dillon, Michael. "Uighur Resentment at Beijing's Rule" *BBC Worldnews*. July 6, 2009. Accessed July 7, 2009. http://news.bbc.co.uk/2/hi/asia-pacific/8137206.stm.

Ding, Ke Jia. "On Hui Merchants Culture and Its Significance of the Times." *Journal of Hui Muslim Minority Studies* 2 (2008): 5-9. (In Chinese)

Gladney, Dru C. "Hui Urban Entrepreneurialism in Beijing: State Policy, Ethnoreligious Identity and the Chinese City." In *Urban Anthropology in China*, edited by Gregory E. Guldin and Aidan W. Southall, 296-307. Leiden: Brill, 1993.

Gladney, Dru C. *Dislocating China: Reflections on Muslims, Minorities, and Other Subaltern Subjects*. London: Hurst, 2004.

Gladney, Dru C. "Islam in China: State Policing and Identity Politics." In *Making Religion, Making the State: The Politics of Religion in Modern China*, edited by Yoshiko Ashiwa and David L. Wank, 151-178. Stanford: Stanford University Press, 2009.

Hong, Meixiang and Liu Wei. *Hui Zu Qing Zhen Mei Shi Wen Hua*. Yinchuan: Ningxia ren min chu ban she, 2010. (in Chinese)

Israeli, Raphael. *Islam in China: Religion, Ethnicity, Culture and Politics*. Lanham: Lexington, 2002.

Jankowiak, William. "Ethnicity and Chinese Identity: Ethnographic Insight and Political Positioning." In *The Cambridge Companion to Modern Chinese Culture*, edited by Kam Louie, 91-114. Cambridge: Cambridge University Press, 2008.

Kim, Hondong. *Holy War in China: The Muslim Rebellion and State in Chinese Central Asia, 1864-1877*. Stanford: Stanford University Press, 2004.

Lipman, Jonathan. *Familiar Strangers: A History of Muslims in Northwest China*. Seattle: University of Washington Press, 1997.

Ma, Ping. "Hui Entrepreneurship: The Fall and Rise in a Thousand Year." *The Communists*, 21(2010): 53-54. (in Chinese)

Ma, Ping. "Middle East Political Instability Impact on China." *Journal of Hui Muslim Minority Studies* 83, no. 3 (2011): 13-16. (in Chinese)

Mackerras, Colin. "Xinjiang and Central Asia, since 1990: Views from Beijing and Washington and Sino-American relations." In *China, Xinjiang and Central Asia, History, Transition and*

Crossborder Interaction into the 21st Century, edited by Colin Mackerras and Michael Clarke, 133-150. Routledge: London, 2009.

Matsumoto, Masumi. "Rationalizing Patriotism Among Muslim Chinese: The Impact of the Middle East on the *Yuehua* Journal." In *Intellectuals in the Modern Islamic World: Transmission, Transformation and Communication*, edited by Stephane A. Dudoignon, Komatsu Hisao and Kosugi Yasushi, 117-141. London: Routledge, 2006.

Simpfendorfer, Ben. *The New Silk Road: How a Rising Arab World is Turning Away from the West and Rediscovering China.* New York: Palgrave, 2011.

Wang, Zheng Ru. "On the Hui Merchants of Wuzhong Doing Business in Baotou." *Journal of Hui Muslim Minority Studies* 3(2009): 96-103. (In Chinese)

Wang, Fu Ping. "Research on Hui Trader and Business House of Wuzhong in the Period of Republic of China." *Journal of Hui Muslim Minority Studies* 3(2009): 140-145. (In Chinese)

Zhao, Suisheng. "The China Model: Can It Replace the Western Model of Modernization?." *Journal of Contemporary China* 19, no. 65 (2010): 419-236.

Chapter Eleven

China and the Gulf: The Social and Cultural Implications of their Rapidly Developing Economic Ties

Jacqueline Armijo

1. Introduction

Over the past five years, China's relations with the major GCC countries (Saudi Arabia, the UAE, Kuwait, and Qatar) have developed rapidly, in both the scale and range of joint ventures, investments, and trade. Billions of dollars worth of manufactured goods, fossil fuels, and sovereign wealth investment funds are traveling back and forth between the Gulf and China, and increasing numbers of people and cultural exchanges are accompanying them. And although these exchanges are based on present-day economic and development needs, both the Chinese and the Gulf countries are well aware of the historic ties between these two regions and regularly refer to these ties when announcing new initiatives.

Although trade was the foundation of relations between China and the Gulf that began during the Tang Dynasty (618-907 CE), over the centuries these relations evolved into a wide range of exchanges including scientific knowledge (of astronomy, medicine, pharmacology); engineering expertise (military, architectural, and hydraulic); Islamic scholarship; knowledge of Arabic and Persian, and artistic skills and craftsmanship. Today, although trade once again dominates relations between these two regions, cultural, artistic, and scholarly exchanges have begun to develop as well.

This chapter focuses on the lives, legacies, and present-day influences of the people who in the past, and again today, are travelling back and forth between China and the Gulf. Beginning with traders, from the earliest days of Islam to the present rush of businessmen today, the chapter then focuses on the growing number of Chinese workers in different fields coming to the Gulf. The next section describes the rapid development of the tourism industry and its related fields, followed by a section on educational exchanges and initiatives. The final section deals with cultural exchanges, using the recent extraordinary exhibit by the Chinese modern artist Cai Guo-qiang, at Mathaf: The Arab Museum of Modern Art, as a case-study.

2. Trading

Traders from the Gulf had been traveling to China since the earliest days of Islam, first settling in Guangzhou (Canton), and later in Quanzhou. So many Arab and Persian traders made Quanzhou their home that they gave it a new name *Zaytun*, or "olive". These traders made the long and often treacherous trip to China on traditional *dhows* built in the Gulf region. The boats were packed with frankincense and other local aromatics from the region before setting off to the main ports of India and Sri Lanka where they picked up pearls, gemstones, ivory, spices, and other lightweight luxury goods, before heading up through the Straits of Malacca where additional spices were added to their cargo, and finally into the South China Sea and the port cities of China.

As for the trade items that the Gulf traders brought back with them, it was not until 1998 and the discovery of a 9th century shipwrecked *dhow* off the coast of Indonesia, that the extent of the Chinese manufacturing for export industry was revealed. The *dhow* was on its way home, fully packed with over 70,000 pieces of pottery and porcelain when it went down off the Indonesian island of Belitung.

When the captain of the hand-sewn *dhow*[1] set off for China, he must have been well aware of the goods available for manufacture there, as many of them appear to have been commissioned with certain regional tastes in mind. The small boat, only 60 feet in length, was able to hold the 70,000 objects as they were carefully stored in large earthenware jugs that were then tightly packed in layers of rows along the bottom of the boat.

The logistical details and extent of the range and quality of the porcelain and precious metal cargo of this small ship were carefully documented in an exhibit that took place at ArtScience Museum in Singapore in 2011. A small replica of the *dhow* as well as a selection of the 60,000 surviving pieces was displayed. In addition to ceramics of various sizes and patterns, the cargo also included finely crafted works of gold and silver.[2]

The cargo was destined for the major *entrepôt*s of the Gulf in the ninth century: Siraf and Basra. And while the mass-produced ceramic bowls were most likely bound for the *souq*s of Baghdad and Shiraz, the ornate and delicate carved silver and gold pieces may have been intended for the royal courts of the Abbasid empire.

2.1. Yiwu

Today, over a millennium later, ships from China laden with layers and layers of custom-made goods, are once again setting off for the Gulf and the marketplaces there. But today the container ships are mostly filled with inexpensive mass-produced goods manufactured in the small city of Yiwu. Located 250 km south of Shanghai, and 150 km inland from the major port of Ningbo, the city of Yiwu, more than any other place in China, has customized its manufacturing output to the designs and desires of the residents of the Gulf and the Middle East.

Although Guangzhou is still the largest and most important trade center in China, over the past decade Yiwu has been able to develop a multi-billion dollar export market by specializing in mass-produced inexpensive custom-made goods. Yiwu boasts the largest small commodities wholesale market in the world, with 62,000 booths that sell more than a million different products. According to recent Chinese government statistics, in 2010 the annual market turnover in Yiwu reached $9.6 billion.[3]

Small business owners from throughout the world and especially the Middle East began flocking to Yiwu in 2001, shortly after China's admission to the WTO. Some businessmen were fleeing unrest at home, while others were entrepreneurs quick to take advantage of China's supportive policies regarding export trade. In addition, the growing demand for consumer goods in the Middle East in general and the Gulf in particular has created an ideal environment for trade to flourish. A further factor facilitating the strong trading ties between the local Chinese manufacturers and the Arab traders is the presence of several Arab businessmen in Yiwu who graduated from China's top universities, are completely fluent in Chinese, and decided to stay in China after completing their studies to promote business ties.

Approximately 200,000 Arab businessmen travel to Yiwu every year to place manufacturing orders, and there are now over 20,000 Arab residents living in Yiwu.

Some have brought their wives with them, while others have married Chinese women. Their children attend local schools where they learn both Chinese and Arabic. While some families plan to stay in Yiwu indefinitely, others plan to move back to the Middle East when their children are older.

Although Yiwu does not have a local Chinese Muslim population, over the past few years, thousands of Chinese Muslims from other regions of China have moved there to take advantage of the job opportunities created by Arab owned businesses. Many are graduates of Islamic Colleges who have studied Arabic and work as translators and interpreters, whereas others work in the restaurants, cafes, and stores that have been set up to cater to Muslim and Arab visitors and residents.

2.2. Yinchuan, or Yiwu with Muslim characteristics

Yiwu has proven so successful as an economic development model that another region of China is presently in the process of building itself up as a center of trade and manufacturing. But in this case, Yinchuan, the capital of Ningxia, in Northwest China, is starting its development plan by systematically and carefully developing economic ties with the Arab world. Wang Zhenghui, a Hui Chinese Muslim official who is Chairman of the People's Government of Ningxia Hui Autonomous Region, has taken the lead in brokering economic alliances with Arab countries and Southeast Asian Muslim nations. In an interview in early 2011, Wang described his long-range goals for Ningxia: "We are setting up mechanisms with Arabic countries one by one and these are proceeding smoothly. Our ultimate purpose is to build Ningxia into a design center, certification center, producing center, exhibition center, and logistic distribution center of Muslim products. The products from Ningxia, even from other provinces will be able to enter Arabic and other Muslim countries through the platform. This is not only good for Ningxia, but also good for other provinces in China."[4]

While Ningxia's historic role as a major trading stop along China's historic Silk Road is often mentioned in its current development plans, the main reason Ningxia was selected was due to its large Muslim population (approximately 20 per cent of China's more than 20 million Muslims live there). It is also one of China's poorest provinces and most in need of development funding.

3. Working

Although traders had been traveling back and forth to China for centuries, it was not until the rise of the Mongolian Empire and their establishment of the Yuan

Dynasty in China (1260-1368), that hundreds of thousands of Muslims from the Middle East and Central Asia were relocated, first to Mongolia, and then to China.

The rapid rise of the Mongolian Empire resulted in a period of unprecedented trade and the transfer of peoples, ideas, technologies, and goods from the Gulf and Middle East, across Central Asia, into China and back.

The new emperor Qubilai hired tens of thousands of Arabs, Persians, and Central Asians to build up and govern his empire. Expertise in certain fields, specifically engineering, medicine, and astronomy were especially sought out. Muslim architects were recruited to design the new capital (now known as Beijing), as were Muslim hydraulic engineers, military munitions experts, medical physicians, astronomers, military officials, and civilian officials. An Islamic Astronomical Bureau was established in 1271 that included an observatory built to meet the specifications of the Muslim astronomers. A Muslim Medical and Pharmaceutical Bureau was also established, and in order to meet the growing demand for translations into Chinese of Arabic and Persian scientific and medical texts, the Muslim Imperial College was established to translate texts as well as to teach Arabic and Persian.

Thousands of other foreign Muslims with administrative skills were hired to serve as officials and bureaucrats and assigned to every region of the empire. Many of these Muslims settled where they were sent, and most of China's Muslims today are the descendants of these Yuan period immigrants.

Just as China needed hundreds of thousands of workers and trained experts to assist them in establishing their new empire, the wealthy countries of the Gulf today are in need of hundreds of thousands of workers and professionals to help them develop their economies.

By far the largest group of workers coming from China to the Gulf region is construction workers. Over the past three years, China's major construction companies have been awarded contracts for some of the largest building projects in the UAE, Saudi Arabia, and Qatar. One of the most interesting stories related to construction workers in the Gulf concerns the workers responsible for the hugely successful Hajj railway. Completed by Chinese workers just in time for the Hajj season of 2010 (mid-November), the 11-mile Al-Mashaaer railway project transports pilgrims between Mina, Arafat, and Muzdalifa. Over the years, this section of the Hajj has become increasingly clogged with tens of thousands of buses and cars backed up for miles, causing both long delays as well air pollution. In its first year of operation, the train was limited to Saudi and GCC citizens. Passengers were impressed with the ease and convenience of the trip; what might earlier have taken as long as five hours, could now be made in five minutes. According to one journalist who rode the train, "The state-of-the-art rail system is changing peoples' perceptions about China almost as fast as it is whisking passengers around Mina."[5] Over the next few years, as the total number of passengers increases, the train will be made available to all pilgrims, and a line linking Mecca to Medina will be added.[6]

Although the rail system proved to be an unequivocal success, the use of Chinese workers to construct it caused two interesting twists. There were reports that between 600 and 8,000 workers were hastily converted to Islam before beginning work within Mecca. The question arises as to why China does not simply recruit Chinese Muslim construction workers for this part of the project. In addition, there were reports that 16 Chinese workers were arrested and deported for organizing a riot demanding better pay and working conditions. The mass conversions were apparently an effort to quell rising local complaints about the large number of non-Muslim workers entering Mecca. The strikes were a rare case of workers violently lashing out against bad conditions.[7]

Given the overall success of the project, it is likely that China will play an increasing role in the construction of the over $385 billion infrastructure projects (including highways and railways) the Saudis announced in 2009 as part of their five-year plan.

Another of the most important major projects recently completed in the region is the Habshan-Fujairah pipeline. Construction on this project began in 2008, and it resulted in the first major influx of Chinese engineers and workers into Abu Dhabi. As many of the engineers brought their families, it also meant the creation of a Chinese community in Abu Dhabi. The pipeline is 370 km in length, beginning in Habshan on the Gulf coast of Abu Dhabi, crossing the peninsula and on to Fujairah on the coast of the Arabian Sea, thus avoiding the vulnerable Strait of Hormuz. The completion of the pipeline comes at a critical time, as sanctions and pressure on Iran increase, and Iran in response threatens to close off the Strait. The initial flow through the pipeline was 600-700 thousand barrels per day, but by July 2012 it reached 1 million barrels a day, with an eventual target of 1.7 million barrels, representing about 70 per cent of the UAE's total oil production.[8]

4. Leisure Travelling

One area in which one sees a vast difference between the historical period and the present day is leisure traveling. Although in the past there was a handful of travelers who made their way across the seas without the goal of trading in mind (most famously Ibn Battuta), today hundreds of thousands of Chinese are making their way to the Gulf as tourists.

4.1. Chinese tourists to the UAE

The past three years have seen a huge increase in the number of Chinese tourists traveling to the Gulf, almost all headed for Dubai. Given Dubai's fame for having the best of everything, be it the seven-star Burj al-Arab, or endless options for luxury shopping, it was inevitable that China's rapidly growing numbers of international tourists would eventually find their way there. Further facilitating tourism was the Chinese government's September 2009 decision to grant the UAE approved destination status. This designation not only made it easier for Chinese to travel to the UAE, it also allows the UAE to advertise itself as a tourist destination in China. In 2010, approximately 150,000 Chinese were guests in Dubai, and it is estimated that in 2011 the number rose to 300,000.[9] Chinese tourists have quickly become some of the biggest spenders in the designer stores found in Dubai's malls. So much so, that in the past year many of the most famous designer stores and luxury hotels have hired Chinese-speaking staff to cater to the recent influx of Chinese customers. One of the most popular activities of the Chinese tourists is a stay at Dubai's iconic Burj al Arab. According to Gerald Lawless, executive chairman of the Jumeirah Group, during the Chinese New Year in 2011, 80 per cent of the hotel's occupancy was Chinese.[10]

4.2. Airlines and Linkages

Over the past five years, there has been a significant increase in nonstop flights between the major cities of the Gulf and China. At present there are three Gulf-based carriers with direct flights to China and three China-based carriers with direct flights to the Gulf.[11]

In late 2011, both Etihad (Abu Dhabi's official carrier) and Qatar Airways inaugurated flights to the most populous cities in Western China: Chengdu (the capital of Sichuan Province) and Chongqing (formerly a part of Sichuan, but now its own city/province). While some might have wondered about these two choices, especially as neither is a major tourist destination, in fact in both cases the airlines were thinking very strategically and had linked their decisions to China's long-term development plans for Western China. In addition, this region of China has for decades been the largest single source of the hundreds of millions of workers who leave the countryside in search of work in distant cities.

Although China has experienced rapid economic development, almost all of it has been along its eastern coast. In recent years, in an effort to balance out the economic reform in China, the government has focused on development projects in Western China and encouraged corporations to do the same. This 'Look-West' policy has taken several approaches.

In a *Wall Street Journal* article, Greg Lindsay reports that, "In the Western city of Chongqing, huge swaths of countryside have been paved in preparation for the arrival of China's electronics manufacturers, which are pulling up stakes along the coast. Led by Hewlett-Packard and Foxconn, the maker of Apple's iPhones and iPads, Chongqing aspires to produce nearly half the world's laptops by 2015, all of which will leave the city by air."[12] Although it will be a couple of years before this huge amount of cargo starts to leave this region, large numbers of construction workers are already heading to building sites in the UAE, Qatar and Saudi Arabia on these flights.

The Chinese airlines have also been planning strategic connections between China and the Gulf. In March 2011, China Eastern, China's second largest airline, inaugurated direct flights from Dubai to Yinchuan (with a stopover in Kunming, a city in Southwest China with a large Muslim population). In this case, the choice of a relatively unknown city in China's far Northwest bears witness to a specific dimension of the China-Gulf relationship. Yinchuan, as mentioned earlier, has for several years been building up a range of businesses geared toward markets in the Middle East and in the Muslim countries of Southeast Asia. Most of the industry revolves around the production of halal foods. In order to encourage trade, the province has organized large annual trade shows that cater to the needs of Middle Eastern and Southeast Asian markets. To further promote products from Ningxia, in 2009 the Chinese government announced it would be investing $27 million dollars in a sales complex and trade office in Dubai.[13] For more on the halal food industry in Northwest China, see the chapter by Ho Wai-yip in this book.

5. Exchanging Knowledge and Culture

As mentioned earlier, medical and pharmacological knowledge from the Muslim world was especially valued in China beginning in the Yuan period. Today, it is traditional Chinese medicine that has become extremely popular throughout the Gulf, where traditional Chinese medicine clinics can be found in all of the major cities. One explanation for its growing popularity is that certain traditional Chinese medical treatments, especially cupping or moxibustion (Arabic *al-hijama*, or *kasat hawa* in the local Gulf dialect) are considered *sunnah* as they are mentioned in Islamic texts. Traditional Chinese medicine has become so popular in the UAE that in 2011 China's most famous company in this field, Tong Ren Tang, opened a major clinic and pharmacy in Dubai's Health Care City.[14]

5.1. Abu Dhabi Model Chinese School – Mushrif School

Around 2005, articles started appearing in the US and British press about the phenomenal rise in demand for Chinese-speaking nannies in the homes of the super-wealthy in New York City. Ambitious and successful parents were beginning to realize the importance of China in the future and wanted to give their children a head start. Meanwhile, in Abu Dhabi, the ruling family was taking an even more ambitious approach. In 2006, a tri-lingual (Chinese, Arabic, and English) kindergarten was established in Abu Dhabi. Catering for Emirati families, the school started with a kindergarten program, and then added a grade every year. In the autumn of 2012, there were approximately 300 students at the school, going up to Grade 5. By 2019, it expects to have over 800 students, and have classes all the way up to Grade 12. The school has proven to be very popular and there is a waiting list for entrance. In July 2011, during the visit of a high level Chinese official to the UAE, Shaikh Mohammad bin Zayed, Crown Prince of Abu Dhabi, mentioned that he saw the school "as a bridge of cultural communication and civilizational interaction" between the two countries.[15]

5.2. Confucius Institutes

In the last two years, two Confucius Institutes have been established in the UAE. In September 2011, the first Confucius Institute in the region was established at Dubai University. Public interest in the Chinese languages courses being offered has been high.[16] A second Confucius Institute opened in March 2012 at the Zayed University campus in Abu Dhabi. It also provides language courses to the general public that have proven to be quite popular. In the summer of 2012, the Confucius Institute in Dubai hosted a group of Arabic teachers from Ningxia as part of a two and half month intensive study program to improve ties between the two regions. The teachers from Ningxia took courses on Arabic literature, Arab culture, politics, diplomacy, and economics.[17] This project is just one of the ways in which both China and the Gulf countries are hoping both to improve ties and, at the same time, opportunities for China's large Muslim minority population. In August 2012, Qatar University announced it was planning to establish a Confucius Institute there as well.

5.3. Zayed Centre in Beijing

Although recent efforts to support language training between China and the Gulf have focused on Chinese language instruction in the UAE, in fact it was Shaikh Zayed who almost 20 years ago financed a project in Beijing to promote Arabic language training. In 1994, the UAE Centre for the Study of Islamic Culture and Arabic Language was established at Beijing Foreign Studies University. Originally intended to assist Chinese diplomats being posted to the Middle East, the program now attracts students eager to engage in all aspects of China's growing political and economic ties with the region. In 2010, the UAE government spent $2.8 million to refurbish and expand the center, which has been renamed the Shaikh Zayed Centre for Islamic and Arabic Studies. The number of Chinese universities offering Arabic language programs has increased dramatically over the past few years. Today close to 30 universities offer Arabic classes, whereas just a decade ago only seven universities did.[18]

5.4. Saudi students studying in China

Saudi Arabia, on its side, has taken a very different approach to enabling its citizens to engage with China. Instead of focusing on Chinese language instruction in Saudi Arabia, it has been encouraging its students to attend universities in China. Since the 1970s, China has engaged in a 'soft-power' educational initiative, sponsoring thousands of students from developing countries to attend universities in China. Saudi Arabia first sent students to China in 1986, however, it was approximately 10 years ago that more systematic efforts began. Among the most important of these was Saudi Aramco's program for sending its employees and Saudi students to study at several universities in China. There are now over 1,100 Saudi students studying in universities throughout the country.[19]

After spending a year completing an intensive Chinese language program, these students then begin their studies in a range of fields. Although petrochemical engineering is one of the most common majors, students major in other degree programs as well. Saudi universities have signed numerous research and exchange agreements with different universities in China, and even before the King Abdullah University of Science and Technology (KAUST) opened its doors in 2010, research agreements and student exchanges with China had already been developed.

Many of the tens and thousands of Middle Eastern and African students who graduated from China's top universities have played a prominent role in facilitating China's successful inroads in their home countries, as they rose in their careers upon their return home. It will be interesting to see whether or not, over the next few years, other Gulf countries will follow the lead of Saudi Arabia, and encourage their students to study in China.

5.5. Saraab – Cai Guo-qiang's Exhibit at the Mathaf: The Arab Museum of Modern Art in Doha

At present, as has been noted, businessmen from the Middle East and the Gulf seeking to do trade with China can take any one of the dozens of daily direct flights that have sprung up over the past three years from Dubai, Abu Dhabi, and Doha to China's major cities. However, for the Muslim traders from the Gulf who made their way to China over a millennium ago, the journey was a long and dangerous one. After passing through the Strait of Hormuz, traders would follow the Monsoon winds across the Indian Ocean, through the Strait of Malacca and up into the South China Sea.

In late 2011, the souls of dozens of Muslims from the Gulf who had died centuries ago in Quanzhou (an ancient port city along China's Southeast coast) made a symbolic return to their homeland, through the art of Cai Guo-qiang. Cai Guo-qiang is perhaps the most famous modern Chinese artist of our times. In addition to having major exhibits of his work throughout the world, in China, he is regarded as the brilliant mastermind behind the hugely successful fireworks and theatrical extravaganzas featured in the opening and closing ceremonies of the 2008 Olympic Games in Beijing.

As a child growing up in Quanzhou, Cai had played in the Muslim cemeteries along the hillsides just outside the city and had noticed the strange designs on the headstones. Decades later, when he was asked by Shaikha Mayassa, head of the Qatar Museum Authority, to create a series of artworks for his first major exhibit in the Middle East, Cai Guo-qiang not only remembered the tombstones, but decided to reunite them with their homeland. Cai had local artisans in Quanzhou carefully reproduce epitaphs from the Muslim tombstones by engraving them onto 60 large boulders, shipping them all the way to Qatar, and then having them installed around the entry of the museum in Doha.

The engravings not only carefully replicate the epitaphs and the different styles of Arabic calligraphy that evolved in China over the centuries, they also evoke the sense of distance and solitude that comes from dying so far away from home. One of the most common inscriptions engraved on the boulders is, "Whoever dies as a foreigner, dies a martyr."

Cai's six-month exhibit in Doha (December 2011 – May 2012) not only attracted visitors from all over the Gulf, but more importantly a significant sector of Qatari society. Museums in Qatar have generally not been as successful as expected in attracting local residents. The Saraab exhibit, however, started off with a bang (actually a series of explosion works) and many local residents who visited the museum expressed their appreciation for the extraordinary art work Cai had created for the exhibit. Qatari visitors were moved and delighted at Cai's ability to incorporate so many traditional symbols of Gulf society into works of art that were decidedly Chinese. In addition, works such as the collection of boulders with descriptions, the three boats floating in a giant wave tank, and the huge re-interpretation of a 15th century Ming Dynasty maritime map detailing the route from China to the Gulf, acted as powerful reminders of the historic links between these two regions.

Another work involved gunpowder and the use of half a dozen *shayla*s and *abaya*s. In one especially striking installation piece, a cast of falcons carry a life-size baby camel away. In another work, 640 intricately created porcelain tiles covered with floral creations are connected in a massive work that then has the Gulf Arabic term for "fragile" written in a gunpowder explosion across it. But the piece of artwork that proved to be the most popular was "99 Horses." Another massive work created with gunpowder and the work of dozens of local volunteers, the painting portrays a herd of 99 horses galloping across the desert. However, the scale of the representation is accentuated by a miniature herd of gold-plated horses suspended in front of the top of the painting with its shadow adding an ethereal element to the painting.

Cai's work left a lasting impression on the visitors to the exhibit, and there was also a reciprocal change in the artist's own vision. Cai found himself gaining insight into both Qatari society and Chinese society, as well as into the history of his hometown. During his two-month stay in Doha creating these works, Cai frequently spoke about his work. With regard to the "Homecoming" collection of boulders, he stated that it was not his intention to express sorrow or grief over the ancient Arabs' passing away in a foreign land. Instead, he wanted to offer solace and closure by bringing them back home after a thousand-year journey. He said that this was also a journey that brought him back to his hometown Quanzhou by exploring its history and culture.

6. Conclusion

Virtually every day, new reports appear about major new developments in China-Gulf relations. In 2012 alone, the Habshan-Fujairah pipeline went into operation and Qatar announced it had applied for permission to invest $5 billion dollars in China's stock market and government bonds. In a recent trip to Beijing virtually every Chinese person I spoke with had heard of Dubai, and most had heard of Qatar. Flights going back and forth between China and the Gulf are full, and the government of the UAE appears to have lost track of how many Chinese are now living in the Emirates. This chapter focused on just a few of the ways in which the lives of Chinese and Gulf Arabs are once again crossing paths, with individuals living in each others' homelands, and slowly but surely influencing each other's societies. At this point in time, it is difficult to predict in what ways China-Gulf relations will develop in the future: how will the focus be shared between joint ventures developing renewable and alternative energy sources, joint food security and development projects in Africa, educational exchange projects, military alliances, intra-Asia rail systems? The possibilities are almost endless as these two dynamic economic systems continue to thrive and expand and seek new ways to invest their multi-billion dollar sovereign wealth funds to insure their economic futures.

Endnotes

1   The _dhow_ is believed to have been built in one of the seaports of the Gulf. Like other traditional _dhow_, this one was constructed without the use of nails.
2   The exhibit, entitled "Shipwrecked: Tang Treasures and Monsoon Winds," was jointly curated by the Smithsonian's Freer-Sackler Gallery and the Asian Civilizations Museum of Singapore.
3   Bi Mingxin (ed.), "Yiwu's Transformation to International Trade Market," _Xinhua_, 21 December 2011. Retrieved from the Chinese Government's Official Web Portal, 20 March 2012, http://english.gov.cn/2011-12/21/content_2026085.htm.
4   Wang Yanfang. "Wang Zhengwei: Build a golden bank along the Yellow River," China.org.cn, 14 February 2011. http://www.china.org.cn/travel/Ningxia/2011-02/14/content_21917688.htm
5   Siraj Wahab, "China Earns Newfound Respect with Mashair," _Arab News_, 20 November 2010.
6   Imran Garda, "Red Workers, Green Trains Make Hajj Easier—For Some," _Al Jazeera_, 13 November 2010.
7   UPI, "Chinese Railway Workers Arrested," 14 October 2010.
8   Shehab Al Makahleh, "Habshan-Fujairah Pipeline Starts Pumping Crude Oil," _Gulf News_ [UAE], 21 June 2012.
9   Vicky Kapur, "Dubai among Top 10 Tourist Destinations," _Emirates 24/7_, 2 June 2011.
10 Aya Lowe, "Hospitality Firms Target Newly Affluent China," _Gulf News_ (UAE), 25 May 2011. In addition, the Jumeirah Hotel Group has recently opened a luxury hotel in Shanghai, in part as a strategy to introduce more Chinese to its brand.
11 Qatar Airways has flights to Beijing, Shanghai, and Guangzhou; Emirates flies to Beijing, Shanghai, and Guangzhou; and Etihad has flights to Beijing and Chengdu, with flights to Shanghai that began in March 2012. China's largest airline, Air China, has regular flights from Beijing to Dubai and flights to Kuwait via Karachi. China Southern has flights from Guangzhou to Dubai, and China Eastern recently inaugurated direct flights from Yinchuan to Dubai, via Kunming.

12 Greg Lindsay, "Cities of the Sky." *The Wall Street Journal*, 26 February 2011.
13 Yazad Darasha, "Dragon Breathes Fire Again: China Uses Three-Pronged Strategy to Become Mideast's Top Investment Partner," *Gulf News* [UAE], 8 August 2010.
14 "Traditional Chinese Medicine Company Lands in Middle East," *Xinhua News Service*, 19 October 2011.
15 "UAE Gives Full Attention to Ties With China," *WAM* (Emirates News Agency), 13 July 2011.
16 Rania Moussly, "Chinese Language, Culture Classes on Offer in Dubai," *Gulf News* (UAE), 22 August 2010.
17 "Ningxia Hui Sends Students to Dubai for Cultural Training," *Xinhua News Service*, 2 June 2012.
18 Daniel Bardsley, "A Two-Way Trade in Languages." *The National* (UAE), 1 September 2010.
19 Shahid Ali Khan, "More Saudis Seek to Study In China," *Saudi Gazette*, 24 April 2011.

Bibliography

Al Makahleh, Shehab. "Habshan-Fujairah Pipeline Starts Pumping Crude Oil," *Gulf News* [UAE], 21 June 2012.

Bardsley, Daniel. "A two-way trade in languages." *The National* [UAE], 1 September 2010.

Bardsley, Daniel. "Yiwu is the 'fastest growing Muslim community' in China," *The National* [UAE], 12 August 2012.

Bi Mingxin (ed.), "Yiwu's Transformation to International Trade Market," *Xinhua*, 21 December 2011. Retrieved from the Chinese Government's Official Web Portal, 20 March 2012, http://english.gov.cn/2011-12/21/content_2026085.htm.

Darasha, Yazad. "Dragon breathes fire again: China uses three-pronged strategy to become Mideast's top investment partner." *Gulf News* [UAE], 8 August 2010.

Garda, Imran. "Red workers, green trains make Hajj easier - for some." *Al Jazeera*, 13 November 2010.

Kapur, Vicky. "Dubai among Top 10 Tourist Destinations," *Emirates 24/7*, 2 June 2011.

Kemp, Geoffrey. *The East Moves West: India, China, and Asia's Growing Presence in the Middle East.* Washington, D.C.: Brookings Institution, Press, 2010.

Khan, Shahid Ali. "More Saudis seek to Study in China." *Saudi Gazette*, 24 April 2011.

Kumar, Himendra Moah. "Fujairah poised to become oil export hub." *Gulf News* [UAE], 12 June 2011.

Lindsey, Greg. "Cities of the Sky: From Dubai to Chongqing to Honduras, the Silk Road of the future is taking shape in urban developments based on airport hubs." *The Wall Street Journal*, 26 February 2011.

Lowe, Aya. "Hospitality firms target newly affluent China." *Gulf News* [UAE], 25 May 2011.

Moussly, Rania. "Chinese language, culture classes on offer in Dubai." *Gulf News* [UAE], 22 August 2010.

Rahman, Saifur. "China-UAE trade likely to touch $100b by 2015." *Gulf News* [UAE], 11 July 2008.

Shaheen, Abdul Rahman. "Over 600 Chinese nationals working in Saudi embrace Islam." *Gulf News* [UAE], 27 September 2009.

Simpfendorfer, Ben. *The New Silk Road: How a Rising Arab World is Turning Away from the West and Rediscovering China.* New York: Palgrave Macmillan, 2009.

UPI, "Chinese Railway Workers Arrested," 14 October 2010.

Wahab, Siraj. "China earns newfound respect with Mashair." *Arab News* [Saudi Arabia], 20 November 2010.

WAM (Emirates News Agency). "UAE Gives Full Attention to Ties With China," 13 July 2011.

Wang Yanfang. "Wang Zhengwei: Build a golden bank along the Yellow River," China.org.cn, 14 February 2011. http://www.china.org.cn/travel/Ningxia/2011-02/14/content_21917688.htm

Xinhua News Service. "Ningxia Hui Sends Students to Dubai for Cultural Training," 2 June 2012.

Xinhua News Service. "Traditional Chinese Medicine Company Lands in Middle East," 19 October 2011.

Chapter Twelve

Beyond Food for Fuel:
The Little Red Dot in GCC-ASEAN Relations

Sofiah Jamil

1. Introduction

In a press conference following the first meeting between foreign ministers from the Association of Southeast Asian Nations (ASEAN) and the Gulf Cooperation Council (GCC) in 2009, ASEAN Secretary-General Surin Pitsuwan summed up the growing trade ties between the regions with, "You have what we don't have, and we have plenty of what you don't have, so we need each other."[1] By this, he was referring to the abundance of energy sources in the Arabian Gulf and the agricultural potential of Southeast Asia. Indeed, growing concerns over energy and food security have been a prominent topic in the discussions, which took place about a year after the global food crisis of 2007-2008. Given the fact that Gulf Arab countries imported 80% of their staple foods at a cost of $20 billion in 2008, they have shown an increasing interest in Southeast Asia's fertile farmland. Conversely, Southeast Asian countries continue to demand more energy resources such as oil and liquefied natural gas (LNG) to facilitate their economic development plans. While the meeting did herald a start to accelerating exchanges between the two regions, it is important to take into account existing developments that have contributed to this milestone.

Understanding GCC-Singapore relations is interesting in this regard as Singapore does not fit neatly into this 'food for fuel' arrangement, but has nevertheless played a significant role in facilitating this inter-regional exchange. Unlike its Southeast Asian neighbours, Singapore only covers a land space of 710 sq km, has no natural resources, and was historically a highly water-stressed nation.[2] Nevertheless, within the past 40 years, Singapore has leveraged on its strategic location, adopted pragmatic development policies, and has emerged as one of the most highly industrialised East Asian nations. As such, despite being a "little red dot"[3] on the map, the Singapore story has demonstrated how great things come in small packages. It is therefore not natural resources that Singapore has to offer the Gulf Arab region, but rather its wealth of human resources and expertise in various sectors to facilitate economic – and more importantly – human development. Conversely, while the Gulf Arab region has been an important source of fossil fuels for Singapore, the increased interest from the Middle East will help to sustain Singapore's economic growth and development, primarily by providing a range of business and investment opportunities for Singaporeans.

That said, there are also several socio-political lessons to be learnt from the Singapore story beyond the realm of national economic development. This paper will therefore assert that Singapore plays a significant role for the Gulf Arab region in not only providing examples of commendable developmental policies and strategies, but also acting as a conduit for engagement with the wider East Asian region, and sharing lessons relating to the challenges in managing diversity and the limits of conventional economic development.

2. The Singaporean Experience in Human Development Strategies

The character of Singapore's interaction with other states is moulded by its success in devising and pursuing effective human development strategies. This is as important in the country's relationship with the Gulf states as with other states, and it is therefore worth giving some attention to these strategies before examining the course taken by Singapore-Gulf relations.

Human development – as defined by the 1998 Nobel Laureate in Economics, Prof. Amartya Sen – is an approach that seeks to advance "the richness of human life, rather than the richness of the economy in which human beings live, which is only a part of it."[4] This definition highlights the importance of going beyond materialistic and economic values by including social development. To understand both the social and the economic aspects of development, the United Nations'

Human Development Index (HDI) provides a measurement for it based on three dimensions: health, education and living standards. These are in turn determined by four indicators: life expectancy at birth, mean years and expected years of schooling, and gross national income per capita.[5]

While there are only 3 dimensions to the HDI, meeting them requires input in other fields. The health dimension, for instance, implies taking into account factors such as the availability of clean water and the provision of food, which would be essential for proper nutrition and ensuring high life expectancy. Access to immunisation and other forms of infant and maternal healthcare are equally important. Ensuring good education for children not only requires accessibility to educational resources but also proper training of qualified teachers. In light of these requirements, substantial investments in good social infrastructure are vital.

A reasonable measure of economic development is therefore needed to generate the necessary financial capacity to provide for these social needs. Several studies have shown a strong relationship between gross domestic product (GDP) per capita and various indicators of development (including life expectancy and literacy),[6] as well as the co-relation between free trade and the HDI.[7] That said, however, such success would only be possible by balancing economic development with good governance that channels a sufficient proportion of the country's wealth to human development.

Singapore is an example of such success given its pragmatic development policies, which have integrated the human development needs of its people since gaining independence in 1965. From its export-oriented strategies in developing its manufacturing and service industries to an emphasis on manpower development through training, and concretising legal standards for businesses, the Singaporean government also ensured sufficient funds devoted to healthcare and education.[8] The result has been deemed to be an "economic miracle," as Singapore, Taiwan, Hong Kong and South Korea were East Asia's highly developed economies by the 1990s, known as the Asian Tigers.

In terms of human development rankings, Singapore ranks in 26th position globally, well ahead of the Gulf Arab countries and of its Southeast Asian neighbours (see Table 12.1). Several points are worth noting from Singapore's achievement in this ranking. First, a lack of natural resources is not necessarily an impediment to a country's growth and development. Second, good governance is key to ensuring that sufficient resources are channelled to meeting these human development needs. The HDI is also a good indicator of examining national policy choices, by questioning how it is that Singapore, with a lower Gross National Income (GNI) than its Gulf

Arab counterparts such as Qatar, the UAE and Kuwait, is able to fare better in its human development outcomes.[9] A possible explanation to this would be to examine public spending on education as a percentage of total government expenditures, of which Gulf countries trail behind East Asian countries such as Singapore and Korea.[10] That said, Gulf Arab countries have recognised the success stories of such East Asian economies and have sought to learn from them, particularly in recent years. This is reflected in the account of the development of economic links in the two sections which follow. There is, however, an important caveat to mention in Singapore's success story. While Singapore's economic development is remarkable, its success has been more of an exception, as Singapore's size and population is far smaller than other industrialising countries. To illustrate this point, Singapore's population of about 5 million is comparable to that of the city of Bangalore alone in India. As such, managing development in other countries would be much harder than in Singapore, as the former would have to operate on much larger scales.

3. Growing Economic Links between Singapore and the Gulf Region

The last decade has seen a steady development in the relationship between Singapore and the Gulf states. In part this reflects a wider phenomenon: a strengthening Middle Eastern interest in Singapore's experience and expertise. After the September 11th attacks of 2001, in particular, there has been an increasing number of high-level visits to Singapore by Middle Eastern leaders and officials. These visits have led to increased economic engagement and exchange, as will be demonstrated.

Three main factors account for the growing interest. First, a growing consciousness among Middle East governments of the need to diversify their economies and ensure long-term sustainability. These are areas where Singapore has proven experience. Second, the rapid growth of the Chinese economy has opened up new markets in Asia generally, with Singapore being a key part of this. Third, the events of 9/11 demonstrated the vulnerability of Middle Eastern states in the face of tighter security restrictions and waves of Islamophobia in Western countries. Singapore constitutes an alternative avenue for trade and investment, as do Asian states.

Singapore has made extensive efforts to respond to the increased interest from the Middle East. Under the auspices of Senior Minister Goh Chok Tong, Singapore has strengthened diplomatic and economic relations with Middle Eastern countries. One initiative was to establish the Middle East Business Group (MEBG) in 2007 as a means of providing assistance to Singaporean companies and businessmen to venture into the Middle East. The MEBG – part of the Singapore Business Federation – fills an important gap by sensitising Singaporean companies to the business environment in the respective Middle Eastern countries with a series of workshops, seminars and people-to-people exchanges.[11]

Another major development in Gulf Arab and Singapore relations, specifically, occurred in December 2008 with the establishment of the Gulf Singapore Free Trade Agreement (GSFTA). This was a significant milestone as it was the first free trade agreement signed by the GCC as a collective body with another country.[12] The GSFTA would allow Singapore to reduce the net import trade deficit that it has with GCC countries. With Saudi Arabia alone (its major Gulf Arab trading partner), Singapore had a net trade deficit of $14 billion in 2010. The GSFTA thus entitles Singapore to tariff-free concessions for 99% of its domestic exports to the GCC, thereby increasing the competitiveness of Singapore's goods vis-à-vis other foreign imports entering the GCC.[13] In addition to this, the GSFTA states that Singapore's *halal* certification under the Majlis Ugama Islam Singapura (MUIS) would also be recognized by GCC member states. It is predicted that if successful, Singapore's *halal* food exports will garner a bigger share of the GCC's food import market, which is worth S$18 billion (US$13 billion) annually.'[14] As such, the GSFTA provides the necessary support needed to increase trade opportunities and reduce the pressure on Singapore's import expenditure.

Positive effects from the GSFTA are slowly materialising. In terms of the level of trade, the extent of Singaporean trade with individual GCC member states varies from as low as $424.2 million with Bahrain to $16.4 billion with Saudi Arabia.[15] The UAE and Saudi Arabia are Singapore's main trading partners in the Gulf – understandably for oil imports. That said, there has been an increasing trend in non-oil trade such as with the UAE.[16] Moreover - although not a GCC member state - Singapore's trade with Iran is also fairly significant with up to $3.47 billion, making Iran Singapore's 30th largest trading partner in 2010. The Middle East in aggregate is currently Singapore's 6th largest trading partner with a total trade volume reaching S$65.5 billion in 2011.[17]

What is also interesting is that despite being a latecomer in tapping the Gulf Arab market, Singapore has been able to establish an FTA before other Southeast Asian countries – particularly Indonesia and Malaysia – which have had longer ties with the Arabian Gulf. There are two contributing factors to this. Firstly, from the outset, Singapore has focused on boosting its relations with the Arab Gulf on trade. Singapore's Middle East Eminent Persons Programme (MEEPP), [18] for instance, was launched in early 2007 as a means of inviting distinguished leaders from the

Middle East to have a better understanding of Singapore and, in turn, facilitate discussions on bilateral cooperation. Neighboring Malaysia, on the other hand, had historically emphasized religious affinity and was initially a recipient of loans from the Arab Gulf before boosting economic ties.[19] Secondly, Singapore's pro-business environment with its track record of clean and efficient governance processes makes the island state an attractive partner for establishing an FTA.

Singapore's strategic location and pro-business environment have continued to be attractive assets for attracting foreign direct investments. As of December 2009[20], Singapore has been home to 310 companies from the Middle East, including Dubai Drydocks, AlJaber and the Emirates National Oil Company from the UAE, Kuwaiti-listed Agility Logistics and the Saudi Basic Industries Corporation. Of particular mention for Singapore would be two landmark investment deals in the manufacturing sector. The first would be the acquisition of Singapore's Chartered Semiconductor Pte Ltd. by Advanced Technology Investment Co. (ATIC), part of Abu Dhabi's state-owned conglomerate, Mubadala. The US$3.9 billion (S$5.4 billion) deal marked the largest investment made by Abu Dhabi in Singapore. The second would be the formation of a joint venture company by Qatar Petroleum International and Shell Eastern Petroleum.

Boosting trade with the Gulf region would also work hand-in-hand with Singapore's efforts to ensure energy security. The joint venture company between Qatar Petroleum International and Shell Eastern Petroleum, for instance, would complement Singapore's efforts to diversify its energy mix and increase demand for LNG imports from Qatar. This is due to Shell's stake in the Qatargas LNG projects, which is seen as a means of facilitating Qatar's vision to become the world's largest LNG supplier.[21] In addition to this, Singapore has also been looking into other plans to facilitate LNG imports such as assessing the feasibility of LNG bunkering for sustainable growth in Singapore's maritime industry.[22] Such forward-planning would not only enhance Singapore's attractiveness as a trading port, but also a means of engaging other suppliers of LNG in the future.

Growing GCC-Singapore ties have also contributed to Singapore's tourism industry, with a steady increase of visitors from the Gulf Arab states, many of whom come as part of health tourism. Singapore's commitment to providing efficient and advanced healthcare systems has also contributed to the increase in visitors to Singapore seeking medical treatments. Overall, Emiratis make up a substantial number of West Asian visitors to Singapore (see Table 12.2). Iran, Saudi Arabia and Kuwait are also major visitors from the Arabian Gulf. That said, however, critics note that the island state is a latecomer in attracting the Middle East market, since neighboring Muslim countries – Malaysia and Indonesia – have been the common Southeast Asian holiday destinations for Middle Easterners. Nevertheless, with the increasing availability of halal food and Muslim amenities in Singapore – on top of its established tourism industry – it is likely that Singapore will continue to see a steady inflow of visitors from the Middle East in the future.

Aside from these conventional modes of trade and economic cooperation, Singapore's expertise in various forms of infrastructure has also been increasingly sought after by Gulf Arab countries. The potential for this was highlighted by Singapore's Former Minister Mentor, Mr. Lee Kuan Yew, who noted that the GCC offers Singapore "many opportunities for consultancies and to transmit [its] various management skills in managing cities, airports and enterprises."[23] Recent consultancy projects on public infrastructure include the operation of Dubai's The Palm Jumeirah Rail Transit system,[24] and the planning of the Sudair Industrial City, one of the seven economic cities planned in Saudi Arabia.[25]

Improving education standards in Gulf Arab states has been another form of social infrastructure co-operation that has seen extensive engagement. This has involved Singaporean academics and experts as consultants in enhancing educational institutions in the Arabian Gulf. Such interest is clear given Singapore's track record in primary, secondary and tertiary education.[26] There has also been interest in how Singapore has integrated the use of information and communication technology into their educational institutions to facilitate learning.[27] Singapore has consequently provided technical assistance and facilitated exchanges with several Gulf Arab counterparts. In particular, Singapore's National Institute for Education has trained Emirati teachers in Abu Dhabi,[28] provided advisory services in Bahrain's education reforms initiatives and was also involved in setting up the Bahrain Teachers College from 2007 to 2010. Other engagements in the Gulf Arab region include partnership with the King Saud University in Saudi Arabia to develop its leadership program and reforms in its mathematics and science curriculum, as well as discussions to provide advisory services to Qatar University's College of Education.[29] This is a good start and if deemed successful, would likely be further expanded in other areas of education in the future.

Another field of greater Gulf Arab and Singapore cooperation has been the health sector. In Saudi Arabia, for instance, several Singaporean companies have been engaged to improve aspects of the Saudi health system[30] while technical cooperation in improving dengue control measures was carried out in Jeddah in 2006. Such efforts in health security, particularly in terms of addressing communicable diseases in Saudi Arabia would be vital given the potential outbreak of diseases during the annual Hajj pilgrimage that brings close to 2 million Muslims from around the world to the cities of Makkah and Medina. Such concerns became even more pressing during the period when Avian Influenza was apparent in several Muslim countries worldwide,[31] which not only resulted in human fatalities, but also a depletion in livestock, which is the main source of livelihood for many citizens in developing countries. This, therefore, affects a country's economic productivity. Hence, by improving a country's capacity to address transnational security issues such as pandemics, it would not only ensure the security of its people, but can potentially serve to protect the security needs of the wider region.

Given the above mentioned economic projects and numerous technical cooperative arrangements between Singapore and GCC countries, there is certainly a strong start in boosting economic relations. However, it remains to be seen how long the positive trajectory in trade thus far will last and to what extent it would be significant. That said however, the relations have definitely given a further boost to Singapore's international image and business community via sharing its development experience and providing opportunities to untapped markets respectively.

4. Singapore's Human Presence in the Gulf States

The growing economic relations between Singapore and the Gulf States have also resulted in a growing number of Singapore companies and businessmen venturing to the Middle East. Some of Singapore's major firms have been engaged in various national planning or public infrastructure projects. In Oman, for instance, Singapore's Sembcorp has invested $1bn in water and power projects in Salalah (for which Hyflux will design and supply the desalination facility),[32] while Top Great Engineering and Marine Pte Ltd is helping to develop Duqm's Drydocks[33] - both of which are valued at nearly RO10 mn. As of 2011, close to 65 Singaporean companies have set up shop in Oman.[34]

Efforts to improve tertiary education systems in the Gulf have also meant engaging Singaporean academics to teach in or even manage Gulf Arab education institutions. One of the most notable developments has been the appointment of the former President and Vice-Chancellor of the National University of Singapore, Professor Shih Choon Fong, as the Founding President and Professor of Electrical Engineering at the King Abdullah University for Science and Technology (KAUST) in Saudi Arabia. As such, Singaporeans residing in the Gulf region are not just from the private sector, but also comprise academics and other practitioners related to the public sector.

Despite the expanding socio-economic links, the number of Singaporeans in the Gulf region is still relatively small, although growing and varying substantially in the different Gulf Arab states. The UAE accounts for the largest proportion of Singaporeans in the Gulf Arab region with up to a thousand Singaporeans in 2011 compared to less than 50 in the 1980s. At the other end of the spectrum, Oman has been home to about 50 Singaporeans in 2009.[35] In Qatar, the Singapore Association known as *Reddotters @ Qatar* had about 200 registered members in 2007,[36] while Bahrain had approximately 200 Singaporeans in 2011.[37] It is likely that with a burgeoning middle class with greater mobility and willingness to venture globally, the number of Singaporeans in the Middle East will increase in the future.

Increasing the number of Singaporeans in the Gulf States will be facilitated by the growing openness of the Gulf Arab states' development policies. Kuwait, for instance, while only Singapore's 4th largest trading partner in the GCC, has seen its bilateral trade with Singapore exceed 20 per cent year-on-year to reach S$4.7 billion in 2011. Moreover, with Kuwait's commitment to liberalizing its economy since 2010 and projected plans worth more than $115 billion in the pipeline (including privatization of public firms and construction of mega-projects through public-private partnerships) as of early 2012, it sets itself as one of the most promising project markets in the region.[38] Oman has also been investing heavily in the sea-ports sector with more than 12 ports in the pipeline, as well as opportunities in services sectors - IT, oil and gas and tourism.[39] In light of these developments, coupled with the available support structures in Singapore, there are many prospects for Singaporeans to venture into the Gulf Arab region.

5. A Conduit for engaging East and Southeast Asia

Singapore's engagement with the Gulf and the Wider Middle East can also be seen in terms of its role as a conduit for, and facilitator of, wider Asian engagement with the Gulf: working with other Asian countries to promote relations with the Gulf, and working with Gulf countries to enhance their engagement in Asia and their understanding of the region.

Two multilateral efforts are particularly noteworthy. The first is the Asia-Middle East Dialogue (AMED), for which Singapore mooted the idea in 2004, to increase inter-regional exchange and greater cooperation via the formation of working groups.[40] In 2005, Singapore jointly co-chaired the Working Group on Social, Educational, Scientific, Cultural, Environmental and Media (SESCEM) Issues, which examined three areas: human resource development and media;

promotion of co-operation in science, technology and research; and tradition and modernity. In all of these areas, Singapore has been active in sharing its experience with other Asian and Middle Eastern countries.

The AMED process was also a means of facilitating greater technical cooperation between the two regions. Singapore's contribution to technical cooperation under AMED has largely been in terms of human resource development via regional training centers that had been established under the AMED.[41] Some of the training that Singapore has jointly conducted with the regional training center in Qatar include courses related to improving public administration, enhancing skills in negotiating FTAs, and land-use planning based on Singapore's experience.[42] In addition to this, Singapore has also developed new training courses on aviation security, port management and intellectual property protection under the Singapore Cooperation Program.

While the initial AMED meetings focused on conventional areas of cooperation, Singapore has raised the importance of recognizing and addressing contemporary transboundary challenges in subsequent AMED meetings. In 2009, Singapore hosted the first AMED Media Roundtable, which brought together 34 journalists from the Middle East and Asia to discuss how media organizations from the two regions could better cooperate[43] and, in some respects, reduce the dependency on Western-based media sources. In addition to this, during the second AMED meeting in Sharm El Sheikh, the then foreign minister of Singapore, Brig-Gen. George Yeo, expressed the importance of discussing pertinent contemporary issues such as energy security, climate change, religious conflict, maritime security and pandemic outbreaks.[44] In view of the contemporary challenges in those fields, the experiences of Singapore and other East and Southeast Asian countries are clearly relevant to the Gulf states.

The second multilateral engagement has been through the Association of Southeast Asian Nations (ASEAN).[45] On the basis of its existing relations with the GCC and as a founding member of ASEAN, Singapore has been in a good position to provide a voice to other less developed ASEAN member states and thereby galvanize cooperation between the GCC and ASEAN. Singapore's FTA with the GCC, for example, has served as a stepping stone for establishing a GCC-ASEAN FTA.[46] Like Singapore, other Southeast Asian countries suffer from a trade deficit with Gulf Arab countries, despite the growth of overall trade.[47] This led to a series of high level meetings between GCC and ASEAN member states, and culminated in the formulation of the GCC-ASEAN Plan of Action (2010–2012). The plan focuses on three fields: trade and investment; economic and development cooperation; and education, culture and information. It has been a starting point for future substantial inter-regional cooperation including the possibility of a GCC-ASEAN FTA. While these areas of cooperation are an important start, there is a long way to go for the two regions to understand the intra-regional nuances of their counterpart.

In a more diffuse manner, Singapore has also been in a position to facilitate Gulf understanding of East Asian countries. This is possible given Singapore's strong political and economic links with China, and its shared experiences with South Korea and Japan as highly developed economies.[48] Moreover, many of the above-mentioned non-traditional security challenges – such as disaster management, transnational crime and pandemic outbreaks – are addressed cooperatively by East and Southeast Asian countries. A case in point would be the extensive cooperation between ASEAN and China in curbing pandemic outbreaks such as Avian Influenza,[49] where Singapore contributed its experience in controlling the SARS outbreak in 2003. What these developments point to is the fact that East and Southeast Asian states acknowledge the possible socio-economic (and at times political) ramifications of not addressing non-traditional security challenges effectively. Such lessons may provide significant insights for the GCC in its long-term national and regional planning.

As such, there is much in Singapore's unique position in the East and Southeast Asian regions that the Gulf Arab region can take advantage of. That said, however, Singapore is also facing considerable challenges which may not always be highlighted at the international level. The next section will discuss these challenges. As the Gulf states share many of the same challenges, there is room for experience to be shared here.

6. Managing the Challenges

While Singapore has been able to pride itself as being highly developed and has the capacity to address many socio-economic and transnational issues, there are still significant mid- to long-term challenges. These are essentially challenges in managing the regional environment and in coping with cultural and economic diversity. They have become increasingly apparent to Singaporeans in recent years.

6.1 Managing the Regional Environment
Singapore's security is ultimately dependent on regional security. If we examine security as being a concept that encompasses human development aspects,

then regional security in this regard does not merely refer to territorial security but also to securing basic needs such as food and water, and economic well-being. While Singapore has been boosting its efforts to diversify its sources of food imports and increase its local produce, much of the demand will still ultimately have to be met from external (mainly other ASEAN) sources. The problems coming from this were evident in the 2008 food/fuel crisis when Thailand, a primary producer of rice in Southeast Asia, temporarily ceased its rice exports. In addition to this, the increasing intensity of weather-related disasters also exacerbates the fluctuations in the level of the region's agricultural productivity.

Regional environmental issues can also adversely impact on Singapore's economic well-being. The annual trans-boundary haze, for instance, which is a result of forest fires in neighboring Indonesia, has been a major factor causing poor air quality and thus affecting people's health. The visibility on the trading routes is also impaired. Estimates on the damage from the 1997-1998 haze, for instance, range from $4.47 billion[50] to more than $9 billion.[51] Some 70 million people throughout the region were affected.[52] The 2006 haze is estimated to have cost Singapore about $50 million.[53] Efforts to address the trans-boundary haze remain unsatisfactory, as Indonesia has still not ratified the ASEAN agreement on trans-boundary haze pollution due to opposition at the national level as well as perceptions that local capacity impedes effective implementation of the solutions.[54] A common criticism of ASEAN is the fact that while various regional frameworks have been established, very little of it gets implemented nationally. ASEAN member states have varying levels of resource capacity, which has implications for the implementation of frameworks and operational costs of the regional organization.

These above-mentioned examples indicate that while national development policies may drive Singapore's economic well-being, the country is still vulnerable to non-traditional security (NTS)[55] developments in the region. The GCC states face some similar problems, and these may become yet more complex if the GCC seeks to expand its membership to include countries that are less developed than the six founding member states.

Another NTS challenge for Singapore arises from regional inequalities. Regional economic inequalities lead to flows of migrant workers from one ASEAN country to another. The lack of rights given to migrant workers has been a point of contention between those ASEAN member states which send migrant workers (such as Indonesia and the Philippines) and those which receive them (such as Singapore and Malaysia). Singapore has attempted to make inroads on this matter, including recently passing a bill to legislate a day off for domestic helpers.[56] Even so, the issue continues to be hotly debated, with some sections of Singapore society arguing that such measures compromise the rights of employers.[57] This is clearly a teething period, as it still remains early days for the legislation to effectively take root on the ground, coupled with the fact that information and media coverage – whether global or national – has to be critically assessed.

Issues regarding the treatment of migrant labor have also been of considerable importance to all Gulf Arab countries. This has, moreover, a specific relevance to relations with Southeast Asian countries. The GCC states are prominent recipients of migrant workers from Southeast Asia, and the governments have in some instances been criticized for issues relating to migrant rights. It is understandable that the issue of migrant rights is a highly sensitive topic, but if Gulf Arab and Southeast Asian relations are to be set on a stable basis the issue must be addressed, or at least broached, at some point. There have been moves to address the issues, such as proposals to abolish the employer-based sponsorship system,[58] but there needs to be more frank discussion between Gulf Arab governments and their Southeast Asian counterparts on managing migrant worker issues, particularly in terms of the actual processes of employing migrant workers and the rights given to them. As a first step, the Gulf Arab states may benefit from hearing Singapore's experiences in managing migrant rights issues – not only from government officials, but more importantly from civil society organizations in Singapore working with migrant workers.[59]

6.2 Coping with Cultural and Economic Diversity

Singapore's cultural and economic diversity can provide GCC countries with useful points for consideration and reflection, particularly in aspects or dynamics that are less apparent in official negotiations/exchanges. There is a need, on the Singaporean side, to acknowledge more fully the history and diverse backgrounds of Singaporeans, as well as demonstrate greater sensitivity towards different levels of economic well-being.

The first point to note is that unlike its immediate neighbors – Malaysia and Indonesia – the proportion of Muslims in Singapore's population is a minority. In this regard, Singapore Muslims are wired somewhat differently from their Malaysian and Indonesian counterparts, given the circumstances that they are in. The Singapore Muslim community[60] also exhibits nuanced differences from Muslim minorities in the West, stemming from the fact that they are operating in East

Asian circumstances and were integral to Singapore's national and regional history long before independence. As such, the experiences of Singapore's Muslim minority can potentially provide GCC countries with subtle insights to human development in Singapore as well as understanding the concerns of minority groups.

There has been some acknowledgement of the unique cultural position of Singapore's Muslim community in facilitating the country's relations with Gulf Arab countries.[61] Some members of Singapore's local Arab community, who are largely third and fourth generation descendants of Arab settlers and have assimilated with the larger Malay Muslim community, are contributing to Singapore's bilateral relations with Yemen. Singapore's Non-Resident Ambassador in Sanaa is a Singaporean of Hadrami descent, who still maintains family ties with his ancestral land.[62]

That said, however, Singapore's Arab connection should not be overstated, and more could be done to embrace the significance of Singapore's cultural diversity in its entirety. The changing landscape of Kampong Glam[63] with more arabized features is a case in point. This is an area which reflected the local Malay/Muslim culture that was prevalent in the area in the early days of Singapore history, and which merited conservation and recognition. However, some Singapore Muslims feel that economic interests are changing the character of the area. This, in fact, is part of a broader trend in Singapore in recent years, where transformed landscapes are encountering criticism. With governmental efforts to constantly improve Singapore's economic competitiveness, new infrastructural developments have in some cases meant the loss of some historical and (the few remaining) natural areas in Singapore. There is thus the concern that the rapidly changing physical landscape (to accommodate growing bilateral and multilateral economic ties) undermines the sentimental value that Singaporeans feel towards their homeland.

GCC countries could also consider domestic developments that have manifested themselves as a result of economic growth and development in Singapore. In spite of the high levels of economic development, socio-economic inequality has also increased in Singapore in recent years, particularly seen in the rising costs of living[64] (such as skyrocketing prices of public housing). Societal concerns rising from these increasing costs have been exacerbated by the influx of migrants as part of government policies to address the pressures of Singapore's aging population. Understandably, such trends are evident in other development countries, but what is striking in the Singapore context are the effects that it has had on the ruling government. Social media has played a significant role in amplifying these concerns including assertions by some sections of Singapore society that the government has lost touch with sentiments on the ground. The accumulation of these developments has led to a major loss in public confidence, as witnessed in the results of the general elections in 2011.[65] While the incumbent People's Action Party (PAP) was able to maintain the majority of seats in Parliament, it won only 60.41% of the total votes, which is the lowest percentage it has ever received since independence. It was also the first time in Singapore's history that the PAP lost a multi-member constituency (known as a "group representative constituency" or GRC) to an opposition party. As such, it is clear that while achieving high levels of human development are a basic requirement at the national level, it must be reviewed periodically at the sub-national level – so that individuals and communities are able to accommodate or adapt to the growing economic inequality that may result from economic development. Such developments would require further analysis and understanding of Singapore's domestic scene, but would nevertheless provide a good comparison for Gulf Arab countries that are experiencing similar trends, particularly in the wake of the Arab Spring.

7. Conclusion

It is clear that while the "little red dot" is generally a glowing example of national development and political stability, and an advocate for cordial international ties, Singapore's domestic limitations and regional vulnerabilities need to be recognized. The Gulf Arab region has the opportunity to learn both from Singapore's achievements and its challenges. This constitutes not only a means to enhance development levels in the Gulf Arab states, but also a medium through which they can better understand the political and socio-economic dynamics of the East Asian region. Moreover, the importance of increasing inter-regional people-to-people contact should not be understated, as it serves to fill in gaps which conventional notions of development have failed to cover. Student exchanges and professional study visits are already proving to be an effective means of cultivating these personal interactions between Singapore and the Gulf States, but more can be done, such as increasing the level of interaction between expatriate Singaporean communities in the Gulf and locals. Enhancing such ties would not only provide a means of approaching sensitive issues, but may also serve to "dispel negative stereotypes of each other."[66] Such elements are therefore necessary in ensuring deep relations between the GCC and Singapore (and in extension GCC-ASEAN) beyond diplomatic missions and economic interactions.

Tables and Figures

Table 12.1: Human Development Index Ranking of Gulf Arab and Southeast Asian Countries[67]

Singapore	26
UAE	30
Brunei	33
Qatar	37
Bahrain	42
Saudi Arabia	56
Malaysia	61
Kuwait	63
Oman	89
Thailand	103
Cambodia	139
Philippines	112
Yemen	154

Table 12.2: Visitors to Singapore, by year

Year	Iran	Israel	Kuwait	Saudi Arabia	UAE	Other West Asian countries	Total visitors
2002	2,530	10,288	7,113	6,753	20,784	9,466	**56,934**
2003	3,089	7,779	3,174	3,477	15,686	5,204	**38,409**
2004	5,363	10,546	8,160	7,288	25,158	11,721	**68,236**
2005	6,083	10,670	4,977	6,993	28,062	13,167	**69,952**
2006	9,350	10,148	4,635	9,549	34,013	14,536	**82,231**
2007	14,235	11,025	5,242	10,555	41,054	16,497	**98,608**
2008	19,083	11,402	4,838	10,096	51,170	17,348	**113,937**
2009	23,917	10,884	5,750	10,815	49,529	16,114	**117,009**
2010	36,930	12,831	8,368	12,631	56,474	19,310	**146,544**
2011	32,434	12,137	8,278	17,041	62,736	21,667	**154,293**

Source: Singapore Tourism Board

Endnotes

1 Brian McCartan, "Farmers forgotten in oil-for-food deals", Asia Times, July 31, 2009, accessed October 3, 2012, http://www.atimes.com/atimes/Southeast_Asia/KG31Ae04.html
2 Poh Onn Lee, 2005, Water Management Issues in Singapore, Paper presented at Water In Mainland Southeast Asia, 29 November – 2 December 2005, Siem Reap, Cambodia. accessed

April 20, 2012, http://www.khmerstudies.org/download-files/events/Water/Lee%20Nov%20 2005.pdf

3   The term "little red dot" first gained currency when former Indonesian President B. J. Habibie described Singapore in a disparaging manner, as quoted in an article published in the Asian Wall Street Journal on 4 August 1998. Singapore has however turned it on the flipside and sees the term as being a positive characteristic of overcoming challenges despite its small size. See Keynote address by Deputy Prime Minister, Mr. Lee Hsien Loong at the Network Conference 2003, May 3, 2003, Singapore Government Press Release, http://stars.nhb.gov.sg/stars/public/viewHTML. jsp?pdfno=2003050301

4   "About Human Development", United Nations Development Programme, accessed April 21, 2012, http://hdr.undp.org/en/humandev/

5   "Human Development Index Statistics", United Nations Development Programme, accessed April 21, 2012, http://hdr.undp.org/en/statistics/hdi/

6   See Chapter 4: World Resources 1998-99: Environmental change and human health, World Resources Institute, the United Nations Environment Programme, and The World Bank, May, 1998, accessed April 21, 2012, http://www.wri.org/publication/content/8372

7   Antony Davies & Gary Quinlivan, A panel data analysis of the impact of trade on human development, *Journal of Socio-Economics*, 35: 5, (2006): 868-876

8   Habibullah Khan, 2001, "Social Policy in Singapore: A Confucian Model?", World Bank Institute, accessed April 21, 2012, http://siteresources.worldbank.org/WBI/Resources/wbi37165.pdf

9   World Development Indicators database, World Bank, 1 July 2011, accessed April 21, 2012, http://siteresources.worldbank.org/DATASTATISTICS/Resources/GNIPC.pdf

10 Samia Satti and O. M. Nour, Science and Technology Development Indicators in the Arab Region: A Comparative Study of Arab Gulf Countries and Mediterranean Countries, *Science Technology & Society*, 10 (2005): 260.

11 For more information, please see the online resources available on the Middle East Business Group's website http://www.sbf-mebg.org.sg/newsroom.aspx

12 The GSFTA is Singapore's second FTA with a Middle Eastern country – the first being with Jordan in 2005. See "GCC-Singapore FTA", Ministry of Foreign Trade, United Arab Emirates, accessed April 20, 2012, http://moft.gov.ae/wto/index.php?option=com_content&view=article&i d=11&Itemid=18&lang=en

13 Overview of The Gulf Cooperation Council (GSFTA)" International Enterprise Singapore, accessed April 21, 2012, http://www.fta.gov.sg/fta_gsfta.asp?hl=32

14 "Singapore's business ties with the Middle East grows from strength to strength," Economic Development Board of Singapore, accessed April 28, 2012, http://www.edb.gov.sg/edb/sg/en_uk/ index/news/articles/singapore_s_business.html

15 See figures in Introductory chapter by Prof Tim Niblock. Also see International Enterprise, Singapore statistics,http://www.iesingapore.gov.sg/wps/portal/MI_MiddleEast_Bahrain

16 Trade Figures, Abu Dhabi-Singapore Joint Forum, http://www.adsjf.com/en/trade/figures

17 "Middle East", Ministry of Foreign Affairs, Singapore, accessed April 21, 2012, http://www.mfa. gov.sg/content/mfa/countries_and_region/middle_east.printable.html?status=1#tabs-3

18 Since 2009, the MEEPP has been managed by the Middle East Institute at the National University of Singapore. For more information on the MEEPP, see http://www.sif.org.sg/programmes/19/ middle-east-eminent-persons-programme.html

19 For more on Malaysia's relations with the Arabian Gulf, please refer to the chapter by Fauzi Abu-Hussin.

20 Economic Development Board of Singapore. "Singapore's business ties with the Middle East grows from strength to strength." Accessed April 28, 2012, http://www.edb.gov.sg/edb/sg/en_uk/index/news/articles/singapore_s_business.html

21 "Qatar Petroleum International acquires first downstream overseas assets in deal with Shell in Singapore", News and Media Releases, Shell, November 11, 2009, accessed April 23, 2012, http://www.shell.com/home/content/media/news_and_media_releases/archive/2009/qatar_petroleum_international_11112009.html

22 Singapore Joint Industry Project on Future LNG Bunkering, The Maritime Executive, 16 April 2012, accessed on 18 April 2012, http://www.maritime-executive.com/pressrelease/singapore-joint-industry-project-on-future-lng-bunkering

23 "GCC-Singapore FTA plan backed", *Gulf Daily News*, July 18, 2007, accessed April 21, 2012, http://www.gulf-daily-news.com/NewsDetails.aspx?storyid=188071

24 Nakheel and SMRT Engineering Pte Ltd enter partnership for the operation of The Palm Monorail", *AMEinfo*, August 1, 2007, accessed April 23, 2012, http://www.ameinfo.com/128151.html

25 "Gulf opportunities attract Singaporean companies", *Gulf News*, June 30, 2010, accessed April 23, 2012, http://dubaimetro.eu/palm-jumeirah-monorail/5413/gulf-opportunities-attract-singaporean-companies

26 'Our Achievements', Singapore education, Government of Singapore, accessed April 20, 2012, http://www.singaporeedu.gov.sg/htm/abo/abo0202.htm

27 "Kuwait eyes greater educational cooperation with Singapore," *Kuwait News Agency*, June 19, 2010, accessed on April 27, 2012, http://www.kuna.net.kw/ArticlePrintPage.aspx?id=2095669&language=en

28 "NIE Flying High in Mid-East on S'pore Brand", *Business Times*, March 15, 2007, pg. 12

29 Annual Report on NIE's Internationalisation efforts through NIE International for AY 2009/2010, National Institute for Education, Singapore, accessed April 15, 2012, http://www.nie.edu.sg/niei/about-us/annual-report

30 Singapore companies contribute to development of healthcare in Kingdom of Saudi Arabia, *AME Info*, April 24, 2010, accessed April 21, 2012, http://www.ameinfo.com/230564.html

31 Mely Caballero-Anthony, Sofiah Jamil and Julie Balen, 2009, "Ensuring Good Health During the Hajj in a Time of the H1N1 Pandemic", NTS Alert, accessed April 21, 2012, http://www.rsis.edu.sg/nts/HTML-Newsletter/alert/NTS-alert-nov-0902.html

32 Alex Adams, "GCC-Singapore FTA on Final Leg, Says Official," *Muscat Daily*, 12 Sept 2011, http://www.muscatdaily.com/Archive/Business/GCC-Singapore-FTA-on-final-leg-says-official

33 "RO87m deals signed for developing ports, aviation", *Oman Tribune*, accessed April 28, 2012, http://www.omantribune.com/index.php?page=news_main_page&id=917

34 Alex Adams, "GCC-Singapore FTA on Final Leg, Says Official."

35 Hoe Yeen Nie, "Singaporeans in Oman urged to uphold country's brand name," *Channel NewsAsia,* March 14, 2009, accessed April 28, 2012 http://www.channelnewsasia.com/stories/singaporelocalnews/view/415279/1/.html

36 "Singaporeans to mark National Day", *Gulf Times*, August 7, 2007, accessed April 21, 2012, http://www.gulf-times.com/site/topics/article.asp?cu_no=2&item_no=165832&version=1&template_id=36&parent_id=16

37 "S'poreans in Bahrain remain vigilant amid protests", *Channel News Asia*, February 16, 2011, accessed April 23, 2012, http://news.xin.msn.com/en/singapore/article.aspx?cp-documentid=4646949

38 "Singapore Minister: Try expanding to Kuwait," *Singapore Business Review*, March 15, 2012, accessed April 27, 2012 http://sbr.com.sg/markets-investing/news/singapore-minister-try-expanding-kuwait

39 http://www.asiaone.com/Business/News/SME+Central/Story/A1Story20100203-196426.html

40 Keynote Address by Senior Minister Goh Chok Tong at the Opening Session of the Inaugural Asia-Middle East Dialogue (AMED), 21 June 2005, Shangri-La Hotel, Island Ballroom, Singapore, http://app.amed.gov.sg/internet/amed/read_content.asp?View,180,

41 The AMED Regional Training Centre for Public Administration (RTCPA), located in Qatar, focuses on the training of civil servants and developing skills and strategies for excellence in public service, while the AMED Regional Vocational Training Centre (RVTC) in Jordan focuses on developing skills in air-conditioning and heating systems maintenance and diagnostics for the construction industry.

42 "Update on the AMED Regional Training Centres", Asia-Middle East Dialogue, access April 20, 2012, http://app.amed.gov.sg/internet/amed/WorkingGpUpdateTrgCenter.asp

43 "Report on the AMED Media Roundtable", Asia-Middle East Dialogue, August 6, 2010, accessed April 20, 2012, http://app.amed.gov.sg/internet/amed/AMEDMediaRoundtableReport.asp

44 Mr George Yeo, Minister for Foreign Affairs, Singapore, at the AMED II meeting in Sharm El Sheikh in April 2008, accessed April 20, 2012, http://app.amed.gov.sg/data/internet/amed/pdf/Singapore.pdf

45 ASEAN is a regional organisation with 10 member states – Brunei, Cambodia, Indonesia, Laos, Malaysia, Myanmar, Philippines, Singapore, Thailand and Vietnam.

46 Jumana Al Tamimi, "Singapore wants free trade pact for GCC and ASEAN", *Gulf News*, March 23, 2010, accessed April 20, 2012, http://gulfnews.com/business/economy/singapore-wants-free-trade-pact-for-gcc-and-asean-1.601608

47 While trade between GCC and ASEAN member states was valued at $83.25 billion in 2010 (an increase of 23.64%) from 2009, ASEAN experienced a deficit of $42.99 billion due to imports overwhelming exports. See Linda Yulisman, ASEAN to improve cooperation with GCC, *The Jakarta Post*, August 25, 2011, accessed April 20, 2012, http://www.thejakartapost.com/news/2011/07/25/ascan-improve-cooperation-with-gcc.html

48 Singapore, along with South Korea, Hong Kong and Taiwan were known as the *Asian Tigers*, for their high economic growth rates in the 1980s to 1990s, following suit of Japan.

49 "China, ASEAN agree to step up cooperation on curbing bird flu virus", ASEAN, accessed April 20, 2012, http://www.aseansec.org/afp/23.htm

50 James Schweithelm, Timothy Jessup and David Glover, 2006, "Conclusions and Policy Recommendations", in David Glover and Timothy Jessup, eds, Indonesia's Fires and Haze: The Cost of Catastrophe, Singapore, Markono Print Media, pp. 130-44.

51 Nopporn Wong-Anan,"Q+A: Why has Southeast Asia's haze returned?", AsiaOne News, Oct 22, 2010, accessed April 20, 2012, http://news.asiaone.com/News/Latest+News/Asia/Story/A1Story20101022-243730.html

52 Schweithelm, Jessup and Glover, 2006.

53 *Channel News Asia*, Oct 12, 2006

54 Adianto P. Simamora, 'Govt wants haze agreement ratified', The Jakarta Post, Jan 22, 2011, accessed April 20, 2012, http://www.thejakartapost.com/news/2011/01/22/govt-wants-haze-agreement-ratified.html

55 "Non-traditional security (NTS) issues are challenges to the survival and well-being of peoples and states that arise from non-military sources, such as climate change, resource scarcity, infectious diseases, natural disasters, irregular migration, food shortages, people smuggling, drug trafficking

and transnational crime. These dangers are transnational in scope, defying unilateral remedies and requiring comprehensive – political, economic and social – responses, as well as the humanitarian use of military force." (http://www.rsis-ntsasia.org/ourConsortium/history.html) For more on NTS, please see http://www.rsis.edu.sg/nts/system.asp?sid=130

56 Leah Hyslop, March 8, 2012, Singapore's foreign maids to get day off, The Telegraph, accessed http://www.telegraph.co.uk/finance/personalfinance/offshorefinance/9128243/Singapores-foreign-maids-to-get-day-off.html

57 Cheers and Jeers for Maids' Day Off in Singapore', March 7, 2012, The Jakarta Globe, accessed April 20, 2012, http://www.thejakartaglobe.com/home/cheers-and-jeers-for-maids-day-off-in-singapore/502985

58 Saudi Arabia: A Step to Aid Migrant Workers, Human Rights Watch, April 10, 2012, Accessed April 20, 2012, http://www.hrw.org/news/2012/04/10/saudi-arabia-step-aid-migrant-workers

59 These include the Humanitarian Organization for Migration Economics (H.O.M.E) and Transient Workers Count Too (TWC2)

60 While the large majority of Muslims in Singapore are categorized under the Malay race (which includes various ethnic groups from the Malay Archipelago such as Minangkabau, Javanese, Bugis, Bawean), there are also Muslims of Indian and Arab ancestry. It is also common to find Muslims being a mix of these various backgrounds, who are historically referred to as *Jawi Peranakan*.

61 Sofiah Jamil, S'pore can play unique role in the Muslim world, *The Straits Times*, June 9, 2007, accessed April 20, 2012, http://www.rsis.edu.sg/news/S%27pore%20can%20play%20unique%20role%20in%20the%20Muslim%20world.pdf

62 Ministry of Foreign Affairs, June 11, 2008, ' Transcript of the doorstop interview with Foreign Minister George Yeo and Deputy Governor of Hadramout Ahmed Janned Al Janned at Tepak Sireh Restaurant on 11 June 2008', accessed April 20, 2012, http://app.mfa.gov.sg/2006/press/view_press_print.asp?post_id=4085

63 Hidayah Amin, 'Tell Real Story of Kampong Glam', Forum, *The Sunday Times*, pg. 42, June 17, 2012, accessed June 20, 2012, http://www.gedungkuning.com/inthenews/pdf/35.pdf

64 Cost of living likely to rise further this year, *Asia One*, April 14, 2012, accessed, April 20, 2012, http://news.asiaone.com/News/Latest%2BNews/Singapore/Story/A1Story20120414-339703.html

65 Raju Gopalakrishnan and Kevin Lim, Singapore PM makes rare apology as election campaign heats up, Reuters, May 4, 2011, accessed April 20, 2012 http://in.reuters.com/article/2011/05/04/idINIndia-56766220110504

66 Keynote Address by Senior Minister Goh Chok Tong at the Opening Session of the Inaugural Asia-Middle East Dialogue (AMED), 21 June 2005, Shangri-La Hotel, Island Ballroom, Singapore, http://app.amed.gov.sg/internet/amed/read_content.asp?View,180,

67 Human Development Report 2011, "Sustainability and Equity: A Better Future for All", accessed April 21, 2012, http://hdr.undp.org/en/reports/global/hdr2011/

Bibliography

Adams, Alex "GCC-Singapore FTA on Final Leg, Says Official," *Muscat Daily*, 12 Sept 2011, http://www.muscatdaily.com/Archive/Business/GCC-Singapore-FTA-on-final-leg-says-official

Al Tamimi, Jumana, "Singapore wants free trade pact for GCC and ASEAN", *Gulf News*, March 23, 2010, accessed April 20, 2012, http://gulfnews.com/business/economy/singapore-wants-free-trade-pact-for-gcc-and-asean-1.601608

Amin, Hidayah, 'Tell Real Story of Kampong Glam', Forum, *The Sunday Times*, pg. 42, June 17, 2012, accessed June 20, 2012, http://www.gedungkuning.com/inthenews/pdf/35.pdf

Annual Report on NIE's Internationalisation efforts through NIE International for AY 2009/2010, National Institute for Education, Singapore, accessed April 15, 2012, http://www.nie.edu.sg/niei/about-us/annual-report

Caballero-Anthony, Mely, Sofiah Jamil and Julie Balen, 2009, "Ensuring Good Health During the Hajj in a Time of the H1N1 Pandemic", NTS Alert, accessed April 21, 2012, http://www.rsis.edu.sg/nts/HTML-Newsletter/alert/NTS-alert-nov-0902.html

"China, ASEAN agree to step up cooperation on curbing bird flu virus", ASEAN, accessed April 20, 2012, http://www.aseansec.org/afp/23.htm

Davies, Antony and Gary Quinlivan, 2006, A panel data analysis of the impact of trade on human development, Journal of Socio-Economics, Vol 35, Is 5, pp 868-876

"Cheers and Jeers for Maids' Day Off in Singapore", March 7, 2012, *The Jakarta Globe*, accessed April 20, 2012, http://www.thejakartaglobe.com/home/cheers-and-jeers-for-maids-day-off-in-singapore/502985

"Cost of living likely to rise further this year", *Asia One*, April 14, 2012, accessed, April 20, 2012, http://news.asiaone.com/News/Latest%2BNews/Singapore/Story/A1Story20120414-339703.html

Economic Development Board of Singapore. "Singapore's business ties with the Middle East grows from strength to strength." Accessed April 28, 2012, http://www.edb.gov.sg/edb/sg/en_uk/index/news/articles/singapore_s_business.html

"GCC-Singapore FTA plan backed", *Gulf Daily News*, July 18, 2007, accessed April 21, 2012, http://www.gulf-daily-news.com/NewsDetails.aspx?storyid=188071

Gopalakrishnan, Raju and Kevin Lim, "Singapore PM makes rare apology as election campaign heats up", *Reuters*, May 4, 2011, accessed April 20, 2012 http://in.reuters.com/article/2011/05/04/idINIndia-56766220110504

"Gulf opportunities attract Singaporean companies", *Gulf News*, June 30, 2010, accessed April 23, 2012, http://dubaimetro.eu/palm-jumeirah-monorail/5413/gulf-opportunities-attract-singaporean-companies

Hoe Yeen Nie, "Singaporeans in Oman urged to uphold country's brand name," Channel NewsAsia, March 14, 2009, accessed April 28, 2012 http://www.channelnewsasia.com/stories/singaporelocalnews/view/415279/1/.html

Human Development Report 2011, "Sustainability and Equity: A Better Future for All", Available from: http://hdr.undp.org/en/reports/global/hdr2011/

"Human Development Index Statistics", United Nations Development Programme, accessed April 21, 2012, http://hdr.undp.org/en/statistics/hdi/

Hyslop, Leah, March 8, 2012, Singapore's foreign maids to get day off, *The Telegraph*, accessed http://www.telegraph.co.uk/finance/personalfinance/offshorefinance/9128243/Singapores-foreign-maids-to-get-day-off.html

Jamil, Sofiah, S'pore can play unique role in the Muslim world, *The Straits Times*, June 9, 2007, accessed April 20, 2012, http://www.rsis.edu.sg/news/S%27pore%20can%20play%20unique%20role%20in%20the%20Muslim%20world.pdf

Keynote address by Deputy Prime Minister, Mr Lee Hsien Loong at the Network Conference 2003, May 3, 2003, Singapore Government Press Release, http://stars.nhb.gov.sg/stars/public/viewHTML.jsp?pdfno=2003050301

Keynote Address by Senior Minister Goh Chok Tong at the Opening Session of the Inaugural Asia-Middle East Dialogue (AMED), 21 June 2005, Shangri-La Hotel, Island Ballroom, Singapore, http://app.amed.gov.sg/internet/amed/read_content.asp?View,180,

Khan, Habibullah, 2001, "Social Policy in Singapore: A Confucian Model?", World Bank Institute, http://siteresources.worldbank.org/WBI/Resources/wbi37165.pdf

"Kuwait eyes greater educational cooperation with Singapore," *Kuwait News Agency*, June 19, 2010, accessed on April 27, 2012, http://www.kuna.net.kw/ArticlePrintPage.aspx?id=2095669&language=en

Poh Onn Lee, 2005, Water Management Issues in Singapore, Paper presented at Water In Mainland Southeast Asia, 29 November – 2 December 2005, Siem Reap, Cambodia. access April 20, 2012, http://www.khmerstudies.org/download-files/events/Water/Lee%20Nov%202005.pdf

McCartan, Brian, "Farmers forgotten in oil-for-food deals", Asia Times, Jul 31, 2009, accessed October 1, 2012, http://www.atimes.com/atimes/Southeast_Asia/KG31Ae04.html

Middle East Business Group's website http://www.sbf-mebg.org.sg/newsroom.aspx

Ministry of Foreign Affairs, June 11, 2008, ' Transcript of the doorstop interview with Foreign Minister George Yeo and Deputy Governor of Hadramout Ahmed Janned Al Janned at Tepak Sireh Restaurant on 11 June 2008', accessed April 20, 2012, http://app.mfa.gov.sg/2006/press/view_press_print.asp?post_id=4085

"Nakheel and SMRT Engineering Pte Ltd enter partnership for the operation of The Palm Monorail", *AMEinfo*, August 1, 2007, accessed April 23, 2012, http://www.ameinfo.com/128151.html

"NIE Flying High in Mid-East on S'pore Brand", *Business Times*, March 15, 2007, pg. 12

Nopporn Wong-Anan,"Q+A: Why has Southeast Asia's haze returned?", *AsiaOne News*, Oct 22, 2010, accessed April 20, 2012, http://news.asiaone.com/News/Latest+News/Asia/Story/A1Story20101022-243730.html

'Our Achievements', Singapore education, Government of Singapore, access April 20, 2012, http://www.singaporeedu.gov.sg/htm/abo/abo0202.htm

"Overview of The Gulf Cooperation Council (GSFTA)" International Enterprise Singapore, accessed April 21, 2012, http://www.fta.gov.sg/fta_gsfta.asp?hl=32

"Qatar Petroleum International acquires first downstream overseas assets in deal with Shell in Singapore", News and Media Releases, Shell, November 11, 2009, accessed April 23, 2012, http://www.shell.com/home/content/media/news_and_media_releases/archive/2009/qatar_petroleum_international_11112009.html

"Report on the AMED Media Roundtable", Asia-Middle East Dialogue, August 6, 2010, accessed April 20, 2012, http://app.amed.gov.sg/internet/amed/AMEDMediaRoundtableReport.asp

"RO87m deals signed for developing ports, aviation", *Oman Tribune*, accessed April 28, 2012, http://www.omantribune.com/index.php?page=news_main_page&id=917

Samia Satti O. M. Nour, "Science and Technology Development Indicators in the Arab Region: A Comparative Study of Arab Gulf Countries and Mediterranean Countries", Science Technology & Society, 10 (2005): 260.

"Saudi Arabia: A Step to Aid Migrant Workers:, Human Rights Watch, April 10, 2012, Accessed April 20, 2012, http://www.hrw.org/news/2012/04/10/saudi-arabia-step-aid-migrant-workers

Schweithelm, James, Timothy Jessup and David Glover, 2006, "Conclusions and Policy Recommendations", in David Glover and Timothy Jessup, eds, Indonesia's Fires and Haze: The Cost of Catastrophe, Singapore, Markono Print Media, pp. 130-44.

Simamora, Adianto P. "Govt wants haze agreement ratified", The Jakarta Post, Jan 22, 2011, accessed April 20, 2012, http://www.thejakartapost.com/news/2011/01/22/govt-wants-haze-agreement-ratified.html

"Singapore's business ties with the Middle East grows from strength to strength," Economic Development Board of Singapore, accessed April 28, 2012, http://www.edb.gov.sg/edb/sg/en_uk/index/news/articles/singapore_s_business.html

Singapore Joint Industry Project on Future LNG Bunkering, The Maritime Executive, 16 April 2012. Available from http://www.maritime-executive.com/pressrelease/singapore-joint-industry-project-on-future-lng-bunkering, accessed on 18 April 2012

"Singapore companies contribute to development of healthcare in Kingdom of Saudi Arabia", *AME Info*, April 24, 2010, accessed April 21, 2012, http://www.ameinfo.com/230564.html

"Singaporeans to mark National Day", *Gulf Times*, August 7, 2007, accessed April 21, 2012, http://www.gulf-times.com/site/topics/article.asp?cu_no=2&item_no=165832&version=1&template_id=36&parent_id=16

"S'poreans in Bahrain remain vigilant amid protests", *Channel News Asia*, February 16, 2011, accessed April 23, 2012, http://news.xin.msn.com/en/singapore/article.aspx?cp-documentid=4646949

"Singapore Minister: Try expanding to Kuwait," Singapore Business Review, March 15, 2012, accessed April 27, 2012 http://sbr.com.sg/markets-investing/news/singapore-minister-try-expanding-kuwait

Trade Figures, Abu Dhabi-Singapore Joint Forum, http://www.adsjf.com/en/trade/figures

"Update on the AMED Regional Training Centres", Asia-Middle East Dialogue, access April 20, 2012, http://app.amed.gov.sg/internet/amed/WorkingGpUpdateTrgCenter.asp

World Development Indicators database, World Bank, 1 July 2011, http://siteresources.worldbank.org/DATASTATISTICS/Resources/GNIPC.pdf

World Resources 1998-99: Environmental change and human health, World Resources Institute, the United Nations Environment Programme, the United Nations Development Programme, and The World Bank, May, 1998, Available from: http://www.wri.org/publication/content/8372

Yeo, George, Minister for Foreign Affairs, Singapore, at the AMED II meeting in Sharm El Sheikh in April 2008, accessed April 20, 2012, http://app.amed.gov.sg/data/internet/amed/pdf/Singapore.pdf

Yulisman, Linda, "ASEAN to improve cooperation with GCC", *The Jakarta Post*, August 25, 2011, accessed April 20, 2012, http://www.thejakartapost.com/news/2011/07/25/asean-improve-cooperation-with-gcc.html

Chapter Thirteen

What Determines Malaysia's Interest in the GCC?

Mohamed Fauzi Abu-Hussin
Mohamed Afandi Salleh

1. Introduction

The mutual interests and relationships between Gulf Arab and South East Asian countries are rooted in history. Relations can be traced back to ancient times when the Silk Route served as a connecting network of trade routes across the Asian continent linking Eastern, Southern, Central and Western Asia with the Mediterranean. These links were constituted not only by trade and commerce, but also by cultural and civilizational contacts (where the Gulf region played a key role). Islam traveled to Southeast Asia, especially the Malay world, comprising the areas now constituted by Malaysia, Indonesia, Philippines, Singapore, and their surroundings. Arabian and Persian culture has had a profound and deep influence on the evolution of the Southeast Asian civilization. Despite close relationships, changing global economic and geo-political relations over the centuries have led to the two regions failing to deepen their contacts, but rather taking each other for granted.

However, important changes have been taking place in the last quarter of the 20th century and the early 21st century. The shifting nature of the global economic order, particularly with the rapid growth in the economies of China and India, are mainly responsible for this. The events of 9/11 and the invasion of Iraq in 2003 have also played key roles in transforming the geo-political and geo-economic balance in the Gulf.[1] Asian countries in general have developed a stronger economic interest in the Gulf region, and this includes Malaysia and other Southeast Asian countries. Economic diversification policies in the Gulf and industrialization in Southeast Asia have laid the basis for transformed relationships. Malaysia's policy of adapting its international trade strategies by shifting from dependency on traditional exports markets (US, Japan and EU) to greater involvement in Asian and Middle Eastern ones, shows why the Gulf market is increasingly important for the Malaysian economy.[2]

Over the years, then, Malaysia's bilateral relations with the individual Arab Gulf Countries have been intensified with the impact of globalization and the increasing importance of trade and commerce. This has been bolstered by the religious affinity that was established through historical ties between Malaysia and the Gulf region. Frequent visits by Malaysian leaders to the Arab Gulf countries provide evidence of the importance of these countries to Malaysia.

2. The Development of Political Relations between Malaysia and the GCC Countries

Political relations between Malaysia and the GCC countries can be examined at both the individual state level and the GCC level. In the early stages, only the former was relevant as the GCC was not formed until 1981. The relationship with individual countries has in fact been the major dimension of the Malaysia-Gulf relationship.

Relations with Gulf countries began shortly after the independence of Malaysia in 1957. The first Malaysian Prime Minister, Tunku Abdul Rahman, visited Saudi Arabia in 1958 to perform the *hajj*, giving thanks to God for the independence of Malaya (later to become Malaysia). His presence in Saudi Arabia was symbolically important.[3] Nevertheless, for a few years after independence there were few developments in relations between Malaysia and the Gulf Arab countries.

The conflict between Malaysia and Indonesia, which began in 1963, however, created the need for Malaysia to broaden its international support. According to Ruhanas Harun,[4] this led the Malaysian government to seek to regain the friendship and support of Arab countries. In 1965, the Malaysian King visited Saudi Arabia and Kuwait to strengthen Malaysia's relations with those countries.[5] This marked the beginning of wider diplomatic and economic relations between Malaysia and the Arab Gulf. Several agreements in economic and technical cooperation were signed in the 1960s and 1970s. Among the latter was the Cultural and Scientific Cooperation Agreement with Saudi Arabia in 1975,[6] the Memorandum of Understanding (MoU) in Education with Saudi Arabia in 1978, the Trade Agreement with the UAE in 1962, and the Air Services Agreement with Kuwait in 1975.[7]

Relations continued to develop, but the most significant developments occurred during the 1980s when Mahathir Muhammad was Prime Minister of Malaysia. Under Mahathir's era as prime minister (between 1981 and 2003), there had been much emphasis on closer relations with Islamic countries[8] and this meant specifically countries in the Arab Gulf.[9] Mahathir's visit to the Gulf States in 1982, a year after the establishment of the Gulf Cooperation Council, was a remarkable effort from the Malaysian leader to augment Malaysia's relations with the Arab Gulf. The visit that began in Jeddah was to purposely achieve two objectives. First, to seek economic and investment prospects as well as financial assistance from the Gulf States, and second to discuss and to mediate on the Iran-Iraq war (where the Saudi government was the host to discuss the war).[10] Among the Arab Gulf countries visited by Mahathir were Bahrain, Oman, the United Arab Emirates (UAE) and Saudi Arabia.

Mahathir's visits to the Arab Gulf in the 1980s were fruitful, particularly in obtaining financial aid to speed up Malaysian economic development. Financial assistance was secured during these visits, for example,

- a $10.6 million loan from the Saudi Fund to build five hospitals in the states of Kedah, Kelantan and Terengganu;

- a promise to contribute $58 million to the construction of the East-West Highway (in 1986 the Saudi Fund approved SR189.00 million, equivalent to RM132.2 million);

- financial aid for the second phase of two projects, the port project in Penang Island and the East-West Highway.

It was recorded that until 1984, the overall loan from the Saudi Fund was $252.2 million.[11]

The long term of Mahathir's regime of administration and his determination in maintaining relations with Muslim countries as well as being active in promoting Islam, had definitely given a valuable outcome to Malaysia's relations with the Arab Gulf. It is also argued that Mahathir has successfully changed the pattern of relations "from one to two way communication between Malaysia and the Arab Gulf," particularly during the 1990s. For example, he encouraged the Arab Gulf States' economy to open up more markets for Malaysian products and suggested that Malaysia should not merely depend on Saudi's loan.[12] During this period (the 1990s), there were huge improvements in the bilateral relations between Malaysia and individual Arab Gulf States, where further economic and cooperation agreements were successfully concluded. At the same time, in 1991, the Malaysia-Saudi Arabia Friendship Society (MBFS) was established and this further contributed to Malaysia's aim to strengthen Malaysia–Arab relations.

From the year 2000 onwards, there was a dynamic shift in the Malaysia-Saudi relationship. Following visits by the Deputy of Defense Minister of Saudi Arabia to Malaysia in May 2001 and the Second Saudi-Malaysian Commission meeting in Kuala Lumpur, on May 10–12th, 2001, both Malaysia and Saudi Arabia agreed to foster economic cooperation. Furthermore, in 2001, a visit by the deputy prime minister Abdullah Ahmad Badawi (who later became the Malaysian Prime Minister in 2003) to meet King Fahd, was a stepping stone for a new chapter in Malaysia's relations with the Arab Gulf, where various issues and events were discussed, specifically on economic, investment opportunities, and tourism.[13] Soon after the new Prime Minister, Najib Razak, took over the government in 2009, King Abdullah of Saudi Arabia invited him for an official visit to the Kingdom. The visit definitely cemented the long-standing relations. In his visit to Qatar on May 15th, 2011, Najib Razak mentioned that Malaysia and the Arab countries are like a family, therefore relations are expected to become closer in the near future.

Although the diplomatic relationship with Arab Gulf countries has been promising, the issue is how to translate this into a more productive and beneficial one for both Malaysia and the GCC member states. This is also a main concern raised by the Prime Minister of Malaysia in his visit to Qatar: "The challenge now is how to translate this close relationship into visible development and economic progress."[14] Therefore, in the following section, economic relationships will be further investigated and discussed, which will shed light on the importance of the Arab Gulf Economies to Malaysia.

3. Malaysia's Economic Relationship with the GCC Countries

As noted above, Malaysia's policy of diversifying its economic and trade relations away from its traditional markets and into new potential markets, has led to new directions for Malaysia's trade. Arab Gulf markets are among the aims of Malaysia's trade and investment.[15] Middle East markets, especially those of the Arab Gulf countries, are seen as potential emerging markets for the Malaysian economy to tap. For Malaysia, the Arab Gulf has been a "gateway" for capturing the Middle East market.[16]

The economic liberalization and openness in the GCC countries has provided Malaysia with huge opportunities to tap this new emerging market. At the institutional level, Malaysia and the GCC signed the Framework Agreement on Economic, Commercial, Investment and Technical Cooperation in 2011. By having this new agreement, it is expected to further strengthen economic relations, improve the business environment and increase bilateral trade. This is also a stepping stone for the Free Trade Agreement (FTA) with the GCC.[17]

Meanwhile, economic cooperation between Malaysia and the individual GCC countries had begun before the establishment of the GCC economic group. At the individual state level, bilateral agreements covered issues such as: avoidance of double taxation, and agreements for the promotion and protection of investment, economic and technical cooperation (see Table 13.1 for further details). However, Malaysia's involvement in strengthening its economic relations (especially bilateral relations) with individual GCC countries has focused mainly on two Gulf countries: Saudi Arabia and the UAE. The next section will further discuss the trade relations between Malaysia and individual GCC countries.

3.1 Trade Relations

Despite the desire to expand trade, trade relations between Malaysia and the Gulf Cooperation Council countries have remained relatively small, compared to their 'traditional' trading partners.[18] Trade relations between Malaysia and West Asia as a whole only accounted for 3 to 4 per cent of Malaysia's total trade in 2008. Nevertheless, the growth of this trade is significant. In 2008, Malaysia's exports to West Asia grew by about 38%.[19]

Overall trade between Malaysia and GCC member countries has in fact been growing since 2000; reaching a $3 billion mark in 2003. In 2010, total trade with the GCC reached $10.5 billion, five times greater than in 2000. Total trade between Malaysia and the GCC in 2008 has reached the highest level, amounting to $12.32 billion, which is believed to be due to the increase in world oil prices in 2008. This is depicted in Figure 13.1 and Figure 13.2. The growth of Malaysia's trade with the GCC outpaced its total trade with the world. Between 1990 and 2008, Malaysia's trade with GCC grew at an average of 20.34 %, while the average growth of Malaysia's total trade with the world was only around 12.45%.[20] It is also observed that Malaysia's trade balance with the GCC was in surplus from 1990 to 2005, except in 2001. The rise of oil prices between 2006 and 2008 had affected the trade balance between Malaysia and the GCC countries.

Malaysia's strategy in the expansion of new international markets and the GCC countries' economic diversification strategy assist the increasing bilateral trade volume. This can be seen from the expanding and outstanding relations with the United Arab Emirates in particular. The Emirate has been Malaysia's main export destination in the Arab Gulf, especially exports for manufactured products that mainly come from electrical products. Malaysia's exports to the UAE increased from $859 million in 2000 to approximately $3.7 billion in 2010. As for the trade structure, Malaysia's bilateral trade relations with individual GCC countries have been predominantly influenced by the huge imports of oil and its products, in particular Malaysia's imports from major oil producers such as Saudi Arabia, the UAE, Kuwait and Oman. This can be seen in Figure 13.2, which shows Saudi Arabia and the UAE to have been Malaysia's major import sources. Since 2007, there has been significant shifting in import sources from the Arab Gulf, where the UAE have been a major source of import.[21] This is due to an increase of oil imports from the UAE while Malaysia has reduced imports of oil from Saudi Arabia.[22] Imports of those products cover more than 70 per cent of Malaysia's imports from these countries, whilst jewelry, electrical, electronic and palm-oil based products were among the largest exported products to the GCC countries.

3.2. Capital Flows and Investment in Malaysia: from Aid to Investment

Capital flows from the Gulf Arab countries into Malaysia began with Saudi financial aid. Between 1975 and 1990, Malaysia received SR312.30 million in financial aid[23] from Saudi Arabia for its socio-economic infrastructure.[24] Among the projects funded by the Saudi Development Fund were the development of the University of Technology, the Medical Faculty of the National University of Malaysia, the Ulu Kelantan Land Settlement Project, and the Pahang Tenggara Land Settlement Project.[25] Over this period, the Kuwait Fund also financed $8.5 million to a similar rubber plantation project at Ulu Kelantan and to the conversion of jungle areas into palm oil plantations.[26]

Affiliation with the Organization of Islamic Cooperation (OIC) and good personal relations between the first Prime Minister of Malaysia, Tunku Abdul Rahman, and King Faisal of Saudi Arabia contributed to easy access to the Saudi Development Fund.[27] Although the Gulf Arab countries' aid had helped Malaysia to provide some economic infrastructures for the countries' development, the amount was still smaller than other established financial aid such as Japan's Official Development Assistance (ODA) and the World Bank.[28]

The capital flow from the Gulf Arab countries entered a new phase when the petrodollar funds of the Gulf turned towards major investment in Malaysia's development. In the 1990s, Malaysia was successfully carrying through an industrial transformation of the country. Saudi's investment in Malaysia's development project between 1990 and 1997 was RM139.6 million and the investments were poured into eight Malaysian projects mostly in the industrial-manufacturing sectors like food processing, plastic materials, textiles and textile products, electrical and electronic goods.[29] Furthermore, the UAE, Kuwait and Bahrain also participated in Malaysian industrial development. Between 1995 and 2000, Malaysia secured several investments from those countries amounting to RM43 million, RM4 million and RM 31 million respectively (see Table 13.2).

Table 13.3 shows that an increasing amount of investment came from the GCC countries to Malaysia between 2004 and 2009. The incoming investment from Saudi Arabia and the United Arab Emirates in 2008 reached more than RM1 billion due to the significant contribution of these countries' investments in Iskandar Malaysia and Islamic banking as well as property ventures.[30]

It is also noted that Saudi Arabia and the United Arab Emirates were among the top investors in Malaysia in 2008 and 2011 respectively and in fact were the largest contributors from the Middle Eastern countries.[31] Saudi's investments in new manufacturing projects which involve the production of polycrystalline silicon, sodium hydroxide, chlorine, hydrogen, hydrochloric acid, silicon tri-chloride, silicon tetra-chloride, mixed chlorosilane, oxygen and nitrogen, were worth RM2.2 billion and account for 6 per cent of the total Foreign Direct Investment in Malaysia in 2011.[32]

It is noticeable that Malaysia's economic development has been very much concentrated on the West coast of the Malaysian peninsula. This significantly affected the direction of investments and the distribution of economic growth. Being aware of these circumstances and the need for economic reform, in 2007 Malaysia announced several clusters of economic regions, namely the Eastern, Southern, Northern and Borneo "economic corridors". Development in these economic regions that concentrates on tourism, oil & gas, manufacturing, services, properties, agriculture and education requires fresh and huge investment locally and from abroad.[33]

As financial turmoil hit the United States and Europe in 2008, Malaysia's dependency on investments from these countries diminished. Therefore, the sources of investment to develop Malaysia's new regional economic corridors have been shifted to petrodollar investors.[34] It is noticed that these new regional economic centers, which comprise the Southern Johor Economic Region (SJER), the East Coast Economic Region (ECER), the Northern Corridor Economic Region (NCER) and the Sarawak Corridor of Renewable Energy (SCORE), have obtained new fresh investment from the Arab Gulf countries, which were blessed with skyrocketing oil prices.[35]

In the Southern Johor Economic Region (SJER) for example, companies such as the Millennium Development Company (MDIC), Kuwait Finance House (KFH), and the Mubadala Development Company have established a consortium agreeing to inject initially $1.2 billion into the new projects.[36] Investments from the UAE in this economic area were also contributed by Aldar Properties and Millennium Development International (they were among one of Iskandar Malaysia's first investors) with investment which amounted to RM4.2 billion to develop the Financial District in Medini Iskandar.[37]

Apart from the investment in the real estate and manufacturing sectors, investment flow from the Arab Gulf was also poured into Malaysian financial industries. It is argued that Malaysia's economic liberalization strategy has encouraged capital movement from the Arab Gulf, particularly investment in the Islamic financial service sector. For instance, in 2007, the first Islamic bank in Malaysia, Bank Islam Malaysia Berhad (BIMB), received a massive fund from the Dubai Islamic Investment Bank. The Dubai Islamic Investment Bank is a subsidiary of the Dubai Group and it has purchased 40 per cent of stake in the BIMB valued at RM828 million[38] or 40 per cent of the bank's share. A few other funds in Islamic banking and the financial sectors have also received a significant injection from the Arab petrodollar. The Kuwait-based Gulf Investment Cooperation (GIC) has recently launched a RM 500 million issuance of *sukuk*.[39]

In strengthening the Islamic Financial sector through the Malaysian Islamic Finance Council (MIFC) and with strong support from the Central Bank of Malaysia (BNM), the government encourages foreign Islamic banks especially from the Middle East to set up their business here. Up until now, the BNM has given licenses to several bank operators from the Middle East such as Al Rajhi Banking & Investment Banking, Kuwait Finance House (KFH), and ACR ReTakaful Holdings (a joint venture between Khazanah Nasional Berhad[40] and Dubai Group).

Only a small number of the Gulf Arab investments in Malaysia have been in the energy sector, although this is a field in which Gulf Arab countries have great expertise. In 2010, however, the Malaysian National Petroleum Company (PETRONAS) went into a venture in gas exploration in offshore Sarawak with involvement from the UAE investment organization Mubadala.[41]

It can be concluded that recent investment funds from the Arab Gulf Countries are mainly directed to develop Malaysia's new economic regions and injected to support its Islamic financial service sector. The most active investors, Saudi Arabia and the UAE, are expected to increase their investment in Malaysia. Indications are that investment from the Arab Gulf countries, especially the UAE, may flow into Malaysia in large quantities and it has been reported that in 5 years' time the UAE investment in Malaysia is to expand 4 to 5-fold.[42] It is also argued that an increase in investment from the Arab Gulf is a manifestation of close relationships that have been long established, in addition to huge investment opportunities in Malaysia, specifically in its new regional economic development.

3.3 Participation in the Gulf Economies

Recent development shows that Malaysia's interest in Arab Gulf economies has been overwhelming. This is particularly seen in investment activities in the United Arab Emirates and Saudi Arabia. Due to the rapid development in the construction and financial sectors in these countries, there is a significant presence of Malaysian companies in these particular sectors. The total of Malaysia's investment in the GCC countries can be seen in Table 13.4.

Over the years, Malaysian investments have been consistent in the United Arab Emirates, Bahrain, Qatar, and Saudi Arabia. The outflow investment from Malaysia shows a similar trend with inflow investment from the Gulf. Saudi Arabia and the UAE have been major investment destinations in the Arab Gulf and 2005 was marked as the milestone for Malaysia's investment in the Arab Gulf. The liberalization strategies and economic reforms implemented across the Gulf region have positively affected this massive investment flow in the GCC.

In 2007, the Saudi Arabian General Investment Authority (SAGIA) reported that Malaysia was a major investor, particularly in developing Saudi Arabia's new Jazan Economic City. The MMC Corporation Berhad (MMC) - a Malaysian utilities and infrastructure company - was the largest investor in developing infrastructure facilities in the new city[43] and in 2009, another Malaysian company had secured a project in developing the Shaiba Water and Electrical facilities in Saudi Arabia.[44] According to SAGIA, in 2006 Malaysia was a major investor in the Kingdom along with giant investors such as Japan, the United Arab Emirates, Bahrain, France, and the Netherlands. The United States of America captured the largest share of FDI inflows in the same year.[45]

In the meantime, it is also reported that up until 2008, the total number of Malaysian companies registered with the Saudi Arabian General Investment

Authority was 87, of which 17 are involved in the industrial sector with a total investment of $4.3 billion. The rest are actively involved in the services sector with investments worth $238.6 million. This made Malaysia the 18th largest investor in Saudi Arabia in 2008.[46] Malaysia's experience in developing its economy in the past has attracted GCC countries to cooperate more. Diversification of economic sources and continuous efforts in developing knowledge and a research-based economy has led Saudi Arabia and the remaining Arab Gulf countries to imitate this success.[47]

3.4. Foreign Workers

Since Malaysian companies actively participate in the economic development in the Arab Gulf, there is a significant presence of Malaysian workers and expatriates, particularly in the UAE and Saudi Arabia. In the UAE for example, there are almost 6,000 Malaysian professionals working with foreign and local companies.[48] Given the strong presence of the Malaysian community in the UAE, the Prime Minister of Malaysia has urged the community to build a good name for Malaysia and to promote Malaysian brands in the region.[49]

In 2004, Malaysian expatriates in Saudi Arabia were estimated to be around 1000, of which 80 per cent work as nurses, and the other 20 per cent work in various sectors including banking, hospitality, telecommunications, and the petroleum industries.[50] Nonetheless, the Malaysian presence is still small compared to other Asian workers in the region.[51] The workers from these countries are mainly in the domestic sectors. Malaysia is not one of the exporters of domestic workers to other countries; instead, it is in need of migrant workers from those countries in South East Asia.[52]

4. Potential and Challenges

Over the years, Malaysia has been actively involved in bilateral and multilateral ties with both developed and developing countries at the regional and international levels; there are no reasons for the current government to change that policy. In short, pragmatism will continue to dominate Malaysian foreign policy in matters pertaining to Malaysia's interest abroad. Malaysia's relations with the Muslim world and its strategy to expand its economic relation with Muslim countries might assist to boost Malaysia's bilateral relations with the GCC countries. Statistically and empirically, it shows that Malaysia-GCC economic ties have been sustained by current investment, oil, trade and expatriate dynamics. There are also huge opportunities for both parties to expand their relations and economic ties. There are some areas of cooperation and future economic opportunities where Malaysia and the Arab Gulf could expand their ventures. These include Halal Food industries, tourism and educational sectors.

4.1. The Roles of Halal[53] Industries

Sharing religious values has been an advantage for Malaysia's relations with the GCC countries and it has significantly affected political relations and economic ties alike. Although scholars might argue that religious affinity would not directly influence economic relations,[54] religious affinity is exceptional in Malaysia's relations with Middle Eastern economies. Highlighting the importance of religious values that might shape economic relations between Malaysia and the Arab Gulf, halal products and food securities, being a major concern in the Muslim community, has encouraged cooperation between Malaysia and GCC to boost economic opportunities in this sector. Malaysia has been promoting this industry by implementing halal standards and developing halal parks. Saudi Arabia, being aware of this issue, has expressed its willingness to gain expertise with Malaysia in building halal parks in the Middle East.[55] In the meantime, Mohammed Al-Rabea from the Council of Arab Economic Unity also recognized the importance of the halal industry:

I am proud that Malaysia has achieved a high standard in the concept of halal products. We should develop the halal products in the Muslim and Arab countries. At the same time, we should strengthen the halal-based products in the hospitality industry in all the Arab countries.[56]

In the recent Economic Development Plan, Malaysian government has allocated more than RM100 million for the development of the halal food industry by establishing halal parks as a part of Malaysia's halal hub framework. Malaysia is now looking forward to facilitating a one-stop center/platform for activities related to halal. These activities include: inspection, certification, R&D, analysis, legislation, enforcement, sampling and laboratory facilities, marketing, management, consumerism, reference, education, information technology and networking.

The demand for halal products is ever increasing and expected to continue with the increasing Muslim population all over the world. It was estimated that the value of the global halal trade is around $150 billion, thus giving huge opportunity for this new emerging industry to expand.[57] The Muslim awareness of the obligation to consume products based on Islamic requirements also contributes to a greater demand for halal food and non-food products. Importantly, the halal market does not focus on Muslim countries only; however, non-Muslim countries that have a significant Muslim population also have huge potential for the halal products.

Becoming an international halal hub might strengthen Malaysia's trade with the Islamic countries and on the other hand may attract huge investment from rich Muslim countries, particularly the Gulf countries. In the meantime, Malaysia also has a Showcasing Mart in Dubai that promotes products from Malaysian small and medium enterprises (SMEs) as well as Malaysian processed halal foods and beverages to buyers in the region.

4.2 The tourism sector

Over the past few years, Malaysia has received huge numbers of Middle-Eastern tourists particularly from Gulf states and this at the same time encourages Malaysia's tourism industry. According to Mohamed Khalid,[58] the tourism sector in Malaysia has experienced declining numbers of tourists after 9/11 and has been badly affected by terrorist propaganda. The Bali bombing, Southern Thailand and other Islamic militancy issues in the last ten years have also contributed to a significant drop in tourists from Western countries. Therefore, strengthening ties with the Muslim countries is seen as a practical strategy to stimulate the country's tourism sector.

Since 2001, Malaysia has been actively promoting tourism among Muslim countries. The Malaysian government, through the Ministry of Tourism, has been highly passionate in promoting Malaysia as a tourist destination to Middle Eastern tourists, especially from the Gulf countries. Consequently, the efforts have been quite successful, as indicated in recent statistics (see Table 13.5). The table shows the increasing number of visitors from the Middle East between 2002 and 2007 and tourists from Arab Gulf countries have contributed a considerable percentage of tourists coming to Malaysia. In fact, the data shows that tourists from the GCC countries have increased by almost 100 per cent during the 7-year period.

4.3 Attracting Gulf countries' students

In the National Higher Education Action Plan 2007-2020, Malaysia aims to be an educational hub for international students by achieving the target of having 100,000 foreign students in the country's institutions of higher education by 2010.[59] In putting that objective into the action plan, Malaysia has placed emphasis on attracting international students to further their study in this country and gives attractive initiatives for international scholars to be part of its higher education institutions. Among the efforts taken by the Ministry of Higher Education, Malaysia established the Malaysian Education Promotion Council (MEPC) with a branch located in Dubai. This is specifically to attract students from the Gulf region as well as its neighboring countries.

Given the fact that the enrolment of foreign students might help Malaysian higher education institutions to achieve a reputable position in the world university rankings, the Ministry of Higher Education put extra efforts into increasing the number of foreign students in Malaysian academic institutions. Prior to 2007, the total number of international students in Malaysia's higher education institutions was around 40,000 to 45,000 and it has now almost tripled to around 85,000 students.[60] In 2010, more than two-thirds of the international students were studying at Malaysian public universities (see Figure 13.3).

Knowing that Malaysia is a developing country, it is widely accepted that it is hard to get students from advanced and developed economies to study there. The low ranking of Malaysian universities is also one of the factors that lead to a lack of interest from international students to study in Malaysia. Therefore, it is the Malaysian Higher Education Council's strategy to invite students from neighboring countries, as well as from other developing and under-developing countries. Thus, it is not peculiar that most of the international students come from Indonesia, China and Middle Eastern countries, which accounted for 60% of the total of international students in Malaysia. According to the Malaysian Ministry of Higher Education (MOHE), in 2010 there were approximately 31,000 Middle Eastern students studying in Malaysian public and private universities. This accounted almost 31% of the total number of foreign students in Malaysia. Iranian students constituted the largest single national contingent of students pursuing their degrees in Malaysian higher education institutions. Among the Arab Gulf Countries, students from Saudi Arabia were the largest group in Malaysia with a total number of 2,500 students in 2010. However, given the efforts taken by the Malaysia Education Promotion Council, which has a branch in the United Arab Emirates, this number of students is considerably small.

The increasing interest of foreign students, especially those from Iran and Saudi Arabia, to complete their studies in Malaysia, is believed to be due to several factors. According to a survey by Rohani Jani et al.[61] and Badaruddin[62], competitive program fees, cheaper living costs, political stability and most importantly the international recognition of Malaysian universities, contributed to the decision of those students to come to Malaysia. Moreover, it is also argued that Malaysian public universities' participation in recognized world university ranking systems, such as the Times Higher Education System (THES), influences international students' preference to pursue their degree in Malaysian higher education institutions.[63] The significant numbers of students from Iran and Saudi Arabia are attributed to the support of their governments to increase expertise in some major technical fields, for example, engineering and management. This can be seen in the students' course preferences in studying in Malaysia.

In response to the less significant presence of students from the Arab Gulf, apart from Saudi Arabia, it is believed that it is due to the educational advancements and reforms in their home countries.[64] The UAE, for example, established its own educational centers known as the Dubai International Academic City and the University City in Abu Dhabi, that attracted well known international academic institutions such as Harvard University's Medical School, Johns Hopkins University, Massachusetts Institute of Technology (MIT), and many more. These significant developments might attract students from all over the world, including Malaysia, to come to the Arab Gulf to pursue their degree in these reputable and recognized academic intuitions. Although there have been significant developments in the education system in the Arab Gulf countries, up until now, there are limited numbers of Malaysian students pursuing their degree in the Gulf countries.

5. Economic Cooperation: A Way Forward

Economic cooperation between Malaysia and the GCC has been on the rise. The Malaysian government has formed a number of individual economic agreements with Saudi Arabia, the UAE, Kuwait and Oman. Progress on these agreements is satisfactory and previous discussion proved the implementation of this economic cooperation.

Since the economic agreements and cooperation between Malaysia and the GCC date from the 1970s and the 1990s, further cooperation and economic liberalization agendas between Malaysia and the GCC are needed in order to boost current economic relations which had been stagnant prior to the establishment of the GCC economic union. In 2007, Malaysia realized the potential of the GCC economies, and thus proposed the agenda of the FTA. This will definitely open a new phase of Malaysia-GCC economic relations.

Despite the time taken to bring in a new phase of Malaysia-GCC economic cooperation, it was recently reported that this liberalization strategy between the two has been moving forward. In January 2011, Malaysia and the GCC agreed on a framework agreement leading to an FTA.[65] The present low level of trade between these countries may represent unexplored trade opportunities[66] and a bilateral Malaysia-GCC FTA could increase the current bilateral trade by 41 per cent.[67]

Investments in halal-based products and education are seen as potential areas for economic cooperation between Malaysia and the Arab Gulf.

There is no doubt that economic relations between Malaysia and the GCC are entering a new phase. It is also realized that Malaysian companies will have greater and freer access to the GCC markets. Nevertheless, other countries also have huge interests in the GCC market. Thus, an increase in economic competition is to be expected. The GCC implementation of the customs union and its current economic agenda with Malaysia can potentially deliver meaningful benefits to Malaysia–GCC economic cooperation.

TABLES AND FIGURES

Table 13.1: List of Agreements between Malaysia and the Arab Gulf

Malaysia with Saudi Arabia
Cultural & Scientific Cooperation Agreement (19/05/1976);
Economic & Technical Cooperation Agreement (29/01/1975);
Air Services Agreement (18/07/1993);
Sponsorship of the International Islamic University (08/08/1985);
MoU on Education (20/10/1978);
MoU on Programme of Action for Cooperation in Field of Information (16/12/1982).
Malaysia with United Arab Emirates
Cultural & Scientific Cooperation Agreement (25/01/1975);
Trade Agreement (26/02/1962);
Investment Guarantee Agreement (11/10/1991);
Double Taxation Agreement (28/11/1995);
Economic & Technical Cooperation Agreement (25/01/1975);
Air Services Agreement (04/05/1993).
Malaysia with Kuwait
Cultural & Scientific Cooperation Agreement (21/01/1975);
Agreement for the Promotion and Protection on Investment (1987);
Avoidance Double Taxation Agreement (DTA) (2003);
Economic & Technical Cooperation Agreement (21/01/1975);
Air Services Agreement (07/05/1975).
Malaysia with Oman
Cultural & Scientific Cooperation Agreement (22/01/1975);
Air Services Agreement (19/04/1993);
Information Protocol (28/11/1988).

Source: Ministry of International Trade and Industry, Malaysia.

Figure 13.1: Malaysia Exports to the GCC 2000 – 2010

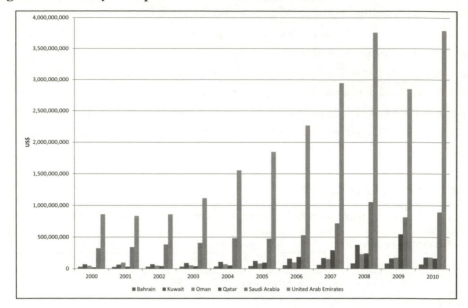

Source: Data obtained from World Integrated Trade Solution (WITS - COMTRADE database) – www.worldbank.org/WITS

Figure 13.2: Malaysia's imports from the GCC 2000 – 2010

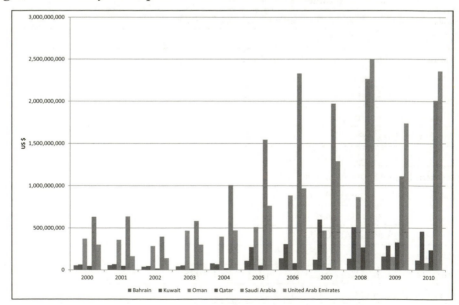

Source: Data obtained from World Integrated Trade Solution (WITS - COMTRADE database) – www.worldbank.org/WITS

Table 13.2: Total Investment from GCC countries between 1995 and 2000 (figure in million Malaysia Ringgit)

Country	Total investment / year					
	1995	1996	1997	1998	1999	2000
United Arab Emirates	3	1	2	5	23	9
Kuwait	...	-	2	-	2	...
Saudi Arabia	5	22	7	21	17	18
Bahrain	8	23	-	-		

Source: Monthly Statistical Bulletin January 2002, Central Bank Malaysia (BNM)[68]

Table 13.3: Total Investment from GCC countries, 2004-2009 (figure in million Malaysia Ringgit)

Country	Total investment / year					
	2004	2005	2006	2007	2008	2009
United Arab Emirates	11	35	976	425	1,411	674
Bahrain	n/a	6	5	19	66	67
Kuwait	17	58	6	363	1,064	612
Qatar	n/a	1	176	15	158	15
Saudi Arabia	14	8	216	315	18	434

Source: Bank Negara Malaysia Monthly Publication, January 2010.

Table 13.4: Malaysia's Investment in the GCC countries (figure in million Malaysia Ringgit)

Country	Total investment / year					
	2004	2005	2006	2007	2008	2009
United Arab Emirates	7	384	25	109	121	655
Bahrain	44	29	10	191	49	350
Kuwait	-	-	-	-	-	4
Qatar	18	372	472	364	98	-
Arab Saudi	2	6	25	223	209	140

Source: Bank Negara Malaysia Monthly Publication, January 2010.

Table 13.5: Tourist Arrivals in Malaysia from Selected Markets (2002 – 2007)

Country of Residence	2002	2003	2004	2005	2006	2007	% Change 2006 - 2007
Saudi Arabia	45,007	20,077	39,432	53,682	67,679	78,298	16
Bahrain	0	0	0	0	-	6,874	n/a
Oman	8,432	5,703	7,983	9,228	11,905	19,525	64
Kuwait	10,470	3,599	12,063	11,506	13,369	17,650	32
UAE	14,124	6,047	21,161	29,606	35,118	38,170	9
Qatar	0	0	0	0	-	11,782	n/a
Singapore	7,547,761	5,922,306	9,520,306	9,634,506	9,656,251	10,492,692	9
Syria	21,109	16,776	8,367	5,613	5,772	7,481	30
USA	127,920	131,071	145,094	151,354	174,336	204,844	17
United Kingdom	239,294	125,569	204,409	240,030	252,035	276,213	10
Japan	354,563	213,527	301,429	340,027	354,213	367,567	4

Source: Tourism Malaysia (http://www.tourism.gov.my/corporate/research.asp?page=facts_figures)

Figure 13.3: Malaysia's top ten source countries of International Students

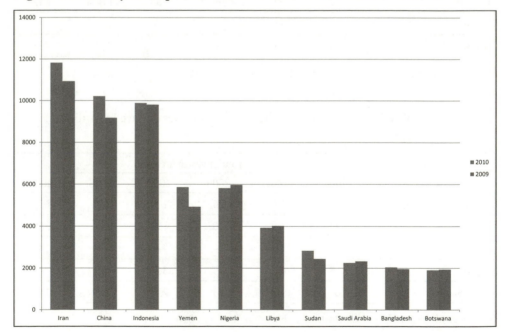

Endnotes

1   Zhang Mei,"China's Interests in the Gulf – Beyond Economic Relations?," in Perpectives 004, November 2009, Middle East Institute, National University of Singapore, 2009.

2   Bank Negara Malaysia BNM,"Bank Negara Malaysia Annual Report 2009," Bank Negara Malaysia (BNM), 2010. See also, Malaysia National Economic Advisory Council,"New Economic Model for Malaysia," National Economic Advisory Council (NEAC), 2010.

3   Asmady Idris, "Key Determining Factors Influencing Small States' Relationships: A Case Study of Malaysia's Relations with Saudi Arabia" (PhD Thesis, University of Newcastle upon Tyne, UK, 2006).

4   Ruhanas Harun, "Re-looking Malaysia's Foreign Policy Towards the Middle East" (Paper Presented at the National Seminar on Malaysia-West Asia Relations: Prospect and Challenges, Insitute of West Asian Studies, Universiti Kebangsaan Malaysia, December 1-2, 2008).

5   During the visit, Malaysian king had also had official visit to Jordan and Egypt. See Ruhanas Harun, "Re-looking Malaysia's Foreign Policy Towards the Middle East" (Paper Presented at the National Seminar on Malaysia-West Asia Relations: Prospect and Challenges, Insitute of West Asian Studies, Universiti Kebangsaan Malaysia, December 1-2, 2008).

6   Similar agreements were also signed with the United Arab Emirates, Kuwait and Bahrain.

7   Interview with Mrs Ho Siew Ching, Director of Economic and Trade Relations (West Asia Section), Ministry of Trade and Investment (MITI), Malaysia, November 21, 2008, 9.00 am – 10.30 am, Kuala Lumpur.

8   Asmady Idris, "Malaysia's relations with Saudi Arabia under Tun Dr. Mahathir era, 1981-2003" (paper presented at the Seminar on Nasional Resilience (SNAR 2010), Bayview Hotel Langkawi, Malaysia, July 13-15, 2010)

9   Mahathir's strategy in political relation that stressed on the ASEAN regional co-operation (security, political and socio-economic fields), closer relations with Islamic countries (especially with the Middle Eastern counterparts), and implementation of the Look East Policy has been fruitful particularly to promote the country's economic growth and strengthening political and economic relations with the developing nations.

10 Ibid., Idris, 147.

11 The loan given by the Saudi Fund (along with the Kuwaiti Fund amounted $137.8 million) was mainly utilized in agriculture projects, education, land development and medical facilities. This loan may exclude the loan for the second phase as it was only approved in 1986. See Fariza Hanum Ahmad Ramli, "Sejarah Hubungan Malaysia- Asia Barat Sehingga 1985" (Undergraduate Project Paper, Universiti Kebangsaan Malaysia, 1986) in Ibid., Idris, 115-118.

12 Ibid. Idris., 157.

13 Ibid. Idris., 150

14 BERNAMA, "Lawatan Ke Qatar Berjaya Tingkat Hubungan, Kata Najib," Bernama.Com, May 15, 2011, accessed April 12, 2012, http://web6.bernama.com/bernama/v3/bm/news_lite.php?id=586604.

15 National Economic Advisory Council, Malaysia,"New Economic Model for Malaysia," National Economic Advisory Council (NEAC), 2010.

16 Mohd Fauzi Abu-Hussin, "Exploring International Trade between Malaysia and GCC Countries: Empirical Analysis on Trends, Developments and Challenges" (PhD Thesis, University of Durham, 2010).

17 "Malaysia - GCC Framework Agreement on Economic, Commercial, Investment and Technical Cooperation," Ministry of International Trade and Industry, Malaysia, accessed March 30, 2012, http://www.miti.gov.my/cms/content.jsp?id=com.tms.cms.article.Article_db099c37-c0a8156 f-23072307-3c9d8b44. See also, "Malaysia Enhances Economic Relations with the Gulf Cooperation Council (GCC)," Ministry of International Trade and Industry, Malaysia, accessed 30 March 2012, http://www.miti.gov.my/cms/content.jsp?id=com.tms.cms.article.Article_ dad77bf1-c0a8156f-23072307-5fe7c5f7.

18 Mohd Fauzi Abu-Hussin et. al. "Capturing Arab gulf market: An analysis of Malaysian Exports Competitiveness in The Market." African Journal of Business Management 5, 21 (2011): 8521-8535, available at: http://www.academicjournals.org/AJBM.

19 Bank Negara Malaysia,"Bank Negara Malaysia Annual Report 2008," Bank Negara Malaysia (BNM), 2009.

20 Abu-Hussin, "Capturing Arab gulf market: An analysis of Malaysian Exports Competitiveness in The Market."

21 Numerous visits by Malaysian Prime ministers and Trade Ministers to UAE between 2006 and 2010 reflected the change of direction in Malaysia's bilateral trade with this country.

22 Data obtained from COMTRADE confirmed this.

23 The aid given was in the form of a loan.

24 The Saudi Fund Development SFD,"The aid, in fact, ended in 1983," (The Saudi Fund Development, Annual Report (20), 1993 (1413/1414H)) in Asmady Idris. "Malaysia's Economic Relations With Saudi Arabia." Journal of Southeast Asian Studies (JATI) 12(1), 2007, 31-54.

25 Idris, "Malaysia's Economic Relations With Saudi Arabia," 31-54.

26 John Lawton. "Arab Aid in Malaysia." Saudi Aramco World Magazine, no. 6 November/ December 1979, accessed April 3, 2012, http://www.saudiaramcoworld.com/issue/197906/arab. aid-in.malaysia.htm

27 Idris, "Malaysia's Economic Relations With Saudi Arabia," 31-54.

28 Idris, "Malaysia's Economic Relations With Saudi Arabia," 31-54.

29 Malaysia Industrial Development Authority (MIDA), 2003 in Idris, Idris, "Malaysia's Economic Relations With Saudi Arabia."

30 Danny Yap, "Foreigners still find good values in M'sia," The Start Online, July 7, 2008, accessed February 18, 2012, http://biz.thestar.com.my/news/story.asp?file=/2008/7/7/ business/21745793&sec=business.

31 "Malaysia: Prestasi Pelaburan 2011," Malaysian Investment Development Authority (MIDA), accessed February 11, 2012, http://www.mida.gov.my/env3/uploads/PerformanceReport/2011/ Laporan.pdf.

32 "Malaysia: Prestasi Pelaburan 2011."

33 In the ninth Malaysian economic plan, the government announced several clusters of economic regions namely, Eastern, Southern, Northern and Borneo economic corridors. Developments in these regions concentrate on various aspect of economy including tourism, oil & gas, manufacturing, services, properties, agriculture and education.

34 Reuters, "Malaysia's Iskandar eyes Gulf Funds As Crunch Bites," The National, December 24, 2008, accessed January 15, 2011, http://www.thenational.ae/business/economy/malaysias-iskandar-eyes-gulf-funds-as-crunch-bites.

35 BERNAMA, "ECER eyes more gulf investments." Bernama.Com, January 31, 2011, accessed February 15, 2011, http://www.bernama.com/bernama/v5/newsindex.php?id=560723.

36 "Iskandar Development Region ("IDR") attracts major landmark development of an initial investment of USD1.2 billion," South Johor Investment Corporation Berhad (SJIC), accessed January 18,2011, http://www.iskandarmalaysia.com.my/content/iskandar-development-region-idr-attracts-major-landmark-development-of-an-initial-investment.

37 "Promoting Iskandar Malaysia to the Middle East," Iskandar Region Developmenr Authority (IRDA), accessed April 18, 2012, http://www.iskandarmalaysia.com.my/press/promoting-iskandar-malaysia-to-the-middle-east-irda-participates-in-invest-malaysia-abu-dhabi.

38 BERNAMA, "Bank Islam Set To Expand Its Financial Services." Bernama.Com, Sept 4, 2007, accessed December 12, 2010, http://www.bernama.com/finance/news.php?id=217924., see also, http://www.bankislam.com.my/en/pages/Milestones.aspx?tabs=1

39 Sukuk is an Islamic bond that is asset based bond and structured according to Syariah principles.

40 The Khazanah Nasional is a government-owned investment organisation that manages the sovereign wealth fund.

41 "Mubadala oil & gas signs development & production sharing agreement with Petronas," Mubadala Development Company PJSC, accessed February 15, 2012, http://mubadala.ae/media/news/mubadala_oil_gas_signs_development_production_sharing_agreement_with_petron.

42 "Malaysia: Prestasi Pelaburan 2011," Malaysian Investment Development Authority (MIDA).

43 "Malaysia pelabur keempat terbesar Arab Saudi." Malaysian Investment Development Authority (MIDA), accessed December 12, 2011, http://bmweb.mida.gov.my/cms/eBerita2.jsp?id=com.tms.cms.article.Article_a7b4dc91-d2bb29d0-a097f700-92622184.

44 BERNAMA, "Bank Islam Set To Expand Its Financial Services," Bernama.Com, Sept 4, 2007, accessed January 18, 2012, http://www.bernama.com/finance/news.php?id=217924.

45 BERNAMA, "ECER eyes more gulf investments," Bernama.Com, January 31, 2011, accessed February 15, 2011, http://www.bernama.com/bernama/v5/newsindex.php?id=560723.

46 "SEDCO eyes investments in Malaysia." The Saudi Gazette, May 18, 2010, accessed December 13, 2010, http://www.saudigazette.com.sa/index.cfm?method=home.regcon&contentID=2010051872634.

47 "Promoting Iskandar Malaysia to the Middle East," Iskandar Region Developmenr Authority (IRDA).

48 "FAQ Arising from Official Visits to Saudi Arabia, UAE and India (20 Jan 2010)" Ministry of International Trade and Industry, Malaysia, accessed October 3, 2012, http://www.miti.gov.my/cms/content.jsp?id=com.tms.cms.article.Article_563ec500-c0a81573-2f1d2f1d-32c2ae22_my.

49 Leong Shen-Li, "Looking to the Middle East," The Star Online, January 25, 2010, accessed March 15, 2012, http://thestar.com.my/news/story.asp?file=/2010/1/25/nation/5536408&sec=nation.

50 Idris, "Malaysia's Economic Relations with Saudi Arabia."

51 Andrzej Kapiszewski,"Arab Versus Asian Migrant Workers In The GCC Countries," United Nations Expert Group Meeting On International Migration and Development In The Arab Region, UN/POP/EGM/2006/02, Population Division, Department of Economic and Social Affairs, United Nations Secretariat, 2006.

52 Idris, "Malaysia's Economic Relations with Saudi Arabia."

53 Halal, is an arabic/Quranic term which means "permissible" or "allowed" and it is confined in various aspect of Muslim life whether it is muamalah practices or activities that relates to ibadah etc. However, in the Muslim majority, the concept of halal refers to Muslim daily consumption that includes food, medicine, pharmaceutical etc.

54 M. Helble. "Is God Good For Trade?" *Kyklos* 60, 3 (2007), 385-413.

55 BERNAMA, "Malaysian Expertise Sought To Set Up Halal Parks In Gulf Countries," Bernama. Com, May 15, 2010, accessed December 22, 2010, http://www.bernama.com/bernama/v5/newsbusiness.php?id=498418

56 Dalila Abu Bakar, "Huge Opportunities for Malaysian Businesses in Arab Countries," Bernama. Com, February 23, 2012, accessed October 3, 2012, http://web6.bernama.com/bernama/v3/news_lite.php?id=647395.

57 "Halal Food Products Market Report", Ottawa, Canada: Agriculture and Agri-Food Canada, 2006.

58 Khadijah Md. Khalid. "Malaysia's Growing Economic Relations with the Muslim World," Kyoto Review of Southeast Asia 2004, accessed June 9, 2008, http://kyotoreview.cseas.kyoto-u.ac.jp/issue/issue4/article_362.html>.

59 "National Higher Education Action Plan 2007-2010," Ministry of Higher Education, Malaysia, accessed May 3, 2012, http://www.mohe.gov.my/transformasi/.

60 "Statistics of Higher Education of Malaysia 2010," Ministry of Higher Education, Malaysia, 2011.

61 Rohana Jani, et. al. "International Students' Views of Malaysian Higher Education"(paper presented at the Internationalisation And Marketing Of Higher Education Malaysia Seminar, Putrajaya, Malaysia, Ministry of Higher Education Malaysia, 17 Jun 2010).

62 Badaruddin Mohamed, "Kajian Pelajar Antarabangsa Di Malaysia," Higher Education Research Institute (IPPTN), USM, accessed May 17, 2012, http://jpt.mohe.gov.my/PENYELIDIK/penyelidikan%20IPPTN/Laporan%20akhir%20KajPeljAntrbgsa_TNR_ipptnformat.pdf.

63 Jani, et. al., "International Students' Views of Malaysian Higher Education."

64 Wan Chang Da, et al.,"Higher Education: Middle East (Part 1) Overview, Saudi Arabia and Qatar," No. 30. 15 May 2008, Higher Education Research Institute (IPPTN), Universiti Sains Malaysia, 2008. See also, Wan Chang Da et al.,"Higher Education: Middle East (Part 2) United Arab Emirates, Bahrain and Iraq," No. 31. 15 May 2008, Higher Education Research Institute (IPPTN), Universiti Sains Malaysia, 2008.

65 "Malaysia Enhances Economic Relations with the Gulf Cooperation Council (GCC)," Ministry of International Trade and Industry, Malaysia.

66 Evelyn S. Devadason et. al. "Leveraging Trade Opportunities with Non-Traditional Partners: The Malaysia-GCC Perspective," *SSRN eLibrary,* accessed May 21, 2012, *http://papers.ssrn.com/sol3/papers.cfm?abstract_id=1960470#.*

67 "Malaysia Enhances Economic Relations with the Gulf Cooperation Council (GCC)," Ministry of International Trade and Industry, Malaysia.

68 "Monthly Statistical Bulletin January 2002". Bank Negara Malaysia (BNM), January 21, 2012, http://www.bnm.gov.my/index.php?ch=109&pg=294&ac=242&mth=1&yr=2002&lang=bm&eId=box1.

Bibliography

"Malaysia - GCC Framework Agreement on Economic, Commercial, Investment and Technical Cooperation," Ministry of International Trade and Industry, Malaysia, accessed March 30, 2012, http://www.miti.gov.my/cms/content.jsp?id=com.tms.cms.article.Article_db099c37-c0a8156f-23072307-.

"Malaysia Enhances Economic Relations with the Gulf Cooperation Council (GCC)," Ministry of International Trade and Industry, Malaysia, accessed 30 March 2012, http://www.miti.gov.my/cms/content.jsp?id=com.tms.cms.article.Article_dad77bf1-c0a8156f-23072307-5fe7c5f7.

"Malaysia sets to receive more investments from GCC," Malaysian Investment Development Authority (MIDA), Februari 7, 2011, accessed February 15, 2012 http://www.mida.gov.my/env3/index.php?mact=News,cntnt01,print,0&cntnt01articleid=1104&cntnt01showtemplate=false&cntnt01returnid=144.

"Monthly Statistical Bulletin January 2002". Bank Negara Malaysia (BNM), 2002, accessed January 21,2012, http://www.bnm.gov.my/index.php?ch=109&pg=294&ac=242&mth=1&yr=2002&lang=bm&eId=box1.

"Mubadala oil & gas signs development & production sharing agreement with Petronas," Mubadala Development Company PJSC, accessed February 15, 2012, http://mubadala.ae/media/news/mubadala_oil_gas_signs_development_production_sharing_agreement_with_petron.

"Promoting Iskandar Malaysia to the Middle East," Iskandar Region Developmenr Authority (IRDA), accessed April 18, 2012, http://www.iskandarmalaysia.com.my/press/promoting-iskandar-malaysia-to-the-middle-east-irda-participates-in-invest-malaysia-abu-dhabi.

"Halal Food Products Market Report". Ottawa, Canada: Agriculture and Agri-Food Canada, 2006.

Abu-Hussin, Mohd Fauzi "Exploring International Trade between Malaysia and GCC Countries: Empirical Analysis on Trends, Developments and Challenges." unpublished PhD Thesis, University of Durham, 2010.

Abu-Hussin, Mohd Fauzi, Ahmad Azam Sulaiman Mohamad, and Mohd Yahya Mohd Hussin. "Capturing Arab gulf market: An analysis of Malaysian Exports Competitiveness in The Market." *African Journal of Business Management* 5, 21 (2012), 8521-35.

Bank Negara Malaysia,"Bank Negara Malaysia Annual Report 2008," Bank Negara Malaysia (BNM), 2009.

Bank Negara Malaysia,"Bank Negara Malaysia Annual Report 2009," Bank Negara Malaysia (BNM), 2010.

Da, Wan Chang, Sarjit Kaur, and Muhamad Jantan,"Higher Education: Middle East (Part 1) Overview, Saudi Arabia and Qatar," No. 30. 15 May 2008, Higher Education Research Institute (IPPTN), Universiti Sains Malaysia, 2008.

Da, Wan Chang, Sarjit Kaur, and Muhamad Jantan,"Higher Education: Middle East (Part 2) United Arab Emirates, Bahrain and Iraq," No. 31. 15 May 2008, Higher Education Research Institute (IPPTN), Universiti Sains Malaysia, 2008.

Devadason, Evelyn S., Ahmad Zubaidi Baharumshah, and Thirunaukarasu Subramaniam, "Leveraging Trade Opportunities with Non-Traditional Partners: The Malaysia-GCC Perspective." *SSRN eLibrary*, accessed May 21, 2012, *http://papers.ssrn.com/sol3/papers.cfm?abstract_id=1960470#*.

Fasano-Filho, Ugo, and Zubair Iqbal, "GCC Countries: From Oil Dependence to Diversification," IMF Working Paper, Washington D.C.: International Monetary Fund, 2003.

Harun, Ruhanas. "Re-looking Malaysia's Foreign Policy Towards the Middle East" paper presented at the National Seminar on Malaysia-West Asia Relations: Prospect and Challenges, Insitute of West Asian Studies, Universiti Kebangsaan Malaysia, December 1-2, 2008.

Helble, M. "Is God Good For Trade?" Kyklos 60, 3 (2007): 385-413.

Idris, Asmady "Malaysia's Economic Relations With Saudi Arabia," Journal of Southeast Asian Studies (JATI) Vol. 12, 1 (2007): 31-54.

Idris, Asmady "Malaysia's relations with Saudi Arabia under Tun Dr. Mahathir era, 1981-2003" paper presented at the Seminar on Nasional Resilience (SNAR 2010) "Political Managements and Policies in Malaysia", Bayview Hotel Langkawi, Malaysia, July 13-15, 2010.

Idris, Asmady. "Key Determining Factors Influencing Small States' Relationships: A Case Study of Malaysia's Relations with Saudi Arabia." PhD Thesis, University of Newcastle upon Tyne, 2006.

Jani, Rohana., et. al., "International Students' Views of Malaysian Higher Education," paper Presented at the Internationalisation and Marketing of Higher Education Malaysia Seminar, Putrajaya, Ministry of Higher Education Malaysia, Jun 17, 2010.

Kapiszewski, Andrzej,"Arab Versus Asian Migrant Workers In The GCC Countries," United Nations Expert Group Meeting On International Migration and Development In The Arab Region, UN/POP/EGM/2006/02, Population Division, Department of Economic and Social Affairs, United Nations Secretariat, 2006.

Lawton, John. "Arab Aid in Malaysia." Saudi Aramco World Magazine, no. 6 November/December 1979, accessed April 3, 2012, http://www.saudiaramcoworld.com/issue/197906/arab.aid-in. malaysia.htm.

Md. Khalid, Khadijah. "Malaysia's Growing Economic Relations with the Muslim World," Kyoto Review of Southeast Asia (2004), accessed June 9, 2008, http://kyotoreview.cseas.kyoto-u.ac.jp/issue/issue4/article_362.html>.

Mei, Zhang,"China's Interests in the Gulf – Beyond Economic Relations?," Perpectives 004, November 2009, Middle East Institute, National University of Singapore, 2009.

Ministry of Higher Education, "National Higher Education Action Plan 2007-2010." Ministry of Higher Education, Malaysia, accessed May 3, 2012, http://www.mohe.gov.my/transformasi/.

_____ "Statistics of Higher Education of Malaysia 2010," Ministry of Higher Education, Malaysia, 2011.

Mohamed, Badaruddin. "Kajian Pelajar Antarabangsa Di Malaysia." Higher Education Research Institute (IPPTN), University Science Malaysia, accessed May 17, 2012, http://jpt.mohe.gov. my/PENYELIDIK/penyelidikan%20IPPTN/Laporan%20akhir%20KajPeljAntrbgsa_TNR_ipptnformat.pdf.

National Economic Advisory Council, Malaysia,"New Economic Model for Malaysia," National Economic Advisory Council (NEAC), 2010.

The Saudi Fund Development,"The aid, in fact, ended in 1983," The Saudi Fund Development, Annual Report (20), 1993.

Tong, Goh Chok. "Asia and the Middle East: A New Era of Cooperation," GULF ASIA - Research Buletin, February 2008: 20-23.

Yong, Ong Keng. "Strengthening Ties between Asia and The GCC." ASEAN Website, accessed November 20, 2011, www.aseansec.org/18163.htm.

Chapter Fourteen

Small is Beautiful: South Korean-Gulf Relations as an Example of Strategic Engagement by Players in Different Arenas*

Joachim Kolb

1. Introduction

For a mid-sized, linguistically and ethnically homogeneous East Asian nation surrounded by vastly more powerful neighbors, the emergence of South Korea as a significant player in the Gulf region runs counter to received wisdom on the ingredients of international success in the concert of nations. But contractors, energy companies and cultural institutions alike have had to recognize South Korea (also referred to as the Republic of Korea or ROK) in recent years as a significant regional competitor.

This chapter assesses the political and strategic dynamics of the South Korean role in the Gulf region, with particular emphasis given to the strategic "games" the country has engaged in since the end of the Cold War, and with greater intensity over the last decade. Like other East Asian nations, South Korea relies on the Gulf region for most of its fossil energy, in particular petroleum products and liquefied natural gas (LNG). Unlike other OECD members, it is a relative newcomer to the region, which it first entered during the construction boom of the 1970s and 1980s. After a lull in the 1990s, South Korean decision-makers have over the past 10 years cooperated closely with the country's business community to upgrade the relationship. As a result of this, relations between Korea and its GCC partners have become more comprehensive than before. This chapter seeks to document and explain the relationship, providing a systematic overview which can explain both the astonishing successes and the limits of South Korea's role in the Gulf.[1]

Three overarching theoretical themes will be pursued throughout this chapter. First, the means whereby a country that is firmly inserted in a regional environment where it constitutes a weaker partner can devise autonomous strategies to pursue its interests outside this area are examined. Second, the dichotomy between planning and emergent spontaneous development is discussed, focusing on the extent to which South Korean engagement is planned and coordinated. Third, the interplay between the soft power of public diplomacy and interest-driven traditional *realpolitik* is traced in a region where such coordinated efforts have been the exception, rather than the rule.

Section 2 outlines the character of the playing field in which South Korean decision-makers are operating. Policy games played by South Korea in the Gulf region, it is suggested, are games in an "out of area" arena. Opportunities arise from the interaction with local partners pursuing their own strategic games. Data on the economic bases of the relationship between South Korea and the Gulf, as well as the development of population numbers, are briefly reviewed, and Korean capacities in information aggregation, sustained investment and planning are assessed.

Section 3, the empirical core of the chapter, investigates the dynamics of political and strategic relations between South Korea and the Gulf on a country-by-country basis, covering both long-term strategic constants of the relationships and opportunities for decision-makers on both sides to engage in interactions, giving precedence to developments in the UAE, which has witnessed the most significant recent developments.

Section 4 then analyzes the interaction between South Korea and other Asian actors in the Gulf, and identifies limits, as well as possibilities, of the Asian perspective on Korea-Gulf relations: to a significant extent, South Korea's engagement in the Gulf arena relates not only to the strategic position of other Asian players, but to the more global orientation of Korean politics and business strategies, including with extra-regional partners. Section 5 concludes with an overview of Korea's possible contribution to the Gulf region.

2. South Korea's Strategic Position: Observations and Data

In international relations, the relationships between major powers normally take center stage. Marginal relationships may, however, hold definite attractions for players precisely because of the initially weak bond between both parties. In game theory, such situations have sometimes been addressed as games in different arenas. In these cases, actions whose benefit in one arena may not be particularly evident display a far more convincing payoff structure for the actors involved once the overall rewards in different arenas are considered.[2] As engagement in different arenas thus gives players the option to circumvent certain constraints prevalent in their original environment, it may motivate partners to cooperate, rather than defect, if their interaction extends to more than one arena.

The following pages analyze Korea-Gulf relations in the light of a "multiple arenas" perspective in which partners from two relatively distinct regions devise mutually beneficial win-win games that enable both of them to improve their payoffs with limited scrutiny by veto players operating in the region. It will be shown how the Korean side strategically extends the arenas in which it is active so as to strengthen its overall position.

2.1 South Korea in its Regional Context

South Korea is part of a close-knit network of strategic relationships in North-East Asia that include both antagonisms and cooperative relations. The character of the relationships is determined by powers significantly larger than itself: the US, China, Russia, and Japan, as well as an eccentric smaller power in its immediate vicinity, North Korea.

In order to deal with this challenging neighborhood, the ROK has historically relied on a very close alliance with the United States, which has provided a security umbrella since the Korean War ended in 1953. With 28,500 men permanently stationed in the ROK, the US has maintained a significant military presence since the end of the Korean War, and is the ROK's closest ally.[3] Before 1990, South Korea's exposed position as a Cold War front state meant diplomatic non-engagement with the Soviet Union and its allies, a constraint that also precluded an early establishment of relations with Iraq and Egypt. Today, the range of diplomatic relationships has been extended, but within the framework of the American alliance, since South Korea's own potential for projecting military power autonomously outside the Korean peninsula is limited.

In the sub-regional North Asian context, South Korea is suspended between three larger powers, China, Japan, and Russia, while the unpredictability, the aggressiveness, and the nuclear status of its erratic Northern neighbor elevate it to a focal point of international and regional politics that is far larger than North Korea's intrinsic economic and political relevance would lead to expect. All four relationships, and particularly that with Japan and North Korea, are highly loaded in the public arena. The ROK is embroiled in low-intensity territorial disputes with Japan and the so-called "Koguryo dispute" with China, and wages a cold war that occasionally turns hot against the North.

China is both an extremely important economic partner and, as the only major backer of North Korea and an overwhelmingly stronger power, a strategic threat. Unlike the ROK, it can project significant military power in the region, where it has entered into spats over sovereignty over remote islands and the suspected mineral wealth of the surrounding seabed with both Japan and its Southeast Asian neighbors. Japan, strategically most similar to South Korea (in terms of countenancing the rise of China in the region as a major industrial power while itself having limited military potential), continues to be resented because of its former role as a colonizer of its smaller neighbor between 1910 and 1945.

South Korea is thus surrounded by a strategic field in which it is exposed to the action of four larger powers, but does not, in its turn, constitute a significant political or military threat to them. To counter these threats, it maintains armed forces that are very large in relation to the country's population, and has introduced compulsory military service for its male population. Korean troops have participated in the wars against Iraq in 1991 and 2003, as well as in a large number of peace-keeping missions around the world. But since the Vietnam War numbers of troops devoted to extra-territorial missions have tended to be relatively low, and casualties minimal. To the extent that its policymaking is subject to public scrutiny, the focus here is on East Asia. The Gulf largely remains outside the public view.

2.2 A Global Economic Playing Field

By contrast, in the economic sphere the ROK has become a major industrial and high-tech champion catering to global markets, albeit as a relative latecomer. It only gained prominence as an industrial power from the 1980s onwards. This makes it dependent on others for the security of shipping lanes, open trade regimes, access to raw materials and fossil energy, and an international governance regime that secures property rights and supplies. In this sphere, the ROK acts globally, and has made considerable efforts to gain kudos in the international arena: if the 1988 Olympics marked the transition to tiger status and democracy for what many had seen as an underdeveloped country under an authoritarian regime, the November 2010

G-20 summit in Seoul highlighted the augmented role of this country which, with significant educational and economic success and considerable soft power, craves international recognition.[4] While before 1991 South Korea had no diplomatic relations with China and the Eastern bloc and was not even a UN member state then, it now tends to a far larger portfolio of diplomatic relationships.[5]

However, regarding energy policy, investments into the general global governance infrastructure are insufficient to ensure long-term security. Energy prices fluctuate significantly, and smaller, resource-poor powers with significant energy needs such as South Korea lack the commercial bargaining power and military ability to extend their writ, should established rules of commercial exchange be called into question. Although radically different in its regional context, South Korean energy security necessitates a move from arms-length relationships to building strong common interests with Gulf partners that accounted for 64% of its oil consumption and 43% of its LNG in 2010.[6]

South Korea's late industrialization meant that the country could make its mark in the Gulf energy sector only after other major industrial powers, including the US, the UK and France, but also Japan, had already staked their claims in the region. This presented South Korea with the challenge of having to break into preexisting arrangements between resource-rich states and established developed partners. During the Lee presidency, an explicit resource diplomacy was proclaimed to support this ambition, directed not only at the Gulf, but also at the resource-rich countries of Central Asia, Africa and Latin America.[7]

Another strategic dilemma stemming from industrialization lies in South Korea's apprehension about being "sandwiched" one day between a restructured Japan that has managed to reduce costs and a learning China, which may expand into the higher value-added activities, reducing South Korean competitive advantage.[8] This threat can also be countered by a relationship-based strategy of binding the client by multiple bonds. A further, less immediate, challenge in the global arena arises from the very success of South Korean industrialization: not unlike the Gulf states, South Korea has one of the most massive carbon footprints worldwide, but it has also recently been among the most vocal about tackling it.[9]

In the Gulf region, the rapid development of South Korean trade and investment illustrate the increased role of South Korean enterprises. The Gulf-South Korea trade figures, while lagging behind those of China, India, and Japan, have seen robust growth over the last two decades, as illustrated by Table 14.1, and would appear to point to a prominent role for Saudi Arabia in South Korean economic activities in the Gulf.

Table 14.1: Total South Korean Trade with the Gulf States in $ (bn)

	1990	2000	2005	2008	2009	2010	2011
Bahrain	0.1	0.3	0.4	0.8	0.6	0.6	0.9
Saudi Arabia	2.4	9.8	16.8	36.5	22.2	24.3	41.3
UAE	1.5	5.5	12.1	23.8	13.9	15	21.4
Qatar	0.2	2.1	8.1	13.5	9	10	19.4
Oman	0.2	1.6	4.1	6.9	4.3	4.8	5.9
Kuwait	0.6	2.7	5.9	11.8	8	9	17
Iraq	0	0.7	0.7	4.2	4.3	4.3	10
Iran	1.1	2.9	5.3	12.2	9.6	10.3	18.2
TOTAL	6.1	25.6	53.4	109.7	71.9	78.3	134.1

Source: IMF figures as cited in Niblock, this volume

While trade figures thus highlight the role of Saudi Arabia, by far the single most important trading partner, South Korean FDI in the Gulf region paints a different picture. Insignificant before 2004, it has since seen a rapid increase, particularly in Oman, where it started from the highest base in the region, and in the UAE. In spite of its towering role as a trade partner, Saudi Arabia has not been a favored destination for regional South Korean FDI. Here, it is the UAE that has seen the most dramatic increases, although in 2010, the country still lagged behind Oman in absolute terms.

Table 14.2: South Korean FDI Stocks in the Gulf Region in $ (mn)

	2004	2005	2006	2007	2008	2009	2010
Iran	13.4	..	10.569	1.098	18.398	17.486	34.201
Bahrain	0.1	..	0.133	45.45	46.178	45.45	189.897
Iraq	0	..	0	1.253	1.253	85.665	327.009
Kuwait	0.5	..	1.2	5.845	16.897	16.3	4.8
Oman	97.4	..	164.957	233.614	303.669	325.133	762.142
Qatar	0.6	..	1.37	2.505	9.374	19.803	17.654
Saudi Arabia	34.3	..	41.047	26.98	93.546	166.077	221.271
UAE	15.5	..	120.681	278.228	371.721	291.204	564.011

Source: OECD StatExtracts by partner country

2.3 Cultural Affinity and Previous Experience of the Gulf

The recent increase in South Korean engagement in the Gulf has been facilitated by the fact that, for the older generation, the Gulf had already been a game changer once in their economic fortunes: from the mid-1960s onwards, South Korean construction companies expanded abroad as low-end contractors competing primarily on price. While it left South Korean society largely unaltered and ended temporarily as increasingly sophisticated manufacturing gained precedence over construction from the late 1980s onwards, this expansionary phase was transformational for both individual livelihoods and corporate growth of the powers involved, two spheres that were to be united in the charismatic figure of President Lee Myung-Bak.

According to Seok (1991:56), the first group of 218 South Korean construction workers arrived in the Gulf in 1976. Their headcount peaked in 1982 with over 170,000 workers in the Arab world, which had dropped to 107,000 by 1985. More dramatically, the value of the construction contracts these individuals were involved in peaked at $13bn in 1981 and had dropped to $4bn by 1985. In 1988, it appeared that the first wave of the Korean construction presence on the Gulf market had exhausted itself, but for the Korean construction industry, the Gulf construction boom had come at a defining moment, propelling it from a completely local industry to a global range of activities.[10] As living standards in South Korea rose, these companies increasingly priced themselves out of the market by the end of that decade.[11] In 2010, the South Korean construction industry contributed around 6% to GDP and won overseas contracts valued at $491.5bn on international markets, including 60 percent of EPC-contracts in the Gulf.[12] Table 14.3 illustrates the extent of this massive Korean presence in the late 1970s and early 1980s, which dwarfes the numbers found today.

Table 14.3: South Korean Residents in the Gulf Region, 1974-2011

	1974	1978	1982	1985	2011
Saudi Arabia	218	56,161	122,606	58,924	2,670
UAE	0	2,689	1,414	1,268	6,000
Oman	0	n.a.	n.a.	n.a.	600
Qatar	0	1,915	1,309	699	2,146
Bahrain	0	n.a.	n.a.	n.a.	278
Kuwait	0	8,646	5,644	4,127	1,000
Iraq	0	428	19,920	10,607	260
Iran	177	7,418	455	3,669	506
Total	359	77,257	151,348	79,294	13,460

Source: Seok (1991:58) for historical data, MOFAT for 2011 figures

While most of the participants in this first mass migration of South Koreans to the Gulf lived in tightly controlled labor camps without much interaction with the local inhabitants and their culture, this first expansion phase certainly left corporate Korea's business community acutely aware of what the Gulf had to offer.[13]

One of the business community's most experienced representatives changed jobs in 2008. Born in Osaka to Korean parents in 1941, Lee Myung-Bak, nicknamed "the Bulldozer," entered Hyundai Construction shortly after graduation in 1967, soon rose through the ranks to become its CEO, and remained with the company until 1992. His tenure saw the rise of Hyundai Construction from a relatively small outfit to an international construction behemoth, with an initial overseas contract in Thailand followed by engagements in Bandar Abbas in Iran and Jubail, spanning the period of the Gulf construction boom. His uncommon appreciation of both the potential of Gulf relations and the needs of the Korean construction industry was clearly apparent in an announcement he made in Dubai at the onset of his campaign for presidency in 2007, declaring that a "second Gulf construction boom" was needed.[14] Through this very public announcement, a clear commitment to a sustained development of South Korean-Gulf relations was articulated in public, and as will be seen below, this has been followed through by a very active role of the president in promoting Gulf relationships.

A representative of the conservative Hannara (now Saenuri) party, salient points of his internal stance in South Korean politics include the adoption of major construction projects, including that of a controversial canal connecting South Korea's two major river systems, a more confrontational stance towards North Korea, as well as an emphasis on green policies, including a widely published ecological reclamation project in Seoul, in the course of which a river that had been completely removed from view was brought to the light of day again. At the same time, the Lee presidency has also been associated with austerity measures and a cutback on social security measures.[15]

2.4 Soft Power, Educational Excellence, and Policy Coordination

In rankings of contemporary education systems such as the OECD Pisa project, South Korea regularly scores very highly, documenting the excellence of its education system, and this perceived excellence carries over to its leading universities.[16] While this increases South Korea's attractiveness as a partner to MENA countries striving to establish a knowledge society, it also means that the country is in a far better position to systematically generate an academic knowledge base on the Gulf region than the region is reciprocating: bilateral interactions thus are largely subject to asymmetric information.

Table 14.4: The Knowledge Society in South Korea and the Gulf

	Human Development Index (HDI 2011, Value and Rank)	Patents (Number of resident patent filings per million population in 2010)	PISA–Score (2009)
South Korea	0.897 (15)	2696.78	539
Dubai	n.a.	n.a.	459
Jordan	0.698 (95)	7.44	405
Bahrain	0.806 (42)	n.a.	n.a.
Kuwait	0.760 (63)	n.a.	n.a.
Oman	0.705 (90)	n.a.	n.a.
Qatar	0.831 (37)	n.a.	n.a.
Saudi Arabia	0.770 (56)	10.49	n.a.
UAE	0.846 (30)	n.a.	n.a.

Sources: UNDP for HDI, WIPO Statistics Database and World Bank (World Development Indicators), December 2011 for patent data, OECD for PISA-Scores

The establishment of a first Middle Eastern Studies department at the Hankuk University of Foreign Studies in 1976 and of the Korean Association of the Middle East (KAMES) in 1979 constitutes a first academic investment into the relationship during the first construction boom. At a more political level, South Korea's efforts to widen its knowledge base regarding the MENA region led to the establishment of the annual Forum for Korea-Middle East Cooperation, held for the first time in 2003 with the support of the South Korean Ministry of Foreign Affairs. The 8th edition of the forum was held in October 2011 at the Jeju Peace Institute, enjoyed the sponsorship of the Emirates Center for Strategic Studies (ECSSR) and included numerous high-level GCC decision makers among its attendees. This has provided MENA academics and decision makers with regular opportunities to interact with South Korean counterparts, and has ensured increased levels of information on the South Korean side. At a less academic level, these networks were to be extended further into civil society by the establishment of the Korean–Arab Friendship Society in 2008.[17] The brainchild of a retired South Korean diplomat, the society, which has the government of South Korea and 22 Arab governments as its members, promotes the spread of mutual cultural understanding and cultural activities.[18] Cultural diplomacy has played a role in South Korea's engagement with Gulf partners since its beginnings. During the first construction boom, this appears to have been most pronounced in Iran, an important early site of South Korean construction efforts, the importance of which decreased, however, as South Korean resident numbers fell in the 1980s and policy positions shifted.[19]

2.5 South Korean Priorities and their Gulf Counterparts

The material presented in this section shows that from a South Korean perspective, the following objectives are given priority in South Korean engagement in the Gulf:

- Securing access to energy resources from the Gulf;
- Acquiring, extending and defending markets for South Korean goods and services;
- Supporting the US alliance as a political and military security arrangement that provides for South Korean protection from strategic threats; and
- Strengthening South Korea's soft power and green credentials, so as to preclude charges of environmental neglect and over-consumption of energy.

From a Gulf perspective, a complementary picture emerges. Here, American power has also provided the dominant strategic framework for decades, and as the 1991 Gulf War demonstrated, this vital alliance has afforded reliable protection against outside aggression against the GCC states. Within this overall structure, however, tensions remain: the antagonism between Iran and the GCC states and that between regional Shia and Sunni groups, the continued repercussions of confrontation between Israel and its Arab neighbors, the need to placate and contain the claims of the more populous, but poorer Arab states outside the GCC, and the paradox of large sub-continental populations without any political representation are just a number of strategic relationships that determine policy making in the Gulf region and remain closely watched. Further prominent issues include the need to develop national human resources and alternative sources of energy so as to postpone the day when national mineral resources are exhausted and the Gulf states are singled out by advocates of a greener development path for excessive energy consumption.

Among the strategic objectives of the GCC side, the following inductively generated list of both frequently voiced and quietly held aims are apparent:

- Maintaining stable relationships with major energy clients;
- Upgrading military capabilities without increasing dependence on external actors;
- Preserving the vital alliance with the US;
- Upgrading of national human resources;
- Cultivation of research, R&D and entrepreneurial activity;

- Knowledge transfer with a view to making these succeed;
- Maintaining credibility within the Arab world; and
- Balancing the demographic structure so as not to endanger the Arab character of the polity, a specific GCC problem caused by large numbers of foreigners.

3. The Dynamics of Bilateral Political and Strategic Relations

As discussed above, the historical experience of the construction boom in the Gulf region and the South Korean energy needs constitute two constants of South Korean relations in the Gulf region in the 21st century. The increased importance given to the conduct of resource policy in the Gulf Region finds its expression in the intensification of political relations in recent years. That said, as will be seen, the Gulf countries fall into three different categories in this respect: (1) relations with Iran and Iraq have been subject to constraints due to the continued precedence of the US relationship, (2) Bahrain and Oman receive relatively little attention, (3) Kuwait, Qatar, and Saudi Arabia are most closely sought out, but the multidimensional engagement with the UAE puts it in a category of its own.

The greater importance accorded to the Gulf is reflected in the total number of high-level exchanges between ROK and the region, which increased from a total of 32 and 17 for South Korean visitors to the Gulf and Gulf visitors to South Korea, respectively, in the four-year period between 2000 and 2003 to 58 and 65, respectively, since January 2008.

Table 14.5: High-Level Contacts between South Korea and the Gulf

High-Level Visits from South Korea to the Gulf Region			
	Minister	President	Total
2000-2003	19	0	32
2004-2007	20	5	37
2008-2012/4	22	4	58

High-Level Visits from the Gulf Region to South Korea			
	Minister	President, King, Emir of Prime Minister	Total
2000-2003	14	0	17
2004-2007	24	3	35
2008-2012/4	28	5	65

Source: MOFAT-Webpage (www.mofat.go.kr), accessed 2012-04-13.

In spite of this clear general tendency, the development differs markedly for different Gulf countries. As documented in the following sections on individual country cases, only low-level South Korean politicians have visited Iran, Iraq and Bahrain, where the absolute level of contacts has also been considerably lower. However, a clear expansion could be observed in Saudi Arabia, Qatar, and most prominently the UAE.

Regarding high-level exchanges, a presidential visit to Saudi Arabia in 1980 remained the only appearance of a South Korean head of state in the Gulf, and during the early 2000s, only a single visit by Roh Moo Hyun to the Korean Zaitoun Unit in Iraq in 2004 is on record.

Then, in May 2006, President Roh visited the UAE, followed by Saudi Arabia, Kuwait and Qatar in March 2007. Since that time, South Korea-Gulf relations have developed with particular dynamism during the presidency of Lee Myung-Bak, who took office in 2008, after his 2007 announcement of a "second Gulf construction boom" had been widely heard. While President Lee's domestic and regional policy initiatives are subject to intense political scrutiny in South Korea, he has had far more leeway in developing cooperation in the Gulf, where public scrutiny was less pronounced and no inner-Korean distributive struggles were decided. While President Lee's engagement has been most pronounced in the UAE, visited in December 2009, March 2011 and February 2012, he also visited Riyadh and Kuwait during his February 2012 tour of the region.

These visits correspond to an explicitly articulated South Korean policy. On 17 March 2010, the South Korean government endorsed a proposal for *Building a Partnership with the Middle East in the Post-Oil Era* with a view to economic cooperation. In it, it stated that large infrastructure export projects were to be encouraged, cultural links expanded, higher value-added activities increased, and that South Korea Eximbank facilities for companies expanding into the MENA region should double from Won 11trn ($9.7bn) in 2009 to Won 22trn ($19.4bn) in 2013.[20] Support for economic expansion into the Gulf region was further strengthened by the establishment of the *Middle East Infrastructure Order Support Center* in Abu Dhabi in September 2011 by the South Korean Ministry of Land Transportation and Maritime Affairs, which brought together eight entities in a joint venture between the private and the public sector in South Korea.[21]

More recently, cultural activities have concentrated on the UAE, where academic and cultural exchanges have flourished and a number of institutions established, as will be discussed in section 4.2 below. Politically, the most significant initiative over the last year concerned a series of trips undertaken by President Lee and Prime Minister Kim with a view to receive pledges from the GCC countries regarding their willingness to replace Iranian oil supplies. The positive echo this initiative has met with reflects South Korea's increased standing among GCC member states and vindicates its recent policy initiatives.

3.1 Iran

The ROK has had diplomatic relations with Iran since 1962. During the first Gulf construction boom, the number of South Korean residents in Iran peaked at 7,500 in 1978, but dropped rapidly after the establishment of the Islamic Republic. In the early years of the relationship, significant cultural exchanges were initiated, including the agreement by the mayors of Seoul and Teheran to name a street in the South Korean capital Tehran Street and a street in Teheran Seoul Street, names they retain to this day. A Korean-Iranian friendship society was established in the 1970s. Academically, the establishment of South Korea's only Iranian studies department at Hankuk University in 1975 and the opening of an Iranian Cultural Center at the same university constituted further South Korean investment in the relationship.

South Korea has been maintaining its economic ties (9% of South Korean oil imports, and $15bn in bilateral trade in 2010), and political relations, which result in a significant number of bilateral visits, albeit at a lower level of protocol. Cultural exchanges have also continued, including official invitations to Iranian artists to visit South Korea and a recent cooperative agreement between the Teheran National Library and its South Korean counterpart.

Table 14.6: High-Level Contacts between South Korea and Iran

High-Level Visits from South Korea to Iran			
	Minister	President	Total
2000-2003	6	0	7
2004-2007	1	0	5
2008-2012/4	0	0	16

High-Level Visits from Iran to South Korea			
	Minister	President, King, Emir of Prime Minister	Total
2000-2003	3	0	3
2004-2007	2	0	7
2008-2012/4	1	0	15

Source: MOFAT-Webpage (www.mofat.go.kr), accessed 2012-04-13.

Until recently, neither alleged Iranian cooperation with North Korea nor the Iranian alliance with China were allowed to disturb the relationship.[22] However, intense US pressure forced the ROK in early 2012 to consider a discontinuation of its energy trade with Iran. Faced with significant bilateral trade volumes and the expected higher cost of sourcing these from other regional producers such as Saudi Arabia and Iraq, ROK was initially loath to accept US demands and tried to settle for a voluntary reduction leading to a waiver from the application of the US law, rather than a complete interruption of these trades, while soliciting pledges from other Gulf states, in particular Saudi Arabia and Iraq, to act as alternative providers.[23] However, by the summer of 2012, South Korea had yielded to overwhelming US pressure and, having successfully activated regional networks to replace Iranian supplies in the meantime, discontinued imports from Iran.

More than any other Gulf country, Iran thus illustrates the constraints the close alliance with the US imposes on ROK. A principled South Korean stance on non-proliferation in North-East Asia is incompatible with a point-blank refusal of the American demands in the Gulf. At the same time, ROK pragmatism tolerated links with North Korea for the sake of resource trade. Currently, ROK is under pressure to come to an arrangement with the US regarding its economic relationship with Iran, and is soliciting support from alternative providers.[24]

3.2 Iraq

South Korea and Iraq established significant commercial contacts during the first Gulf construction boom, with 19,920 South Koreans residents in Iraq in 1982.[25] Nevertheless, there were no diplomatic relations until July 1989, and they have been neither continuous nor intensive. The newly opened embassy was closed again in 1993, and only reopened after the 2003 war. While the late establishment of diplomatic relations reflects Baghdad's role as a regional geo-strategic rival and sometime USSR client, the short time window between the end of the cold war and the Iraqi invasion of Kuwait in August 1990 thus proved too short for establishing sustainable diplomatic relations.[26]

Having maintained a military presence in Iraq between 2003 and 2008, South Korea has since engaged moderately in construction and oil projects in Iraq, but the main channel for mutual exchanges remain petroleum exports that reached S9.9bn in 2011. With ROK a net buyer, it maintains cordial relations at a rather low intensity, although recently more high-level visitors have been arriving in Seoul in search of deeper ties. During Prime Minister Nuri Al Maliki's visit in 2011, Iraq pledged to provide emergency supplies of 250,000 tons per day to South Korea in case it could not buy oil elsewhere, and in March 2012, this pledge was reiterated with a view to replacing Iranian supplies should ROK be forced to cease buying from Iran.

Table 14.7: High-Level Contacts between Korea and Iraq

High-Level Visits from South Korea to Iraq			
	Minister	President	Total
2000-2003	0	0	0
2004-2007	0	1	1
2008-2012/4	3	0	3

High-Level Visits from Iraq to South Korea			
	Minister	President, King, Emir of Prime Minister	Total
2000-2003	0	0	0
2004-2007	0	1	1
2008-2012/4	1	3	7

Source: MOFAT-Webpage (www.mofat.go.kr), accessed 2012-04-13.

3.3 The United Arab Emirates

The UAE have been the Gulf country where the relationship with South Korea has developed with the greatest degree of dynamism. If the combined efforts of public and private South Korean actors achieved more in the UAE than elsewhere, this is due to a greater coincidence of interests and strategies which allowed each country to integrate the other into its developmental strategies. Although both countries have contributed actively to this development, the South Korean side has clearly taken the lead and given impulses, by pitching its offerings very directly to the demands of the UAE market and of policy priorities. This engagement has stretched across a wide variety of activities, with the December 2009 accord on the construction of four nuclear reactors in the UAE between Seoul and Abu Dhabi acting as a game changer in the relationship.

Table 14.8: High-Level Contacts between South Korea and the UAE

High-Level Visits from South Korea to the UAE

	Minister	President	Total
2000-2003	3	0	3
2004-2007	6	1	10
2008-2012/4	7	2	13

High-Level Visits from the UAE to South Korea

	Minister	President, King, Emir of Prime Minister	Total
2000-2003	2	0	2
2004-2007	4	1	5
2008-2012/4	7	1	9

Source: MOFAT-Webpage (www.mofat.go.kr), accessed 2012-04-13.

During his election campaign, in 2007, Lee Myung-Bak, then still mayor of Seoul, visited Dubai and declared that a "*Second Gulf Construction Boom*" was needed, expecting this to include both Gulf infrastructure investments in South Korea and increased South Korean construction activity in the Gulf.[27] Since then, a transformational nuclear power deal has allowed the players to put the relationship on a far broader footing.

3.3.1 The Nuclear Power Deal of December 2009 and Other Developments in the Energy Sector

When President Lee visited the UAE in December 2009, both sides pledged an upgrade of relations to a strategic level. The most momentous announcement was that of South Korea's success in its bid to construct four nuclear power plants, to be built by a consortium led by Korea Electric Power (KEPCO) and also including Hyundai Construction and Engineering, Samsung, and Doosan Heavy Industries. This success was perceived to result from a number of factors:

1. The South Korean bid of $20bn was 40% lower than that of the nearest competitor and considerably below market expectations.

2. The bid received comprehensive South Korean government support, including a series of related phone calls of President Lee to UAE Crown Prince Muhammad and export guarantees provided by Korea EXIM Bank.

3. The South Korean side expressed its readiness to engage in technical knowledge transfers. After the conclusion of the deal, four South Korean professors were sent from KAIST (formerly the Korea Advanced Institute of Science and Technology) to Khalifa University in Abu Dhabi to assist in establishing a nuclear academic infrastructure. KAIST also awarded an honorary doctorate to Abu Dhabi Crown Prince Mohammad when he toured South Korean nuclear installations in May 2010.[28] In due course, South Korean specialists were also sent to the newly founded regulatory body, the Federal Authority for Nuclear Regulation (FANR).

4. Simultaneously, South Korea committed to military cooperation and knowledge transfer, albeit not in the nuclear field.

5. Apart from commercial aspects, analysts also noted at the time that the fact that South Korea was not in a geopolitical position to sanction the UAE drive for nuclear power was bound to be perceived as an advantage in the Gulf: as was pointed out at the time, *"there's one political dimension which may have played a role in at least the US consortium not winning. This is a very long-term contract and the UAE has had some negative experiences with the US,"* referring to the opposition of the American Congress in 2006 to the Dubai Ports World acquisition of US ports, which ultimately forced DP World to dispose of its stake. Officially, the UAE side emphasized South Korean commitment and readiness to transfer knowledge as important contributing factors.[29]

It is not yet clear whether the nuclear deal will gain South Korea a permanent place in the nuclear power construction market, given that South Korean bids failed in Vietnam, Turkey, India, and Jordan in 2011, leading to critical questions among Seoul MPs as to the economic rationale for the 2009 deal. In November 2011, however, South Korea became one of a series of strategic partners of Saudi Arabia in the nuclear field.[30] Negotiations with South Africa are also ongoing. Overall, the deal, while possibly unprofitable in itself, has certainly given South Korea a place in the exclusive club of nuclear power plant exporters, and, as will be seen below, has been catalytic in strengthening South Korea-UAE relations. A closer academic and cultural engagement followed on the heels of the nuclear deal, military cooperation was intensified, and payoffs in the oil sector were seen in 2012.

3.3.2 Cultural Diplomacy in Higher Education and Beyond

In October 2010, a "King Sejong Institute", one of only 15 South Korean cultural centers worldwide, was founded at Zayed University in Abu Dhabi. King Sejong institutes follow the approach of the PRC's Confucius Institutes in establishing themselves inside existing universities. Such institutes are highly attractive for local academic institutions, particularly when budgets are tight. The academic engagement is, however, not limited to this university, but is followed up by the establishment of Korean language classes at UAE University in the second city of Al Ain, by the establishment of Korean student clubs at both universities, a landmark in an educational landscape where more current western languages such as German or Spanish are hardly taught, language study is not encouraged, and English predominates.

In the hard sciences, a number of South Korean professors in the field of nuclear technology have been delegated to the Khalifa University of Science and Technology, one of Abu Dhabi's most prestigious and research-oriented institutions. Similarly, South Korean specialists have been seconded to the fledgling regulatory organization in charge of nuclear energy. Outside the academic sphere, an Emirati-Korean Friendship Society was established and, rare for an NGO in the UAE, received official status speedily in March 2012. Two Korean film festivals were held in Abu Dhabi in December 2010 and April 2012 under the auspices of the South Korean embassy, which provided focal points for Emirati-Korean public engagement, with Emirati individuals and institutions intimately linked to the effort. Also, the Korean Tourist Organization (KTO) has maintained an office in Dubai since 2006.

At the leadership level, there were mutual symbolic exchanges between UAE and South Korean leaders. As noted above, the Abu Dhabi Crown Prince was awarded an honorary doctorate by the Korean Advanced Institute for Science and Technology, while President Lee was awarded the Zayed Environment Prize in March 2011.[31] The prize was in recognition of the president's green growth policy, which was incorporated into South Korean law in 2010. The law committed 2% of South Korean GDP to developing eco-friendly businesses. In response, the South Korean Global Green Growth Institute (GGGI) opened an office in Abu Dhabi's Masdar City in July 2011. The institute was to design a Green Growth Plan strategy for the UAE and engage in related training measures.[32]

Finally, in 2011, healthcare became another piece in the ever more complex web of UAE-South Korean relations: with a MoU on medical cooperation signed in March between ministries in both countries, a more detailed agreement on medical tourism, specifying partner hospitals in South Korea and reimbursement mechanisms, was concluded in November 2011 at the Ministry of Health in Seoul.[33]

3.3.3 Military Cooperation

While South Korea had long been active in the region as an arms supplier, one month before the nuclear contract was signed, Defense Secretary Kim visited the

UAE twice to discuss the contracts and military cooperation. In January 2010, an agreement related to the transfer of drones, unmanned vehicles, and other high-tech military applications was signed, and in January 2011, in response to a UAE request, a training unit of 130 Korean elite soldiers, the so-called Akh Brigade, was sent to the UAE to train UAE special forces in fighting terrorism and special operations. A second contingent of 140 soldiers arrived in July 2011.[34] This was the first overseas deployment of Korean troops in a non-conflict zone, and was clearly intended to support and deepen the overall bilateral relationship, rather than achieve any narrowly military objectives.[35]

3.3.4 Oil Diplomacy

On 13 March 2011, the Korean National Oil Company (KNOC) and Abu Dhabi National Oil Company (ADNOC) signed a MoU, which was to guarantee South Korea at least 1 billion barrels of oil. Commenting on the deal, which was signed during his visit to the UAE, President Lee said: "The partnership for 100 years, which started between the two countries thanks to the nuclear deal, has been strengthened more by today's deal."[36] In early March 2012, KNOC announced that it had won three oil and gas concessions in the UAE, joining Western majors and Japan as UAE concession holders for the first time. The concessions include one offshore area and two onshore areas.[37] During the South Korean diplomatic initiative to obtain pledges from GCC powers that they would be willing to replace Iranian oil, South Korea received a corresponding pledge from Crown Prince Muhammad.[38]

Figure 14.1: South Korean Engagement with the UAE

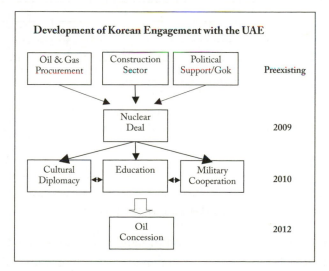

3.4 Saudi Arabia

The ROK established diplomatic relations with Saudi Arabia in October 1962, and in 1963 the Kingdom became the first Arab state to open an embassy in Seoul. South Korea opened its embassy in Jeddah in 1973, and later moved it to Riyadh, with the Jeddah consulate continuing to exist, but closed between 1999 and 2008.

During the first construction boom, the country was a major recipient of South Korean workers, who largely lived in camps and had limited contact with the general population. Labor relations were not always harmonious. During a strike in a camp in Jubail, South Korean management reportedly brought in Saudi guards, who ended up executing those who had been identified as strike leaders.[39] The South Korean presence dwindled during the 1980s.

Saudi Arabia has long been the single most important supplier of petroleum products to South Korea, with South Korean imports reaching $36.97bn in 2011 and exports $6.9bn. One of South Korea's major refiners, S-Oil, has had Saudi Aramco as its largest shareholder since 1991, and its CEO is a Saudi.[40] By contrast, OECD statistics show the country to be of limited importance as a destination in terms of South Korean FDI.[41] Diplomatic exchanges have intensified over the past decade and reached their highest level yet over the past four years, but remain below the levels of engagement seen in the UAE.

Table 14.9: High-Level Contacts between Korea and Saudi Arabia

High-Level Visits from South Korea to Saudi Arabia			
	Minister	President	Total
2000-2003	1	0	1
2004-2007	3	1	4
2008-2012/4	4	1	10

High-Level Visits from Saudi Arabia to South Korea			
	Minister	President, King, Emir of Prime Minister	Total
2000-2003	1	0	2
2004-2007	5	0	5
2008-2012/4	5	0	8

Source: MOFAT-Webpage (www.mofat.go.kr), accessed 2012-04-13.

The economic relationship has gone hand in hand with an increased engagement in the cultural field. While short exchanges of youth groups have occurred frequently since the 1980s, arrangements under the King Abdullah Scholarship program have brought more than 100 Saudi students to South Korea since a MoU between the two governments was signed in 2007.[42] In February 2012, South Korea was made the "guest of honor" at the annual Janadriya cultural festival in Saudi Arabia.

In November 2011, Saudi Arabia and South Korea signed an agreement on the peaceful uses of nuclear energy. This followed similar Saudi agreements with France and Argentina, as well as cooperation efforts with numerous other partners including the US and China, with which a similar agreement was signed in early 2012.[43] During President Lee's February 2012 visit, he sought and received reassurances concerning secure oil supplies, agreed to significantly increase bilateral defense cooperation, and focused reportedly on lifting "cooperation in noneconomic areas to the level of the economic sector."[44]

In comparison to the UAE, the South Korean-Saudi relationship thus has been less broadly based, although of longer standing and more important in purely economic terms, but the government of South Korea seems to be about to upgrade its presence in the Kingdom. It is to be expected that UAE developments will provide a blueprint for the further development of the Saudi-South Korean relationship.

3.5 Kuwait

Although Kuwait is an important trade partner and supplier of petroleum products, and diplomatic relations have been in place since 1979, the relationship is rather staid. While the country was visited during President Roh's tour of the region in March 2007, this apparently did not act as a catalyst for the broader relationship. However, Kuwaiti representatives joined the Korea Arab Society (KAS) in 2008, and the Kuwaiti state has been providing scholarships to Korean students learning Arabic. The press coverage paints a picture of an important economic partner, with regard to whom expressions of mutual goodwill are articulated regularly.

3.6 Qatar

Diplomatic relations with Qatar were established in 1974, during the first construction boom, but Qatar's role remained relatively limited. The number of South Koreans in the country remained below 2,000. The relationship has gained traction in the 1990s. From 1995 onwards, South Korean distribution companies became parties to the Ras Laffan LNG project in Qatar (RASGAS), entering long-term purchasing contracts. This relationship was reinforced when KORAS took a 5% equity stake in RASGAS in 2005. On 10 February 2010, President Lee agreed to establish a high-level cooperation committee spanning all concerns "from oil and energy to science and technology, military and security, and green growth." On 18 April 2012, the South Korean Ministry of Land, Transport and Maritime Affairs announced that it would sign a MoU with the Qatar Investment Authority, concerning joint investment in overseas construction projects.[45]

3.7 Oman

Relations with Oman, established in 1974, are positive and friendly, with a fair number of lower-level diplomatic exchanges in both directions, where the number of Omani visitors to South Korea is slightly higher than that of comparable South Korean visitors to Oman. Following important gas contracts concluded in the 1990s and corresponding South Korean imports volumes that reached $5.36bn in 2011, Oman is also the prime recipient of South Korean FDI in the region.[46] Nevertheless, as a rather small economy, it has not been given the same strategic importance as the UAE.

In 2007, a group of South Korean businessmen established the Oman-Korea Friendship Association in Seoul, and in March 2008, a group of Oman businessmen followed suit. In 2010, an Omani-Korean Business Council was established.[47] Existing educational exchanges are small-scale, but in April 2012, a MoU on expanding bilateral cooperation in Education was signed between both sides.[48] In January 2012, Oman was one of the countries receiving a South Korean appeal for energy supplies, should the Strait of Hormuz be closed.[49]

3.8 Bahrain

The relatively low economic importance of resource-poor Bahrain for South Korea is reflected in a low number of South Korean residents and high-level visits. Although diplomatic relations were established in 1976, South Korea closed its Manama embassy in 1998 due to budget restraints resulting from the Asian Financial Crisis. It reopened in 2011.[50] South Korean involvement in the Combined Maritime Forces (CMF), headquartered in Manama, provides some room for military contacts with the country, which are, however, not specific to the bilateral relationship. The bilateral relationship does not appear to be a priority for either country.

Table 14.10: High-Level Contacts between South Korea and Bahrain

High-Level Visits from South Korea to Bahrain

	Minister	President	Total
2000-2003	0	0	0
2004-2007	2	0	3
2008-2012/4	0	0	1

High-Level Visits from Bahrain to South Korea

	Minister	President, King, Emir of Prime Minister	Total
2000-2003	0	0	0
2004-2007	2	0	2
2008-2012/4	1	0	3

Source: MOFAT-Webpage (www.mofat.go.kr), accessed 2012-04-13.

3.9 The Gulf Cooperation Council

In seeking to conclude a South Korea–GCC Free Trade Agreement, an unsuccessful effort was made to engage with the GCC as a group. During Roh Moo-Hyun's visit to the Gulf in March 2007, a consensus was reached with Gulf partners that such an agreement was desirable, but although three different rounds of talks followed between July 2008 and July 2009, no significant progress appears to have been realized since. As of early 2012, the free trade agreement is classed as under consideration by the South Korean Ministry of Foreign Affairs.

No further indications have been found that the GCC was considered a central player by South Korean policy makers: while several South Korean-EU summits have been held in recent years and there are numerous contractual relations with ASEAN, no similar collective events were held with the GCC as a partner. The relative organizational weakness of the GCC is reflected in this subordinate part played in South Korea-Gulf relations.

4. South Korea and other External Players in the Gulf: Competition and Complementarity

Strategic relationships in their immediate regional environment may shape the way in which other Asian powers relate to the Gulf, but South Korea is an exception. Asian regional dynamics have little effect on South Korea's strategies in the Gulf.

In particular, the North Korean presence in Kuwait, the UAE and Qatar (each of which hosts several thousand North Korean construction workers), has not been an issue for South Korea. Even the supposed presence of cooperation in the nuclear field between Iran and North Korea, while unwelcome, has little impact on South Korea's relationship with Iran.

The South Korean presence in the Gulf is based mainly on market competition, and as such the competition is global - not specifically Asian. Thus, in the construction sector, not only Japanese, but also German and American companies find it increasingly difficult to maintain project volumes in the face of Korean competition, and in the nuclear power field, the main competitors for major construction contracts are French (Areva) and American as well as Japanese companies. Similarly, in the military sphere, a presence on the ground is also maintained by the UK, the US, and France in the UAE, and the significant regional South Korean arms sales also compete in a global market.

There are, however, two areas where specifics of the East Asian arena have dictated the South Korean stance. These are (a) the choice of partner countries - particularly in relations with Iran and Iraq, and (b) cultural diplomacy in higher education, where South Korea's strategy closely follows that of China.

4.1 Choosing Partners: The Shadow of the Hegemon

Iran and Iraq were treated in very different ways by South Korea. Iran was engaged at an early stage, and the relationship was quickly developed to cover commercial, cultural and political relations. This persisted to some extent even when the favorable political conjunction which created the relationship was no longer in place. Iraq, on the other hand, did not have diplomatic relations until 1989, even though commercial relations were significant and significant numbers of South Korean migrants were present in the country. Even after 1989 the relationship remained weak. This different treatment can be explained by South Korea's near-total reliance on its US alliance during the Cold War era. This made Pahlavi Iran, a staunch US-ally, an acceptable partner, while Iraq, for much of the 1970s seen as a Soviet client state, was not. At the time without any diplomatic relations with the Eastern bloc or mainland China and a UN-non-member, South Korea observed this restriction obviously also with respect to the MENA region.

When, somewhat belatedly, South Korea was ready to engage with Iraq after the end of the first Gulf War, the window of opportunity was closed too rapidly with the Iraqi invasion of Kuwait, following which the imperative not to jeopardize the US-alliance made it necessary to put relations on hold within a year of their establishment.

In turn, in early 2012, South Korea had to limit its commercial relationship with Iran due to its regional dependence on the US alliance. In practice, South Korea made a virtue of necessity: it used this move to launch a regional diplomatic initiative to secure its energy supplies. By contrast, Asian powers without this strategic dependence on an alliance with the US, such as China and India, had leeway to profit from lower prices for Iranian oil resulting from a drop in international demand.[51]

That said, within the red lines of the US-South Korean relationship, constant bargaining remains ongoing, and with the exception of core US demands, pragmatism and commercial self-interest prevails in South Korea's foreign relations. Other restraints of the regional environment, such as the historically charged and strategically problematic relationships with China, Russia, and Japan, have no obvious reverberations in the Gulf region.

4.2 Institutional Embedding: the East Asian way of Building Cultural Capital

Generally a latecomer in the Gulf, the uphill struggle that South Korea engages in is nowhere more pronounced than in the cultural sphere. In a region where multiple languages are spoken, but only English and Arabic have official status, efforts to engage in cultural diplomacy by teaching a complex East Asian language with a limited international footprint may appear to be doomed. Following the Chinese example, however, South Korea has taken up the challenge with some success. Internationally, China has established cultural centers through the integration of fully-financed so-called Confucius Institutes in prestigious universities in the host country.[52] Analogously, South Korea established the first regional King Sejong Institute at Zayed University in Abu Dhabi. In unison with other efforts, the East Asian languages have thus become an offering of choice in UAE academe, and as in the case of construction contracts, more established providers of linguistic services will have to go the extra mile in order to beat the disruptive competition from South Korea.

With Korean an unlikely candidate for *lingua franca* of the Gulf, the linguistic route has nevertheless provided the South Korean side with a vehicle for transporting cultural contents, and the activities of such institutes have managed to overcome cultural barriers that might be expected to be insurmountable between the Confucian culture of an industrial powerhouse in East Asia and the post-Bedouin Islamic culture of the Gulf. One of the academics involved stated: "As the students become more educated about Korea, they are realizing the economic incentives for learning about the culture and the language, which could be a road for them to get involved in many Korean companies here, including the nuclear power plant."

At the 2010 Korean Film Festival in Abu Dhabi, the documentary "*Old Partner*," portraying an elderly farmer's relationship with his aging ox in a rapidly modernizing world, struck a chord with the Emirati audience: here was the poignancy of a traditional lifestyle lost to rapid modernization, but also the reassurance that somewhere in the East, there was a country that had successfully bridged the gulf between tradition and modernity and succeeded in a knowledge society, the establishment of which in the Gulf remains to date a work in progress.[53]

5. Conclusion: South Korea's Expected Contribution to the Gulf Region

A disruptive game changer from a Western economic perspective, South Korea has proven adept at providing carefully chosen Gulf partners with a wide variety of benefits from a relationship that it is set to sustain in the long term. In the process, South Korea has been willing and able to invest significant intellectual and financial resources into understanding its partners, building its relationships and making complex, multidimensional offerings that engage the local partner not in an isolated deal, but in an ongoing, long-term relationship that may span the levels of commerce, culture, medical, military and political cooperation.

As has been observed in the UAE case, South Korean policy-makers have been able to leverage an existing relationship of long standing as a buyer of Gulf mineral resources into a more far-reaching mutual engagement. Assiduous support by the South Korean side has transformed the contract for the construction of nuclear reactors in the UAE, awarded in late 2009, into a game changer, which opened doors in sectors as diverse as cultural exchange, academic cooperation, security and regulatory cooperation, as well as military exchanges, and finally a stronger foothold in the petroleum industry. These are not accidental outcomes of economic processes or familiarity with certain MENA environments. Rather, they are strategic achievements which would not have been possible without either the strategic competence of South Korean policy-makers, who managed to assess the needs of their counterparts in the Gulf, and the willingness of the Emirati side to build a multidimensional relationship when it was offered on favorable terms and with a long-term commitment. By initially focusing its limited resources on a single country, South Korea is now in a position to expand its franchise elsewhere in the region.

From a Gulf perspective, the rewards from such a relationship are clear: a reliable buyer, South Korea has proven that it is also willing to transfer knowledge through academic and vocational cooperation. Moreover, it can do so without posing either a demographic challenge or a military threat to its Gulf hosts. Itself a dwarf among giants in the geo-political hotspot it calls home, South Korea's very innocuousness becomes an advantage. For its Gulf partners, a secure alternative to patterns of cooperation with traditional Western patrons, but also with more demanding Eastern newcomers, has thus arisen in a variety of fields without additional cost. For all other players looking to build relationships in the Gulf, however, the bar has just been raised.

Endnotes

* The views and opinions voiced in this paper are the author's own and do not represent an official position of the German Academic Exchange Service (DAAD)

1 See Yamada, Makio *"Kinnen no kankoku GCC shokokukan kankei,"* JIME中東動向分析(JIME Chutodokobunseki), November 2011:15-21, and Shahandeh in this.

2 Tsebelis, George. *Nested Games in Multiple Arenas.* Berkeley, Oxford: University of California Press, 1991.

3 Campbell, Kurt M. *"The Security Situation on the Korean Peninsula,"* Statement before the Senate Armed Services Committee. Washington DC, 16 September 2011

4 On Korea's soft power, see Nye, Joseph. *"South Korea's Growing Soft Power"* Gulf News, 16 November 2009

5 www.mofat.go.kr documents the duration of diplomatic relationships.

6 EIA Country Analysis Brief Korea, as of 11 October 2011

7 Snyder, Scott. *"Lee Myung-bak's Foreign Policy: A 250-Day Assessment"* Korean Journal of Defense Analysis, Volume 21 Issue 1, March 2009, p. 22ff.

8 Yamada. *"Kinnen,"* p.20, citing an article in *Chosennippou.*

9 The Guardian. *"South Korea lights the way on carbon emissions,"* 21 April 2009

10 Kim, Sooyong. *"The Korean Construction Industry as an Exporter of Services"* World Economic Review, May 1988, Vol.2, Issue 2

11 Seok, Hyunho *"Korean Migrant Workers to the Middle East"* in Gunatilleke, Godfrey Migration to the Arab World: Experience of Returning Migrants, Tokyo, Japan, United Nations University Press, 1991. :56-102; Kim, *"Construction Industry"*

12 UK Trade and Invest. *Sector Briefing Construction in Korea,* 1 December, 2011, accessible at http://www.ukti.gov.uk/de_de/export/countries/asiapacific/fareast/koreasouth/sectorbriefing/227160.html?null

13 Seok. *"Korean Migrant Workers,"* 73

14 Yamada. *"Kinnen"*

15 Snyder. *"Lee"*

16 OECD. *The Pisa 2009 Results.* Paris, 2010.

17 http://www.korea-arab.org. The society was established by the Korean government in 2008 to engage with 22 Arab countries.

18 Korea Times, "*Korea-Arab Society actively builds up cultural bridges*," 1 April 2012

19 Section 3.1

20 Yamada, "*Kinnen*," 19; Yonhap News, "*Chuutoo wo tukame: kankoku, chuutookeizaikyouryokuan wo kakutei*" (「『中東をつかめ』韓国・中東経済協力案を確定」), 17 March 2010

21 Electric Times, "*Ministry of Land Transportation and Maritime Affairs opens Middle East Infrastructure Order Support Center*,"14 October 2011; Yamada "Kinnen," 19

22 Chang, "*China's Policy Toward Iran and the Middle East*" and Lewis, "North Korea – Iran Nuclear Cooperation"

23 BBC, "*Iran Oil Sanctions Divide Asia's Four largest Economies*," 15 January 2012

24 Bloomberg, "*US Says Iran Crude Buyers Must Pledge Cuts to Avoid Sanctions*," 23 March 2012

25 Seok, "*Korean Migrant Workers*"

26 Fukuyama, Francis. *The Soviet Union and Iraq since* 1968, Rand Corporation, Santa Monica, July 1980

27 Yamada. "*Kinnen*"

28 KUSTAR, "H.H. Sheikh Mohammed Bin Zayed receives an honorary PhD from KAIST, Korea," news release, 27 May 2010

29 Gulf News, "*Korea's political low profile and commercial track record won nuclear bid*," 29 December 2009, the quote is by As Christian Koch of the Gulf Research Center in Dubai.

30 The National, "S. Korea makes its presence felt in the Middle East," 22 September 2011

31 The National, "Zayed Environment Prize Awarded," 2 March 2011

32 GGGI, "*GGGI opens office in Masdar City*," press release, 8 July 2011

33 Khaleej Times, "*S. Korea, UAE ink pact on healthcare*," 14 March 2011; Korea Times, "Medical Korean Wave ripples in Pact with Abu Dhabi," 27 November 2011

34 Yamada, "*Kinnen*," 21

35 Yamada, "*Kinnen*," 21

36 Gulf News, "*Korea secures Abu Dhabi oil deal,*" 14 March 2011

37 The National, "*Korea oil deal makes capital history*," 6 March, 2012

38 Chosunilbo, "*UAE Pledges Priority Oil Supply to Korea*," 18 January 2012

39 Collins, George Francis, *Goodbye Saudi Arabia*, Bloomington, 2003, p. 101

40 Reuters, "*S-Oil inks 20-yr deal with Aramco to secure oil supplies,*" 8 February 2012

41 See Table 14.2 in Section 2.2.

42 Korea Times, "*Saudi Arabia always open for exchange*," 9 September 2009

43 World Nuclear News, "*Saudi Arabia and Korea Agree to Cooperate*," 15 November 2011; World Nuclear News, "*Saudi Arabia widens Horizon*," 16 January 2011

44 Asia Security Watch, "*South Korea strengthens defense ties with Saudi Arabia*," 9 February 2012

45 Korea Times, "*Korea, Qatar to jointly tap global construction markets*" 19 April 2012

46 See Table 14.2 in Section 2.2

47 MenaFN, "*Oman, S. Korae to boost ties*," 6 May 2011

48 Korea Times, "*Oman, Korea sign MoU on education cooperation*," 17 April 2012

49 Bloomberg, "*South Korea seeks Omani cooperation if energy supply disrupted*,"15 January 2015

50 Korea Times, "*Korea to Open New Missions in Three Nations*" 30 April 2011

51 Reuters. "*India overtakes China as Iran's top oil client*," 12 April 2012

52 Starr, Don. "*Chinese Language Education in Europe: the Confucius Institutes*" European Journal of Education, Vol. 44, issue 1, pages 66-82, March 2009

53 The National, "*Korean film series seen as way to deepen ties*," 16 December 2010

Bibliography

Aoki, Masahiko "Toward a Comparative Institutional Analysis" MIT Press, Cambridge, Massachusetts, 2001

Aoki, Masahiko "Corporations in Evolving Diversity. Cognition, Governance and Institutions." Oxford, 2010.

Barbieri, Rita "Energy Security: The Diplomacy of South Korea in Latin America" UCLA, 2011.

Bustelo, Pablo "Seguridad energética con alta dependencia externa: las estrategias de Japón y Corea del Sur" Real Instituto Elcano, Working paper, 2008.

Campbell, Kurt M. "The Security Situation on the Korean Peninsula," Statement Before the Senate Armed Services Committee. Washington DC, 16 September 2011, available at http://www.state.gov/p/eap/rls/rm/2010/09/147210.htm

Chang, Parris H. "China's Policy towards Iran and the Middle East" Journal of East Asian Affairs, Vol. 25, Issue 1, Spring/Summer 2011, pp. 1-15

Collins, George Francis, Goodbye Saudi Arabia, Bloomington, 2003

Fukuyama, Francis, The Soviet Union and Iraq since 1968, Rand Corporation, Santa Monica, July 1980

Kim, Sooyong "The Korean Construction Industry as an Exporter of Services" in World Economic Review, May 1988, Vol.2, Issue 2

Lee, Min Yong "Securing Foreign Resource Supply: the Resource Diplomacy of South Korea" in Pacific Focus, Vol. 3, Issue 2, 1988

Lewis, Jeffrey, "North Korea-Iran Nuclear Cooperation," CFR Interview, December 14 2010, retrieved at http://www.cfr.org/proliferation/north-korea-iran-nuclear-cooperation/p23625

MOFAT, Diplomatic Whitepaper 2011, Seoul.

Nye, Joseph S., Soft Power: the Means to Success in World Politics, 2004

Nye, Joseph S., "South Korea's Growing Soft Power" Gulf News, 16 November 2009

Seok, Hyunho *"Korean Migrant Workers to the Middle East"* in Gunatilleke, Godfrey Migration to the Arab World: Experience of Returning Migrants, Tokyo, Japan, United Nations University Press, 1991. :56-102

Snyder, Scott *"Lee Myung-bak's Foreign Policy: A 250-Day Assessment"* Korean Journal of Defense Analysis, Volume 21 Issue 1, March 2009

Snyder, Scott and Choi, Seukhoon Paul "From Aid to Development Partnership – Strengthening US-Republic of Korea Cooperation in International Development" Council of Foreign Relations, New York, 2012

Starr, Don "Chinese Language Education in Europe: the Confucius Institutes" European Journal of Education, Vol. 44, issue 1, pages 66-82, March 2009

Woo-Cumings, Meredith "South Korean Anti-Americanism" JPRI Working Paper No. 93, July 2003

Yamada, Makio "Kinnen no kankoku GCC shokokukan kankei," JIME中東動向分析 (JIME Chutodokobunseki), November 2011:15-21

Newspapers Sources Used:

Gulf
Khaleej Times
The National (Abu Dhabi)
Gulf News
Saudi Gazette

Korea

Hankyoreh
Korea Herald
Korea Times
Electric Times

Websites:

Korean Ministry of Foreign Affairs (www.mofat.gov.kr)
Yonhap News (www.yonhapnews.co.kr)
Korea Economic Institute (www.keia.org)

Chapter Fifteen

Japan's Engagement in the Gulf

Yukiko Miyagi
in collaboration with Yoshikazu Kobayashi, Akiko Yoshioka, and Koji Horinuki

1. Introduction

Japan's relations with the Gulf are both intensifying and distinctive. The constants in the relationship are shaped by Japan's unique position in the global political economy as a developed economy with an Asian geographical and historical position. As a developed economy (as manifested in its position as an inaugural member of G8 and the International Energy Forum (IEF)) it has in common with the Western developed states the ability to build trade ties based on its high technology and sales of its high-value-added products. But Japan is also the developed country with the highest level of energy scarcity: Japan's domestic supply of energy sources met only 4% of its total consumption, and together with nuclear power, 18% in 2004. Japan relied on oil for 26% of its energy consumption in 2005, and on the Middle East for about 90% of its oil imports in 2005.[1] Furthermore, Japan's unique character under its Peace Constitution, as a demilitarised trading state, shaped its approach to the Gulf. It has made Japan exceptionally dependent on the US for its territorial security in East Asia and also for the stability of the Gulf and this has required Japan to cooperate with the US in the Gulf region, thereby limiting its ties with Gulf oil producers at odds with the US. Also, in the relative absence of 'hard' power, such as a UN Security Council veto or the arms sales used by 'normal' great powers, Japan's Gulf relations must rely on 'soft' approaches, such as technology, trade, diplomacy and culture. In this respect, Japan's non-Western character, free of the heritage of imperialism in the Middle East, gives it certain advantages. However, Japan shares the challenges common to other Asian states of having to secure its energy supplies without the security of firm ties with the producers that the Western 'oil majors' enjoy; in particular, the relatively small capital of the Japanese oil industry compared to the Western majors disadvantages Japan in gaining up-stream oil contracts.

Japan's special features arguably differentiate the nature of Japan's relationship with the Gulf states from both Western oil importers and also Asia's emerging hydrocarbon consumers such as China and India. This has produced a mixture of approaches, some in common with the Western hydrocarbon importers, especially in terms of setting up frameworks of cooperation for problem-solving between the Gulf producers and the major consumers, but also in using bilateral approaches taken by states such as China, India, and Korea, often in competition with them.

Japan's relations with the Gulf have changed significantly over time, progressively intensifying. For Japan, the Gulf states were initially mere economic markets and energy suppliers, their relationship limited to the exchange of Gulf crude oil for Japanese manufactured goods. However, as Japanese policy-makers became increasingly aware of the country's vulnerability to the Gulf oil producers, beginning at the time of the 1970s oil embargo, Japan's direct diplomatic and commercial contacts with them intensified. More recently, Japan's sense of energy insecurity and vulnerability to the Gulf was again heightened by several factors, notably the rise of oil prices since 1999, the end of the 40-year drilling contract of the Japanese oil company Arabian Oil Company in the Khafji oil field in Saudi Arabia in 2000, the tightening of the oil market after 2004, and increased East Asian competition in the Gulf. The major earthquake and the nuclear disaster Japan experienced in March 2011 both set back Japan's efforts to reduce dependency on oil imports and increase dependency on natural gas from the Gulf.

These challenges have generated a feeling of urgency regarding the need for a new energy policy and proactive approaches towards the Gulf producers. As a result, Japan started promoting diversification and deepening of relationships with the Gulf beyond the one-dimensional trade relation, towards policy consultation over issues of common concerns, promotion of other forms of economic relations such as investment and tourism, and intensifying exchanges at various levels ranging from high-ranking officials to business representatives to the youth of both countries. As such, newly emerging ties are deepening interdependency between the two sides, but not necessarily making them overly vulnerable towards each other, due, as will be argued, to a relative balance in their mutual dependencies.

2. Japan's Engagement in the Gulf

Japan's engagement in the Gulf was activated by awareness of its vulnerability to the Gulf hydrocarbon producers. Indeed, the threat from the Arab oil boycott in October 1973 produced what was termed 'resource diplomacy' in the 1970s and early 1980s, by which the Japanese government increased the budget of its official economic assistance for the Gulf states' development and for support of the Palestinians in order to strengthen the relationship with the Arab states in general. The war between Iran and Iraq in 1980-8 led to a new Japanese diplomatic initiative attempting to bring an end to the continuous devastation and disruption which had been suffered by Japanese business in the two countries and threatened oil supplies from the Gulf. Both the Gulf War of 1990-1 and the war in Iraq in 2003 saw Japan's significant support for the US coalition, for the former providing $13 billion and for the latter political support towards the passage of a UN resolution and the despatch of its military forces to Iraq.[2] Importantly, the tightness of the oil market since 2004 has shaped the current Japanese approach towards the GCC states, termed by the government as efforts 'towards multilayered relationship' and 'strategic partnership' (as seen in joint statements made with Saudi Arabia in 2006, and the Japan-GCC Strategic Dialogue held in September 2010).

Japan's approach towards the regional states is differentiated between those where there are international security and political obstacles to the relationship (such as Iraq in the past and Iran currently) from the US, and those free of such obstacles. Regarding the former states, Japan typically attempted to balance between its US alliance and its relationship with the Gulf country. Japan would seek to accommodate US wishes, often trying to arrange a compromise or urging on the Gulf state compliance with US demands (both Iraq in 2002-3 and Iran since 2002), but might continue some reduced level of economic assistance, trade and high-level dialogue. Depending on the gravity of the US-led international pressure for isolation of the Gulf country, and the level of Japan's vulnerability towards the two sides, Japan has tilted towards support for one or the other (e.g. over the passage of UN sanctions and the terms of the sanctions).[3]

In cases where there were no political obstacles, Japan's relationship used to be largely limited to trade. However, Japan increasingly perceives a challenge to its long-term primacy as the Gulf states' leading source of industrial goods posed by the rise of its East Asian neighbors as major hydrocarbon importers. China's threat is particularly emphasized by Japan's elites and media because of its aggressive energy resource acquisition drive not only in the Gulf but also in Africa.[4] However, closer observers point to the challenge posed by South Korea, whose engineering and construction companies have established high reputations in Gulf countries, and whose automobiles and electric appliances, being competitive in quality and more affordable, are gaining popularity at the expense of Japan's products. On the other hand, Japan views the current projects pursued by GCC states, such as economic diversification, development of human resources, energy conservation and water resource development as presenting opportunities for Japanese firms and collaborative undertakings. Overall, these rising challenges have stimulated Japan's more active and multi-dimensional engagement in the region, via diplomacy, soft power, and government-private sector collaborations.

In diplomacy, the areas of policy for exchanging views and consultation have become more diverse, covering various political and security issues of common concern, such as the stability of Iraq and Iranian nuclear developments, consumer-supplier cooperation in energy markets, and global issues such as reduction of CO_2 emissions. For example, Japan co-organized with Qatar COP18, and established a Joint Committee to explore new areas of economic cooperation and institutionalized regular policy consultation with Saudi Arabia, UAE, Qatar and Kuwait. Contacts also intensified at the high political level, with more frequent visits of Japanese ministers and invitations to Gulf monarchs and ministers to visit Japan as a result of the Japanese observation of the top-down nature of Gulf counterparts' decision-making, which makes the role of the Japanese government particularly important for the finalization of a business deal. In this respect, Japan was also emulating the approaches of Asian rivals such as China and South Korea, where political leaders are actively involved with Gulf leaders.[5] The Japanese government has also exploited the diplomatic advantage of having a monarchy to promote dealings with Gulf monarchies, as in the visit of the Japanese Crown Prince to the Gulf monarchies in 1994, the reception of Gulf monarchs by the royal family in Japan, and most recently, the attendance of the Japanese Crown Prince both at the funerals of the late Saudi King Fahd in 2006 and of Saudi Crown Prince Sultan in October 2011 (which was reciprocated by the Saudi royal family's hospitable reception at the occasion, implying that it was appreciated).[6] Finally, Japanese policy-makers are exploring the possibility of a new role for the Japanese Defense Forces in multilateral piracy control in the area surrounding the Strait of Hormuz.[7] In April 2012, Japan and Bahrain signed a memorandum of defense exchanges, by which the chiefs of staff of the two national forces would discuss regional and international security conditions and joint exercises would be conducted. Furthermore, they agreed to assist each other in multilateral security forums.[8]

The Japanese government has also promoted cooperation between the Japanese public and private sectors in expanding business relations between Japan and the Gulf states. The Japanese government initiated negotiations for agreements on promoting mutual investment (signed with Kuwait in March 2012; under negotiation with Saudi Arabia), on aviation (Saudi 2008; Qatar 2009), and regulating taxation of foreign business (Saudi 2010; Qatar 2009; Kuwait 2010; and the UAE under negotiation). It has also held international joint public-private economic forums with Arab states, the Japan-Arab Economic Forum in 2009 and 2010, promoting Japanese business interest in the Middle East market. The close cooperation can be seen in the financial assistance of the Japan Bank for International Cooperation (JBIC) for major Japanese Gulf contracts, the establishment of a special task force in the Japan Centre for the Cooperation for the Middle East (JCCME) for promoting Japanese business (Saudi Arabia and Iraq respectively), and the offices of the Japan External Trade Organization (JETRO) in Riyadh and Dubai. Japan is emulating other Asian states such as China whose firms have benefited from the support given by their governments in acquiring business contracts.

To compensate for its lack of hard power, whether military or having an international oil major as enjoyed by Western states, Japan has developed alternative soft approaches. Technological assistance has been provided by Japanese companies to their Gulf counterparts and is seen by the Japanese government as a major Japanese strength and driving force for the expansion of Gulf relationships. The current development plans in Gulf states are seen as an opportunity. Vocational training has been provided both by sending experts to training institutes in the Gulf as well as receiving trainees in Japan.[9] Japan's high reputation in the petrochemical sector is also viewed as a strength which could be utilized.[10]

In the field of education, Japanese methods are particularly valued and Gulf states are particularly interested in introducing Japanese-style education at an earlier stage in primary schools.[11] The Japanese school in Abu Dhabi has been holding events with local school students. The exchange of university students between Japan and the Gulf states has generated a group of Gulf youth who are interested in studying the Japanese language and culture. King Saud University's Men's Division in Saudi Arabia has been offering a BA degree in the Japanese language since 1994, and Princess Noura University is opening a course in September 2012. A two-way exchange of university students between Japan and the Gulf has also been taking place[12] although Japan lags behind its Asian neighbors in establishing university branches and exchange programs in the Gulf, most probably because of a lack of sufficient capability for teaching in English. Japanese culture, such as flower arrangement, traditional music, calligraphy, and traditional costumes has been promoted by embassies and consulates. Pop culture, such as cartoons and pop music, which have become increasingly popular among Gulf youth, are promoting 'soft' ties with the Gulf.[13]

It is also worth noting that the Japanese soft approach is not a one-way transmission. Since the Japanese Foreign Minister Kono's initiative for dialogue between civilizations launched on his visit to GCC states in 2000, the Japanese government has been hosting forums between intellectuals from Japan and the Islamic world for the purpose of mutual understanding of history and culture. The lack of a colonial legacy in the Gulf and Japan's image of having recovered from war devastation to achieve high economic development has facilitated its soft power, particularly in Iraq and Iran.[14]

In the following sub-sections, three cases are used to highlight the variations in Japan's approaches depending on the political context. The GCC states all fall within one category. Iran, with the constraints of being subject to Western sanctions, falls into another. Iraq, in effect moving from one orientation to another, constitutes a third category.

2.1. The GCC States

GCC hydrocarbon producing states are important for Japan's energy, given the size of its reserves, production and relative political stability. The vast majority of Japan's imports from the GCC have been hydrocarbons such as crude oil, natural gas, and oil products. While Saudi Arabia's crude oil has consistently taken the largest proportion in Japan's total oil import (29.2% in 2010), the UAE's proportion has also increased since its production became substantial in the 1970s. Until the 1990s, the UAE had also been Japan's main supplier of natural gas within the Gulf (average of 8.6% between 1977 and 2010) until Oman and Qatar began production.[15] Currently, Qatar has replaced the UAE as Japan's supplier of natural gas. Imports from Oman were 3.8% in Japan's total imports in 2010; imports from Qatar were 10.9% in 2010.

Regarding the acquisition of overseas upstream equity, Abu Dhabi is among Japan's most important partners. The Japan Oil Development Company (JODCO) holds a 12% share of Abu Dhabi Marine Operating Company (ADMA-OPCO), the biggest offshore oil producing concession in Abu Dhabi. The concession agreement of ADMA-OPCO, originally made in 1977, will expire in 2018, and its extension is the first priority of Japan's resource diplomacy.

The main destinations of Japan's exports to the GCC are also Saudi Arabia and the UAE, although the proportion of exports to Qatar has been on the rise. The major sectors of Japan's exports include infrastructure, such as petrochemical plants, and transportation, such as a subway system and a monorail system.[16] Japanese firms in real estate investment and finance are interested in the UAE market and are active there.

Following the defeat of a Japanese-US consortium of Hitachi and General Electric (GE) by a South Korean consortium in a bid for a nuclear power plant building in December 2009 (named the 'Abu Dhabi shock'), Japan has tried to strengthen the cooperation between the government and the private sector in promoting Japan's business to the Gulf states. Although Kuwait decided to discard its plan of introducing nuclear power following the earthquake disaster in Japan in March 2011, the UAE's current nuclear project and Saudi Arabia's plan to open a project to bidding have been continued. Currently, a Japanese company, Toshiba, is forming a consortium with US partners, Shaw and Exelon in bidding for a Saudi contract. A joint venture in a more traditional sector is the Emirates-Japan Pearl Cultivation Trading Company formed in 2005 to revive the pearl agriculture in the UAE. The introduction of Japanese pearl cultivation techniques resulted in the production of 40,000 pearls annually.

It can be argued that the Japan-GCC economic relationship has been one of mutual dependency. While Japan has constituted a major market and a source of revenue for the Gulf hydrocarbon producers, its business has also benefited from the growth of their markets and the sectors of a mutually beneficial economic relationship have been expanding. For Japan, the establishment, maintenance and further development of such interdependence, mutual interests are very important for the stability of the bilateral relationship. How the relationship was valued by the Gulf counterparts can be seen in their responses to the major earthquake disaster in Japan in March 2011, when many GCC states provided assistance in various forms, many of which were in the form of hydrocarbon resources (a grant of crude oil from Kuwait; a grant of LP gas from Saudi Arabia; an increase of LNG and LPG sales from Qatar; an increase of LNG sale from the UAE, and an increase of LNG sale from Oman). Kuwait's grant in crude oil was the largest of all, which was extended with the words that it was in return for Japan's assistance in the evacuation of the Iraqi forces from Kuwait in 1990-1.[17]

For a long time, the Gulf had been an alien distant part of the world for the Japanese which only business men working there knew about. However, following the visit of the Japanese Crown Prince and Princess to the Gulf in 1994-5 and the opening of the flight service by Emirates Air, GCC countries and especially Dubai have become a destination for Japanese tourists. There has also been a growth in grass-root exchanges. The Japan-UAE Association has sent Japanese students to UAE University between 1999 and 2004 and the UAE has also sent its students to Japan. There is a Japanese language club in Zayed University's Dubai and Abu Dhabi campuses. In May 2012, the first Japanese-language speech contest was held at the Japanese embassy in the UAE.

Japan has also become familiar within the Gulf. A Saudi TV program called "Hawatir" ("improvement", the translation of a Japanese word, *kaizen*), introducing Japanese culture and manner, has promoted the Gulf people's image of Japan. A Dubai branch of the Japanese nationwide bookstore chain, *Kinokuniya*, has become a gathering place for UAE fans of Japan, youths in their 20s and 30s, including university students, since it opened in 2008. The major and primary source of interest in Japan among the people in the UAE was Japanese cartoons,[18] but other pop culture items such as Japanese TV dramas, Japanese pop music and Japanese pop stars have also started to attract them.

2.2 Iran

The Islamic Republic of Iran is important for Japan in that it provided around 12% of Japan's total oil imports until 2007 and, as one of the few countries whose oil industry is not dominated by the Western majors, is a potential opportunity for Japan to acquire upstream oil development contracts. Because of political conflicts between the US and Iran, however, Japan has had to constantly balance between its US alliance and its oil interest in Iran. The Iranian nuclear issue has complicated matters because of Japan's anti-nuclear norms and its interest in eliminating North Korea's nuclear weapons capability.

Japan's overall approach towards Iran has traditionally been economic-oriented and politically low-key in an attempt to avoid offending the US while, at the same time keeping links with Iran through the provision of economic assistance and political impartiality. However, the level of Japan's engagement in Iran has shifted according to the level of Japan's immediate stake there and its vulnerability to (largely US) pressure over the relationship. For example, during the Iran-Iraq war in the 1980s when Japan had a large stake in an oil joint venture, the Iran-Japan Petrochemical Company (IJPC), Japan attempted high level diplomatic mediation between the two states and advocated Iran's case in the UN. With the moderation of Iran's foreign policy under Muhammad Khatami's presidency starting in 1997, the decline of the US ability to isolate Iran, and the beginning of exploration in Iran's Azadegan oil field in 1999, Japan saw a new opportunity and renewed its official loans to Iran, with a view to acquiring an Azadegan contract. With the enthusiastic backing of the Ministry of Economy, Trade and Industry (METI), a Japanese consortium was formed to bid for a contract.

With the parallel rise of the Iranian nuclear development issue, Japan has come under US pressure to end the relationship. It has, however, shifted between a more Iran-friendly and a more US-friendly tangent.[19] During the initial period after Iran's nuclear development first became an issue, when the US campaign to isolate Iran had not yet prevailed, Japan sought to prevent an escalation in the dispute, while continuing to pursue the Azadegan contract. The Japanese government obtained US approval for signing of the contract if Iran agreed to sign the IAEA's Additional Protocol, thereby allowing the international community's inspections. However, as European states lined up with the US to isolate Iran and Japan came under concerted US pressure, Japan tilted toward the US and supported a warning issued to Iran by the IAEA Board of Governors on the assumption that Iran would give in and remove the obstacles to Japan's taking up of the Azadegan contract. When, however, Iran resisted and warned Japan it would lose the contract, Tokyo tilted toward Iran and opposed the US drive to refer it to the United Nations Security Council (UNSC) for economic sanctions. As Iran subsequently faced increasing international isolation after 2005 with the hardening of the position of European states during the radical presidency of Mahmoud Ahmadinejad, Japan's approach shifted to the support of limited and incremental sanctions on Iran. In parallel, Japanese business had become more cautious about re-entering the Iranian market under conditions of political insecurity and, as the possibility of economic sanction on Iran loomed in October 2006, Japan reduced its share in the Azadegan project from 75% to 10%. It withdrew fully in May 2010 as the UN Security Council resolution 1929 called for UN member states to refrain from entering into new energy contracts with Iran. Thereafter, Japanese media and elite circles expressed frustration at China's non-compliance with US demands for withdrawal from the Iranian energy sector and its taking up of 70% of the Azadegan oil field project.

2.3 Iraq

Iraq is another significant Gulf oil producer, with the world's third largest oil reserves, and with which Japan long sought close relations. As Iraq undertook large-scale infrastructure-building from the 1970s on, Japanese businesses entered the Iraqi market and in 1982, Japanese exports to Iraq amounted to 15.4% of its total exports to the Middle East, a majority of which (between 60-70%) was machinery. Japan was Iraq's top market for its oil exports between mid-1975 and the mid-1980s,[20] which also amounted to a share of 6.1% of Japan's total oil imports by 1979. However, the Iran-Iraq war of 1980-8 reduced Japanese economic activities and the Gulf War of 1990-1 and the following UN economic sanctions on Iraq terminated most of these relations.

Iraq then became a case of an oil producer under political isolation by the US until the 2003 US invasion. The regime change in the 2003 war presented Japan with an opportunity to renew the relationship. Supporting the US-led war on Iraq, Japan's government was enthusiastic about post-war assistance as a way of building business ties; it extended reconstruction assistance amounting to $5 billion, including infrastructure-building, which included a number of power plants and the vocational training of several thousand Iraqi people. Japan's Self-Defense Forces were used between February 2004 and July 2006 to implement reconstruction assistance where security conditions were not suitable for civilians. Assistance immediately after the war was focused on short-term relief such as water supply and humanitarian support, but in the medium-term, programs included human exchanges such as training civil servants in Japan. After the establishment of a post-war Iraqi authority in May 2006, larger infrastructure projects began, including port maintenance, an irrigation system, renovation of Al-Musaib thermal power station, and bridge and road construction in al-Samawa province.

The impact of Japan's reconstruction assistance in Iraq on the relationship at the grass-root level was mixed. Japanese forces were welcomed overall, with the recognition that they were not engaged in combat operations but were only used for implementing humanitarian support and reconstruction. Although the support of the local Iraqi people was high at consistently between 70 and 80% in opinion polls, there was some disappointment with the level of job creation by it and a perception that assistance was concentrated on limited geographical areas, certain tribes, and individuals.[21] Furthermore, the divisions in Iraqi society meant that there were also those who strongly opposed the presence of Japanese forces in the country, such as Muqtada al-Sadr's faction and the Sunnis, who were sympathetic to the old regime. Neither did the Arab people outside Iraq see it favorably.

Now that wars, sanctions, and the worst period of insecurity have ended, Iraq's encouragement for Japanese business participation has strengthened, as the quality of Japanese products and work practices are highly valued. However, Japanese business participation, needed to establish enduring economic relations, has not expanded as much as the Japanese and Iraq governments wish because security conditions are still not satisfactory for the standard of the Japanese private business.[22]

In response to this situation, several measures to encourage private business in Iraq have been taken. The enthusiasm of the Japanese government for the establishment of economic ties with Iraq was manifest in the visits of the Japanese Minister of Economic Affairs to the country in June 2008 and January 2011, in response to the encouragement by the Iraqi government of Japanese investment in Iraq. The Japan-Iraq Economic Forum was held twice, in July 2008 in Amman and in December 2009 in Baghdad airport, for the purpose of matching businesses from the two countries. In 2011, a Japanese delegation comprising official and private sector's representatives visited the country three times, where the officials supported the private sector's exchanges and exploration of business opportunities. In 2008, the Japanese government established the Iraq Committee, which comprises intellectuals, officials from the Ministry of Economy, Trade and Industry, the Ministry of Foreign Affairs, and other governmental institutions, in the view that there is a need for a permanent organization which assists Japanese businesses' entry into the Iraqi market by providing information, support with visas, and facilitating contacts between Iraqi and Japanese representatives. With the initiative of the ministry of economics, JCCME has set up an Iraq Desk and opened an office in Baghdad in 2012 to support businesses. The Japanese government's aid agency, Japan International Cooperation Agency (JICA), opened an office in Erbil in March 2009 and one in Baghdad in August 2011 for the provision of reconstruction assistance and facilitation of the entry of Japanese firms engaged in such assistance. Lastly, consideration is being given to tying a part of Japanese official economic assistance to Iraq with contracts to Japanese businesses. There is a movement among Japanese companies toward opening offices in Iraq but as of November 2011, less than 10 companies had done so, although more companies are moving in that direction.

The Japanese government's long-standing goal is for Japanese firms to acquire upstream oil field development contracts. However, the Iraqi government bidding process in allocating such large-scale contracts made Japan's post-war assistance largely irrelevant to its chances. Out of three biddings for 13 oil or gas fields (July 2009, December 2009, and October 2010) only one contract has been obtained by a Japanese company so far.[23] Nevertheless, Japan thinks that it can pursue more indirect approaches, namely, construction of oil refineries or infrastructure linked to energy development.[24] There has also been a case in which old business relations were revived by Japan's official reconstruction assistance, namely the reconstruction of the Harsa thermal power plant in Basra by Mitsubishi, which had built the plant in 1977.

Although security concerns and political uncertainty have obstructed the renewal of economic ties between Japan and Iraq, Iraq's importance as a major hydrocarbon producer with undeveloped fields will not change. Japan's import of Iraqi crude oil has been on the rise for the last several years and in 2010 exceeded 3% of its total oil imports for the first time in 21 years.[25] It is expected that it will continue to rise along with Iraq's plan for major increases in oil production.

3. Post-Earthquake Change in Japan's Energy Policy and Relations with the Gulf

It is expected that major changes in Japan's energy policy will result from the 2011 earthquake. A committee was established to revise the existing Strategic Energy Plan and to consider to what extent nuclear power generation will remain a component of future power generation. The following considerations are crucial in assessing Japan's energy interests in the Gulf.

Nuclear power is a prime domestic energy source for Japan and has the advantages of no carbon dioxide emissions and lower generation costs compared to other energy sources. However after the earthquake, Japan's nuclear power generation plunged and, as a result, thermal power generation increased, with its historical share of around 60%, rising to above 70% in 2011. Also as a result of the earthquake, safety was added to the traditional 3Es, namely, energy security, environment, and economic competitiveness, as an element in making choices between energy sources. It would not, however, be realistic to abandon nuclear energy in the short run in view of the negative impact on the macroeconomics, the size of required supply capacity for alternatives, and carbon emissions under a no-nuclear energy supply composition. A large increase in the consumption of coal is not likely because of its high carbon emissions. Japan's energy efficiency is already at the highest level among the developed countries and there is little room to achieve further improvement in industry, although in the residential and commercial sectors, additional energy conservation measures are being implemented. Renewable energy, such as solar and wind power generation was still low at 2.9% in 2010,[26] although post-earthquake incentives for investment in it are expected to yield a breakthrough in the long-term. Therefore, a prudent and gradual shift away from nuclear seems the only realistic option and this inevitably means increased dependence on Gulf hydrocarbons.

Natural gas is the most effective solution for filling the short-term gap from reduced nuclear power generation, as it has benefits compared to other fossil fuels, namely, lower carbon emission, a competitive price (compared to oil), and its availability in the world. Japan, having little domestic gas production, has increased imports from various countries. Qatar is an ideal supplier in times of unexpected additional demand, having the world's largest production capacity of seventy-seven million tons of Liquefied Natural Gas (LNG). The fact that Qatar's gas is not tied to a specific buyer on a long-term contract unlike most other LNG exporters and can increase its exports, having completed production expansion in 2010, is particularly attractive to Japan. Qatar increased its LNG export to Japan from 7.6 million tons in 2010 to 11.8 million tons in 2011, covering half of the total increase in Japan's LNG imports in 2011. LNG is expected to play a larger role in quenching the future energy thirst of Japan.

The role of oil is the most uncertain. Japan's belief that long-term dependence on imported oil is undesirable from the viewpoint of energy security was replaced by an appreciation of the importance of a sufficient supply capacity of oil products in case of emergency, since the 2011 earthquake revealed that oil products such as kerosene could be effectively delivered in quake-hit areas without an extensive supply network infrastructure such as transmission grids or pipelines. Its disadvantage is its high cost (compared to natural gas - LNG), particularly with Japan's oil-fired power plants requiring an even higher-cost "sweet," or low-sulphur (typically below 0.20%) oil, and also given the inefficiency of most of Japan's existing old oil-fired power plants. Other factors such as the introduction of a carbon pricing policy could further increase the price, while increased geopolitical risks and continuing high prices on the oil market may discourage oil consumption. The role of oil will vary subject to various policy and market factors, but, given its dominant position in Japan's total energy demand (44%), compared to natural gas (18%) or coal (22%),[27] it will remain the largest energy source for Japan, at least in the next two decades.

Thus, the fundamental tone of Japan's foreign policies toward the Gulf will not greatly change as a result of Japan's energy policy reassessments, but may be altered. Firstly, Japan will pay more attention to LNG supply. Recognizing its growing importance, Japan plans to launch the first Asian LNG producer–consumer dialogue in Tokyo in September 2012,[28] and aims to further tighten relationships with the Gulf LNG-producing countries, particularly Qatar, the UAE and Oman. Secondly, since it is becoming evident that Japan's oil and gas dependence will continue, growing energy consumption in the Gulf countries has become a source of concern for Japan because such demand growth may eventually limit export capacity in the Gulf. As warned by a Chatham House report on Saudi Arabia, runaway energy demand may result in serious energy shortages in the Gulf, and eventually may even eliminate oil and gas exports.[29]

Therefore, Japan is assisting Gulf countries to improve energy efficiency and conservation based on its own experiences and new technological developments. Several workshops on energy conservation and efficiency have been organized in Tokyo and Riyadh involving both countries' governments and think tanks. JICA has produced a master energy plan for the Saudi Ministry of Electricity based on a study conducted in 2007-8. Tokyo Electricity Corporation devised a National Energy Efficient Program (NEEP) of technical cooperation with assistance for planning and implementation.[30] Also for Saudi Arabia, JGC Corporation conducted an experiment in constructing a "smart house" - pre-engineered houses which will save 70% of power for cooling in the heat in the Gulf countries with heat-insulating technology and architecture in July 2011.[31] In the UAE, multiple Japanese companies are currently participating in the country's early-stage experimental platform project for the development of Masdar City, an environmentally friendly city. This is perceived by Japan as a new business opportunity. For example, Cosmo Oil Company, in cooperation with the Tokyo Institute of Technology, has built an experimental solar power generation plant, and Mitsubishi Heavy Industry, jointly with Masdar (the Abu Dhabi Future Energy Company), has been experimenting with electric automobiles. Japan has been cooperating in developing integrated solar combined cycle power generation, discharged thermal energy conservation (utilizing heat from refineries), in a desalination project using ocean thermal power in Qatar initiated in 2007[32] and in lowering sulphur in oil (Kuwait). Japanese technological support is not only making new energy available but also more affordable for the Gulf. Cooperation in such areas will acquire more importance in Japan's foreign policy toward the Gulf in the coming decades.

4. Conclusion: New directions in Japan-Gulf relations

Japan's high dependence on the Gulf region for its oil supply will persist, regardless of how the debate over nuclear power will be settled. While the size of future oil demand in Japan is uncertain, the share of Gulf countries in its total oil supply will remain dominant. Japan's engagement with the Gulf has been shaped and expanded as a means of ensuring its energy supply. History shows that both sides felt vulnerable to each other in the energy supplier-consumer relationship: Japan was increasingly aware of its insecurity as a major consumer reliant on external supplies in an increasingly tight market (and its dependence on the Gulf has actually increased); the Gulf producers, for their part, felt vulnerable due to their heavy reliance on the sale of hydrocarbon. However, the nature of their relationship is likely to see a significant change in the future due to the new developments on both sides.

Firstly, successful economic diversification currently pursued by most of the Gulf states plus an incremental increase in non-hydrocarbon energy sources in Japan will mean that eventually, the level of their interdependence will be somewhat reduced. Diversification of their economic relations, if successful, is also likely to make the relationship more multi-dimensional. Japan's transferring of technology to and nurturing skilled workers from Gulf states might also lay the foundation for further development of economic relations due to increased familiarity of business styles and cultures between the two sides, and Japanese businesses' transfer of some stages of manufacturing to the Gulf, in a similar form to that in East Asia. The Japanese government's new emphasis on the move towards establishing 'mutually beneficial,' hence more enduring, relationships holds great implications for their future relationship. Overall, such changes will mean an eventual move away from a hierarchical one between a raw material producer and an advanced economy, and a partial moderation of a highly political one between a vulnerable consumer and a major producer of a strategic commodity.

However, there is some reason for caution in assessing the significance of Japan's new engagement. Firstly, the political constraint on Japan's involvement in politico-strategic issues in the region will continue to limit its options, hence the range of interdependencies with Gulf counterparts. The lack of security support, cooperation, or arms supply is, from a geopolitical point of view, a significant disadvantage in consolidating ties with Gulf counterparts. Also, a faulty use of 'soft' power can have an adverse effect: the introduction of Japanese styles of education and work, and Japanese pop culture to the youth should be done with sensitivity to avoid giving the kind of offense that elicited a Saudi fatwa against a Japanese cartoon game, Pokemon in 2001. In the current climate where more full democracy might be realized (as seen in Kuwait and Iraq, where parliaments can have a strong influence on the approval and disapproval of foreign business), Japan's political stance (such as Japanese support for a US war in the Gulf) might carry more damaging baggage for its relationship with these countries.

Table 15.1: Japan–Gulf States Trade Statistics

Exports

	1996	1997	1998	1999	2000	2001	2002	2003	2004	2005	2006	2007	2008	2009	2010
Bahrain	141	189	440	133	127	165	256	346	391	428	540	678	961	436	589
Iran	713	880	858	574	572	793	779	1,124	1,119	1,340	1,173	1,332	1,908	1,649	2,078
Iraq	-	5	10	36	43	190	283	76	70	130	199	121	206	316	310
Kuwait	858	949	1,192	705	584	658	865	1,052	936	1,179	1,189	1,670	2,109	1,245	1,418
Oman	655	739	789	673	742	787	859	969	1,162	1,385	1,730	2,531	3,947	2,355	3,113
Qatar	257	378	537	226	288	305	370	476	593	988	1,458	1,844	2,031	1,628	1,141
Saudi Arabia	3,010	3,072	3,992	3,323	3,089	3,593	3,766	3,733	3,677	4,168	4,639	6,725	7,899	5,392	6,481
UAE	2,308	2,533	2,863	2,533	2,532	2,563	2,950	3,638	4,610	4,842	6,041	8,062	10,888	6,493	7,330

Imports

	1996	1997	1998	1999	2000	2001	2002	2003	2004	2005	2006	2007	2008	2009	2010
Bahrain	432	411	248	197	235	223	160	142	276	315	508	430	419	526	659
Iran	3,255	3,524	2,453	3,179	5,356	5,017	4,742	7,441	8,267	10,298	10,875	12,758	18,246	9,307	11,162
Iraq	-	118	89	708	661	141	106	109	1,172	442	1,034	1,092	1,504	1,405	3,427
Kuwait	3,173	3,713	2,348	3,061	4,978	4,430	4,207	4,563	5,751	7,627	9,481	10,221	15,227	8,995	10,287
Oman	1,951	1,832	1,110	1,705	2,031	2,356	2,101	2,513	1,624	2,722	2,825	3,583	5,566	3,320	4,508
Qatar	2,470	3,014	2,785	3,438	5,857	6,030	5,251	6,516	7,887	10,629	15,049	16,964	26,426	15,931	21,695
Saudi Arabia	10,672	11,886	7,176	8,394	14,188	12,316	11,638	14,565	18,484	28,575	36,986	35,593	50,847	29,204	35,879
UAE	11,506	12,309	8,341	8,898	14,815	12,850	11,607	14,327	18,324	25,175	31,720	32,550	46,763	22,723	29,276

Unit: Millions of US Dollars

Sources: IMF Direction of Trade Statistics (2003, 2008, 2011)

Table 15.2: FDI Statistics

Japanese FDI in the Gulf

	1990	1991	1992	1993	1994	1995	1996	1997	1998	1999	2000	2001	2002	2003	2004
UAE	-	46	48	159	93	18	7	196	-	5	-	8	30	2	3
Iran	-	1	378	-	-	-	-	-	-	-	-	-	-	-	-
Saudi Arabia	-	0	100	-	1	-	10	27	3	19	-	-	-	18	-
Bahrain	-	9	67	-	-	31	-	-	-	-	-	-	6	-	-
Qatar	1	2	12	34	85	8	102	130	20	-	-	-	-	-	-
Kuwait	-	-	-	-	-	-	6	-	-	-	-	-	-	-	-
S Arabia/ Kuwait	26	26	98	22	93	96	102	105	117	87	-	-	-	-	-

Gulf FDI in Japan

	1990	1991	1992	1993	1994	1995	1996	1997	1998	1999	2000	2001	2002	2003	2004
UAE	0	0	0	-	-	-	-	-	-	-	-	0	-	-	1
Iran	0	0	0	5	0	0	-	-	-	0	-	-	-	-	-
Saudi Arabia	-	-	2	-	-	-	-	-	-	-	-	-	-	-	-
Bahrain	1	0	-	-	0	-	-	-	-	-	-	-	-	-	-
Kuwait	0	0	2	-	-	-	-	-	-	-	-	-	-	-	-

Unit: Millions of US Dollars

Source: JETRO Statistics http://www.jetro.go.jp/world/japan/stats/fdi/

Endnotes

1   Ministry of Economy, Trade and Industry, Agency for Natural Resources and Energy, "*Nihon no Enerugi Josei to Seisaku* (Japan's Energy Condition and Policy)", 16 February 2008, accessed on May 14, 2008, *tech.edu.nagasaki-u.ac.jp/tech/energy/home/data/enekan5.pdf.*

2   Chapter 2 in Yukiko Miyagi, Japan's Middle East Security Policy: Theory and Cases (London: Routledge, 2008).

3   Chapter 2 in Miyagi, Japan's Middle East Security Policy.

4   Particularly compared to India, another rising hydrocarbon consumer. China's energy exploration and acquisition activities near the disputed maritime zone between China and Japan is a major source of such a view.

5   Normally in oil-producing Gulf states, the Japanese embassy has staff sent from the Ministry of Economy, Trade and Industry (METI) who will support energy source acquisition as well as Japanese business activities as well as representatives of oil businesses and manufacturing plants for liaising between the government and the business. The oil companies such as INPEX and JAPEX are partially owned by the Japanese government and their CEOs and chairmen are retired METI officials, therefore such companies are particularly under the influence of the government policy.

6   Ministry of Foreign Affairs, "*Sauji Arabia Okoku Surutan Kotaishi no Hogyo: Gaiyo to Hyoka* (The Demise of Crown Prince Sultan of the Kingdom of Saudi Arabia: general overview and assessment)", 26 October 2011, accessed on May 12, 2012, http://www.mofa.go.jp/mofaj/area/saudi/visit111026_gh.html.

7   Research Institute for Peace and Security (RIPS) "*Dai Nikai Kokusai Kaigi: Wangan Chiiki ni Okeru Nihon no Yakuwari: Gaiyo* (The 2nd International Conference: Japan's Role in the Gulf Region, General Report)", March 2011, p. 31, accessed on May 14, 2012, https://ssl60.secureserver.jp/~**rips/rips**.or.jp/etc/pdf/2010JPN.pdf.

8   Ministry of Foreign Affairs, "Meeting between Prime Minister Noda and H.M. Hamad bin Isa Al-Khalifa, King of the Kingdom of Bahrain", 11 April 2012, accessed on May 12, 2012, http://www.mofa.go.jp/region/middle_e/bahrain/meeting1204_pm.html.

9   The Japan Cooperation Centre, Petroleum (JCCP) has provided various training courses under METI's policy. Japan Centre for Cooperation, Petroleum (JCCP), "Training Programs", accessed on June 26, 2012, http://www.jccp.or.jp/english/training/dispatch/performance; Ministry of Education, Culture, Sports, Science and Technology (MEXT) "*Chuto ni Okeru Jinzai Ikusei ni Tsuite* (On Human Resource Development in the Middle East)", METI, July 2011, accessed on 15 August, 15 2011 http://www.mext.go.jp/b_menu/shingi/chousa/kokusai/010/shiryou/__icsFiles/afieldfile/2011/11/08/1312142_03_1.pdf.

10 A major petrochemical project undertaken by the Japanese businesses in the Gulf is Petro Rabigh in Saudi Arabia, which began operation in 2009. Among its technological advantages is the installation of the world's largest High Olefins Fluid Catalytic Cracker (HOFCC), whose yield of lighter petrochemical feedstock is 20%, more than double of that of a conventional FCC plant, which is less than 10%.

11 Research Institute for Peace and Security (RIPS) "*Dai Nikai Kokusai Kaigi: Wangan Chiiki ni Okeru Nihon no Yakuwari: Gaiyo* (The 2nd International Conference: Japan's Role in the Gulf Region, General Report)", March 2011, p. 31, accessed on May 14, 2012, https://ssl60.secureserver.jp/~rips/rips.or.jp/etc/pdf/2010JPN.pdf.

12 The Japan-UAE Association *Gaiyo oyobi Shusai Shuyo Gyoji* (General View and Major Events Hosted), accessed on June 11, 2012, http://www.uaesociety.jp/gaiyo.html.

13 In May 2011, on invitation of Saudi Arabia to participate in its annual Janadriya Festival with its cultural exhibitions, the Japanese government emphasised its pop culture. The promotion of Japanese pop culture by various Japanese embassies in the Gulf, such as those in UAE, Oman has also been seen.

14 Based on the author's personal conversation with an Iraqi civil servant in September 2008. The same view was also expressed in a speech by the Director of the Middle East and European Bureau of JICA, Jun'ichi Yamada. Jun'ichi Yamada, "*Koen 4 Nihon no Tai Iraku Fukkoshien to JICA no Torikumi* (Lecture 4: Japan's Assistance for Iraq Reconstruction and JICA's Tackling)" 14 June 2010 p. 2, accessed on May 14, 2012, www.iraq-jccme.jp/pdf/20110203_b5.pdf.

15 Although Qatar's share in Japan's LNG imports increased significantly to meet Japan's energy demand between 2010 and 2011, a large part of Japanese imports of natural gas still comes from Indonesia and Malaysia.

16 Companies contracted for Dubai Metro are Mitsubishi Corporation, Mitsubishi Heavy Industries, Obayashi Corporation, and Kajima Construction. The vehicles are provided by Japan Turkey Metro Joint Venture (JTM-JV), comprising Turkey's Yapi Merkezi and five Japanese companies.

17 Ministry of Foreign Affairs, "Meeting between Prime Minsiter Yoshihiko Noda and H.H. Sheikh Sabah Al-Ahmad Al-Jaber Al-Sabah, Amir of the State of Kuwait", 22 March 2012, accessed on April 12, 2012, http://www.mofa.go.jp/region/middle_e/kuwait/meeting1203_pm.html.

18 The first volume of a Japan-UAE joint cartoon, "Sawar al-Dahab (Gold Ring)" was published in 2008, and the second volume is to be published in 2012.

19 For details see Chapter 5 in Miyagi, Japan's Middle East Security Policy.

20 International Monetary Fund (IMF) Direction of Statistics Yearbook (various issues).

21 According to the poll taken by another local paper, Uruk, together with Kyodo in 2006.

22 Corruption in the Iraqi government is blocking the proper transfer of oil revenues into the nation's reconstruction, and the growth of the independent Iraqi economy is another factor.

23 JAPEX will participate in the Garraf oil field project as a non-operator.

24 Ensuring stable imports on a commercial basis is another possible approach.

25 Petroleum Association of Japan, "*Tokei Joho* (Statistics Data)", accessed on July 7, 2012, http://www.paj.gr.jp/statis/.

26 The percentage excludes hydro-electricity. International Energy Agency, *Energy Balances of OECD Countries, 2011 edition* (Paris: International Energy Agency, October 2011).

27 Energy Data and Modeling Centre, The Institute of Energy Economics, Japan, Handbook of Energy & Economic Statistics in Japan (Tokyo: Energy Conservation Centre, Japan, March 2012), 36.

28 *Yomiuri Shimbun*, April 17, 2012.

29 Glada Lahn and Paul Stevens, Burning Oil to Keep Cool: The Hidden Energy Crisis in Saudi Arabia (London: Chatham House, December 2011).

30 Jun Hagiwara, '*Sauji Arabia ni Okeru Sho Enerugi no Torikumi* (Copying with Energy Conservation in Saudi Arabia)', Japan Institute of Middle East Economy (JIME) Analysis of Middle East Climate, October 2011, p. 28.

31 JGC Environment Report 2011, accessed on July 6, 2012, http://www.jgc.co.jp/en/40_csr/06_environment%20rpt/pdf/2011/enviroment_report_2011.pdf.

32 Sadayuki Torahara, "*Ondosa Hatsuden Purojekuto no Kaigai Joukyou* (Report on Overseas Thermal Power Generation Project)", OPOTEC News Vol. 4 No.1, August 2008, Organization for the Promotion of Ocean Thermal Energy Conservation), accessed on April 12, 2012, www.opotec.jp/japanese/opotec_news/004.pdf.

Bibliography

Books

Energy Data and Modeling Centre, The Institute of Energy Economics, Japan, Handbook of Energy & Economic Statistics in Japan. Tokyo: Energy Conservation Centre, Japan, March 2012.

International Monetary Fund, Direction of Statistics Yearbook, (various issues).

International Energy Agency, Energy Balances of OECD Countries, 2011 edition. Paris: International Energy Agency, October 2011.

Lahn, Glada, and Stevens, Paul. Burning Oil to Keep Cool: The Hidden Energy Crisis in Saudi Arabia. London: Chatham House, December 2011.

Miyagi, Yukiko. Japan's Middle East Security Policy: Theory and Cases. London: Routledge, 2008.

Articles

Hagiwara, Jun. "*Sauji Arabia ni Okeru Sho Enerugi no Torikumi* (Copying with Energy Conservation in Saudi Arabia)", Japan Institute of Middle East Economy (JIME) Analysis of Middle East Climate, October 2011:.28-30.

Online sources

Japan Centre for Cooperation, Petroleum (JCCP), "Training Programs", accessed on June 26, 2012, http://www.jccp.or.jp/english/training/dispatch/performance.

The Japan-UAE Association *Gaiyo oyobi Shusai Shuyo Gyoji* (General View and Major Events Hosted), accessed on June 11, 2012, http://www.uaesociety.jp/gaiyo.html.

Ministry of Economy, Trade and Industry, Agency for Natural Resources and Energy, "*Nihon no Enerugi Josei to Seisaku* (Japan's Energy Condition and Policy)"16 February 2008, accessed on May 14, 2008, *tech.edu.nagasaki-u.ac.jp/tech/energy/home/data/enekan5.pdf.*

Ministry of Education, Culture, Sports, Science and Technology (MEXT) "*Chuto ni Okeru Jinzai Ikusei ni Tsuite* (On Human Resource Development in the Middle East)", METI, July 2011, accessed on 15 August, 15 2011 http://www.mext.go.jp/b_menu/shingi/chousa/kokusai/010/shiryou/__icsFiles/afieldfile/2011/11/08/1312142_03_1.pdf.

Ministry of Foreign Affairs, "*Sauji Arabia Okoku Surutan Kotaishi no Hogyo: Gaiyo to Hyoka* (The Demise of Crown Prince Sultan of the Kingdom of Saudi Arabia: general overview and assessment)", 26 October 2011, accessed on May 12, 2012, http://www.mofa.go.jp/mofaj/area/saudi/visit111026_gh.html.

Ministry of Foreign Affairs, "Meeting between Prime Minister Noda and H.M. Hamad bin Isa Al-Khalifa, King of the Kingdom of Bahrain" 11 April 2012, accessed on May 12, 2012, http://www.mofa.go.jp/region/middle_e/bahrain/meeting1204_pm.html.

Ministry of Foreign Affairs, "Meeting between Prime Minsiter Yoshihiko Noda and H.H. Sheikh Sabah Al-Ahmad Al-Jaber Al-Sabah, Amir of the State of Kuwait", 22 March 2012, accessed on April 12, 2012, http://www.mofa.go.jp/region/middle_e/kuwait/meeting1203_pm.html.

Petroleum Association of Japan, "*Tokei Joho* (Statistics Data)", accessed on July 7, 2012, http://www.paj.gr.jp/statis/.

Research Institute for Peace and Security (RIPS) "*Dai Nikai Kokusai Kaigi: Wangan Chiiki ni Okeru Nihon no Yakuwari: Gaiyo* (The 2nd International Conference: Japan's Role in the Gulf Region, General Report)" March 2011, accessed on May 14, 2012, https://ssl60.secureserver.jp/~rips/rips.or.jp/etc/pdf/2010JPN.pdf.

Torahara, Sadayuki. "*Ondosa Hatsuden Purojekuto no Kaigai Joukyou* (Report on Overseas Thermal Power Generation Project)", OPOTEC News Vol. 4 No.1, August 2008, Organization for the promotion of Ocean Thermal Energy Conservation pp.2-5. Accessed on May 2012 14, 2012 www.opotec.jp/japanese/opotec_news/004.pdf.

Yamada, Jun'ichi. "*Iraku Fukko Shien: JICA no Torikumi to Kongo no Tenbo* (JICA Assistance for Iraq Reconstruction: JICA's Tackling and Prospect)", June 14, 2010, accessed on May 14, 2012, www.iraq-jccme.jp/pdf/20110106_4.pdf.

Yamada, Jun'ichi, "*Koen 4 Nihon no Tai Iraku Fukkoshien to JICA no Torikumi* (Lecture 4: Japan's Assistance for Iraq Reconstruction and JICA's Tackling)" 14 June 2010, accessed on May 14, 2012, www.iraq-jccme.jp/pdf/20110203_b5.pdf.

Chapter Sixteen

Japan and the Gulf:
Balancing the Business Relationship

Yoshio Minagi

1. Introduction

The Gulf countries are critical for Japan's energy security. Nearly 90% of Japan's crude oil supply is imported from the Gulf. Hence, strengthening the relationship with the Gulf is of utmost importance, particularly now as changes in government policy on nuclear energy will inevitably be revised in the light of the Great East Japan Earthquake on 11th March 2011. Japan will need to exert additional efforts to diversify its bilateral relations with the Gulf States.

Since the 1970s, Japanese companies in the electronics, automotives, trading, engineering, energy and financial sectors have been heavily involved in the Gulf. In the 1970s and 1980s Japan was evolving into one of the world's major exporting countries. The relationship between Japan and the Gulf was reciprocal in so far as manufactured products were exchanged for oil and gas. In the early 1990s, Japan's bubble economy collapsed and subsequently the country suffered the effects of the Asian financial crisis in the late 1990s. Consequently, the business flow with the Gulf changed and Japan's relative position among other Asian countries gradually decreased. It became difficult for 'Made in Japan' products to compete in terms of price with the products of emerging Asian countries. It was, in addition, important for the Gulf countries to strengthen their relations with emerging Asian countries so as to diversify their markets for oil and gas. Where there were large-scale projects not requiring high-end technologies, lesser Japanese companies could nonetheless participate in the tenders. Japanese government and companies have not yet found appropriate countermeasures to prevent Japan's position, relative to other Asian countries, from declining.

Japan faces, on the one hand, the expectation that in the long-term both its economy and its population will shrink, and on the other, the immediate impact of the 2011 earthquake and the more recent appreciation of the yen against other major currencies. In the light of the trade deficit recorded in 2011 (the first time the trade balance had been in deficit since 1980), many economists recommended that Japan should rebuild itself as an investing nation. The emphasis then would be on maintaining the current account surplus rather than seeking a trading surplus. This argument indicates that the Japanese economy is now reaching a structural turning point. In the last decade, the Japanese manufacturing industry has become heavily engaged in other Asian countries, with an accelerating number of bilateral business arrangements. In the near future, Japanese small and medium enterprises (SMEs) will inevitably follow the same path. It may, therefore, be wrong to place emphasis on competition between Japanese and Asian companies in the Gulf. The reality is that Asian economies are coming to work in a mutually complementary manner.

This chapter will show how the economic relations between Japan and the Gulf have developed over the last two decades, in terms of trade, investment, and corporate activity.

2. Japanese Trade with the Gulf over the Past 20 Years

2.1. Japanese Trade in the Gulf: General Characteristics

Political and economic developments in both Japan and the Gulf States over the last two decades have had a decisive impact on the economic relationship between them. The Japanese economy, which had been booming since the mid-1980s (the so-called 'bubble') burst in the early 1990s. Japan struggled with serious asset deflation in real estate and the stock market for more than 10 years. During this period, banks were forced to make provisions against the flow of non-performing loans. As a result of the forced consolidation of Japanese banks and financial institutions, the number of Japanese financial institutions with offices in the Gulf, especially in Bahrain, decreased dramatically over that period. At the same time, Iraq's invasion of Kuwait led to the Gulf War. Then there was the era of low oil prices through to the early 2000s. Between 1997 and 1998, the Japanese and Asian economic crisis and the cheap oil price (below $10 per barrel at the lowest point) occurred at the same time, marking a particularly difficult time for the economic relationship between Asia (including Japan) and the Gulf. After the Iraq War in 2003, the Gulf economies expanded quickly through to the 2008 financial crisis, due to the benefits of high oil prices. Some Japanese-involved projects in the UAE were negatively affected by the financial crisis. Thus, the last two decades can be described as relatively dark in the first half and relatively bright in the latter half. Trade data show this clearly.

The value of trade between Japan and the eight countries of the Gulf (Bahrain, Iran, Iraq, Kuwait, Oman, Qatar, Saudi Arabia and the UAE) stood at $180.3 billion in 2011 compared to $38 billion in 1990. The volume of Japanese global trade in those years stood at $1,673.9 billion and $521.7 billion respectively. Trade with the Gulf rose manifold between 1990 and 2011: by 4.7 times, compared to global trade by 3.2 times. Figure 16.1 shows trade figures with the Gulf in Japanese overall trade. Due to the nature of the trade relationship - exporting manufacturing products and importing oil and gas - it is clear that the trade figures heavily depended on the market price of oil and gas. Therefore, the Gulf is critically an important trade counterpart for Japan for its energy security. In addition, the Gulf has been a stable export market for Japan.

The ratio of Japanese export to the Gulf varied between 1.6% (in 1995, lowest) and 3.8% (in 2008, highest). On the contrary, the import ratio varied between 8.8% (in 1998, lowest) and 21.7% (in 2008, highest). This means that Japanese trade balance with the Gulf has consistently been negative although Japan has been recognized as an export-oriented country. Figure 16.2 shows Japanese trade balances with the World and the Gulf. Japan recorded a trade deficit with the World in 2011 at $32 billion for the first time since 1980 as well as a huge deficit with the Gulf at $137 billion.

Figure 16.1: The Ratio of the Gulf Countries against Total Japanese World Trade

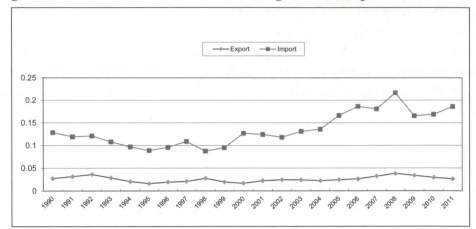

Compiled by the author from JETRO HP

Figure 16.2: Japanese Trade Balances with the World and the Gulf

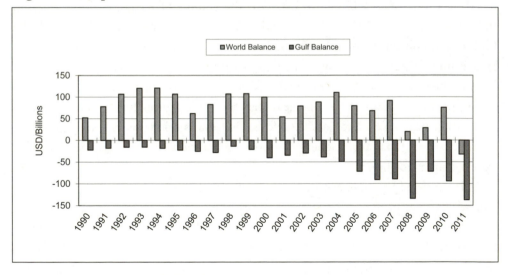

Compiled by the author from JETRO HP

Trade volume between Japan and the Gulf peaked in 2008 – the highest in historical records. The yearly average oil price in 2011 (OPEC basket: $107.46 b/d) was higher than in 2008 ($94.45 b/d), so imports in 2011 should have been larger than in 2008. However, Japan's total imports in 2011 from the Gulf were smaller in volume than in 2008. In addition to that, the oil price mechanism between Japan and the Gulf has not been well reflected by the sharp decline of oil prices in the last quarter of 2008. Japan reduced crude oil imports in 2011 from the Gulf by 13.5% to 181 million kilolitres (kls) compared to 209 million kls in 2008. Japanese reliance on crude oil from the Gulf stood at 87.5% which was almost at the same level in 2008 at 87.6%, as Table 16.1 shows. Japan is one of the most advanced countries in terms of energy conservation which is part of the reason for decreasing crude oil imports.

Figure 16.3: Japanese Trade with the Gulf Countries

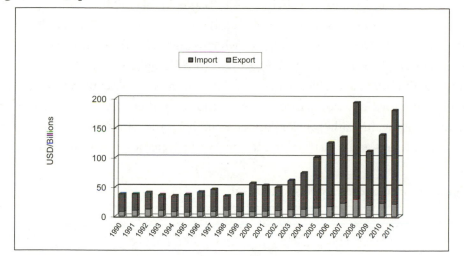

Compiled by the author from JETRO HP

Table 16.1: Japanese Crude Oil Imports (kls/million)

	1990	2000	2008	2011
Saudi Arabia	44.5	62.8	70.2	68.6
UAE	47.8	62.9	58.7	47.8
Qatar	13.1	22.9	25.9	21.9
Iran	22.6	29.6	28.0	18.2
Kuwait	7.9	21.0	18.7	14.0
Iraq	-	3.6	2.3	5.7
Oman	12.3	11.4	5.4	4.8
Bahrain	-	0.1	0.1	-
(Gulf total)	148.1	214.3	209.3	181.0
World	220.7	249.0	239.0	207.0
(Gulf ratio)	67.1%	86.1%	87.6%	87.4

Compiled by the author from JETRO HP

2.2. Trade Relations with Individual Gulf countries: an Overview

In exports, the UAE has been the largest trading counterpart for Japan since 2004. For many years prior to this, its main trading partner had been Saudi Arabia. The reason why the UAE has been in the top position in recent years is because Japanese companies use Dubai as a trading hub and regional marketing center. Likewise, there are many Japanese contractors which have been involved in several infrastructure developments in Dubai since 2004. The total Japanese export in 2011 was at $21.6 billion which consisted of: the UAE (34.4%), Saudi Arabia (30.0%), Oman (12.9%), Iran (7.9%), Kuwait (6.3%), Qatar (4.7%), Bahrain (2.2%) and Iraq (1.6%). Total exports in 1992 were at $12.3 billion, which consisted of: Saudi (39.4%), UAE (22.2%), Iran (21.6%), Oman (6.5%), Kuwait (6.2%), Qatar (2.4%), Bahrain (1.7%) and Iraq (0%). 1990 and 1991 were unusual due to the Gulf War, therefore the 1992 figures were used as a comparison. Due to the strengthened exchange rate of the Japanese Yen against other major currencies in 2011, the Yen-denominated exports such as cars, tires and construction machinery, etc. were negatively affected.

Figure 16.4: Japanese Exports to the Gulf

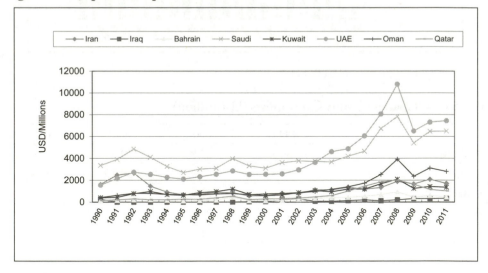

Compiled by the author from JETRO HP

Japanese exports can be characterized as transport-equipment driven. Transport equipment includes: passenger vehicles, large vehicles, motorcycles, construction machinery and parts etc. When the oil and gas proceeds were relatively lower in the 1990s, transport equipment was less than 50% of total exports. However, when oil and gas proceeds were higher in the 2000s, transport equipment made up more than 50%

of GCC imports from Japan. In 2008, almost 55% of imports were in this category. When oil prices contracted from the late 2008, the ratio suddenly declined, to 45.7% in 2009. In 2010, it increased rapidly to 56.2%, however it declined again to 49.7% in 2011 due to supply chain disruption after the earthquake in Japan and serious flooding in Thailand. Thus, exports of transport equipment are generally proportional to the level of economic activities in the Gulf, based on oil and gas proceeds, however, at the same time they are sensitive to any incident causing disruption in global supply chains.

Along with transport equipment, electrical machinery should be regarded as one of the major export items because of the huge presence of large Japanese manufacturing companies, such as Sony, Panasonic, Sharp and Toshiba etc. However, more than 90% of those companies' products in the Gulf come from Asian countries other than Japan. They have globally diversified the production capacities and utilized ideal logistic networks from time to time. Most of the 'Made in Japan' products are no longer exported to the Gulf. Therefore, the ratio of electrical machinery in total exports has decreased recently to around 5% compared to more or less 18% in the early 1990s. It is difficult to estimate the volume of Japanese-branded electrical machinery exported from any third country to the Gulf. Taking into consideration the sales volume of those companies in the Gulf, at least $7–10 billion in trade flows might be assumed. Those figures have been included mainly in the trade data of other Asian countries. Similar trade flows can be seen in transport equipment data, for example, major car manufacturers such as Toyota, Nissan and Honda export some lines of cars to the Gulf from Southeast Asian countries, Australia, and the USA.

Figure 16.5: Segments of Japanese Exports to the Gulf

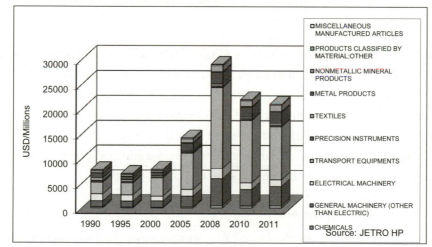

Compiled by the author from JETRO HP

Since 2005, the largest proportion of Japanese imports from the GCC has come from Saudi Arabia, followed in second position by the UAE. From 1990 until 2004, Saudi Arabia and the UAE were almost at the same level because Japanese import volumes of oil and gas and its related products remained unchanged. Total Japanese imports in 2011 were at $158.7 billion, which consisted of: Saudi Arabia (31.8%), UAE (26.9%), Qatar (18.9%), Kuwait (8.3%), Iran (8.1%), Oman (3.2%), Iraq (2.3%) and Bahrain (0.5%). Total imports in 1992 were at $28.2 billion, which consisted of: Saudi (36.2%), UAE (34.6%), Iran (9.2%), Qatar (7.7%), Oman (7.0%), Kuwait (4.2%), Bahrain (1.1%) and Iraq (0%).

Figure 16.6: Japanese Imports from the Gulf

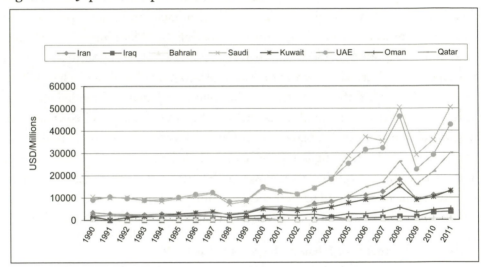

Compiled by the author from JETRO HP

Oil and gas related products constitute almost 100% of Japanese imports. Imports of metal products such as aluminum are minimal compared to oil and gas. As Table 16.1 shows, total Japanese crude oil imports in 2011 came to 207 million kls. Eighty-seven per cent of this total (181 million kls) came from the Gulf, and this figure has remained almost at the same level for the last 15 years. This chapter shows that trade data between Japan and five Gulf countries recorded more than $10 billion in total exports and imports in 2011.

2.3. Trade with Saudi Arabia

Saudi Arabia is now one of the largest importing countries of Japanese passenger cars. Until the early 1990s, American cars dominated in Saudi Arabia, however, market shares of Japanese brands have gradually expanded. The export figure of transport equipment in 2008 was 4.4 times larger than in 1995.

The Japanese Arabian Oil Company had an oil concession in the Al Khafji neutral zone between Saudi Arabia and Kuwait until 2000. For a long time, Saudi Arabia has been one of Japan's most important oil suppliers. As Table 16.1 shows, Japanese crude oil imports in 2011 increased in quantity by 9.2% compared to 2000 and increased by 54.3% compared to 1990.

Table 16.2: Exports to Saudi Arabia ($ million)

	1990	1995	2000	2005	2008	2010	2011	2011 vs 1990	2011 vs 2005
Grand Total	3,341	2,702	3,098	4,192	7,824	6,459	6,487	94%	55%
TRANSPORT EQUIPMENTS	1,319	884	1,432	2,208	3,903	3,369	2,782	111%	22%
GENRAL MACHINERY (OTHER THAN ELECTRIC)	414	549	467	566	1,643	1,042	1,222	195%	116%
METAL PRODUCTS	284	279	332	424	791	753	966	240%	128%
PRODUCTS CLASSIFIED BY MATERIAL OTHER	153	119	159	251	375	371	459	201%	82%
ELECTRICAL MACHINERY	559	377	342	310	413	308	314	-48%	1%
CHEMICALS	59	76	56	73	195	188	266	352%	262%
TEXTILES	248	167	97	92	146	135	124	-50%	35%
PRECISION INSTRUMENTS	122	113	77	73	98	111	114	-7%	56%
MISCELLANEOUS MANUFACTURED ARTICLES	97	90	67	54	65	56	69	-29%	26%
NONMETALLIC MINERAL PRODUCTS	25	26	28	27	41	48	54	116%	99%

Compiled by the author from JETRO HP

Table 16.3: Imports from Saudi Arabia ($ million)

	1990	1995	2000	2005	2008	2010	2011	2011 VS 1990	2011 VS 2005
Grand Total	10,462	9,716	14,241	28,739	50,470	35,763	50,390	382%	75%
PETROLEUM AND PETROLEUM PRODUCTS	8,944	7,740	11,818	25,882	46,302	33,741	47,961	436%	85%
PETROLEUM GAS OTHERS GASEOUS HYDROCARBONS	1,159	1,498	2,104	2,382	3,494	1,501	1,684	45%	-29%

Compiled by the author from JETRO HP

2. 4. Trade with UAE

The UAE is the largest Japanese exporting country in the Gulf. Exports in 2008 recorded over $10 billion and it was the first time that Japanese exports to a single country in the Gulf exceeded this amount. Due to the existence of trading hub functions in Dubai, exporting items are well diversified. Some of the exported products have been re-exported to other countries through free trade zones. The transport equipment ratio has never been more than 50% of total exports and it is still the largest component of Japanese exports to the UAE.

Oil and gas trade with the UAE, especially with Abu Dhabi, is important for Japanese energy security because there are a few Japanese oil concessions in Abu Dhabi. Apart from oil and gas, Japan is a regular buyer of the aluminum products produced by Dubai Aluminum.

Table 16.4: Exports to UAE ($ million)

	1990	1995	2000	2005	2008	2010	2011	2011 vs 1990	2011 vs 2005
Grand Total	1,550	2,105	2,540	4,868	10,793	7,306	7,441	380%	53%
TRANSPORT EQUIPMENTS	364	612	1,006	2,160	5,213	3,485	3,170	770%	47%
GENERAL MACHINERY (OTHER THAN ELECTRIC)	190	295	482	747	1,903	1,188	1,629	760%	118%
METAL PROUCTIONS	122	98	96	303	779	610	668	446%	121%

	1990	1995	2000	2005	2008	2010	2011	2011 vs 1990	2011 vs 2005
ELECTRICAL MACHINERY	419	558	442	669	1,249	671	609	45%	-9%
PRODUCTION CLASSIFIED BY METERIAL: OTHER	45	94	135	326	550	557	516	1049%	58%
TEXTILES	180	198	124	126	224	165	177	-2%	40%
CHEMICALS	26	32	36	64	185	128	127	395%	98%
PRECISION INSTRUMENTS	91	65	51	84	108	105	126	38%	50%
MISCELLANEOUS MANUFACTURED ARTICLES	80	85	84	144	144	88	83	4%	-42%
NONMETALLIC MINERAL PRODUCTS	13	24	19	65	101	64	64	390%	0%

Compiled by the author from JETRO HP

Table 16.5: Imports from UAE ($ million)

	1990	1995	2000	2005	2008	2010	2011	2011 vs 1990	2011 vs 2005
Grand Total	9,085	10,172	14,883	25,324	46,415	29,183	42,716	370%	69%
PETROLEUM AND PETROLEUM PRODUCTS	165	8,860	12,405	22,130	40,339	23,626	35,048	21136%	58%
PETROLEUM GAS, OTHER GASEOUS HYDROCARBONS	7,659	1,284	2,271	2,908	5,645	5,114	7,006	-9%	141%
BITUMINOUS & ASPHALT OIL SHALE & TAR SANDS	1.011	-	-	-	-	-	0	-100%	#DIV/0!

Compiled by the author from JETRO HP

2.5. Trade with Qatar

In comparison to the early 1990s, Japanese trade with Qatar has increased dramatically. After two Japanese trading firms, namely Mitsui & Co and Marubeni Corp, started to get involved in Qatar's first LNG development Qatargas, Japan became the first LNG buyer from Qatar. In 2011, oil and gas imports were recorded at $30 billion.

The export figures to Qatar expanded until 2008, but then consecutively contracted to $2.0 billion in 2008, $1.6 billion in 2009, $1.1 billion in 2010 and $1.0 billion in 2011. The decline was caused by a decrease in passenger car sales in 2009 and a decrease in project related machinery exports in 2010. Unlike the UAE, Qatar is a final destination for exports and a relatively small country, therefore exporting figures may change easily due to external factors such as financial crisis or the state of Japanese-related project contracts in Qatar.

Table 16.6: Exports to Qatar ($ million)

	1990	1995	2000	2005	2008	2010	2011	2011 vs 1990	2011 vs 2005
Grand Total	152	270	289	994	2,010	1,137	1,018	569%	2%
TRANSPORT EQUIPMENTS	78	89	184	488	1,185	773	609	680%	25%
GENERAL MACHINERY (OTHER THAN ELECTRIC)	20	57	47	174	428	149	148	658%	-15%
ELECTRICAL MACHINERY	22	24	14	31	115	88	78	253%	147%
PRODUCTS CLASSIFIED BY MATERIAL OTHER	11	11	7	11	29	30	38	238%	240%
METAL PRODUCTS	6	62	19	253	193	47	23	280%	-91%
TEXTILES	3	5	5	8	12	9	13	325%	60%
MISCELLANEOUS MANUFACTURED ARTICLES	4	4	4	3	5	6	12	220%	334%
NONMETALLIC MINIRAL PRODUCTS	2	2	3	4	7	6	7	334%	58
PRECISION INSTRUMENTS	5	7	3	6	11	7	5	11%	-6%
CHEMICALS	1	8	2	7	6	11	5	285%	-33%

Compiled by the author from JETRO HP

Table 16.7: Imports from Qatar ($ million)

	1990	1995	2000	2005	2008	2010	2011	2011 vs 1990	2011 vs 2005
Grand Total	2,153	2.172	5,879	10,692	26,233	21,627	30,057	1296%	181%
PETROLEUM AND PETROLEUM PRODUCTS	2,042	2,003	4,248	8,110	18,064	14,245	16,754	720%	107%
PETROLEUM GAS' OTHER GASEOUS HYDROCARBONS	80	155	1,622	2,515	8,119	7,329	13,191	16348%	425%

Compiled by the author from JETRO HP

2.6. Trade with Iran

Exports to Iran in 2011 were almost at the same level as in 1990. Japan has a unique relationship with Iran. However, due to the recent tension between the West and Iran and related sanctions, the 2011 export figures showed a decrease of 18% compared to 2010.

As Table 16.1 shows, Japanese imports for crude oil varied at: 22.6 million kls in 1990, 29.6 million kls in 2000, 28.0 million kls in 2008 and 18.2 million kls in 2011. The increase in import value was due to increased oil prices, rather than increased volume.

Table 16.8: Exports to Iran ($ million)

	1990	1995	2000	2005	2008	2010	2011	2011 vs 1990	2011 vs 2005
Grand Total	1,617	660	574	1,347	1,889	2,074	1,699	5%	26%
TRANSPORT EQUIPMENTS	133	96	101	218	757	853	601	351%	176%
GENERAL MACHINERY (OTHER THAN ELECTRIC)	417	109	143	405	515	531	422	1%	4%
MATAL PRODUCTS	384	78	135	360	190	316	301	-22%	-17%
CHEMICALS	134	39	35	56	138	106	136	2%	140%
ELECTRICAL MACHINERY	211	164	63	136	67	62	66	-69%	-51%

	1990	1995	2000	2005	2008	2010	2011	2011 vs 1990	2011 vs 2005
PRECISION INSTRUMENTS	65	27	20	51	59	63	62	-5%	23%
PRODUCTS CLASSIFIED BY MATERIAL:OTHER	122	78	22	33	36	38	26	-79%	-21%
NONMETALLIC MINERAL PRODUCTS	14	4	4	12	13	19	21	49%	78%
MISCELLANEOUS MANUFACTURED ARTICLES	17	14	22	26	29	30	21	21%	-21%
TEXTILES	60	3	5	4	4	2	1	-98%	-65%

Compiled by the author from JETRO HP

Table 16.9: Imports from Iran ($ million)

	1990	1995	2000	2005	2008	2010	2011	2011 vs 1990	2011 vs 2005
Grand Total	3,460	2,821	5,380	10,354	18,095	11,127	12,831	271%	24%
PETROLEUM AND PETROLEUM PRODUCTS	3,369	2,613	5,191	10,106	17,344	10,374	12,152	261%	20%
PETROLEUM GAS, OTHER GASEOUS HYDROCARBONS	-	15	93	179	507	617	581	na	225%

Compiled by the author from JETRO HP

2.7. Trade with Kuwait

The trend of exports with Kuwait was similar to Qatar's, peaking in 2008 and heavily decreasing thereafter. Without much Japanese involvement in Kuwaiti projects, transport equipment (mainly passenger vehicles) dominated Japanese exports. After 2005, the ratio of exports accounted by transport equipment recorded extremely high levels, between 65% and 67%.

Japanese crude oil imports varied: 7.9 million kls in 1990 (the year of the Iraqi invasion), 21.0 million kls in 2000, 18.7 million kls in 2008 and 14.0 million kls in 2011. The increase in import value was due to the oil price increase, rather than an increased volume.

Table 16.10: Exports to Kuwait   ($ million)

	1990	1995	2000	2005	2008	2010	2011	2011 vs 1990	2011 vs 2005
Grand total	398	623	585	1,185	2,088	1,414	1,352	240%	14%
TRANSPORT EQUIPMENTS	115	261	338	794	1,359	949	880	668%	11%
METAL PRODUCTS	46	45	36	83	116	129	120	160%	44%
GENERAL MACHINERY (OTHER THAN ELECTRIC)	70	110	57	91	316	84	114	63%	25%
PRODUCTS CLASSIFIED BY MATERIAL: OTHER	25	30	23	40	65	73	84	237%	109%
ELECTRICAL MACHINERY	59	85	80	103	135	90	77	31%	-25%
TEXTILES	34	28	13	15	22	22	24	-30%	62%
PRECISION INSTRUMENTS	18	17	11	12	9	17	12	-34%	5%
NONMETALLIC MINERAL PRODUCTS	2	4	5	7	9	9	12	457%	77%
CHEMICALS	13	13	10	9	15	9	10	-24%	4%
MISCELLANEOUS MANUFACTURED ARTICLES	13	16	8	8	11	8	9	-34%	16%

Compiled by the author from JETRO HP

Table 16.11: Imports from Kuwait

($ million)

	1990	1995	2000	2005	2008	2010	2011	2011 vs 1990	2011 vs 2005
Grand Total	1,711	2,766	5,001	7,667	15,121	10,250	13,098	665%	71%
PETROLEUM AND PETROLEUM PRODUCTS	1,505	2,420	4,549	7,030	13,827	9,297	11,763	682%	67%
PETROLEUM GAS, OTHER GASEOUS HYDROCARBONS	147	298	442	630	1,287	949	1,332	804%	111%
COAL & COAL PRODUCTS	47	38	-	-	-	-	-	-100%	#DIV/0!

Compiled by the author from JETRO HP

3. Japanese Investment in the Gulf

As Figure 16.7 shows, the amount of Japanese investment has fluctuated since 1975. Compared to the total Japanese outward direct investment globally, the Gulf ratio is generally low, less than 1%. However, there were three years that recorded more than a 1% ratio which were: 1992 at 2.1% ($706 million, when Iran was the largest recipient with $378 million, 2005 at 1.2% ($521 million, when Saudi Arabia was the largest recipient with $521 million) and 2007 at 1.2%, ($953 million, when Saudi Arabia remained the largest recipient with $793 million). Although many Japanese were involved in investment projects in the Gulf mainly in the fields of petrochemical, steel and IPP (IWPP), there was no obvious investment in the manufacturing field which is the major field for Japanese Foreign Direct Investment (FDI) globally. A lack of FDI in manufacturing in the Gulf is due to investment circumstances such as foreign ownership limitation, existence of commercial agency laws, lack of proper human resources and the low trade tariff (in the case of the Gulf Cooperation Council - GCC).

Figure 16.7: Japanese Investments to the Gulf after 1975

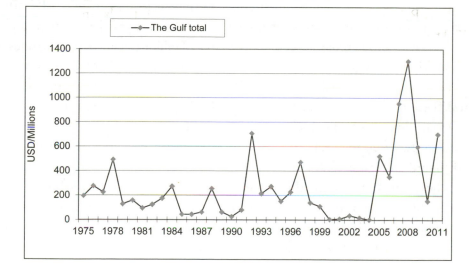

Compiled by the author from JETRO HP and Japanese Ministry of Finance HP

Figure 16.8: Japanese Investments to the World and the Gulf

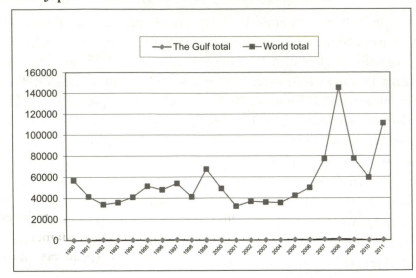

Compiled by the author from JETRO HP and Japanese Ministry of Finance HP

The Petro Rabigh project in Saudi Arabia contributed to the Japanese FDI after 2005. It is a joint venture project between Saudi Aramco and Japan's Sumitomo Chemical with a total project cost of more than $10 billion. Japanese trading houses such as Marubeni Corporation, Sumitomo Corporation, Mitsui & Company and Sojitz Corporation are quite active in IPP or IWPP project participation in the Gulf. These projects have contributed to the FDI figures for the last several years. In Dubai, there are many 100% owned Japanese companies who invested their capital to their free zone subsidiaries. Such investments have been included in the UAE figures in Figure 16.9.

The FDI data from the Japanese Ministry of Finance shows only three individual countries, namely Saudi Arabia, the UAE and Iran. Other countries included in the data are unnamed. These countries are labeled as 'not identified' in Figure 16.9. It is assumed that 'not identified' includes Qatar and Oman.

The investment amounts/numbers from the Gulf are not available from Japanese data. Although some of the sovereign wealth funds in the Gulf for a long time have been making huge financial investments to Japan through overseas funds, there are not many obvious cases, except 15% of investment to Cosmo Oil Company by Abu Dhabi's IPIC in 2007 and also 20% investment to Showa Shell Oil Company by Saudi Aramco in 2004.

Figure 16.9: Japanese External Investments to the Gulf

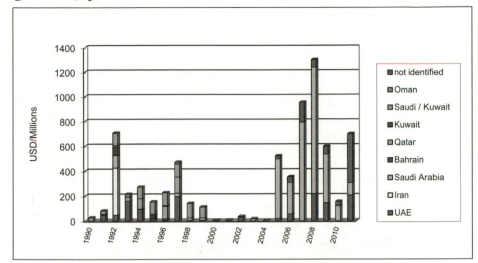

Compiled by the author from JETRO HP and Japanese Ministry of Finance HP

4. Activities of Japanese Companies in the Gulf

4.1. The Number of Japanese Companies in the Gulf

Table 16.12 shows the recent number of Japanese companies in the Gulf. There are 525 offices located in the Gulf including representative offices (39%), 100% subsidiaries (25%), joint ventures (18%), branches (14%) and privates (5%). The largest concentration is in the UAE which accounts for 314 offices (41 in Abu Dhabi and 273 in Dubai) followed by Saudi Arabia with 86 offices (53 in Riyadh/ Eastern Province and 33 in Jeddah). There are 95 100% subsidiaries in Dubai which are located in free zones because 100% foreign ownership is not allowed outside free zones in the UAE. There are 15 100% subsidiaries in Saudi Arabia due to the opening of 100% foreign ownership after the country joined the World Trade Organization (WTO) in 2005. Many Japanese businesses used Bahrain as their regional headquarters, however since 2000 most have moved to Dubai.

Table 16.12: Number of Japanese Companies

	Number of offices	Branches	Reps	100% subsidiaries	Joint Ventures	Privates
UAE (Abu Dhabi)	41	7	24	1	5	4
UAE (Dubai)	273	54	77	95	30	17
Iran	36	1	22	10	2	1

	Number of offices	Branches	Reps	100% subsidiaries	Joint Ventures	Privates
Oman	12	0	6	3	3	0
Qatar	38	0	36	1	1	0
Kuwait	21	0	7	0	14	0
Saudi Arabia (Riyadh+East)	53	7	7	11	27	1
Saudi Arabia (Jeddah)	33	2	15	4	11	1
Bahrain	18	4	9	4	1	0
Total	525	75	203	129	94	24

Compiled by the author from Japanese Ministry of Foreign Affairs HP

4.2. Contracts Awarded to Japanese Companies

Between the late 1970s and the early 1980s, the Gulf ratio in Japanese contracting business was relatively high, at almost one third. Those were mainly downstream projects such as petrochemicals. When the Japanese Yen exchange rate against USD started to appreciate rapidly in 1985, overseas contracts by Japanese companies slumped until the late 1980s. In the 1990s, up until the Asian economic crisis, Japanese contracts recovered, due to the expansion of privatization projects in Asia and the Gulf.

Table 16.13 shows Japanese contracts between 1998 and 2010 in the Gulf. The year 2005 was the highest with contracts totaling $13.4 billion. The Gulf share of global contracts was more than half at 52.2%. In 2005, there were 12 contracts amounting to more than $100 million in: Qatar (two LNG plants), UAE (LRT system, LRT civil construction, LRT trains and the Monorail system), Saudi Arabia (refinery plant, NGL plant, methanol plant and two petrochemical plants), Yemen (LNG plant) and Iran (petrochemical plant and chemical textile plant). In 2005, aside from the Gulf, the second largest area was Asia ($8.0 billion) and the third was Western Europe ($1.5 billion). The Japan Machinery Centre for Trade and Investment stated in its annual survey in 2002 that,

> Competitors of Japanese contracts were European and American companies until the 1980s. However, South Korean and Chinese contractors started to be competitive in Engineering, Procurement and Construction (EPC) businesses after 1990. At the same time, they were

still competing with Europeans and Americans... Japanese companies faced requirements of engineering improvement by efficiently using information technology. Furthermore, Japan needs to prepare global alliances in the future with new financial technology.

Figure 16.10.1: Japanese Contracts Awarded

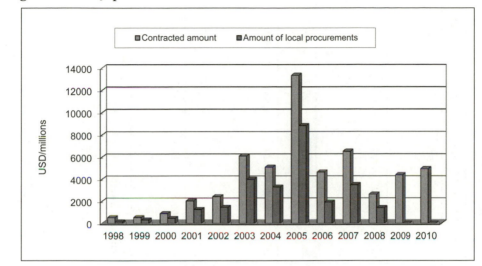

Compiled by the author from the reports of the Japan Machinery Centre for Trade and Investment

Figure 16.10.2: Number of Contracts and Share ratio

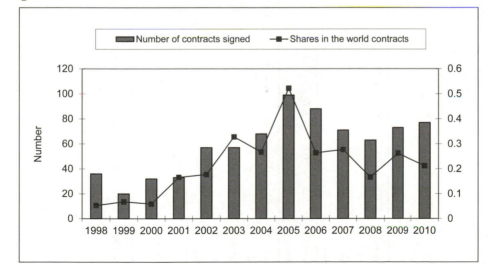

Compiled by the author from the reports of the Japan Machinery Centre for Trade and Investment

Table 16.13: Plants and Engineering Projects Awarded to Japanese Companies

	1998	1999	2000	2001	2002	2003	2004	2005	2006	2007	2008	2009	2010
Number of contracts signed	36	20	32	33	57	57	68	99	88	71	63	73	77
Contracted amount (USD/ millions)	530	540	900	2,040	2,440	6,110	5,100	13,350	4,660	6,530	2,640	4,400	4,950
Shares in all contracts (%)	5.3	6.8	5.9	16.6	17.7	32.8	26.7	52.2	26.4	27.7	16.7	26.3	21.2
Amount of local procurements (USD/ millions)	140	320	460	1,270	1,450	4,000	3,300	8,850	1,920	3,500	1,420	na	na
Local procurements ratio (%)	26.0	58.9	21.6	62.1	59.2	65.4	64.7	66.3	41.3	53.5	53.6	na	na

Compiled by the author from the reports of the Japan Machinery Centre for Trade and Investment

4.3. Banking Exposures to the Gulf

The total amount of Japanese banking exposures to the Gulf as of September 2011 was $24,298 million, which was almost 5 times the figure of December 2000. The top three countries (the UAE, Saudi Arabia and Qatar) occupied an 85% share in September 2011. The largest exposures in September 2011 are with the UAE at $8,593 million which is 22.6 times larger than the figure in 2000.

Figure 16.11: Japanese Banking Exposures to the Gulf

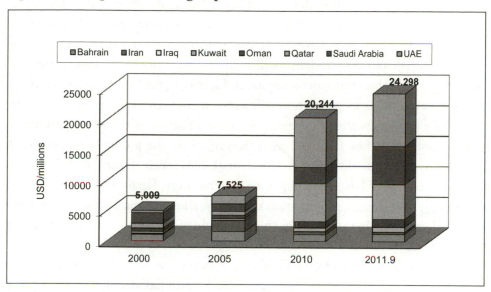

Compiled by the author from BIS WEB

Since the European financial crisis deepened in 2011, Japanese exposures have sharply grown, although Europeans have hurriedly been reducing them. This shows that Japan has the financial capability to support the Gulf economies, not only for Japanese related projects in the Gulf but also for local projects/entities, whereas other Asian countries have only supported their own country-related business in the Gulf.

5. Summary/Conclusion

Japanese trade figures with the Gulf increased significantly especially in the 2000s when the Gulf countries started enjoying higher oil prices, an increasing development budget for public procurements and an increasing private budget for consumption. This was a well-balanced complementary relationship between purchasing oil/gas and selling industrial products. Today, Japan has a huge trade deficit with the Gulf. However, Japan does not have any option to alter the existing energy imports because nearly 90% of its crude oil import comes from the Gulf. Japan being a mature, developed country may be less attractive to the Gulf in terms of economic growth, compared to other emerging Asian countries. Unlike these emerging countries, Japanese energy demands may not be expected to expand.

Transport equipment constituted the major part of Japanese exports to the Gulf. Consumer electronic products of Japanese companies may have been performing solidly, but this does not mean that they originated from Japan. More than 90% of Japanese branded consumer electronics are made elsewhere, mainly in Asian countries. Japanese manufacturing has been spreading to other Asian countries and this tendency will continue not only in electronics but also in other items such as transport equipment. Generally, the Gulf is recognized as a growing economy, as its population will continue to increase. Therefore, there are potentially many new areas for export. The diversification of exporting products is quite important for the Japanese, regardless of where the products are produced. Fortunately there is still value attached to the 'Made in Japan' label, based on the track records of Japanese companies. Furthermore, Japan has room to utilize technologies for energy conservation/efficiency, thus making it one of the most advanced countries in the world in this field, which would be good for attracting business with the Gulf.

Japanese investments to the Gulf are important for both sides. Although the importance of export expansion has been raised, Japan has already entered a phase of transition from a trading country to an investment country, because it is difficult to compete in costs with developing Asian countries. If Japan is able to expand its investment in the Gulf, it may be one of the mitigating factors to reduce trade deficits. For the Gulf countries to accommodate Japanese investment requirements, they need to make an effort to change their investment environment including the introduction and implementation of investment-related laws. Patient negotiations between governments will definitely pave the way for Japanese investments.

Although the volume of Japanese contracts was larger in the 2000s than the 1990s, it is apparent that other Asian companies, especially those of South Korea, are gaining more contracts than the Japanese. Japanese contracting is therefore losing its relative position in the Gulf as a result of serious competition with Asian counterparts. Some Japanese contracting firms, nonetheless, have well-advanced technology and special expertise for management. Japan has financial capabilities in both Export Credit Agencies (ECAs) and commercial banks. The banking exposure expanded by 4.8 times between 2000 and September 2011, which was almost at the same level as trade expansion in both exports and imports. This indicates that the volume of Japanese contracting business did not benefit from the increase in trade and financing. For example in Iraq, Japanese companies are quite cautious and naive in handling securities, even though the Japanese government committed more than $5 billion worth of soft loans to the Iraqi government in 2003. Japanese approaches in different fields need to be coordinated to function effectively so as to develop businesses in the Gulf.

The economic relationship between the Gulf and Japan is based on mutual trust, and has been excellent for many years. Given the existing strong aspirations for an expanding relationship, both the Japanese government and Japanese companies need to consider the direction of their relationship with the Gulf countries strategically.

Bibliography

Trade data: Japan External Trade Organization (JETRO) Website http://www.jetro.go.jp/indexj.html

Investment data: Ministry of Finance in Japan and JETRO Websites http://www.mof.go.jp/international_policy/reference/balance_of_payments/bpfdi.htm, http://www.jetro.go.jp/world/japan/stats/fdi/

Number of companies data: Ministry of Foreign Affairs in Japan Website http://www.mofa.go.jp/mofaj/toko/tokei/hojin/index.html

Japan Machinery Centre for Trade and Investment, Annual Reports

Bank for International Settlements, Quarterly Reviews Website http://www.bis.org/forum/research.htm

List of Contributors

Mohd Fauzi Abu-Hussin is a senior lecturer at the Faculty of Islamic Civilisation, Universiti Teknologi Malaysia (UTM), Malaysia. He is a PhD holder from Durham University with specialisation in Islamic Political Economy. He earned his Master degree in Economics and Bachelor of Syariah Economics from the University of Malaya. His main research interests include the political economy of the Arab Gulf and the Middle East countries' relation relations with Asia. His work has focused primarily on Arab Gulf relations with South East Asian countries and issues of economic development in the Arab Gulf.

Naser al-Tamimi holds a PhD degree in Government and International Relations fromthe University of Durham, England. He is also a UK-based independent political consultant and journalist. He has written/edited several articles and books (Arabic and English) on the most pertinent political and economic issues affecting the Middle East.

Jacqueline Armijo is an Associate Professor in the Department of International Affairs at Qatar University. She has published extensively in the field of Islam in China, and is now focusing her research on the growing importance of China – Gulf relations. Dr. Armijo has also taught at Zayed University (UAE), Stanford, and Cornell. She has lived in the Gulf region for ten years and in China for seven. She received her Ph.D. from Harvard University.

Sara Bazoobandi is a lecturer at Regent's College in London and previously worked for various organisations, including the National University of Singapore, Nomura International and Roubini Global Economic. She has recently published a book on political economy of Gulf Sovereign Wealth Funds. Sara holds an MSc from the University of Reading and a PhD from the University of Exeter.

Koji Horinuki is a researcher of the Japanese Institute of Middle Eastern Economies (JIME) Center, Institute of Energy Economics, Japan (IEEJ) since December 2010. His research interests include contemporary Gulf politics and social affairs.

Sofiah Jamil is an Adjunct Research Associate at the Centre for Non-Traditional Security (NTS) Studies, S. Rajaratnam School of International Studies (RSIS), Nanyang Technological University (NTU), Singapore. Her published works include two co-authored chapters in an edited volume on Energy and Non-Traditional Security in East Asia; and a chapter on "Islam & Environmentalism: Greening Our Youth" in Igniting Thought, Unleashing Youth: Perspectives on Muslim Youth and Activism in Singapore. She holds a Masters in International Relations from NTU and is currently pursuing her doctorate in international, political and strategic studies at The Australian National University.

Yoshikazu Kobayashi is Manager of Oil Group of the Institute of Energy Economics, Japan (IEEJ). Earlier he was an analyst at Tonen General Sekiyu, an ExxonMobil-affiliated company in Japan covering refinery operation planning and marine transportation. His research is on the world oil and gas market and energy security issues in Northeast Asia.

Joachim Kolb is director of the DAAD Information Centre Gulf Region in Abu Dhabi. He holds an MA in Islamic Studies from Tübingen University and an MSc and a PhD from the Center of Financial and Management Studies, SOAS, University of London. Apart from the international relations of the GCC countries, main research interests inlcude economic policymaking and the development of regulatory authorities in the MENA region.

Nikolay Kozhanov is a scholar at the nongovernmental Institute of the Middle East (Moscow, Russia) and a Senior Lecturer at the School of Economics of the St. Petersburg State University. From 2006 to 2009, he served as an attaché at the Russian embassy in Tehran, where his portfolio included socio-economic and energy issues as well as issues related to the nuclear program of Iran. At the end of his tenure with the Russian Ministry of Foreign Affairs, Dr. Kozhanov continued his research with a special focus on modern Iran and the Middle East.

Monica Malik has over 15 years of experience as an Economist specialising in the MENA region. Monica is the Chief Economist at EFG-Hermes and heads the Economics team. Prior to joining EFG-Hermes in 2007, she was the Senior Economist for the MENA region in Standard Chartered (Dubai) and at Dun & Bradstreet (London). Monica has presented at a number of high profile conferences and policy round table discussions. Monica holds a Ph.D. in Economic Development in the Middle East from the University of Durham, focusing on Private Sector Development.

Yoshio Minagi is Executive Director of Mizuho Corporate Bank Ltd Dubai Branch and concurrently Chief Representative of its Bahrain Office since 2008. He previously held a position of Managing Director, Japan External Trade Organization (JETRO), Dubai Office. He has involved Japanese business in the Middle East since 1995 from the viewpoints of both private company and government institution.

Huang Minxing, PhD, was born in April 1958 and is the Professor of Middle East Studies and Director of the Institute of Middle Eastern Studies at Northwest University, Xi'an, Peoples Republic of China. His main publications are on the history of the Middle East.

Yukiko Miyagi is Research Fellow at the Institute of Middle East, Central Asia and Caucasus Studies, the University of St Andrews. Previously she was Lecturer in the School of Government and International Affairs, University of Durham. She is a specialist in Middle Eastern-East Asian relations, Middle East politics, and East Asian politics.

Chen Mo is Associate Professor at the Institute of West-Asian and African Studies (IWAAS) in the Chinese Academy of Social Sciences (CASS). She is also deputy secretary-general of the Chinese Association for Middle East Studies. Her research focus is on energy security, economic relations between China and GCC countries, and economic development of West Asian and African countries.

Tim Niblock is Emeritus Professor of Middle East Politics at the University of Exeter, and Vice-President of the European Association for Middle East Studies. He was formerly Director of the Institute of Arab and Islamic Studies at Exeter, and has also served at the University of Durham, the University of Reading and the University of Khartoum. He works on the Political Economy and International Relations of the Middle East.

Girijesh Pant is Professor and Dean in School of International Studies, Jawaharlal Nehru University India. He specializes on, Development Studies, the Political Economy of International Energy, India's Energy Security, and the Economies of West Asia.

M.A. Salleh is presently a Senior Lecturer at the Faculty of Law and International Relations, Universiti Sultan Zainal Abidin, Terengganu, Malaysia. He obtained his bachelor degree in Political Science from the International Islamic University Malaysia (IIUM), an LL.M in International Law and International Relations form the University of Lancaster, United Kingdom and a Ph.D in International Relations from the University of Durham, United Kingdom. His research interests include religion and international relations, US foreign policy and public international law.

K.M. Seethi is Dean of Social Sciences and Professor of International Relations in Mahatma Gandhi University(MGU), Kottayam, Kerala, India. He is also Director of the KN Raj Centre for Planning, MGU and Editor of *South Asian Journal of Diplomacy*. He also has served as Director of Research, and Director of the School of International Relations and Politics, MGU.

Dr. Özlem Tür is an Associate Professor of International Relations at Middle East Technical University, Ankara, Turkey. Her main expertise include the political economy of the Middle East, and Turkish - Middle Eastern relations (especially Syria, Israel and Lebanon). Her publications include *Turkey - Challenges of Continuity and Change* (Routledge, 2005, with Meliha Altunışık), "Turkish-Syrian Relations in the 2000s – Where are we Going?" (UNISCI 2010), "Political Economy of Turkey's Relations with the Middle East" (Turkish Studies, 2011) and "Turkey and Israel in the 2000s" (Israel Studies, 2012.

Ho Wai-Yip is an Assistant Professor at the Department of Social Sciences, Hong Kong Institute of Education. He has been the Sir Edward Fellow Rotary Ambassadorial Scholar at the Institute of Arab & Islamic Studies (IAIS), University of Exeter; an Endeavour Research Fellow at Australian National University; and Visiting Scholar at the Oxford Centre of Muslim-Christian Studies (CMCS). His recent research interests include Gulf-China relations, China's Christian-Muslim relations, the New Media and Islam in China.

Akiko Yoshioka is a researcher at the Japanese Institute of Middle Eastern Economies (JIME), Institute of Energy Economics, Japan (IEEJ). She was a visiting researcher in the Gulf Research Centre in Dubai during 2007. The fields of her research interests are contemporary Iraqi politics and economy, especially after 2003.